FUNDAMENTALISM
in
American Religion
1880 - 1950

A forty-five-volume facsimile series
reproducing often extremely rare material
documenting the development of one of the
major religious movements of our time

■ *Edited by*
Joel A. Carpenter
Billy Graham Center, Wheaton College
■ *Advisory Editors*
Donald W. Dayton,
Northern Baptist Theological Seminary
George M. Marsden,
Duke University
Mark A. Noll,
Wheaton College
Grant Wacker,
University of North Carolina

A GARLAND SERIES

■ The Youth for Christ Movement and Its Pioneers

Edited by with an introduction
Joel A. Carpenter

Garland Publishing, Inc.
New York & London 1988

For a list of the titles in this series, see the final pages of this volume.

These facsimiles have been made from copies in the Billy Graham Center of Wheaton College.

Library of Congress Cataloging in Publication Data

The Youth for Christ movement and its pioneers/edited with an
    introduction by Joel A. Carpenter.
        p. cm. — (Fundamentalism in American religion, 1880-1950)
    Bibliography: p.
    Contents: God hath chosen/Forrest Forbes — Young man on fire/
    Melvin G. Larson — Reaching youth for Christ/Torrey Johnson &
    Robert Cook — Youth for Christ/Melvin Larson.
        ISBN 0-8240-5045-2 (alk. paper)
    1. Wyrtzen, Jack, 1913-   . 2. Word of life hour (Radio program).
    3. Johnson, Torrey Maynard, 1909-   . 4. Youth for Christ
    International. 5. Evangelistic work. 6. Revivals—Illinois—
    Chicago. 7. Evangelists—United States—Biography. I. Carpenter,
    Joel A. II. Series.
    BV3785.W9Y68 1988
    267'.61—dc19
                                                                88-21249

Design by Valerie Mergentime
Printed on acid-free, 250-year-life paper.
Manufactured in the United States of America.

CONTENTS

INTRODUCTION

"Youth for Christ" was an evangelistic youth rally movement that sprang up during and just after World War II. It featured swing-tempo gospel music, patriotic pageantry, and fast-paced preaching. Led by a younger generation of evangelical (at first, mostly fundamentalist) pastors and business people who had grown up with the new entertainment media, Youth for Christ was a hit with many young people—and their elders—during the domestic upheavals of wartime and early postwar America. By 1947, there were over a thousand of these weekly rallies, which ranged from mid-town Manhattan to LaSalle, Illinois, and on to the "G.I. Gospel Hour," held in Manila. Average weekly attendance at these meetings was estimated to be close to a million. The Youth for Christ movement featured some truly massive "Victory Rallies," such as ones sponsored by Jack Wyrtzen's Word of Life organization, which filled Madison Square Garden twice in the spring and fall of 1944; or Chicagoland Youth for Christ's Memorial Day, 1945 pageant at Soldier Field, attended by some sixty- to seventy-thousand.[1]

Despite the widespread interest that the Youth for Christ movement enjoyed at its peak, it has received very little historical attention until just recently. This evangelistic movement should not be passed over lightly, however, for it was the first wave of the postwar evangelical resurgence.[2] In addition to spawning evangelical youth agencies such as Word of Life, Youth for Christ International, and Young Life, which minister to hundreds of thousands of teenagers today, the movement spun off many of the leading evangelical organizations and personalities of the postwar generation. Out of Youth for Christ came Billy Graham, the world's most prominent evangelist and the personification of the evangelical resurgence. Former Youth for Christ leaders also created World Vision, the massive relief and development agency; Trans-World Radio, now an international network of evangelistic short-wave radio stations; and Greater Europe Mission, Far Eastern Gospel Crusade (now Send, International), and Overseas Crusades—all independent evangelical missionary societies.[3]

Clearly, a movement of such dynamism and formative

influence needs further study, and this volume should provide valuable evidence to researchers who wish to probe the origins of the postwar evangelical resurgence. Contained herein are biographies of the Youth for Christ movement's two most prominent leaders, Jack Wyrtzen and Torrey Johnson; a how-to-do-it manual for prospective rally directors; and a breathless account of the movement's early years.

Forrest Forbes, *God Hath Chosen: The Story of Jack Wyrtzen and the Word of Life Hour* (Grand Rapids: Zondervan, 1948), details the life of Casper John Von Wyrtzen (1913–), known to all as Jack, who was the high-spirited son of a Danish-American family that had settled in Brooklyn, New York. A popular, well-liked young man, Wyrtzen was an insurance salesman who went to church with his friends on Sunday, but hung out with them in bars and dance halls on weeknights. Wyrtzen was an avid pop musician; he played trombone in a twelve-piece orchestra he had organized for fraternity and sorority dances.

Jack's best girl and future wife, Marge Smith, experienced a crisis in her life, however, that fundamentally changed Wyrtzen and his circle of friends. Marge nearly died from appendicitis in 1932, and she began to think about her spiritual condition. Her mother, who liked to listen to the "Young People's Church of the Air," a radio program hosted by evangelist Percy Crawford,[4] prompted her daughter to attend Crawford's new "Pinebrook" youth conference in the Poconos in the summer of 1933. Marge became a "born-again" Christian her first night there. Jack "got saved" too, and began to hand out tracts and to encourage others to be converted; but he struggled over giving up, as evangelical morality demanded, the dance band work he enjoyed so much. Wyrtzen did give it up, though, during the winter of 1933–34, as he and his close-knit circle of friends, who were all becoming converted Christians, began to meet regularly for intensive Bible study and prayer.

This circle evolved into a self-supporting evangelistic squad, which formally organized in late 1939 as the Word of Life Fellowship, a ministry to young people. During the mid-to-late 1930s, Wyrtzen's group played, sang, and preached in churches, in revival tents, on the street, in prisons and reformatories, over the radio, in C.C.C. camps—in short, anywhere they could get a hearing. They developed friendly relations with the network of fundamentalist Baptist, Presbyterian, independent, and Plymouth Brethren preachers who shared their convictions; and they also befriended lay leaders of evangelisitic groups such as the Gideons, the Christian Business Men's Committees, and the

Pocket Testament League. In sum, Wyrtzen's biographer recounts a fascinating story of lay religious initiatives. By allowing the reader to piece together Wyrtzen's friends' increasingly wide range of contacts and ministry, this work provides one of the most valuable records now available of grassroots activity and networking among East Coast fundamentalists in the 1930s.

In 1941, Wyrtzen "stepped out on faith," as fundamentalists put it, and quit his job to devote all of his considerable energies to Word of Life. Soon Word of Life was holding weekly Saturday night rallies in Times Square and broadcasting live over one of New York's leading radio stations. Next came rallies in Carnegie Hall, and then, in April of 1944, a massive "Victory Rally," which brought 20,000 to Madison Square Garden. That feat was repeated the following September. These rallies were the high points of a more fulsome program that by the mid-1940s included weekly Bible clubs scattered throughout the New York metropolitan area, a weekly evening Bible School held at the National Bible Institute in midtown Manhattan, the Word of Life Bookstore, social/evangelistic events such as banquets and Hudson River cruises, a missionary support and recruiting program, and by 1947, a summer youth camp in the Adirondacks, modeled after Percy Crawford's Pinebrook. As early as 1943, youthful pastors and business men and women elsewhere were borrowing this pattern of ministry and beginning "Youth for Christ" rallies in other cities.

One of these emulators was Torrey M. Johnson (1909–), a young preacher in Chicago. His parents were Norwegian immigrants and born-again members of the Evangelical Free Church, a Scandinavian ethnic denomination with strong ties to institutions like the Moody Bible Institute. Torrey was thus a second-generation fundamentalist; indeed, he had been named after Reuben A. Torrey, one of the "founding fathers" of the fundamentalist movement.[5] A stellar high school athlete but also a rather wild teenager, Johnson was sent out to Wheaton College, a fundamentalist liberal arts college in one of Chicago's western suburbs.[6] His parents hoped Torrey would settle down, be converted, and find his life's calling. He was converted, in his freshman year, but he continued to be restless. He entered a premedical program the following year at Northwestern University and struggled with a call to Africa as a missionary. Resolving to follow that prompting after experiencing fierce personal anxiety, Johnson returned to Wheaton in early 1929 and graduated in 1930.

After a year as a Baptist pastor in Chicago, Johnson spent two years touring as an evangelist, holding hundreds of meetings in rural Wisconsin, Iowa, Minnesota, and northern Michigan. Deciding that he wanted to further his doctrinal education, Johnson accepted a call to Midwest Bible Church, a tiny storefront congregation in northwest Chicago, and enrolled at Northern Baptist Theological Seminary, also on the city's west side.[7] Johnson graduated from Northern in 1936, but taught introductory courses there and took advanced coursework toward the Th. D. until 1940, when had only his thesis remaining. At that point, his rapidly growing church asked him to choose between the pastorate and a seminary teaching career, and Johnson chose the pastorate.

By this time, Midwest Bible Church was pursuing an ambitious program of expansion in facilities and ministry. The congregation had built a large, tabernacle-style auditorium that seated 900, remodeled a nearby garage to seat 1,200 for special meetings and house a radio production studio, and converted three storefronts across the street for Sunday School classes. By 1944, this once-tiny congregation was averaging 462 in attendance Sunday mornings and 668 on Sunday evenings, with many programs for children, youth, and adults. It featured a lively musical ministry, led by gospel radio musician Douglas Fisher, and two weekly "Chapel Hour" radio broadcasts. A third program, "Songs in the Night," became too much for Johnson to handle, so he turned it over to a young protégé, a Baptist pastor in suburban Western Springs named Billy Graham.

Johnson's congregation had successfully followed what was by now a well-established fundamentalist pattern of urban evangelism and church growth. "Gospel tabernacle" congregations such as Midwest Bible Church utilized the popular entertainment-shaped revival style made famous by such urban evangelists as Dwight L. Moody and Billy Sunday. But unlike the campaigns of the itinerant evangelists, these gospel tabernacles would not fold up in six weeks and move to the next town. They became ongoing churches, with revival meetings, so to speak, every week. The master of this new style, who added the powerfully attractive ingredient of radio broadcasting, was evangelist Paul Rader. His work at the Chicago Gospel Tabernacle in the 1920s and early 1930s was widely influential.[8] By 1943 and 1944, Johnson's congregation had become a regular stop on the speaking circuit for Rader's generation of fundamentalist leaders.

Johnson was also making connections and trying out new ideas with a younger group of enterprising fundamentalists. Included in this group were several businessmen who were avid supporters of evangelism, and young preachers such as Don

Hoke, who sometimes reported on religion in the *Chicago Tribune* ; Billy Graham, who was broadcasting regularly with gospel singer George Beverly Shea (a veteran of Jack Wyrtzen's New York campaigns); Johnson's brother-in-law, Bob Cook, a Baptist pastor; and Doug Fisher, Johnson's minister of music and the regular organist on WMBI, the radio station of the Moody Bible Institute. Through a variety of contacts, this Chicago cadre learned about and experimented with the new style of young people's ministry pioneered by Percy Crawford, Jack Wyrtzen, and Glenn Wagner of Washington, D.C. Persuaded at last in the spring of 1944 to organize a "Chicagoland" Youth for Christ rally, Johnson's group secured the prestigious home of the Chicago Symphony, Orchestra Hall, for the summer season, and launched their youth rallies.

The balance of this small book portrays the week-by-week unfolding of the first year of Youth for Christ rallies, with details of the planning, the personalities involved, the aspirations of the leaders, and the actual program content of Youth for Christ. The highlight of their first season, a Wyrtzen-style "Victory Rally" that drew 28,000 to the Chicago Stadium, receives vivid treatment. The growing national movement—which by 1944 had rallies springing up by the hundreds and was being treated to increasing publicity in the secular press—is reported here also. In sum, the researcher will find much to document the texture of this movement, and some very suggestive information about the restless, expansive, ambitious younger fundamentalists who led it. They were more eager to bring revival to American and evangelize the world than to carry forward the anti-modernist campaigns of the previous generation.

In the wake of the successful summer campaign, Johnson and his friends began to receive inquiries from people elsewhere who wanted to start rallies in their towns. Johnson and his brother-in-law, Robert Cook, quickly produced a small book, *Reaching Youth for Christ* (Chicago: Moody Press, 1944), which they first presented at the Chicago Stadium Rally. In the first year they sold 15,000 copies. There is probably no more revealing document of the Youth for Christ movement's emerging tactics, strategy, and sense of purpose. *Reaching Youth for Christ* gives the authors' account of the genesis of Chicagoland Youth for Christ, a brief summary of the spread of the movement elsewhere, advice on how to develop an evangelistic youth rally program, and then some transcribed sermons from the Orchestra Hall rallies.

The advice that Johnson and Cook give out is especially

instructive. It reveals how conscious they were of the hackneyed style of much evangelism in their day, and how sensitive they were to teenagers' and young adults' tastes and expectations. They urged prospective evangelists to be "geared to the times" by modeling their program after the entertainment the younger generation found on the radio (p. 37). Johnson and Cook warned that rally directors had to pay special attention to the program's pace, style, and quality of talent if they were to hold entertainment-hungry and radio-jaded young people's attention. Rallies had to compete with what the "world" had to offer. Young people were used to good production and "brother, they'll hold you to it. Dare to offer something shoddy and they'll shun your meeting" (p. 36). So the program needed split-second timing, zippy gospel music instead of slow hymns, "'punchy' announcements," short, rehearsed, "outstanding" testimonies, and brief, timely evangelistic sermons with current-events "lead-ins" (pp. 41–42, 44–45).

The most important ingredient, however, was radio. From it flowed the style to emulate, as noted above; and Johnson and Cook sensed that radio broadcasts of the rallies had immense symbolic and practical value. The authors urged their readers to broadcast their meetings, if at all possible. Not only was radio good for publicity and extended impact, but it added to the legitimacy and eventfulness of what they were doing. It made the audience feel, the authors insisted, that they were "part of something big, and alive, and vital" (p. 37). This striving for an image of significance and eventfulness prompted rally directors to emulate radio celebrities. A *Newsweek* report on Youth for Christ called Johnson "the religious counterpart of Frank Sinatra," the current teen rage, while Wyrtzen and Graham clearly patterned their sermonizing after the clipped, rapid-fire urgency of the radio newscasters.[9]

In sum, *Reaching Youth for Christ* shows modern revivalism at a new point of departure. Fundamentalists were the heirs of a long tradition of crafting evangelistic messages to elicit a positive response from a mass audience. But in the Youth for Christ movement, we see this whole enterprise taken a step further. It was moving, in its efforts to be entertaining, toward the situation of the late twentieth century, when religious television has thoroughly immersed—obscured, some would say—the Christian gospel in the slick style and frothy content of popular entertainment.

Melvin Larson's *Youth for Christ: Twentieth Century Wonder* (Grand Rapids: Zondervan, 1947), which is an action-packed, episodic portray of Youth for Christ at its apogee, reflects the style of the movement itself. Larson (1916–1972) was a sportswriter from Minneapolis who became the chief publicist for Youth for Christ and the many evangelistic enterprises that followed in its wake. He became acquainted with the movement through the Minneapolis rallies, and soon began writing glowing accounts of the Youth for Christ phenomenon for fundamentalist publications. By the late 1940s, Larson was an editor of *Youth for Christ Magazine*, and continued on its staff into the mid-1960s.

Youth for Christ: Twentieth Century Wonder favors vignettes and personal profiles over a continuing narrative; it switches back and forth with fairly little continuity or progression in time, place, persons, or institutional development. Readers may find this frustrating, but the book is filled with information—apparently drawn from the author's first-hand experience and from now-extinct files—that cannot be found anywhere else. Larson sketches brief accounts of Youth for Christ's beginnings in various major cities, small towns, and among the armed forces overseas; often these stories contain valuable information about how the movement's network operated, and what kind of people became rally directors.

Indeed, the impressions Larson leaves about the movement's leadership and character are very instructive. Among Youth for Christ's rally directors, there was a preponderance of former dance band members and radio disc jockeys. Pastors with radio-preaching experience seemed numerous also, as did people with careers in other media fields, such as journalism, printing, and advertising. Youth for Christ was slickly produced and promoted, especially in the larger cities, by people who knew what they were doing. And through the help of a good half-dozen "born-again" stringers, reporters, and cartoonists, the movement received an ample share of news coverage. Such coverage meant more than free publicity. It meant that the movement was newsworthy, that at least for the moment, it *mattered* in American life. Larson's *Youth for Christ* proudly quoted this favorable coverage, and the author fairly crowed whenever he could cite some important government official's kindly expressions toward the movement's goals. For fundamentalists and other evangelicals who had felt the sting of the world's scorn, a good word from President Truman, for example, was heady stuff (p. 64).

In sum, these four little books give the reader a valuable glimpse of the early stages of what would become the postwar evangelical resurgence. The younger fundamentalists who led Youth for Christ voiced some virtually boundless aspirations as their creative efforts paid off in a surge of grass-roots religious interest. These leaders yearned to spread their message beyond the confines of sectarian fundamentalism and to make a difference in American public life. They began to talk of bringing another Great Awakening to America, and of taking the gospel to the entire world (Larson, *Young Man*, 111–14). They gravitated toward mass communications as the way to get their message out, to assert their existence, and to proclaim their legitimacy. They came on the scene at a time of national crisis when the American public responded with more interest toward religion than it had in decades. The result was a religious chain reaction that has continued for a generation.

Joel A. Carpenter
Institute for the Study of American Evangelicals
Wheaton College

NOTES

1. Bruce Shelley, "The Rise of Evangelical Youth Movements," *Fides et Historia* 18 (January 1986): 48–50.

2. For further arguments and evidence in favor of this thesis, see Joel A. Carpenter, "From Fundamentalism to the New Evangelical Coalition," in *Evangelicalism and Modern America*, ed. George Marsden (Grand Rapids, Eerdmans, 1984), 14–16; Carpenter, "'Geared to the Times, but Anchored to the Rock' : How Contemporary Techniques and Exuberant Nationalism Helped Create An Evangelical Resurgence," *Christianity Today* 29 (November 8, 1985): 44–47; and "Youth for Christ and the New Evangelicals' Place in the Life of the Nation," in *American Recoveries: Religion in the Life of the Nation*, ed. Rowland A. Sherrill (Urbana-Champaign: University of Illinois Press, forthcoming).

3. Carpenter, "Geared to the Times," 44–45.

4. Bob Bahr, *Man with a Vision: The Story of Percy Crawford* (Chicago: Moody Press, n.d.), reports Crawford's pioneering work in young people's evangelism and religious broadcasting.

5. H. Wilbert Norton, et. al., *The Diamond Jubilee Story* (Minneapolis: Free Church Publishing, 1959), provides much evidence of links between the Evangelical Free Churches and American fundamentalism.

6. Paul M. Bechtel, *Wheaton College: A Heritage Remembered, 1860–1984* (Wheaton, Ill.: Harold Shaw, 1984), is the standard account of this important fundamentalist-evangelical institution.

7. Northern Baptist Theological Seminary is an evangelical institution that was founded by Chicago Baptist pastors in 1913 to provide an alternative to the theologically liberal University of Chicago Divinity School. James D. Mosteller, "Something Old—Something New: The First Fifty Years of Northern Baptist Theological Seminary," *Foundations* 8 (January-March 1965): 26–48, is a serviceable summary of the school's development.

8. Larry K. Eskridge, "Only Believe: Paul Rader and the Chicago Gospel Tabernacle, 1922–1933" (M. A. thesis, University of Maryland, 1985), gives a vivid account of this paradigmatic ministry; Everett L. Perry, "The Role of Socio-Economic Factors in the Rise and Development of American Fundamentalism" (Ph. D. dissertation, University of Chicago, 1959), contains a wealth of fascinating detail about selected "gospel tabernacle" and "Bible church" congregations in metropolitan Chicago; William G. McLoughlin's *Billy Sunday Was His Real Name* (Chicago: University of Chicago Press, 1955), his *Modern Revivalism: Charles Grandison Finney to Billy Graham* (New York: Ronald Press, 1959), and his *Billy Graham: Revivalist in a Secular Age* (New York: Ronald Press, 1960), remain required reading on revivalism in the first half of the twentieth century.

9. "Wanted: A Miracle of Good Weather, and the 'Youth for Christ' Rally Got It," *Newsweek*, June 11, 1945, 84; Clarence Woodbury, "Bobby Soxers Sing Hallelujah," *American Magazine* 141 (March 1946): 27; John Pollack, *Billy Graham: The Authorized Biography* (New York: McGraw-Hill, 1965), 85.

God hath chosen

The Story of Jack Wyrtzen and the Word of Life Hour

FORREST FORBES

ZONDERVAN PUBLISHING HOUSE
Grand Rapids :: Michigan

INTRODUCTION

We are told by the Apostle Paul that he was made all things to all men, if by any means he might save some. What an encouragement, and how suggestive these words are, to those who are endeavoring today to get the Gospel to the unthinking masses, many of whom will never enter a church door or read the Bible until literally compelled by some special work of the Spirit of God. The Lord has used His servant, Jack Wyrtzen, in a very definite way to reach many by means and methods that may be a bit out of the ordinary and which, unfortunately, shock some who are too conservatively inclined and who forget that while Truth is unchanging, methods may vary from age to age.

Jack Wyrtzen has proved that one can reach vast throngs of people with the message of the Cross, provided it is so presented that their attention is obtained almost without their being conscious of the fact. As a result, not only hundreds but thousands, young and old, have been brought to a saving knowledge of our blessed Lord. Some who do nothing to reach the lost man look on with disapproval, but those in whose hearts God has implanted a love for precious souls will thank Him for the signal way in which He has honored His servant and used him to hold forth the Word of Life. Having known Jack Wyrtzen almost since the inception of his special ministry, I rejoice unfeignedly in the success that has accompanied his efforts, and pray earnestly that he may ever be sustained of God and kept pliable in His hand, clean and faithful, as a vessel meet for the Master's use.

H. A. IRONSIDE

ACKNOWLEDGMENT

Thankful acknowledgment is given for many sources generously made available to the writer: the Chi Beta Alpha Constitution and photographs from George Schilling; the earliest clippings, pictures and programs of the Woodhaven meetings from Dorothy Duchardt; the scrapbooks of Florence Otterbeck and of William Malcolm, the reminiscences of many friends; and the oft searchings of old files by the indulgent Word of Life staff. Gratitude is expressed also for the use of Marge Wyrtzen's revealing diary of the British Isles journey.

FOREWORD

"Can we hold a Christian youth rally in Madison Square Garden, or Yankee Stadium, and win hundreds of persons to Jesus Christ?"

"You can if you begin fifteen years ago," replied Jack Wyrtzen's friend, James E. Bennet, the kindly Christian lawyer who, while maintaining his legal practice, has spent his life teaching the Word of God in thousands of meetings in the New York area.

"Begin fifteen years ago in a young insurance man's bedroom, with a prayerful gang of newly-converted young men saved out of jazz and drunkenness, so hungry for the Word of God and the will of God that they preached Christ on the streets, in night clubs, prisons, hospitals, army camps, boat rides and banquets."

"But what has that to do with filling a stadium?" asked a bewildered interviewer.

"Just this," offered the lawyer, with a quiet smile. "Oaks grow from acorns. God's work doesn't begin with a big flourish. Adam was the only man who sprang full fledged into being. Big branches are nothing unless they have Life in the Vine, Jesus Christ.

"A novice does not set up a big business front, when he has nothing but liabilities and his own advice," he continued. "And yet nothing is impossible when you have a Senior Partner whose assets are unlimited, who assumes your liabilities, and whose directions are specific in every forward move."

"You know," recalled Mr. Bennet, "I have worked with and watched many Christian organizations for more than half a century. They start with a big organization, personalities and a budget. And then they die. Inspiration is what you pump into a tire. It can come out through a puncture. The necessity is Life!"

Salvation is immediate. The fruits of salvation are borne only in faithful living.

The Word of Life Fellowship is composed of many individual believers who have known forgiveness of sins, and new life from heaven, through Jesus Christ, crucified and risen. These have no tie but Christ, and no desire but to bear fruit in Him.

FORREST FORBES

CONTENTS

Chapter 1

"THE FOOLISH THINGS"

> But God hath chosen the foolish things of the world to confound the wise; and God hath chosen the weak things of the world to confound the things which are mighty; and base things of the world, and things which are despised, hath God chosen, yea, and things which are not, to bring to nought things that are: that no flesh should glory in his presence (I Cor. 1:27-29).

THE WAY MEN LOOK at things, there was nothing important in George Schilling's giving Jack Wyrtzen a copy of John's Gospel. For that matter, there was nothing important in Jack's tearing it up, either!

Furthermore, it was an act quite beneath the notice of most current religious groups, what with the new way of looking at things in these days of psychiatry and "self improvement."

Yet George gave Jack a Gospel of John. And Jack gaily tore up the Word of God, and tossed away the pages.

Jack and George were United States Army bandsmen in Brooklyn. And one important fact lay hidden in the incident. George had lived a life of reckless license and sin. His sudden conversion was a mystery to Jack. Nor did he connect it with the Gospel of John. But George kept on praying, and gave him another Gospel of John. Not long after that, Jack also was saved. It was a most uncommon happening in the cavalry band. Who could have predicted the consequences?

9

George Schilling had come to the knowledge of Jesus Christ on January 1, 1932, through the faithful ministry of Dr. Will Houghton, during a watch-night service at Calvary Baptist Church in New York. (For years he has been in the ministry in New York, Vermont and New Hampshire, and God has given him many souls for his hire.) How clearly did he seize upon the way of the Early Church! When he knew the joy of sins forgiven, he went out and won his friend, Jack, just as Andrew went out and brought his brother, Peter, to Jesus. Peter won three thousand to Jesus Christ with one sermon. Ed Kimball, the Boston Sunday-school teacher, won to God a rough jewel whose name was Dwight L. Moody. God used Moody to shake two continents with the Gospel of Jesus Christ.

That is apostolic succession—every living believer linked with every other believer in the body of Christ by a bit of that sacred flame "once delivered." Spiritual genealogies in Jesus Christ are glorious. It is amazing how the results of one soul won to the Lord multiply into infinity.

It was 1932. George asked Jack to play a trombone solo at a Gospel meeting. Willing to do a favor for a pal, Jack played a number, and then listened to the testimonies. It was an artful plot, often used; and it was effective, for the Word of God and the Holy Spirit were doing their convicting work. Jack later dropped beside his bed, in the quiet of his own home, and accepted the Lord Jesus Christ as his Saviour. A sinner was reconciled to God. The month was October.

Jack describes the experience in his own words. This is his personal testimony in the Madison Square Garden Rally, September 29, 1945:

"'For I am not ashamed of the Gospel of Christ: for it is the power of God unto salvation to every one that believeth; to the Jew first and, also to the Greek.' Paul said he was not ashamed of the Gospel of Christ. The word 'gospel,' you know, means 'good news' or 'glad tidings.' My, if there was ever a day when the world needed to hear good news, it's today! But this Gospel that we preach is not only good news but it's the power of God unto salvation. Yes, it's the power of God.

"You talk about atomic power! Well, the Gospel is far more powerful than that. Beloved, it's the power of God to salvage, to reclaim ruined, wrecked, lost, sinful men and women who will but believe on the Lord Jesus Christ and be saved for all eternity. For our 'God commendeth his love toward us, in that, while we were yet sinners, Christ died for us.' Notice I Timothy 1:15 where Paul says, 'Christ Jesus came into the world to save sinners'; I Corinthians 15:3: 'Christ died for our sins'; Romans 5:6: 'Christ died for the ungodly.' But Galatians 2:20 says, 'Christ . . . gave himself *for me.*' It's a wonderful thing to be able to say that Christ died for me. Can you say that?

"I remember the night when I knelt at my bedside and took Christ as my Saviour. That night I became alive unto God through His Son. I became a Christian by receiving the Lord Jesus Christ into my heart as my own personal Lord and Saviour. Little did I realize as I knelt there and asked God to save me that I'd ever have the joy and privilege of standing here in Madison Square Garden before this microphone tonight telling you about the Saviour who came into my heart.

"Oh, the joy that is ours to tell you about the One who is altogether lovely, the fairest among ten thousand, the One who changed our lives, revolutionized our thinking, and gave us joy and peace that we never knew before!

"Before I was saved, in the evenings, I was leading a dance orchestra and playing for fraternity clubs and sorority dances. In the daytime I was working in the insurance business. But along with all this, I joined up with the 101st Cavalry Band in Brooklyn, and there I played my trombone one night a week on horseback in the United States Cavalry Band.

"With a busy life like this I'll tell you that I didn't find very much time for God or the Bible until one night a young fellow by the name of George, who was then my buddy in the United States Army 'Band, came to me and handed be a Gospel of Saint John. I looked at him and asked him what the idea was, for he was the last one I'd ever expect to see with a Bible under his arm. Then he told me how he had taken the Lord Jesus as his personal Saviour and had been wonderfully saved. I told him that I wasn't the least bit interested and I tried to hand the Gospel of John back. He insisted that I at least take it home with me.

"Well, I finally took the Gospel of John to be polite, and I put it in my pocket. Then later, on my way home, while I was standing at the railroad station with my trombone under my arm, I put my hand in my pocket and there I found the Gospel of Saint John. I took it out and read 'Gospel of Saint John.' I thought it would have been bad enough if it had said 'Gospel of John,' but 'Gospel of *Saint* John,' mind you . . . *Saint* John! Somehow that *Saint* business seemed to burn me up. I thought, *Boy what a sissy, what a holy Joe I'd be, carrying around a Gospel of "Saint" John.*

"So I took the Gospel of John and I tore it to pieces and threw it off the railroad station platform.

"Friend, that's what I thought of God's Word a few years back. Little did I realize that night, as I stood there brazenly tearing God's Word to pieces, that it would only be a few months later when this very Book, God's Word, would tear me to pieces and I'd see myself as a sinner, lost and needing the Saviour that the Bible tells of.

"Well, that was in January, one cold winter's night, when I tore up the Gospel of John. The following Monday night at the band rehearsal I met George again and the first question he asked me was, 'Jack, how are you getting along with the Gospel of John I gave you last week?' I said, 'Gospel of John? What Gospel?' 'Oh,' I said, 'you mean that little red book!' He said, 'Yes, have you read it?' I said, 'Read it?

Why, George, I threw it away before I got home.' He said, 'You did? Well, here's another one.' 'Oh,' I said, 'now, look here, George, let's not go into that again.' Week after week George kept handing me tracts and Gospels, and the more he handed me the more I threw away.

"Six months went by and we went off to army camp together. I thought, *Surely this fellow George will forget all about his old religion in this man's army with all the drinking, gambling, cursing, filth and debauchery.* I knew that the summer before, George had committed every sin right down the line that a soldier could commit.

"The first day that we were away there at army camp, I heard several of the fellows using the Name of the Lord in vain, dragging it down into the gutter. I saw George speak to one of them, and he said, 'Listen, fellow, the Name you're dragging down is the Name that's taking me up to heaven.' That hit me! Then, too, I knew that a Christian would read his Bible and get down on his knees to pray before going to bed. And I thought, *Surely George will never read his Bible and pray with these fellows around.*

"Taps sounded, lights out, and George hadn't read his Bible or prayed. And we all lay there on our cots thinking, *He's scared to do it.* But wait a minute! George reached down into his barracks bag and grabbed hold of his Bible and flashlight and there he sat on the edge of his cot! I can see him yet. He read for awhile and then he got down on his knees for prayer. We could curse at him, throw shoes or anything else, but he stayed there until he was through. He was a man!

"And after watching this fellow for two full weeks, twenty-four hours a day, there in that army camp, and noting the marvelous change in his life, I decided he had something that I didn't have, and whatever he had I wanted.

"That summer after we came back from the army camp, I got hold of a Gospel of John. I started to read it through. The following fall the band got together again and my buddy, George, invited me to a little meeting over in Brooklyn where the Gospel would be preached. One after another got to their feet and told what Christ meant to them, just as these did here tonight.

"This was all new to me, for outside of George's testimony I'd never heard anything like it before. But that night, in His grace, God brought me under deep conviction. I got mad. I didn't like the way the preacher talked about sin, righteousness and the judgment to come. He spoke about a real heaven and a real hell, and about the second coming of the Lord Jesus Christ. He spoke to us straight from the shoulder and told us that the only hope of heaven was in the new birth.

"I didn't like it. I left the meeting mad, but that night home, in the blackness of my room as I lay on my bed, it seemed as though all the blackness of eternity loomed up before me, and I realized for the first time in my life that I, too, was a sinner, but that Jesus Christ, God's Son, died and shed His blood on the Cross of Calvary for me. Somehow I slipped out of bed; I got down on my knees and admitted to God above that my life had been stained, marred and blackened with sin. Then I asked Him right there and then to save me for Jesus' sake.

"I don't remember just how or what I prayed that night, but I know that I passed from death unto life, from the power of Satan unto God. My eyes were opened and forgiveness of sins became my portion. That night, Jesus Christ became real to me and what He did for me, beloved, He can and will do for you if you'll only 'behold the Lamb of God, which taketh away the sin of the world.' "

Chapter 2

NEW LIFE AND OLD LIFE

WHEN JACK BECAME a Christian, he was at a loss as to how to witness of his Saviour. For one thing, he had been afraid to tell his girl friend, Marge, and did not know the value of giving an immediate testimony to his loved ones. Marge remarks that Jack continued to attend movies with her, expressing unhappiness in seeing them. He also suggested that it would be better if girls did not smoke. This astonished her, and made her wonder what was "wrong" with him. With a girl's intuition, she blamed George. She decided she didn't like George. He was always hanging around Jack, and both of them looked so upright and queer!

But let's drop the curtain awhile on the future Mrs. Wyrtzen. Love can endure much, and it can be greatly enhanced by the knowledge of Jesus Christ.

Evolution demands a pedigree. If such availed, Christ need not have died for us. There is no doubt that substantial physical and mental advantages accrue to the descendants of godly men and women. By God's decree these count for nothing, however, toward salvation: "For by grace are ye saved through faith; and that not of yourselves: it is the gift of God: not of works, lest any man should boast."

15

If a person has large natural gifts and talents, he is that much more responsible to use these for God, *after* his salvation. A faithful "one talent" man is more pleasing to God than a shiftless "five talent" man.

Jack never talks about his ancestors, but one learns that his people were "Von Wyrtzens" of no mean standing in Denmark. There was a sea captain, for example. During World War I the knightly "Von" on the family name seemed a needless provocation, for it bore too many suggestions of its distant German origin. So the name became simply "Wyrtzen."

Mother and Dad Harry Wyrtzen are a lovely elderly couple, who have reared a family of three sons. Mother Wyrtzen has a radiant testimony of Jesus Christ, stirred anew by the burden of praying for the ministry of her son, and for the entire world. The couple's speech bears the friendly savor of Brooklyn.

Jack was born April 22, 1913, in Brooklyn. His childhood and youth were somewhat penalized by the name "Casper John Von Wyrtzen." It was kindly bestowed, but misunderstood. Many of the boys believed that a fellow with the name "Casper" was a push-over. His stout frame won a general respect from the gang, however. At this present writing it is a bit doubtful that the name will pass the "censor." Even his mother calls him "Jack."

Young Wyrtzen could run the hundred-yard dash in good time, and was not at the foot of his classes, either. But most of all he enjoyed music and sports, and he loved to ride horseback. That was one reason he joined the 101st Cavalry Band.

While a Boy Scout, Jack became a bugler and drummer. Later he played the trombone. Jamaica High School was the natural setting for a dance band. Jack later led a twelve-piece orchestra that played at sorority and fraternity dances. The gay whirling centers of sin were fond of his music.

And this was the life—until Christ overtook him, broke his heart, and shaped him anew.

Jack's willingness to risk his own life to save others was foreshadowed in 1925 during his twelfth year, seven years before he knew salvation. From the Queens Council of Boy Scouts (the president and the assistant executive) are letters (saved by a proud mother) commending him publicly. Jack had entered a home smelling of gas, had opened the windows, shut off the open gas cock, and had rescued a mother and two sons. He personally carried one of the boys to safety.

Jack Wyrtzen recalls three times when he might have accepted the Lord Jesus Christ in early life, but, instead, he went on in the darkness of sin.

When he was a child in a Universalist Sunday school, he sang "Jesus loves me! this I know, for the Bible tells me so." The Universalists do not believe in Christ as the virgin-born son of God, who died for our sins and rose again from the dead. But the little Gospel song touched Jack's heart and made it fallow for the truth that would yet come.

An old-fashioned Y.M.C.A. worker conducted a Bible class attended by Jack. "I know he taught the Word of God, and tried to win us to Jesus Christ," he recalls. "And I do not even know his name, so that I could thank him for trying to tell me of salvation."

The Wyrtzens now attended a different denominational church. There came a new pastor. Unfamiliar with the way of the worldly church and eaten up with the zeal of God, he inquired of the church members whether they knew Jesus Christ as Saviour. This was a most unpopular activity, and the minister did not have a long pastorate.

But he visited the Wyrtzens as he made his faithful rounds. Mother and Dad Wyrtzen were not home, and Jack felt that the pastor would therefore not want to see *him*. He was nervous and indignant when the pastor turned to him and asked *him* if *he* were saved.

"What if I am *not* saved?" Jack inquired with more anger than interest.

"Then you will go to hell," said the fearless minister.

"There is the door," Jack replied grimly, as he pointed the faithful servant of God from his home and from his life.

"I just didn't believe in hell, when I was going there," he explains.

Sin and riotous living reigned in Jack's gang, and if the fourteen neighboring churches ever complained of sin's fatal disease, they were unable to cry forth the remedy: salvation through faith in the death and the resurrection of the spotless Son of God. The gang went to church on Sunday and lived in sin during the week—beer joints, pool halls and dances.

They were considered promising young men. They held excellent positions and were well liked, even in the church. Yet the problem of sin had never been answered. However attractive the appearance of a sinner, the final product of sin is death. Cancer is not cured by talcum powder, and sin is not cured by the polite praises and encouragement of ministers and social workers, nor by psychiatrists who talk about "guilt complexes."

Jack plummeted through five churches. Until his sixth year he was with the Universalists, and then his family moved. The Methodists proved congenial until a feud after class left Jack with a bloody nose. This demanded a new circle of pals with more dignity, so he joined the Presbyterians. When the Baptists started a Boy Scout troop, this was all right, too. He became a Baptist. However, all of these paled to nothing when the delightful daughter of Dr. Sidney Smith was observed to attend the Reformed Church. He suited his taste by immediately becoming Reformed . . . but not converted. Margaret Smith was not yet converted, either.

Margaret Smith was the adopted daughter of a distinguished Brooklyn surgeon, Dr. Sidney Smith. Her name in infancy was Grace Gunn, and she was of Scottish ancestry.

Her mother had died as a result of a fire in the home. Later, Grace was orphaned by the fatal illness of her father.

Dr. and Mrs. Smith named her "Margaret," as there was already a "Grace" in the family. They made every thoughtful and generous provision for their new daughter. Theirs was an English Victorian background that demanded integrity and propriety. There were evidences that their faith was in the Saviour, but great prosperity, and increasing social obligations, had made the things of Christ grow dim.

Margaret was "Marge" to Jack and all his friends, and so she is today, to thousands of Christian associates.

Marge was an unsaved church member. During the week she lived as a host of today's young people live, experimenting with the less offensive forms of sin, but ever sensing that she was being fettered beyond hope. Her kind and indulgent parents did not notice the late hours. Even her mother did not know that Marge smoked constantly while away from home. She attended several movies a day and did all the things her gang thought "fun."

An emergency appendectomy brought her near death. Complications were so serious that she heard her father and a surgical colleague discussing her expected death that night. Though in great pain and weakness, she cried out in desperation for the help of a minister.

"Will I go to heaven if I die tonight?" she asked in agonizing doubt.

The minister, knowing nothing personally about assurance of salvation tried to comfort her. "Your chances are as good as mine," he said. But she was not satisfied. She had no knowledge of the new birth, of sins taken away through the atoning death of Jesus Christ.

Great are the ways of God. Marge's mother liked a certain Gospel radio program, the "Young People's Church of the Air," by which the fiery young radio evangel, Percy Crawford, had ministered faithfully since 1931. The first summer conference at Pinebrook, in July of 1933, was mentioned on the program. Mrs. Smith decided to send the Christian summer camp a gift and to take Margaret there for a few days.

Marge didn't want to go. She feared it would be unfamiliar—and unpleasant. But the camp was near a famous Pennsylvania summer resort, and so she finally consented to make the trip.

Fifteen evening dresses went into Marge's suitcases. When she arrived, she was troubled by the plain appearance of the girls, and she hoped to escape soon to a neighboring hotel. But the young camper decided to stay one night. This concession was rewarded. A spirited Gospel quartet sang of salvation and of heaven. Young people told of a new life in Christ. And then Percy Crawford preached on "Hell"! Marge alternately sneered and trembled. Well known for plain speaking, the evangelist hurled at Marge a stream of Scripture verses concerning judgment and salvation. The Holy Spirit burned them in. Conviction of sin made her wretched. It seemed that a searchlight was upon her. When the invitation was given, several of the girls asked for prayer— and so did Marge.

Marge didn't cry at first. Her heart was too filled with wonderment as she realized that her burden of sin and guilt was gone. The other girls were weeping with their own new-found joy of salvation. Marge stole away to her camp cot and then her heart broke. The hardness of the years melted away, and she knew the sweet peace of the Saviour. The precious blood of the broken body of Jesus Christ had availed for her broken life. His glorious resurrection power had entered her heart.

Life was worth living! She sent a glad telegram of testimony to her boy friend, Jack Wyrtzen. He rejoiced and wired back that he was saved, too. You see, he had been afraid to tell her!

The Word of God was Jack's compass long before he was skilled in the understanding of it. "God said it, Jesus did it,

I believe it, and that settles it!" he often quoted. In the first year of his Christian experience God had begun the proof of His promise: "I will instruct thee and teach thee in the way which thou shalt go: I will guide thee with mine eye" (Ps. 32:8). The promise became exceedingly precious.

And Jack *needed* guidance. The Lord was real and dear to him, but he had not yet sensed that through salvation he was "dead" and "hid with Christ in God" (Col. 3:3). In the years of struggle, 1932 and part of 1933, he had tried to continue in some of his old ways, while denying the power of the resurrection to cleanse his walk.

Jack was still a dance-band leader. Why he should give up this employment did not immediately occur to him. It supplemented his income as an insurance man, and a fellow had to live, didn't he! Anyway, didn't he give out tracts in the subway, and talk to people in the office about the Lord? Didn't he spend his money to help evangelism?

Comforting his soul by giving out tracts, he continued to lead the band. He even asked God to help him with the arrangement of the dance music! God could do all things . . . almost.

One night, carrying his tracts and his trombone, Jack went to play for a sorority dance. The date was December 3, 1933, and the band throbbed with its usual delirious rhythm. But the leader lacked something. The hostess sensed it, and came to Jack with a kind curiosity, devoid of understanding. The hour was twelve-thirty—no time for the temperature of the music to cool. "Don't you feel well, Jack?" she inquired.

"I don't know that I am enjoying myself," said Jack. And that was the end. He never played again for the world, the flesh and the devil.

"'Old things are passed away; behold, all things are become new,'" he had declared in that first street meeting in Philadelphia, December 10, 1933, to which George Schilling had summoned him. It was the only Scripture verse that Jack had learned. George had used it six times in his street-corner exhortation, and it was humbling for Jack to repeat it again. But why not, for now he knew it as a reality, as he was walking by faith with Jesus.

During the winter of 1933-34, Jack, George and Ray were much exercised about studying the Word of God more thoroughly. Where to go for help they did not know. There were fourteen churches in town, but none with an out-and-out, Fundamental, evangelistic fervor. Why, they didn't even have a Sunday-night service, let alone an evangelistic service.

Well, a fellow could meet in his own home, couldn't he? In America there is no law against that.

How could you get the fellows to join you? God would take care of that. Prayer would awaken their interest. Life from heaven would be more attractive than its cheap imitation in the gaiety of sin. The Holy Spirit could warm the soul to Jesus Christ, and without the curse of Satan's counterfeit, liquor. "Why do they put the pretty girls and noble-looking gentlemen in the liquor advertisements?" Jack often asked. "Why don't they show the final product of alcohol, the rotten, gutter-flavored wrecks that are beyond all hope, except in Jesus Christ?"

Chapter 3

PLEDGES OF CHI BETA ALPHA

So GEORGE AND JACK started a little home-meeting. It took the form of a fraternity, a mysterious "secret" group called XBA, Chi Beta Alpha. The Spanish Civil War had not yet brought forth the term "fifth column," but that's what the little XBA was, a fifth column for God, to pray, preach and win souls right in the devil's territory. Fellows "joined"— and they had plenty of surprises. It was a Bible club for prayer and soul-winning.

The "fraternity" was George's idea, and he preceded Jack as the "princeps," or leader, of it. You may smile at this august organization, but you must agree that, according to their old constitution, their purpose was noble: (1) to win others for Christ (Matthew 25:14-29); (2) to study the Bible (II Peter 3:18); (3) to seek the society of Christians (Ephesians 4:11-18); (4) to help and encourage others to read the Bible; (5) to furnish talent for churches, street meetings and missions (speakers, testimonies, male chorus singing); (6) to attend various churches in a group; (7) to distribute Bibles (Gospels, tracts and New Testaments) and present every new member with a Scofield Reference Bible (Luke 24:27); (8) to develop lay talent to work in their respective churches.

You can see plainly that the "Young Men for Christ" (their public name) meant business for God. The statement of their purpose remained virtually unchanged when Chi Beta Alpha became a Pocket Testament League team in 1936 and the Word of Life Fellowship in December, 1939. Thousands of present-day youth rallies across the world have adopted the aim of Chi Beta Alpha.

George Schilling, writes from Rochester, New Hampshire, sending a venerable carbon copy of the constitution, "You can judge our profundity by the fact that the XBA (for us, at least) meant 'Christians Born Again.' What we lacked in scholarship and theological exactness we made up in zeal, I suppose. At least the Lord did use the foolish, weak and base things."

Membership in the active group was restricted to those from sixteen to thirty. A definite born-again experience was a requisite for membership. To become an active member, the prospect had to be "pledged" for a month and attend both meetings (held on the first and third Mondays of the month). At the third meeting the "pledge" was required to give his testimony. (No wolves were permitted in this sheepfold.) A majority vote in the *next* meeting was required to elect the pledgee. And, moreover, each member had to promise to carry a New Testament with him at all times.

The other name for Chi Beta Alpha was "Young Men for Christ," similar to the term "Youth for Christ" which Jack later used in many meetings and rallies around New York.

Jack's date book for 1934 records numerous "frat" meetings. We observe that the women "kept silence" in the meetings, too, for they were completely excluded! Thus was the problem of girls in a young man's life completely solved! This unauthorized severity prevented even Marge from entering her boy friend's house one evening when the fraternity was in session. "The fellows simply wouldn't understand," Jack explained to her with roguish finality.

The girls later countered by forming their own little band,

"Phi Gamma," a "fishing club"—fishing for the salvation of other girls. It was Percy Crawford's idea, and many were the good reports of its chapters.

The fellows had started with four members: Jack Wyrtzen, George Schilling, Ray Studley and Henry Hutchinson. Fairly soon their membership numbered twenty-one. All that winter they studied the Gospel of John. Blessed by their study of the Word, prayer and fellowship, the young men felt the need for the normal consequence of these: witnessing, needful spiritual exercise.

They put it to a vote. Should they actually try street preaching? Jack was doubtful. That was not so easy as being a fraternity member! Everybody would know them, too. The vote was 20 to 1. The fraternity wanted to go all the way. Jack knew that God would not let them down, but he hoped the meeting would be on a back street.

A girl was there on the street, and she was smiling with embarrassment. A girl! Well, they knew why they were there —to speak a good word for the Lord Jesus Christ, the Saviour. The girl's name was Helen. She had come because they invited her. Being a pastor's daughter, she felt she must live up to her reputation. God spoke to her heart, and she yielded her all. Helen later became a member of the girls' quartet.

One of the first to know the Lord through this burning new apostolate was Bill Wiley. Bill was a steady homespun sort in whom God saw fine gold. He was office boy in the Stock Exchange in New York, and the noisy confusion might have unsettled the mind of a less stable person. Jack made a date to sell Bill some insurance. It was cunning strategy. Young Wiley got insurance for eternity, for he accepted the Lord Jesus Christ as his Saviour. He had never known that such a provision had been made by God. Bill's church had an ample program of social suppers and bingo games, but no Gospel message.

Now that Bill was "liberated," he became one of the most

faithful soul-winners, touching thousands of lives through
the "fraternity" and as advance jail-contact man for the
Pocket Testament League teams. Bill was a real missionary,
and proved it when the army placed him in New Guinea.
As master sergeant he used his spare time to give natives
the Gospel message. God gave him a faithful helpmeet in
Marjorie Clarke, of the South America Indian Mission, and
today they are in the heart of Brazil, bringing the Gospel
message.

Jack and his friends hadn't even known how to go about
studying the Word of God. One time they launched into the
majestic ocean of the Old Testament and swam toward any
islands they could find. God helped them. "Trust in the
Lord with all thine heart; and lean not unto thine own understanding. In all thy ways acknowledge him, and he shall
direct thy paths" (Prov. 3:5-6). How important this living
admonition and promise was to become in other years!

They heard of able teachers who were willing to come and
help them, and many of these were Plymouth Brethren. Great
friends these, traveling across metropolitan New York from
Jersey's shore, and farther. J. Arthur Reed was one of the
faithful "missionaries." He lived in Elizabeth and was president of the Newark Gideon Camp. His son, Brandt, joined
the Woodhaven "four" and attended the little meeting every
Monday night. "We sure looked up to Brandt," Jack says.
"He was the only one of us that had a Bible background,
and we drank in everything he had to say."

Brandt Reed gives his first impressions of Jack, as he was in
1933 or 1934. "He came over to Ray Studley's house where
I had been invited to meet the group. Ray had told me of
the converted band leader. He was wearing a white sweater.
I liked his personality lots."

The Reeds introduced another "Brethren" friend to the
group, Alfred Kunz, of Tenafly, New Jersey. He also guided
the young seekers into the priceless riches of God's Word,
advising the fellows when the hard problems of young man-

hood laid siege to them. It was Alfred Kunz who married Jack and Marge on April 18, 1936. (Beverly Shea sang and Brandt Reed served as best man.) And it was Mr. Kunz who years later stood with Jack, weeping silently with joy as he watched the heavenly waves of blessing sweep over the hundreds of souls won at the Madison Square Garden Rally, for they both remembered that it was all of God with whom they had covenanted, through Jesus Christ, in a young man's bedroom, on Long Island.

Alfred Kunz now heads the Pocket Testament League, of which Jack is also a director. But that is a later story. Mr. Kunz says of Jack: "He put legs on his prayers—prayed and obeyed. He had a single eye to God's will. I recall so well the years with him, on the way to hospitals and jails with his red leather Bible. He would talk openly and without shame of the things of God as we traveled along, especially to the bewilderment of the subway crowd.

"Eventually the gang couldn't crowd into the bedroom, so an arrangement was made to use the Republican Club. The fellows went more and more into the open-air work, preaching on the street corners. It was during this time there emerged a prayerfulness and obedience in Jack. He became fearless in whatever project he felt God wanted him to undertake. And his loyal friendship to the humblest of his earliest colleagues in Christian testimony has never altered. He is a hilarious liver in Christ, and God's work is his hobby as well as his calling. I believe he extracts joy from everything."

The girls met with the fellows in the public meetings, but continued to study the Word of God separately in their own "sorority." At the start there were only five girls: Joan Schilling, Marge Smith, Ruth Studley, Helen Cadwell and Anne Lubkemann.

There came a time when the Chi Beta Alpha merged with the Phi Gamma Fishing Club. But that was much later, in 1936, when Marge and Jack were married. That was the beginning of the 1936 to 1940 period in which the fellows and girls put their united effort into the Pocket Testament League project of winning souls and getting thousands to promise they would read God's Word.

In the "dawn days" of 1933-34 the germ ideas of Bible training, soul-winning, banquets and rallies in churches were already developing.

The growing group of earnest young men had experienced salvation and they were willing to fill the lowliest place and do any task for the glory of God. They lived but for one purpose: to win souls for the Lord Jesus Christ. It is no wonder that God today has given them thousands of decisions for Christ and has widened their original mission field in New York until many of the group are now at the ends of the earth.

Fearing dead religious forms, the Chi Beta Alpha group was convinced that obedience to God in winning souls was the only safe way to have continued blessing. The fellows longed to see a revolution that would turn their community upside down for God. They wanted a continuance of the Acts of the Apostles! Were they willing to be broken and blessed for the feeding of a multitude? "Yes, by God's grace," they said.

Jack's favorite illustration of the use of unconventional methods in bringing needy men to Jesus is the picture in Mark 2 where we read that four zealous men, full of faith and cheerful desperation, uncovered the roof of a crowded home where Jesus was and lowered the palsied man to Him for healing. "When Jesus saw *their* faith, he said unto the sick with the palsy, Son thy sins be forgiven thee." Religious leaders, or "scribes," were in the same meeting, reasoning against the Saviour instead of helping sin-sick humanity to meet Him!

"God is not so much concerned with *methods* as with *motives*," Jack has often said, "so we ought to be careful in criticizing those who resolve with the apostle, 'that I might by all means save some'" (I Cor. 9:22).

Top: Second row, Ray Studley, Ernie Lubkemann, Scottie Malcolm, William
    Wiley and Howard Hansman. Front row, Jack Wyrtzen and George Schilling
Center: Taken during the summer when George Schilling first witnessed
    to Jack. Jack is at the left, George on the right
Bottom: The first brass trio. Left to right, Jack Wyrtzen, William (Bill) Wiley
    (now a missionary in Brazil) and George Schilling

Top: Jack speaking to 20,000 people at Madison Square Garden Rally
Bottom: Word of Life Hour Radio Staff. Left to right: Norman Clayton, com-
poser and organist; Harry Bollback, pianist; Jack Wyrtzen; Carlton
Booth, soloist, choir director, song leader and announcer

So the fellows decided to hold a banquet. To secure admission each person must bring one or more unsaved guests! The idea was a good one, and was often repeated in later years. Thus, many heard stirring testimonies who were not otherwise likely to hear the Gospel message. And many were saved.

The first banquet was in May, 1934. (The charge was seventy-five cents a plate in those days.)

Anne Lubkemann was much concerned about bringing her brother, Ernie, for in November of 1932 she had come to know the Lord through Percy Crawford's broadcast. Her heart had been fired by the consecration services at Pinebrook in 1933, the summer that Marge accepted the Lord. And both Anne and Marge were "Phi Gammas."

Ernie didn't want to go. "I get enough of this religion stuff at church on Sundays," he said. Ernie was a young life-insurance employee, who occasionally indulged in a little "innocent mischief."

Anne had told him of her joy in knowing the Saviour, of course, but he was confident that he, too, could give a testimony "just like the rest of them over the radio." Yet he had tried it secretly, and found that he didn't have anything to talk about.

The way of these women! Anne waited until the very evening of the banquet, and then caught Ernie as he came home from work—hungry. "Oh, I'll go," Ernie agreed, languidly. A tasty meal wouldn't make things worse.

The banquet attracted some forty or fifty unsaved persons. Arrangements were made so that it adjourned in favor of a meeting at the Euclid Baptist Church, sponsored by the Chi Beta Alphas. Ernie accepted the Lord Jesus Christ that night. His most earnest desire was to testify of his newly-found peace and joy at the next street meeting. Jack was a little doubtful, or even "pharisaical," he regrets to say. He did not yet know that the babe in Christ not only grows mightily by commencing at once to tell others, but that there is about that fresh testimony of a new convert a glorious and spontaneous quality that breaks open the hearts of many who have not yet seen Jesus.

Ernie never did things half measure. He brought his violin to the very next Chi Beta street meeting. If the instrument had any shortcomings, they weren't Ernie's fault, and the music brought a crowd. (Later Ernie played a trumpet.) Despite Jack's doubts, Ernie begged to testify. "I have to," he said, "because this is my gang—the fellows I have been shooting pool with." So they allowed him to testify, and he learned a valuable lesson. Ernie stood on Jack's orchestra stool and told his former gang how God had saved him and had given him a new heart. There was astonishment and interest on many faces. (An average of ten persons accepted Christ nightly in the street meetings.)

Only power from heaven can make a person eager for a street meeting! But Anne recalls that one night Ernie didn't even wait for the gang. There they were, Anne and Ernie, in front of the five and ten, and numerous people recognized them. Ernie was convinced that he must take advantage of the opportunity. He started playing his trumpet—and Ernie and Anne had a meeting. But God was with them.

All the tasks that God gave Ernie to do—are they not written in His records! Testifying in jails, hospitals, C.C.C. camps, street meetings, offices; leaving his insurance job to attend Columbia Bible College; marrying his God-appointed helpmeet, Leona Shade, of Washington, D. C.—all were part of God's plan. And today this Christian couple are, with their children, in the frontiers of the Xingu Indian country, in the heart of the Matto Grosso, in Brazil. The writer met a senior missionary of the South America Indian Mission who said, "We need more Ernies!"

Chapter 4

"FOOLS FOR CHRIST"

"At the beginning, four of us were preachers, Ray, George, Henry and I," Jack recalls. "We were six months in our bedroom Bible school, and we had only one sermon each. There was quite a question which one should preach, so before we knew any better, we would flip a coin to find out (method not recommended). Happily, we came to know a fellow named Phil Saint, who had lots of sermons. And Charlie Woodbridge (now Dr. Charles Woodbridge, PhD.). We brought them to meetings in local churches, when we could."

While nineteen of the Chi Beta Alpha fellows prayed, Jack and Ray went to the deacons of a certain church and asked permission to hold meetings. Permission was granted and the committee raced back to tell the jubilant group. God answered prayer. In the first meeting there were two hundred, with twenty-two conversions. Three months later, in the closing meeting, there were six hundred and twenty-five persons, with fifty-five decisions for Christ. Two deacons and seven or eight Sunday-school teachers yielded to the Saviour!

31

Among the trophies of grace on the first Sunday in October
was Dorothy Duchardt. Her first concern was for her brother,
John. Three months went by, as she continued to pray
and enlist prayer for him. The fellows earnestly claimed
"Duke" for Christ. He was a butcher and a hard-boiled
truck driver. Also, he was remembered as a star baseball-
catcher during his schooldays. His sister Dot had trembled
to invite him to another Gospel meeting as he had refused
frequently. Duke found himself dodging the meetings, for he
had planned other ways of spending his evenings in riotous
living and in dissipation.

One night, however, he did decide to come to a meeting
and they found a special seat for him, in full sight of the
speaker, who was again—Percy Crawford. The meeting was
over, and before he could escape, Ernie introduced him to
Percy Crawford. Conviction filled Duke's heart with shame
and despair, and he accepted the help of God. Salvation so
changed Duke that neighbors and those who patronized his
delicatessen truck wondered at the cause of it. Duke became a "pickle wagon" preacher, but his message was sweet.
He was added to the "Young Men for Christ," too, and was
soon participating in the street corner, jail and hospital services. When he remembered the wonder of his deliverance
from sin, his eyes often filled with tears. Audiences were
broken with praise to God as his clear tenor voice sang out
"I know of a Name, a beautiful Name, that angels brought
down to earth . . . That matchless Name is Jesus." Among his
favorite songs was *It's Real.*

Gospel revolutions, or revivals, work in all directions. One
saved person in some measure changes the whole course of a
neighborhood, and that through a host of little things. It
was a new development in the history of the local public
library, for example, when Duke brought back an armful
of books he had "borrowed permanently." The Spirit of God
had pointed out to him one day that he had stolen them.
Neither did the fullness of his Christian joy return until

he took them back. The attendant was filled with wonderment, as books are often stolen but never returned. "So *salvation* could do *this* for a person!"

One could write a book about any of the young men in that gang that meant business with God. Duke worked with them for years in the task of reaching souls. He was joined in marriage to one of the group, Doretta Davison, and the couple entered missionary training. At this writing, Duke is teacher of the Missions and the Christian Character Courses in the Word of Life Bible School in New York, and performs his full-time ministry as director of the Christian Business Men's Victory Center, sponsored by the New York Christian Business Men's Committee. Through this organization, thousands of young men from all parts of the world have come to know the Lord Jesus Christ as Saviour.

The year 1934 was indeed a great year of beginnings. The names of Marge, Bill, George, Brandt and "Scotty" Malcolm appear on the yellowing news clippings and programs gleaned from that year. "Scotty," by the way, was a considerable help. He had come to know the Lord one golden day in Dundee, Scotland, when he had gone into a meeting with a gun, to make a malicious disturbance. R. A. Torrey was preaching, and Charlie Alexander was singing. Instead of ejecting him from the meeting, they told him of the Saviour. The message concerned the "New Birth." "The first birth has done me little good," Malcolm said. That night they led him to Christ. And now he was in America as Jack's neighbor and friend.

Jack's record book of 1934 contains notes of faithful efforts: "Tried to reason with a fellow who expects to be a Christian Scientist . . . Tried to speak to C. G. Little interested. Told him to listen to Crawford . . . Gave out tracts . . ."

James E. Bennet, widely-known New York Christian lawyer, was among the first teachers and advisors of the little fraternity of "Young Men for Christ." From the rich experience of a lifetime spent in laboring with Bible Christians, he taught pointedly the high privileges of salvation truth. He was well acquainted with the young people of the New York area, and they liked his humor and forceful Bible challenge. Here was a Presbyterian whose glad acknowledgment of Jesus Christ was in the succession of Jonathan Edwards. The fellows called him "Uncle Jimmy." Speaking of him, Jack declares soberly, "God gave him to us. No one knows how much sorrow and trouble he has saved us through his noble and consecrated advice." Fifteen years later, Brother Bennet is one of the most intimate advisors of the Word of Life Fellowship, as well as a teacher in the Word of Life Bible School.

About this time, Brandt Reed obtained employment in Jack's insurance office in New York, and they had more opportunity for fellowship. Brandt, however, went to Long Island less often. God had raised up the Elizabeth Prayer Fellowship in New Jersey, and there were to be other groups like the high-school "Born-Againers," and, finally, the "High School Evangelism Fellowship" which was to spread the Gospel among a half-million Greater New York young people, 92 percent of whom were without even nominal religious connection!

Brandt told Jack about Bob Moon. Bob was the son of a New Jersey dentist. At college he had taken a few drinks to "please the fellows," and soon he was fettered by the hellish power of alcohol. His conduct was such that he was expelled from college. Moreover, he had been expelled from three other colleges! Bob did not lack brilliance. But he lacked a Saviour. When he was black-listed from all the colleges, he didn't feel happy about going home, so he played the piano for drinks in beer parlors. Bob was a phenomenal piano player. Prayer for Bob was answered. Reports of his salvation brought gladness to many who had known him and prayed for him. God gave him a new heart and a burning testimony of Jesus Christ. He mastered the profitable profession of mechanical dentistry, established a godly home, and traveled widely playing the piano in Gospel meetings. When Jack's Chi Beta Alpha group merged with the Pocket Testament League team, Bob Moon was often the pianist. He also played the piano in the first Saturday-night rallies. Later he prepared for the mission field, learned Spanish in Mexico, and without the support of an organization, entered the needy Putumayo River area of Colombia, South America, the area where he is at this writing, with his wife and five children, bringing the Gospel of Jesus Christ to those who have never heard.

In 1935 the Chi Beta Alpha fellows preached frequently in New York rescue missions, as well as churches. There were street meetings and church programs featuring James Bennet, J. C. Wilson, Dr. Woodbridge and Walter MacDonald. The Young Men for Christ were impressed by the fact that several rescue missions in New York were reporting more souls saved by actual count than the combined results of all the denominational churches in the entire New York area! There was a hint here for the young people. "Build out instead of up. Give out instead of horde. Lose your life in reaching others. In saving others you cannot save or spare yourself." It was a great lesson.

The hunger of these young Christian workers for more of God's Word gratified Alfred Kunz, who had taught them the Bible truths of repentance, justification, atonement and redemption, and the meaning of the names of God. It was providential, therefore, that the Hawthorne Gospel Church in Hawthorne, New Jersey, established an evening Bible-study course, in which Herrmann Braunlin, Alfred Kunz and Arthur Springer would teach. All who could attend this Monday-night class found a spiritual arsenal. Jack attended Hawthorne Evening Bible School two and one-half years, beginning in 1938. Herrmann Braunlin was pastor of Hawthorne Gospel Church. For many years Mr. Braunlin had been employed in a New York office, also. His notebooks became filled with jewels from God's Word as he faithfully studied his Bible while he rode the daily commuter's train from New Jersey.

Jack never found it possible to complete more studies at the evening Bible school, but in 1943 he was given an honorary diploma for the four-year course.

When the marriage of Jack and Marge in 1936 brought a merger of the Chi Beta Alpha Club with the Phi Gamma Fishing Club, there were no sighs of regret. The fellows and girls were so busy in the glad work of carrying the Gospel that there were not enough hours in the day, especially since they were all working or attending school.

Then began a stirring saga of the grace of God. It was a passionate effort to get the Word of God into the hands of the multitudes. Thursday-night prayer meetings stimulated the meetings of the team in churches, jails, reformatories, hospitals, night clubs and C.C.C. camps.

"We knew God could give us strength to do it," Jack said, "because we belonged to Him. Most of us had served the devil all night, while holding down our day employment. We asked that God would give us the strength and guidance to do *more* than that for Him. If the 'pleasures of sin' had been the bait that lured us on before, now truly the 'joy of the Lord' was our strength."

"The hand of the Lord was with them: and a great number believed, and turned unto the Lord" (Acts 11:21). This verse of Scripture became a living testimony to them long before the organization of the more spectacular youth rallies which arrested the attention of the nation and of the world.

What was the recipe for such revival? A broken heart for Jesus Christ; a burning love for the Son of God, "who loved [us] and gave himself for [us]"; fervent prayer for the gain of God's interests, alone; straight-from-the-heart testimonies of deliverance from the filth and guilt of sin, through the blood of Jesus Christ; the Word of God in plain speech, and the entreaty to be reconciled to God through the acceptance of His crucified and risen Son; music, the best obtainable, filled with the praise of Jesus Christ, poured forth as a fountain from the hearts and instruments of those who personally loved Him.

Not only were there the Thursday-night meetings devoted wholly to prayer, ("Without me ye can do nothing"), but prayer meetings were held in the automobiles while the young folks were riding. "Call unto me, and I will answer thee, and shew thee great and mighty things, which thou knowest not" (Jer. 33:3).

"From the beginning," Duke recalls, "Jack emerged as the leader of the group. It wasn't something you voted about: it was a God-given capacity. 'A man's gift maketh room for him' (Prov. 18:16). Nobody was jealous of it. If he led us he was the servant of us all. He humbly counseled with the lowliest of Christians, and thankfully acknowledged help from them."

The testimonies were a vital part of the ministry. Short and straight to the point of redemption and the sure hope of heaven, they were the artillery that softened the field for the sermon attack and the capture of many for Jesus Christ. The Gospel team was made up of young men and women who were close to present-day life, with all its temptations and problems. They were living proof that God could save a dance-band leader, a butcher, a clerk, an office boy, a beautician, a stenographer and a schoolgirl.

Behind the prison bars of Sing Sing, Rykers Island Penitentiary, New Jersey State Prison at Trenton and many other jails and reformatories, unhappy men and women, for whom Christ died, were giving attention to firsthand claims that Christ could save to the uttermost. Could it be for them also? Was it possible? Thank God, many proved it so. The ringing testimony of these young nonprofessional ministers and missionaries commanded the respect of their hearers. Remembering how important Ernie's testimony had been in the conviction of his former associates, Jack now brought with him many newly delivered from lives of sin. In nontheological language they told of their salvation and hope and their words moved hearts strangely, as in the glorious days of old.

Immediately after work, the team assembled and prepared to drive to such needy "mission fields," frequently in adjoining states. When the message had gone forth, and the souls were garnered in, the young witnesses went home again—but often there was little of the night left for rest. "But God gave us strength for the new day," recalls Ruth Elliott Narramore, who was first trumpeter, and a member of the girls' trio in those years. "We didn't seem to miss the sleep, certainly not as much as we would have noticed the loss in staying up late hours for our own purposes."

The group, however, did not always win outward approval for its sincere testimonies and stirring challenge. Some pastors were afraid of revival. They wanted the interest of young people, but not at the price of a spiritual revolution. When their young people accepted Jesus as Saviour, they trembled at the zeal and enthusiasm that quickly changed their little formal and dead pattern. Such timid pastors did not invite Jack to return. But again and again he was invited to revisit scores of churches which were prayerfully seeking every means of bringing their youth into contact with the living Christ.

Prisons were among the most enthusiastic hosts of the traveling team. Those who were saved in the prison chapel meetings often became tireless students of the Word of God. They supplemented the Bible-study lessons by searching for themselves the Scriptures. *The Young Believers' Bible Work*, by Keith L. Brooks, of *Los Angeles*, was a follow-up course used with blessing by the newly-saved prisoners. One of the most earnest and spiritual gatherings in a certain state was not a church congregation but a prayer and Bible-study group in the state penitentiary! Some would never see the outside world again, because of their offenses against society, but God had delivered them from the infinitely

onger fetters of sin. And those who were forgiven much
o loved much.

Jails were not always hospitable at first, however. In a
uthern prison, for example, a large company of women
isoners jeered and mocked the evangelistic party. In such
oments the workers, like foreign missionaries, remembered
at a lost world has never invited the Saviour or His mes-
ngers. "Herein is love, not that we loved God, but that
loved us, and sent his Son to be the propitiation for our
is" (I John 4:10). Being sent of Him enables the evange-
t to know the quietness of His will, even though all mock
id appear to reject the Name.

The jeering cries "Preacher Boy," "Sissy," "Sky Pilot" and
loly Joe" were taken up by the imprisoned women. But a
adual hush settled upon that hostile prison congregation as
e women listened with sullen curiosity to the "Preacher
oy." God's Word, like a spiritual machine gun, began to pierce
arts. There were testimonies that told of deliverance from
n. Sin had imprisoned all mankind. Christ had paid the
ebt to set us free.

The music, the testimonies and the Word of God—these
attered the ridicule. Presently their leader put up her
and for prayer. Fifty women accepted Jesus Christ. The
romise of a new life had become theirs through Jesus Christ!

Those who have traveled with Jack Wyrtzen know that
e is not ashamed to use the same message and illustrations
epeatedly, so long as God honors them with the salva-
ion of souls. For this, however, there is sound precedent,
is Spurgeon, D. L. Moody, Paul Rader, Percy Crawford
nd probably many others have done likewise. Jack's record
books contain notations of his favorite messages: "Five
Fools," "The Boa Constrictor," "Millions Now Living Are
Dead," "Have You Been Born a Second Time?" "The Soon
Return of the Lord Jesus," "Two Thieves," "The Heart of
Man," "The Prodigal Son" and "Sin and Its Cure."

The messages never neglected to declare the hopelessness

of our condition under sin; the blood of Jesus Christ for
our sins; His resurrection and the invitation to come to Him.
Many who thought themselves hardened yielded themselves
to God in new-found faith in His provision.

The arduous schedule of the Gospel team during its years
with the Pocket Testament League frequently called for
missionary journeys that commenced at the close of work on
Friday and continued until Sunday night or Monday morning. In the same manner the fellows took their vacations together in the summer and traveled as far as they could in a
wide circuit from their New York homes. On one of these
trips, services were held eleven times in one day! On one
occasion the group walked into a roadhouse and invited the
customers outside to hear the Gospel. The crowd actually
went out and listened, to the astonishment of the proprietor.

By September of 1937 the group had distributed 15,000
Pocket Testament League Gospels. That summer they traveled
in New England, covering 1,500 miles in ten days, holding
28 meetings, including four broadcasts, and giving out 2,200
Gospels of John. At the close of a meeting at the C.C.C.
camp a man came forward and said, "I am fifty-eight years
old and my life has been spent in sin. I would to God that
I were good enough to go to heaven." They had the joy
of telling him that no one was *good* enough to go to heaven,
but that God had made the way through Jesus Christ.

In the late thirties Carlton Null, of Highway Evangelism,
Inc., gave the group the idea of distributing tracts in a color-
ful wrapping of cellophane. The practice was so novel that
multiple thousands of tracts were thrown from the cars,
and rarely were they unheeded. The write-in cards proved
that many were interested in accepting the Lord and inquiring further into His Word. A decision requesting
a New Testament was received as late as February, 1948, perhaps ten years after it was dropped from a car!

Twenty-seven meetings were held on one trip when Jack,
Bob Moon, Bill Wiley and Phil Worth took a simultaneous

vacation from their jobs. For variety they had spoken in churches, missions, prisons, tents, broadcasts and at a convention. But the glorious reward of the journey came when 225 of the C.C.C. camp boys accepted Jesus Christ. On the same trip they spoke at the women's prison previously mentioned.

A prisoner, serving a life term, wrote the team from New Jersey State Prison: "I'd rather be in prison saved than to be free and lost." This was also the conviction of many who came to know the Lord in other penal institutions where the Gospel was preached. In fact, many young men having come from ungodly homes, believed that their imprisonment had been the means of acquainting them with salvation.

Through the godly Christian warden, Fred Sacher, many opportunities came to present the transforming Gospel of Christ at the New York City Reformatory, New Hampton, New York. Better than all methods of human reform combined were the good results of the meetings wherein the boys accepted Jesus Christ as Saviour from their sins.

One of the loyal friends and teachers to whom the Pocket Testament League group looked with appreciation was Jim Plummer of Rockville Center, Long Island. Not only had Jim encouraged the boys in every Gospel endeavor, but he also supplied practical aid by lending his car for long Pocket Testament League journeys. On these same trips there often traveled with Jack and the gang a young college student, Merrill Calloway, now a missionary en route to Arabia.

During these years of blessing the saintly life and teaching of another eminent Bible teacher influenced the lives of the Woodhaven young people. Dr. Harris Gregg, eminent and humble scholar and colleague of the leading contemporary orthodox authorities, took time to talk of his Lord with any young servant of God eager to learn. Dr. Gregg had come from retirement to pastor the North Shore Baptist Church at Flushing, Long Island, not far from the last resting place of his old friend, Dr. C. I. Scofield. It was ever remembered

of Dr. Gregg that although he was eminent in the world of
learning he was never known to open a conversation without
acknowledging his Lord and humbly praising Him. His
life and testimony left a mark upon Jack Wyrtzen, Jimmy
Johnson and many others.

On one of the P. T. L. trips the Woodhaven fellows met
Tommy Steele, of Raleigh, North Carolina. Tommy had been
challenged in evangelistic services held by Jimmy Johnson.
His joy in being delivered from a life of deep sin was so
great that he wanted to dedicate his all to the Lord Jesus
Christ. Jimmy Johnson had started a radio broadcast and
then had thrust it into Tommy's hands. For many years this
victorious morning testimony has gone out from WPTF,
Raleigh, under Tommy Steele's direction. He had meanwhile remained in the employ of a laundry company, as
Jack remained with the insurance business.

Among the Long Island ministers who showed kindness to
the Woodhaven group from the earliest years was the Spirit-
filled pastor and teacher Charles E. Furman, of Lake Grove,
Long Island, who first introduced Jack to the celebrated
hymn writer George Stebbins. Both Charles Furman and
George Stebbins had served in the Moody campaigns of long
ago. Brother Furman owns a Bible once owned by Moody.

Also of valuable assistance to Jack was Herbert Elliot, a
building contractor who had the oversight of several enthusiastic church groups on Long Island. Among these
meeting places was the Little White Church in Melville,
Long Island. Elliott is a member of the Word of Life Council.

Remembered with thanksgiving also was the friendship of
Dr. Alexander Sauerwein, the outstanding pastor of Flushing
Presbyterian Church, now of Staub Congregational Church,
Portland, Oregon. Dr. Howard Cleveland, pastor of Dover
Congregational Church, in New Jersey, and now of the
Wheaton College theological faculty, also befriended Jack.
Through men and events, God executes His plan for the
lives of His children.

Chapter 5

JUDAEA, SAMARIA AND WBBC

SINCE THEY HAD gone forth as missionaries along their own Atlantic seaboard, it was not surprising that the group should be concerned about the "uttermost parts" also. Among Jack's earliest missionary acquaintances was Ralph Davis, veteran missionary of the Africa Inland Mission. The young people sought a part in getting the Gospel to the lands that had never heard the good news of Jesus Christ.

Through the zeal of a converted taxi driver, John Rippey, several foreign missionaries were given opportunities to speak in New York rescue missions and prayer groups. Thus in 1937 the writer, returning to Asia, met Jack Wyrtzen at the Fulton Street Noon Prayer Meeting. A year later, to the heart of Burma came an unfailing series of short letters signed by "Duke," or "Jack," and accompanied by prayer-empowered missionary gifts. The bond was never broken, and in 1940 it was possible for me to visit the fellows in New York and see the spiritual revolution that was being spread by the business, home and personal contacts of the young men and women.

The missionary interest of Jack Wyrtzen's P.T.L. group was further awakened by the introduction of Bob Williams, who was on the way to a fruitful pioneer witness of Jesus

43

Christ in Borneo. Their missionary zeal was increased also by the later visits of Paul Fleming and Hubert Mitchell, young missionary veterans of Malaya and Sumatra, who, with the other workers mentioned, owed much of their vision of the unevangelized lands to the late missionary leaders Paul Rader and R. A. Jaffray.

So stirring was the missionary challenge to the young Word of Life group that virtually all the original fellows volunteered for the mission field. Three of those in the original team are in South America today: Ernie Lubkemann and Bill Wiley are in Brazil with the South American Indian Mission, and Bob Moon is laboring independently among the Putumayo Indians of Colombia.

The challenge of Paul Fleming, the most disturbing and painfully pointed, hinged on the last command of Jesus Christ. He discussed apostolic precedent, the evidence of a presently unfinished task, and the culminating hope of Christ's return when the Gospel has been taken to the last tribe and tongue. He emphasized the truth that every man, woman and child in the world had a better right to hear the Gospel of Christ once than we had to hear it twice.

Unspoiled by professional or academic views of missions, the young people simply volunteered to go any place in the world where God might want them to serve. Jack tells of the time when all his interest in life was gone until he could know beyond a doubt what God's will was for him. He was so pierced by the challenge of the unevangelized lands that he and Marge were more willing to go there than stay in New York. Yet they could not ignore the fact that there were also millions of unsaved young people in New York. And God was giving a harvest of souls in the meetings. Jack had to be dead to his own preferences. His hands, like George Muller's, had to be off the scales.

In the fierce struggle of heart he told Marge that he must

Top: Word of Life Hour Bible School
Bottom: Word of Life Council and Staff with wives and office force

Top: Word of Life Boat Ride up the Hudson with 4,500 on board
Bottom: Part of the 4,500-voice girls' choir at Madison Square Garden Rally

retire to the attic and wait on the Lord until he could know without a doubt the will of God for himself. He could not go on without that certainty.

The words "Trust in the Lord," came again to his heart. "Lean not unto thine own understanding. In all thy ways acknowledge him, and he shall direct thy paths." The hours of heart-search brought him out of the dark woodland of his own feelings and into the green pastures of God's peace. As they came long ago to the singer of Israel, there came to him the words from Psalm 32:8: "I will instruct thee and teach thee in the way which thou shalt go: I will guide thee with mine eye."

The experience marked a turning point in Jack's ministry. Henceforth he knew that his plans were not to be his own. There were similar crises in the lives of Carlton Booth and Norman Clayton, the consequences of which were seen in tides of new spiritual blessing.

As the Chi Beta Alpha, or "Young Men for Christ," had been Jack's "Jerusalem" or starting point in Christian testimony, so the streamlined team work of the Pocket Testament League had carried him into neighboring "Judaeas" and "Samarias."

And now, near the end of 1939, the name of the group was changed to "Word of Life Fellowship," and the organization began to reach into the "uttermost parts." The name came from the familiar Scripture verse, "Holding forth the word of life; that I may rejoice in the day of Christ, that I have not run in vain, neither laboured in vain" (Phil. 2:16).

The Word of Life Fellowship was a manifest answer to the prayer of the Gospel group, "Oh that thou wouldest bless me indeed, and enlarge my coast, and that thine hand might be with me, and that thou wouldest keep me from evil, that it may not grieve me! And God granted him that which he requested" (I Chron. 4:10).

The annual banquets increasingly influenced every walk of

life as Christians brought unconverted friends and associates into a gathering glowing with Gospel testimonies and climaxed by a time of fellowship. Previous years had proved the worth of the banquets as a means of soul-winning. The "Spring Banquet in April 1940, was attended by 320. Carlton Booth, of Providence Bible Institute, was the soloist and speaker. He was later to become a "Sankey" in the ever-widening ministry granted to the group. The banquets continued through the years, the last being held on February 25, 1947, at the Hotel Astor, New York. There were 494 in attendance. The previous year, 550 had attended. The banquets brought in a harvest of newly-yielded lives, and the idea was utilized in other cities. The increasing costs of the meals, however, prevented the bringing of many additional guests.

Throughout the years, especially at the banquets, boat rides and rallies, the attendance of consecrated Christian businessmen was a sustaining and strengthening force. These men were chiefly from the Gideon camps and the Christian Business Men's Committees. Some of them were·known to Jack in the business world. Many were prominent Manhattan business executives. It was not uncommon to see these influential men in the large cities testify of Jesus Christ in the city parks and distribute tracts. (The writer remembers having been invited to testify with Leon Sullivan, vice president of a brokerage firm, and other business leaders, in a Philadelphia square.)

It is significant that Jack Wyrtzen is still identified with the Gideon and Christian Business Men's groups rather than with the organized ministry. He has never accepted ordination from any human committee or organization. In like manner, God raised up Spurgeon, Moody and Dr. Ironside to minister with great blessing across the English-speaking world, and that without human credentials. Yet, like these humble Gospel preachers, Jack has a host of truly cherished friends in the organized ministry.

An outstanding example of the ardent spending of one's

life for God—an example which was a chief formative influence in Jack's early ministry—was "Uncle Ott," a Christian lawyer of Binghamton, New York. His Scriptural and Spirit-filled ministry, conducted by personal contact and radio, brought many to accept Jesus Christ.

Othniel Brandt, LL.B., was the skeptic son of a pioneer Minnesota Gospel preacher. In the course of his successful career at law, Othniel felt led to write a thesis on the fallacies of the Christian revelation. Like Lew Wallace, author of Ben Hur, he believed it wise to read the Bible first, in order to develop his subject. And like Lew Wallace, he was impaled by the sword of the Spirit, broken by the loving sacrifice of the sovereign Son of God for the sin of man. Othniel became a fervent believer and an immediate witness who delighted in living his remaining days for Jesus Christ.

Heaven beckoned early to him. A heart condition developed, and his doctor warned him to be careful. Othniel Brandt did not dare to conserve that which belonged to God, and he allowed his life to be poured forth in a stream of thanksgiving and testimony. From station WNBF he witnessed across the countryside. His business letterhead bore these Scripture references: Hebrews 2:11; Colossians 3:1; Proverbs 2:3-5. He held meetings in addition to his weekly broadcast. Across his little church was a joyous sign: "The Blood, the Book, the Blessed Hope." And "he was not, for God took him." One day Jack scrawled into his little date book, "Uncle Ott's funeral." But it was like a revival—Uncle Ott's funeral. A group of earthly friends asked the Lord for like privilege in Him, and they kept Othniel's burning motto tenderly in their hearts.

In 1940, Jack's group felt that the next step in "enlarging their coasts" should be a Gospel radio program for the Word of Life Fellowship. The small Brooklyn station WBBC was suggested through the kind help of Mortimer Bowen, a Christian business executive. Jack Wyrtzen, the trio and the quartet undertook this weekly half-hour program literally without purse or scrip—or even script!

Some of the lessons learned were terrifying as well as humorous, and prepared them against the day when a precisely-timed program of testimony and music would go forth from New York on a network to four or five million listeners.

The Young people assembled at WBBC every Tuesday morning. "Duke," parked his delicatessen truck out front and sang his solos while he was dressed in overalls. Ruth Elliott Narramore recalls that the girls' quartet was often a trio, and that she played first trumpet in the "Men's Brass Quartet"! The girls, Anne Lubkemann, Dorothy Duchardt, Ruth Elliott and Helen Cadwell, were coached by Helen's mother, a trained vocalist. The "Men's Brass Quartet" was composed of Ruth Elliott, first trumpet, Bill Wiley, second trumpet, Jack Wyrtzen, first trombone, and Phil Worth, second trombone. Marge Wyrtzen and Bob Moon were pianists.

One day the spirited brass quartet was playing a powerful and dramatic sequence "Thy God Reigneth!" A member of the chorus thought innocently enough that such a blast of melody would cover up while he blew his nose. But the selection called for a sudden rest. Too late! A ripping sound shattered the silence. The astonished band had to continue, and approached a repetition of the dramatic phrase. Now thoroughly bewildered, the unhappy offender thought it would be safe this time, at least. The same indescribable sound filled the musical rest. It was difficult to finish the program.

One of the low moments in the brave attempt to "hold forth the Word of Life" over WBBC was a program in which everything was out of tune. "Keep going! Keep going!" Jack whispered in agony. At last he went humbly to the management to apologize.

The Jewish manager, touched by his distress, made several observations. "In the first place," he said, "you are only human. In the second place, it will keep you humble. And

in the third place, nobody listens to this station, anyway!"
While the Gospel team was meditating on this gloomy homily,
the station ceased to exist, and the team was temporarily
without an opportunity for radio testimony.

Jack Wyrtzen desired to remain a businessman as long
as possible, not for personal gain, but that his contacts with
businessmen might count the more for God. Those who knew
his ability have no doubt that he could have achieved success in the business world.

It was difficult for him to leave his employment, for he
believed that the "nonprofessional minister" had considerable
advantages in soul-winning. Even yet he thinks of himself
as a "businessman too busy to go back to work."

After much prayer Jack handed in his resignation. He
did not think that his round-the-clock schedule was fair to his
job or to the Gospel. His employer expressed disappointment
and told him that he was in line for a raise. The fellows in
his office, who had previously shown little outward response
to his sincere effort in showing them the way of salvation,
gave him an unusual token of esteem, a fountain pen set
with a diamond.

It was 1941 when the Word of Life Fellowship found itself
without a radio program, because of the closing of the Brooklyn station. But there was never an idle moment.

Then came the idea of a Hudson River Boat Ride. True,
other Christian groups had taken excursions; why not make
this a *soul-winning* excursion? Great enthusiasm attended
the plans, and measures were taken to charter the *Peter
Stuyvesant*, a junior vessel of a fleet. The capacity was 1,800
passengers. The cost for this would be high, of course, and
a contract necessary.

Consternation filled the young folks' hearts when a letter
from the excursion-line agents told of an operational change,
and suggested a larger steamer, the largest river steamer in the
world, the *Hendrick Hudson*, having a passenger capacity of
5,253! The company explained the merits of the larger vessel.

The young people's faith, already weak, grew weaker. But they accepted the change and hoped that God was in it.

Great was the victory that night when the throng of Christians and their friends came aboard the *Hendrick Hudson.* The smaller vessel could not have accommodated even half of them, for there were 3,604 passengers. Again, God had gone before them and had provided for these whose paths were committed to Him.

The boat ride proved itself a truly unique opportunity to bring friends to know the Lord Jesus Christ. It offered an unusual attraction of combined outing, "entertainment" and refreshments—all in one evening. And what an opportunity for soul-winning! A splendid program of testimonies, a Bible message, and music offered many their first invitation to the Saviour. Missionaries had, in earlier years, proved the value of shipboard opportunities. The person with whom the soul-winner talked could not escape without jumping overboard!

Other youth movements also sponsored boat rides. One of the earliest of these was the popular Potomac Boat Ride, directed by Glenn Wagner, Jack's close friend and colleague, and president of the Washington D.C. Bible Institute.

In the twelve summer boat-excursions that the Word of Life Fellowship has conducted since that first experiment in 1941, hundreds of young people have accepted the Saviour, and many of these have entered training for full-time Christian service.

An outstanding conversion as a result of the boat rides was that of Thelma Lambert, of Trenton, New Jersey, who had come to the outing with friends. During Carlton Booth's singing of *The Stranger of Galilee,* her heart was filled with sadness that Christ was indeed a stranger to her, despite the fact that she led a Christian young people's society. That night as Larry McGuill explained the way of redemption, she gave her testimony that she had yielded her life to the Lord Jesus Christ for salvation and service. At this writ-

ing she is completing her studies at the Providence Bible
Institute, and is looking forward to carrying the Gospel to
foreign lands.

R. G. Le Tourneau was the speaker at the May, 1941,
banquet, attended by 550 guests. His personal testimony,
as one of the world's leading factory executives, stirred the
unconverted in attendance. Of his Saviour he said, "I love
Him because He suffered for me, and I am trying to serve
Him, not just because He will take me to heaven when
I die, but because I have caught a vision of His marvelous
program and I want to take part in that program both here
and hereafter."

The Word of Life Fellowship Bible Conference was
scheduled for the Labor Day week end, August 29 to Sep-
tember 1, 1941. The speakers were Bob Moon, Frank Vurture,
Ted Fix, Brandt Reed, Charles Anderson, Leon Sullivan
and Vincent Brushwyler. It was held at Dorwillen Bible
Conference grounds, at Suffern, New York. At the Memorial
Day Bible Conference, held earlier at the same place, Dr.
Ironside had been a speaker.

The summer boat ride on the Hudson had brought out a
company of 3,200 and an encouraging number had accepted
the Lord during this last summer of peace in a war-clouded
world.

A plea for Christian obedience and thanksgiving was sent
forth: "These are days when we as young people must realize
our individual responsibility to be foreign missionaries, and
this godless world we are living in today is a foreign missionary field. Only the Lord can tell you whether you are to
go a few feet, a few hundred miles, or a few thousand
miles, but every one of us must become missionaries to this
lost and dying world all about us. Revival must come to us
as believers."

Chapter 6

WHN AND SATURDAY RALLIES

WHEN JACK STOOD in front of his home on Forest Parkway, Woodhaven, and told his old friend Alfred Kunz that he felt led to start a Saturday-night youth rally in Times Square, New York, Mr. Kunz naturally was cautious to advocate such a strange new undertaking. There were too many uncertain and untried problems involved. How could one reach the gay multitudes on Broadway—especially on Saturday night? Would Christian young people support such a movement? Like every untried scheme, it aroused little interest. Who could have imagined that it would become a working pattern for hundreds of Saturday-night rallies across the world?

Jack felt it should be successful because Saturday night was the devil's busiest season. If young people could spend Saturday night in merriment, revelry and vice, then the excuse would not serve that young people were "too tired." Jack knew from personal experience that youth could take a lot more than most Christian leaders would dish out. Youth thrived on a challenge. Why not try it? He applied the couplet often quoted by missionaries:

He cannot have taught us to trust in His Name,
And thus far have brought us to put us to shame!

The first Times Square Rally and the first WHN broadcast were a twin birth. The rally was tailored to the swift
precision and zest of the broadcast. In fact, the broadcast
was the first-born of the twins. Jack had written to WHN,
the powerful New York station, inquiring regarding the
possibility of a far-reaching Gospel broadcast. The station
didn't even answer the letter. Encouraged by many blessings
that God had granted the fellowship team during the summer,
Jack felt led to meet the station manager, through a letter
of introduction from H. N. Willets of Western Electric Company, who had engineered the new 50,000-watt installation.
The manager was not even faintly interested in the program.
The time would cost $450 for a half hour, if a contract
had been possible. There would have been no discount.
But it was stated flatly that the program was not in the
interests of the station. The door was closed. Well might
the Christian group have said, "The Lord does not want
us on the radio."

But couldn't a closed door be opened? Two or three weeks
later Jack's letter of inquiry was found by young Marty
Glickman, a co-operative new salesman, who was delighted
to sell the required time. Marty was unaware of previous
conversations between the station and the Word of Life
Fellowship. He wrote Jack to "come in and talk it over."
The contracts were drawn up—while Jack drew a deep breath
of wonderment at the proceedings. A thirteen-week contract—
unbelievable! One half of the money must be paid down.
There would be a discount, the salesman said: $1,750 would
be due before the first broadcast—a considerable sum for fellows who had nothing. Could God supply it? Afterward, the
puzzled station manager inquired how the program bought
the time. No one was to blame. It was just simply a mistake!
Perhaps after the thirteen weeks . . . But the program is

still going in 1948, and the relations with the station have been most pleasant.

The 1941 Word of Life Fall Banquet, October 18, preceded the broadcast by a week, and was a time of spiritual challenge. It was held at Jamaica, Long Island, Y.M.C.A., and Carlton Booth sang and brought the message. Jack was confident that as God had enlarged their coasts He would also take them over the mountains of difficulty. A Bible note beneath Joshua 1:3 reminded him that the immense spiritual grant "Every place that the sole of your feet shall tread upon, that have I given unto you" had but one qualification. God gives, but we must take! Here was another spiritual battle. Battles will continue until Jesus comes. But God had assured the final outcome of the war.

How about the $1,750 required by the contract before the first broadcast? God works abundantly. The group received $1,760, or $10 extra! The remaining obligations were providentially met, week by week.

Now that there was going to be a broadcast, where should it be held? How would it combine with the rally? Would anyone come on a Saturday night?

The old Alliance Gospel Tabernacle, at 44th Street and Eighth Avenue, Mahattan, offered a hospitable meeting place. It was not only on Times Square, a world-capital of gaiety and sin, with it eighty-three theaters and fifty cabarets, but it was a historic rendezvous of Christian workers from the time of the well-known missionary pastor, Dr. A. B. Simpson.

Thus was the setting for the first Saturday-Night Youth Rally, October 25, 1941, with its now familiar slogan "Youth for Christ," used by the youthful Gospel team. Who could have predicted that this meeting would become a first venture in thousands of similar rallies across the world, in war and in peace!

By a happy providence the already powerful station WHN increased its transmission wattage from 5,000 to 50,000 during the first month of broadcast. This gave the Word of

Life broadcast a potential audience of twelve million within twenty-five miles from Times Square, New York.

"From Times Square, New York, we bring you the Word of Life . . . on the air!" became the glad phrase of attack in these youth broadcasts, timed to split seconds and packed with living testimonies, songs, a plain Bible message and a warmhearted invitation to accept the Lord Jesus Christ.

Wonderful Words of Life became the theme song of the Word of Life broadcast. This song has lost none of its vigorous salvation testimony since its introduction in the Moody-Sankey meetings at New Haven, in 1878. Since then it has become the melodious faith-confession of millions of Bible Christians.

Following the WHN broadcast, by Jack Wyrtzen, the first Saturday-night rally was introduced, with songs and testimonies. Pastor David Fant of the Alliance Church, a beloved personal friend, had encouraged Jack greatly in the project and now assisted in the program. The speaker was Forrest Forbes, a missionary from Asia.

Subsequent speakers at the first Saturday-night rallies, November 1 to December 6, were Erling C. Olsen, Dr. F. A. Robinson, Horace Dean, Dr. Clarence Roddy, Ralph Davis, James Bennet, Brandt Reed, Dr. Stephen Paine and Ted Fix.

If the Saturday-night rallies had looked impossible before the first meetings, there was now at least proof that many would attend, and that among these would be pleasure-bent young people who would find salvation.

However, the faith of the Christians was tried further when attendance of the rallies began to decline in November and December. It fell from 250 to 150. At this point it would have been easy to abandon the project, and few would have condemned them for doing so. But God purposed it otherwise, and put a continuing ray of hope in the hearts of the leaders. By the third Saturday in January the auditorium was packed out, and that situation has continued until now. The singing at the rallies was accompanied by pianists Bob Moon, Harry Bollback, Donald MacDonald and Sam Walters.

Following his return from Marine Corps service, Harry Boll-back resumed this duty, and is presently aided by Bob Post.

The tenor soloist during the first year of the rallies was John Trotter. When he was called into the service, he was succeeded by Horace Davies, who aided Carlton Booth. Both of these popular young singers were well known as members of the Young People's Church of the Air Quartet. Horace Davies continues to sing duet parts with Carlton Booth in the Saturday-night rallies and on the radio broadcasts.

Then came Pearl Harbor, and youth, even more than age, had to give the best of its strength to wage a war by air, land and sea, against ruthless invaders of the remaining democratic lands and Christian freedoms.

"A Word of Life meeting held on board the super-battleship the U.S.S. *North Carolina* on the fateful morning of December 7, 1941, was prophetic of the ministry that would shortly go forth to millions of soldiers, sailors and marines who would soon be called to the colors, many of whom were to lay down their lives in remote lands. That morning the holocaust of Pearl Harbor had already taken place. The alarm had not yet been sounded. It was the last moment of a precarious peace. The Gospel had gone forth with power that opened hearts to salvation. That same day the ship was made ready for battle.

Three outstanding Christian sailors were with the Word of Life team on the *Carolina* that Pearl Harbor morning. They were George Blevins, Harry Blair and Jack Armstrong, all from that group of zealous young service men called the "Navigators." Dawson Trotman, of Los Angeles, had originated the Navigators as a fellowship of Christian service men for Bible study, Bible memory work and soul-winning. During the war years it spread through all branches of service, as a means of reaching and deepening thousands of young men and women for Jesus Christ.

Jack Armstrong, shortly to give his life for his country,

testified that day, and told of his conversion. On the U.S.S. *West Virginia*, an Alabama boy named Johnny Prince (who had been won to the Lord by another sailor, Jim Downing) was on his way to a Gospel meeting where he was to preach. He saw a big good-looking young recruit, and felt led to talk to him. There was a struggle, as he had no time to delay in view of the meeting. But he turned aside from his plans and talked with him about the Bible. How wonderful that he did!

Jack Armstrong put his trust in Jesus Christ, and the Bible became his constant companion. His friends wanted to know what he had that they didn't have. True, he was an outstanding athlete and had a pleasant personality, but they knew that he had something the Navy couldn't give. On the U.S.S. *Atlanta* in the last months of his life he conducted a Sunday school and Bible class that helped many men.

He wrote, "I would not trade my relationship with Him for anything on this earth!" His fears were gone. "If anything ever happens to this ship, it will mean sudden death for me—then sudden glory!" The last words he wrote were: "Many men are turning to the Lord Jesus Christ and being saved."

"General Quarters" was sounded on five cruisers and six destroyers as they approached the enemy ships in Savo Sound, Guadalcanal, on November 12, 1942. The *Atlanta* sank several enemy vessels in withering accurate fire. The numerically superior enemy units responded, finally disabling the *Atlanta* with torpedoes and fire, blasting her guns and slaying her gunners. Jack Armstrong, machinist's mate second class, was serving as captain's repairman on the bridge. His surviving buddies found him lying on the bridge, one leg severed and the other filled with shrapnel. His life ebbed away in a New Hebrides base hospital as he prayed that he might depart and be with his Lord forever.

Thousands of friends who remembered Jack Armstrong in

the New York rallies and meetings felt that his testimony was representative of the glorious transformation wrought by Jesus Christ in the lives of hosts of young service men who testified of God's grace during the war years.

One of the members of the original Woodhaven Pocket Testament League was Bob Hawley, a student who had accepted Christ in the meetings of 1933 when Charlie Woodbridge was the speaker. Bob had seen something in the life of Jack that had made him long for the new life also. The surrender of his own life-plans to God occurred later, and he became a member of the gang that testified in the streets and prisons. He even organized a tent campaign in a vacant lot.

As an officer in the Navy, he traveled 100,000 miles during the war, and lost no opportunity to testify of Christ. Upon returning from the service, Bob married Gladys Schneider, Word of Life office manager. He has a testimony in his employment and in neighboring missionary work.

Overwhelmingly large figures numb one's mind, so that one does not grasp the hugeness of the national debt, the population of China, or even the attendance at four Madison Square Garden Rallies, plus the overflow, plus fifty-two radio rallies a year, plus thousands of Gospel meetings in churches.

So, like the photographer, the architect and the artist, one must look at the towering mountain in soft focus, and then take a sharp picture of a near-by object which will provide a detailed study of the whole. Crowds are composed of real people—not statistics. To study the crowd, we must study first the individual.

Consider, for example, the man who couldn't get into the Madison Square Garden Rally. He was one of thousands. As he sat on the curb, the Spirit of God made the Saviour real to him and he wept brokenheartedly when the message of grace came over the outside loud-speakers. He rejoiced that Jesus Christ had died and risen for him, and that he could be saved then and there, even where he sat.

Christians were outside the rally for the very purpose of helping such as he, so there was one to explain further the way of life to him and to join him in prayer.

Another example is the case of the girl who sang in the Garden Rally Choir, consisting of some thousands of voices. At a rehearsal she told Jack that she and her sister had accepted the Lord the year before. They had both signed up to sing again, but her sister had died two weeks before. She had come to keep her covenant. Jack turned to the choir. It was a volunteer group of 2,500 young women, many of whom had never had a previous opportunity to accept the Saviour. That was part of the purpose in inviting numerous young people to sing. When the Spirit of God reached their hearts with the redemption story, many were gained for God. Jack spoke briefly of the urgency in trusting Jesus, and the shortness of life. More than a hundred in the group requested prayer and committed their lives to the Redeemer. Such a wave of blessing swept across thousands of hearts that the songs became psalms of praise which penetrated the hearts of the vast multitude.

The first Madison Square Garden Rally was the next step from the regular tabernacle rallies, which had already expanded into a First Victory Rally at Mecca Temple, and the weekly Saturday-night rallies in historic Carnegie Hall. Subsequent Garden rallies (there have been four so far) were held when the regular Saturday-night rallies met in the great hall of St. Nicholas Arena, Carnegie Hall, Mecca Temple, Gospel Tabernacle and Town Hall.

As a Christian, one is gratified to discover that Jack and his friends never make decisions of any kind without prayer and the definite leading of the Holy Spirit.

What people think does not disturb or influence Jack, and he has been known to reject exceedingly large "opportunities," replete with flattering inducement, because he felt that they were not for the sole glory of God and of Jesus Christ.

"I don't ever feel that we should hold another super-rally

this year just because we held one last year," Jack explains. "It isn't enough reason. But if God warms our heart to trust Him for the utterly impossible, we will believe Him, however dark the outlook and however weak our ability."

The First Victory Rally was in the definite leading of God, and an occasion of praise for the wonderful blessings during the first six months of the Saturday-night broadcasts and rallies. The gathering was held in the Mecca Temple, New York, May, 1942. Many of the fellows thought it unwise to engage a meeting place so large as this. They hoped for a "good meeting," but a full auditorium seemed too much to expect. Jack had caught a vision of victory for this rally as he lay awake during the previous night. When the rally was held, all the seats were filled, more than three thousand of them, and there were a thousand people turned away. Walter MacDonald. "Happy Mac," was the speaker, and many souls were saved.

Eighteen months later it seemed practical to engage a larger meeting place for a series of Saturday-night rallies, so historic Carnegie Hall was suggested. This seemed an immense undertaking of faith, as the cost of holding a rally there was more than seven hundred dollars. Prayer culminated in the conviction that Carnegie Hall should be used when available.

The blessing and the wisdom of the move were apparent in the great outpourings of grace on the meetings. One of the outstanding Carnegie meetings was that in which "Happy Mac" spoke. So many confessed their need for Christ that there was scarcely sufficient space in the inquiry room.

A leading New York newspaper gave front-page prominence to many of the rallies at the Tabernacle, at Carnegie and later at the Madison Square Garden rallies and the St. Nicholas Arena. Noteworthy messages were brought to large groups at the latter place by Dr. Walter Kallenbach, Fred Sacher, Dr. Donald G. Barnhouse, Leon Sullivan, Herbert Lockyer and others.

Chapter 7

MADISON SQUARE GARDEN

At the first Madison Square Garden Rally Carlton Booth declared that the entire undertaking would have been called a fantastic dream even as early as six months before. He pointed out that the idea came when jocular Irish policemen who were trying to guide an overflow of three thousand persons away from Carnegie Hall on Fifty-seventh Street and Sixth and Seventh Avenues asked the gang why they didn't hire Madison Square Garden. Some laughed, but others were not amused. They remembered that there were 3,500 packed in the meeting from which 3,000 were turned away—and that was nearly a third of the Garden capacity!

The cost of renting Madison Square Garden for a Saturday night was $7,000—so the idea was pigeonholed and dismissed as a whimsy.

Big things hinge on little acts of obedience. Jack has never abandoned the work of Soul-winning during the week, in many spiritually needy towns and villages far from New York. Because of these arduous journeys (he has exhausted relays of helpers accompanying him), many churches have been inspired to go forward in new faith.

This time, the prospects were not pleasing. It was a long

trip, and Jack didn't even have the money to reach his destination. But he went there dutifully, borrowing five dollars from Marge. Thoughtful Christians had given him fifteen dollars toward his expenses.

At this humble meeting there was a man present who was convinced that a great rally should be held in Madison Square Garden. He believed this so sincerely that he told Jack about his prayerful conviction. Moreover, he supported it with a check for a thousand dollars! Jack promised to pray about the matter, though the idea seemed visionary.

Signs are not given to unbelievers, but they are given to believers who are moving in the current of God's will, Jack Wyrtzen declares, with sound Scriptural warrant. It is useless to turn the rudder of a ship in drydock, but a light touch on the tiller of a moving vessel guides it perfectly to its proper destination. The council of the Word of Life Fellowship wanted to be in the center of God's will. This experience, the result of humble obedience to His will in an every-day ministry, was viewed as a sign that God would have them trust Him for a great moving of His Spirit in a large meeting in the sinful heart of the world's greatest city.

Heavy were the buffetings of Satan to deter and hinder the growing plan. Seven thousand dollars! The additional expenses for such a rally would bring the cost near ten thousand dollars. But—they had a thousand!

The sponsors of this great Christian rally encountered several strange expense items: a private chief of police and eleven policemen must be paid; cleaning after the crowd would cost $284.77; mysterious figures called "emergency men" (not personal workers!) would cost $32.63; the watchman was paid $30.36 to guard the rented pianos in the lobby (a painful commentary on present-day society!); the marquee sign "Word of Life—Youth for Christ Rally—Jack Wyrtzen—Gil Dodds—C. Booth" cost $50.00. And these were but a few typical expenses.

The darkest days came just before the rally. Jack's little

son, Donnie John, was extremely ill. Marge was at home, the arrival of the second daughter, Betsy Lee, being close at hand. Doctors had warned that the condition of both Donnie and Marge was serious. The enemy whispered to Jack that perhaps while he was zealous for this Garden rally, he would lose his family.

Then came sudden and crisp word from the head of the office of War Information in Washington that all military personnel would be prohibited from taking part in the rally program. The decision was final. Word of Life headquarters was heartsick.

The rally was called "The Victory Rally," and consisted chiefly of the radiant testimonies of our Christian soldiers, sailors and marines. There were Colonel George S. Clark, the last ground officer to leave bleeding Bataan, and also Lieut. Col. Irwin C. Stoll, Major Hutchins, Chief Gunner's Mate James Downing—all with a glorious testimony for the Lord Jesus Christ.

As at other times, when doors were closed against them to frustrate their jail preaching, the group fell on their knees and waited on the Lord with hearts poured out in helplessness and desperation. They confessed the lack of everything—wisdom, financial means, ability even to obtain a program. There in tears before the Lord whom they loved they asked Him to take over. And He did.

Among the faithful business friends and counselors of the Word of Life Fellowship were a number of God's stewards in places of high business influence. Some of these were discouraged when they learned of the new order from Washington. But Philip Benson (now with the Lord) felt led to reopen the discussion with Washington. Mr. Benson had been president of the American Bankers' Association and was president of the Dime Savings Bank in Brooklyn. He prayed and then called a leading military authority, whom he did not know, in Washington, and explained the importance of the Madison Square Garden Rally, stressing the fact that it would benefit the nation, aid military morale and issue in the salvation of many souls.

The leading military authority to whom he spoke was mildly astonished to hear of the sudden restriction placed upon the testimony of the officers and men, and he promised that it would be removed immediately. Next came a pleasant call from the lesser chief expressing his complete approval of the remedial action.

"Thank God for battles done and victories won!" said Jack, who had been once a Cavalry trombonist but was no match for the War Department. God had defeated the last impediment and opened the way for the rally. To Him be all the glory. Surely now the heavens would open and there would be a showing of His salvation. And it was so.

The mighty Gospel rally, with its emphasis on youth, was one of the greatest gatherings in spiritual history. No one who was there will ever forget April 1, 1944.

"Who's the guy that's running this show?" asked a harassed cop at five p.m. The crowds were lined up for blocks. At six the doors were barred. No one could enter.

A beer concession had called an extra uniformed crew of union bartenders to satisfy the thirst of the crowd. These stared in open-jawed amazement at the orderly Bible-carrying host that swept by without even regarding their barreled sorrow. Old-timers shook their heads.

It was a program that drew youth by the thousands, and many could not even get into the building. Three hundred pastors and laymen were the ushers, led by Bob Swanson, head of a Long Island City bakery.

Gil Dodds was there to testify of his Lord. He had two fresh world-records, established two and three weeks previously at Madison Square Garden and Chicago, where he had run the indoor mile in 4.07.3 and 4.06.4 minutes. (He did it in 4.05.3, Madison Square Garden, in February, 1948.) Gil had been voted by the A.A.U. the most outstanding athlete of the day.

Time would fail to tell of the blessings brought by the immense choir of girls, who after only one rehearsal, under the direction of the gifted and consecrated leader, Carlton Booth, sang gloriously. Besides the testimonies of our officers and men, Lieut. Philip Cheeseman, of the Royal Navy, spoke for his Lord. The Salvation Army Band played. There were also testimonies by Fred Sacher, warden of the New York City Reformatory, and Bob Moon, en route with the Gospel to the Putumayo Indians of Colombia. Norman Clayton played the organ and Samuel Walters the piano. The audience was led in prayer by Dr. Clarence Roddy, Pastor Charles A. Anderson and Pastor Herrmann Braunlin. Donald MacDonald also accompanied at the piano, and Beverly Shea and Carlton Booth sang. Wilmos and Gladys Csehy played the violin, the vibraharp and the piano.

And Jack preached. Approximately eight hundred persons asked for prayer and made public decisions for Jesus Christ. So great was the tide of blessing that the rally was extended to Sunday. All who took part in the program were present at an afternoon rally at Calvary Baptist Church, in New York, and conducted an evening gathering at the Baptist Temple in Brooklyn.

Blessings, like troubles, come in waves. On the very eve of the rally, March 31, Betsy Lee Wyrtzen was born, and Donnie's fever broke. Great was the joy of those days, and it did not diminish.

Exactly six months after the first Madison Square Rally, God led its sponsors to conduct another. The date was September 30, 1944. During the time between the two rallies Jack and his assistants spoke at many church services, conducted the regular Saturday-night rallies, and participated in the Sunrise, Rumney, Pinebrook, Harvey Cedars and other Bible Conferences.

Of this second rally, called The Third Anniversary Rally, the New York *World Telegram* said "It was an old-fashioned meeting—king size," and declared further, "The faithful came from miles around, 20,000 of them, to sing, to pray, and to hear a young man in a tweed suit, a young man with a round face and curly hair, who had once sold insurance and played a trombone in the United States Cavalry band, plead with them, 'Let God come into your hearts.'"

The Garden was filled early. During the four-hour meeting there were testimonies by Percy Crawford, veteran youth evangelist, and president of King's College; Erling Olsen, president of Fitch Publishing Company; Fred Sacher, warden at the New York City Reformatory; and Philip Benson, president of the Dime Savings Bank. Gil Dodds was present, and there was also big Glenn Wagner, Jack's beloved friend and colleague, who had lately resigned the presidency of the Washington D.C. Bible Institute in order to become a Pocket Testament League missionary to China. Glenn had played on Red Grange's famed football team and had known the transient glory of being on the national championship team from the University of Illinois.

Glenn gave the following testimony at one of the rallies:

"About fourteen years ago I was invited to hear a former Denver University fullback preach the Gospel at Peoria, Illinois. I couldn't reconcile an athlete and the Christian ministry so I was curious to find out what this fellow had to say.

"I had joined the church when I was fourteen years of age and went through all the ceremonies, but when I was in the last years of high school and the first years in college I was a thousand miles away from the church and all that there was about it. It seemed that religion was all right for old men and women; it was good to have a preacher to get married and buried. It was all right to have a religion to die by. But for a young fellow, what was there in it? I spent my Sundays in a fraternity house with fifteen other fellows, playing penny-ante poker, and we drank Saturday nights and ran the sorority houses. Religion was something connected with an old maids' society, a pink tea affair. I couldn't get serious about it. I wanted my fling, and was looking every night for some new thrill.

"Then I went to hear this former fullback. That was on a night when my plans went haywire, and the only night in a two week's mid-semester vacation when I was away from booze, women and song. When this fullback walked on the platform, two hundred and twenty-five pounds of man, and preached to sinners that they needed to be born again according to John, chapter three, I sat there saying to myself that if what that fellow is talking about is real, that is just exactly what I want. He talked about Christ who could change a man, forgive every sin he had committed and put a joy inside of one that couldn't be found anywhere else.

"Thrills! I thought that I would never have another like the one I had experienced with thirty other fellows when we were the toast of the country on a November night in '28 at the University of Illinois where thousands gathered. We had just defeated Ohio State University 10 to 0 and became national champions, and that night our coach, Bob Zuppke, was at the microphone giving us the credit. That was a real thrill. But when I heard this Christian athlete and accepted the Christ he preached about, and walked out of that meeting a new man without a sin to my account, that was the greatest thrill of my life and I have been having them in the Christian life ever since. That night I went in there a sinner, with a weight of a thousand pounds of defeat in my soul; I had tried everything this life could offer. But when I left that night I was redeemed; I was saved. The heaviness was gone. God had come into my life to live. The Bible became a new Book. What is there better than this, that Christ liveth in me? Jack, it's great to be here with you on the Third Anniversary of the Word of Life Hour and to look into the faces of these thousands of Bible-loving young people."

Jack brought the rally message. Again, many hundreds accepted Jesus Christ.

A full year went by before the third Madison Square Garden rally, which was called the Fifth Anniversary Radio Rally and commemorated the earlier year of broadcasting from Brooklyn. It was held September 29, 1945, and was preceded by a children's rally held earlier in the day.

There were features that a child would never forget, and all of them pointed up in a clear testimony of the Saviour. The Claus Iroquois Indian family, with their songs and and testimonies, were great favorites. Bev Shea presented the song *This Little Light of Mine,* and Carlton Booth sang also. There were testimonies by Don Robertson and Sam Scales, service men. "Uncle Win" and "Aunt Betty" of Uncle Win's Radio Broadcast Program gave a special Gospel message for the large group of children. They were aided by Pastor Don Marsh. Jack brought the message on the subject *ABC. A* stood for *"All* have sinned," *B* for "The *blood* of Jesus Christ," and *C* showed the importance of *"coming* to Him."

There were 1,500 decisions as a result of that morning service! Jack continues to hear from scores of young people who were born again at the children's rally.

The combined meetings brought out an estimated 27,000 persons that historic autumn day. The Word of Life Fellowship was humbly thankful for the large numbers of curious unbelievers who had come and who were saved.

In his message "Ye Must Be Born Again," Jack gave his personal testimony of salvation through Jesus Christ. The response in numbers who were felled by the impact of God's Word, His Spirit, and the testimony of His children, rewarded the group in terms beyond all human appraisal, for on this day there were, in all, 2,618 decisions!

Jack was confident of the outcome of the first Madison Square Garden rallies. This was not the case concerning the last, however. He had the certainty of obedience to God's will in going ahead, but no beforehand evidences of success. It was one of the most trying experiences in his remem-

brance. He arrived at the Garden thankful for another
privilege to hold forth a salvation testimony. But it did not
appear that the rally would be well attended. His heart sank
as he thought of the contract obligation of thousands of
dollars. The devil crushed him with fear.

He knew he had to face the circumstance, however unpleasant, in half an hour. He asked if the auditorium was
filled, and a friend told him that thousands were again
being turned away and that the doors had long been closed.

The offering was the largest in the history of the Word of
Life Fellowship. After all expenses had been paid, the large
balance was given to Charles Fuller for his world-wide Gospel
radio ministry.

This last Madison Square Rally was the Sixth Anniversary
Radio Rally, held November 14, 1946. Charles E. Fuller
was the speaker. He was accompanied by Mrs. Fuller, their
son Dan, a naval officer, and Rudy Atwood, well-known
Gospel pianist. Norman Clayton played the organ. Beverly
Shea sang *Singing I Go* and *If We Could See Beyond Today*.
Carlton Booth presented the song *The Ninety and Nine* and
led the congregation singing of *All Hail the Power of Jesus'
Name*, *Whosoever Will* and other numbers. At Jack's request, Charles Fuller led in the singing of *Heavenly Sunshine*,
his well-known radio theme song.

Glenn Wagner gave a stirring missionary challenge center-
ing around the desperate spiritual needs of China.

Charles Fuller brought the Gospel message and presented
the invitation to accept Jesus Christ. There were hundreds
of responses, and again the Holy Spirit had used the Word
of Life Fellowship in the salvation of souls once dead in
trespasses and sins.

Chapter 8

SOFTENING UP AND MOPPING UP

JACK VIEWS RADIO Gospel broadcasts as aerial attacks, heavy bombing raids into the very kingdom of Satan. In that sense they soften up enemy citadels where imprisoned souls await release. These broadcasts are more powerful than a thousand planes dropping myriads of tons of high explosives upon enemy emplacements, for it is estimated that the network broadcasts alone reaches four to five million listeners every Saturday night. Scripture declares, "The word of God is quick, and powerful, and sharper than any two-edged sword" (Heb. 4:12). "Is not my word like as a fire? saith the Lord; and like a hammer that breaketh the rock in pieces" (Jer. 23:29).

After much prayerful experimentation with broadcasting outlets over as many as sixty-five stations across the United States and its territories, the Word of Life Fellowship has focused its program on select Eastern and Midwestern stations and around-the-world short-wave from Quito, Ecuador.

In many fervent prayer meetings the Word of Life Fellowship friends have frequently asked the Lord to move upon hearts so that millions will tune in on the radio program. For

70

example, station WHN has guaranteed coverage in an area of 15,000,000 potential listeners. No one, however, can state accurately the exact number of listeners. Many, intrigued by the excellent music, listen to the Gospel also. Millions listen, and the varied testimonies would constitute a book of soul-saving miracles. The mail count for 1947 was 54,185 letters. In a representative high week more than 5,000 letters were received.

More than a fourth of the surviving Jews of the world are in the listening area of the Word of Life program network, it is estimated from recent reports. The chief seats of Catholic power in the United States are likewise covered. (Many of th original Puritan cities of New England are now from 85 to 95 per cent Roman Catholic, the Word of Life Gospel team has discovered in the course of hundreds of meetings with Bible Christians in these areas!). No less in need of the Gospel are the large Christian Science, Unitarian and liberal or Modernistic church groups whose members are without personal knowledge of salvation in Jesus Christ.

Jack at one time considered discontinuing a broadcast outlet in Buffalo because of financial limitations. It was well that he did not! A young aviatrix was driving home from the airport. She liked the music of the Word of Life program, so she dialed in. Previously, she had listened only until the "preaching" began, but this time she heard several Bible passages and testimonies before she realized it. Then like a light shining in a dark place, the Word of God convicted her of her lost estate. When the invitation came to accept the Saviour, she drove to the side of the road and bowed her head in prayer, accepting the Son of God as her Redeemer.

Dolores is now completing her studies at Wheaton college, in preparation for going abroad as a missionary aviation pilot. At a Madison Square Garden Rally she testified, "When I began flying two years ago, I dreamed only of the day when I would be a commercial aviation pilot. But when that goal came in sight, I wondered if I had worked and studied in vain, until I heard the story of Jesus' love for me. Can you see how wonderfully the Lord works? Just when I needed Him most, the Saviour opened my eyes to His power and ability to give me a new life in Him, filled with His benediction."

Statistics show how radio reaches into human need. For example, in 1945, this letter was received from a young actress:

> While back stage in my dressing room in a theater off Broadway, I happened to have tuned in on the radio and recognized your opening hymn *Wonderful Words of Life*. It was a great inspiration to me. A year and a half ago I thought I was the happiest person in the universe when I was offered a position on the stage. My mother, being saved, objected to this. But having a stubborn streak in me, I signed a contract with the agent and on the stage I went. As I said before, I thought I was the happiest person since I had everything my heart desired, money, clothes and the so-called "good times." Everything went fine for about half a year. But within the last year I've been living in misery. I thought I had escaped this by going to Hollywood but my greatest misery took place there, so I returned to New York. If you would ask me what I remembered on your broadcast, I would say nothing except the following words: "Choose you this day whom ye will serve."
>
> Just before curtain time these words were ringing in my ears. When I was told to be ready to go on in three minutes, a fear came over me. Out of all the lines I had memorized I could think of none but "Choose you this day whom ye will serve." That night, instead of going out with the rest of the actors and actresses, I went home wanting to get away from it all. I didn't mean to trouble you . . . but I wish you would help me by praying for me. If possible I would appreciate it if you would sing a song I heard once called *I'd Rather Have Jesus*. Thanking you, and looking forward to this Saturday night . . .

If the radio broadcast can be called the aerial bombing attack to soften up the citadels of unbelief, Jack feels strongly that one can never conquer without the infantry attack of preaching everywhere possible and doing personal work.

He doubts that a message can be given forth in all fullness of heart-to-heart conviction without a flesh-and-blood audience. Hence, even his radio broadcasts are always combined with a visible rally audience. It's the mop-up that wins the war!

Between the weekly rallies of the last seven years Jack has spoken in several thousand local church and mission meetings within driving or flying distance of New York. On such trips he is always accompanied by his pianist, Harry Bollback, or Bob Post, and often by several evangelists, missionaries or new converts.

You can't look at these meetings as you'd view a cold column of type in the *World Almanac*. The rallies are a whirlwind of zeal and joy in the Lord, and the workers never begrudge the time spent in dealing with seekers for God. If you are with Jack, you perhaps sleep in a car or plane. But he doesn't seem to sleep much. When he is not driving he is dictating letters of encouragement to new converts or Christian colleagues (he has a dictaphone machine in the glove compartment of his car). If he is not in a car, he is in a train, plane or telephone booth, talking to someone about Jesus Christ. Or perhaps he is reading the Word, and finding a childlike delight in its glorious application to present problems of living.

Take a glimpse into one of these weeks of which Jack tells in a personal letter sent to the writer last year (where he finds time for personal letters to many mission fields, no one knows). Jack wrote:

Again this week the Lord has surely blessed. On Sunday night we were in Catskill, New York, in the First Baptist Church, which was jammed out to the doors— balcony, Sunday-school room and main auditorium, and at the close there were about forty who gave their hearts to the Lord. You remember that Catskill was the home of George Stebbins, the famous hymn writer. Four years ago he encouraged the preachers, of all kinds, to invite me to Catskill for a meeting. Little did he realize that would be yearly, and that the Lord would abundantly bless with souls.

Tuesday night, in a pouring rain, we journeyed down to Asbury Park for a meeting in the Neptune High School auditorium. There was a great crowd present in spite of the terrific rain; in fact, it looked as though the whole Atlantic Ocean were going to wash in on us. The Lord blessed, and twenty-two gave their hearts to the Lord. Wednesday night, Harry Bollback and Don Robertson were with me in Marcus Hook, Pennsylvania, and we felt that the meeting was clicking along swell and there would sure be a lot of souls saved, but at the close, nobody responded.

How different was the following night in New Jersey! The church was old, hot and stuffy, but cold spiritually. It was half empty. The upright piano was all out of tune, and just about useless for a song service and piano solos. The people wouldn't sing anyway, so I decided to preach. I preached for one hour but couldn't seem to get going. It seemed to me like I was talking to the pulpit and that nobody else was interested in what I was saying. By the time I finished, I thought there were three strikes against me, but I gave an invitation anyway. When I started the invitation I was sure that nobody was going to be saved, but lo and behold, a tidal wave of blessing broke loose on us, and seventeen or eighteen came forward to get saved, including a prominent business executive who was sitting in the last row, last seat, a man of about fifty years of age.

The Lord surely rebuked us for our lack of faith, and I think in the closing prayer I must have said ten times over, "Great is Thy faithfulness." Even when we abide unfaithful, yet He is "ever faithful." Well, we sure took courage, and last night we journeyed clear up to Auburn, New York, near Syracuse, and fifty-two more gave their hearts to the Lord. These are great days to be on the firing line.

One of the most unusual week-night meetings away from New York came to pass through an unlikely circumstance. Jack refused a meeting in a mission about a hundred miles from New York. He rarely felt led to do this, but in this case it seemed to him that the motive was the edification of local Christians rather than the winning of souls. He did not object to the long journey, but he felt that since he could not be everywhere at once, the evangelistic meeting should have first priority. It was a sincere conviction. He offered to come if unbelievers were brought to a united meeting. This caused a ferment in the mission and one lady wrote Jack that she remembered when he was "humble enough to go anywhere." To this he remained silent. No one dared to say that he had refused for money reasons, as he made no financial arrangements with groups large or small.

There was one man in the city who heard of the situation and thought Jack's offer reasonable, so he asked if he could go ahead and engage a large meeting place, then go out into the "highways and hedges" and invite everybody.

Came the night of the rally. It was raining. Then it rained harder. Who would come on a night like this? Jack's group was gloomy. Great was their surprise, however, to see a packed auditorium with twelve hundred persons and three uniformed high-school bands.

When decision time came there were 204 high-school students that came forward in acceptance of the Lord Jesus Christ. The wave of blessing transformed much of the wicked life in the city. A month later another rally was held in the same area. There were about 1,000 present, and 189 made decisions for Christ.

Among the most touching responses in weekly campaign meetings were those in such cities as Mars Hill, Presque Isle, Bangor, Eastport, Waterville, Milo, Sanford and Portland, Maine. Night after night, from as far as 125 miles around, the country folk and villagers came on foot, and by car and bus. At one place, by four o'clock in the afternoon the meeting house was almost full, though the service did not begin until seven-thirty. There was an average of fifty decisions each night in the three Maine campaigns of a week's duration. Jack looks back upon such meetings with deep joy. "I would like to take off a week just to praise the Lord, when I think of His great victories, but there are so many new battles to be won," he says.

Chapter 9

MEXICO AND FOREIGN MISSIONS

EVEN DURING EARLIEST Christian experience Jack Wyrtzen had felt a deep concern for the unevangelized tribes and tongues both in neighboring and remote lands. He met the challenge by prayer, personal sacrifice and, finally, by offering his life for foreign service should such be the will of God.

It was with much enthusiasm that in January of 1945 he accepted an invitation to see the widespread Indian translation work and Gospel witness conducted in Mexico by the Wycliffe Bible Translators. W. C. Townsend, a missionary serving in Central America, had developed phonetic principles that greatly simplified the translating and writing of languages. The Mexican government had invited him and honored him for his help. Aided by Drs. Nida and Pike, and many other assistants, Missionary Townsend was achieving new triumphs in Bible translation.

Arriving at Mexico City by plane, Jack was accompanied by Glenn Wagner, of Washington, D. C., and Larry McGuill, of Ridgewood, New Jersey. The writer joined the party from California. Bob Moon came with the group later, from Southern Mexico. The first part of the trip was conducted

76

Top: The Wyrtzen family: Marge and Jack Wyrtzen and their three
children, Mary Ann, Donnie John and Betsy Lee
Bottom: Part of the Word of Life Rally in Convention Hall, Philadelphia, on
April 3, 1948. Police estimated there were between 17,500 and
18,000 in attendance, with 1,500 turned away

Top: Crowd at LaGuardia Airport saying farewell to team on way to Great Britain, May 29, 1946

Bottom: Part of the 2,000 who attended rally in YMCA Hall, Dublin, Ireland

by Eugene Wolf, a translator from Chicago. But let Jack tell his own story:

"We left at five in the morning from Mexico City and arrived at our destination in the early evening, going by car, an old-fashioned train, and walking. I'll never forget the thrill of the first night, as we walked into an Indian village with a guide and his burro carrying all of our baggage.

"There on this high tableland of the Mazahuas, 9,000 feet above sea level, among lowly Indian huts, we were greeted by a young lady who had spent eight years translating Bible portions and songs into the language. While we were eating dinner with her the Indians started to arrive for the meeting. Her front room was small and it seemed full, when twenty-five Indians had come in. We asked them if they wanted to sing. Which one of the 104 hymns would they like? They wanted all of them beginning with Number 1! We sang for awhile, and then more Indians arrived until there were seventy in the room! It seems it was a nightly affair, lasting from dinner until eleven or twelve o'clock. The indians smiled when we tried to sing in their language. One after another got up with radiant faces and told how the Lord had so wonderfully saved them.

"I learned that about ten years ago a Mexican believer had come to this tribe with prayer and friendliness, winning many to Christ. The price this faithful missionary paid for his testimony would put us to shame. Many times he was beaten and once left for dead after his teeth had been knocked out and his head crushed in. All this for preaching the Gospel to a people in a land where an evil religious system had opposed the light of God's Word for four hundred years.

"This man came back again to minister, and his enemies were put to flight. The blood of the martyrs is still the seed of the Church. Today, among the Mazahuas there are reported to be about five hundred believers!

"The next morning we were up early visiting the homes

of the Indian Christians. The pigs, the sheep and the Indians all live in the same houses, but this didn't seem to bother anyone at all. Finally it came time for us to leave, and we felt like Paul when he left the Ephesian church, for the local elders accompanied us on our hour's walk to the railroad station. The train was an hour late, so we had a little service. After we attempted to minister the Word awhile, we asked them to do likewise. I'll never forget an Indian named Leonardo who stood to his feet and read from Luke 1:1-4. Finally he looked at us and he said, 'There are 77,000 people in my tribe, and they are scattered all through these mountains in little villages!' Then with grim determination he said, 'Brethren, even if it costs me my life, I'm going to carry the Gospel to them, for they have never heard.' It was hard to tell them good-bye when the train came, and we waved until we could not see them any more. What a joy to know that when the roll is called up yonder, we'll be filled with joy and wonder; when we see the blood-bought number, some from every tribe and nation will be there.

"Next day we went to visit the Tarascan Indians, and after twelve hours of travel we came to the home of Mr. and Mrs. Max Lathrop, who have translated the whole New Testament into this ancient language.

"One of the little Lathrop girls asked Larry McGuill where he came from, and he explained that his home was in a place called New Jersey. 'What tribe of Indians do you belong to?' she asked. (Irish Indians, maybe!) We set out for another Indian village, and again we had a five-hour hymn sing and testimony meeting with these Tarascan believers.

"Max took us to the world-famous volcano, Paricutin, which erupted into a two-thousand-foot cone, from a poor man's corn field. It was in the Tarascan country, and he talked with the Indians along the way. I'll never forget that sight! We arrived at the volcano after dark and saw tons of red-hot fireworks being thrown into the air, and rolling down the slope of the cone. On our way we had seen two villages that were wiped out by the flow of mud, lava and brimstone. To see this would be a good lesson for those who do not believe the Genesis story of Sodom and Gommorah's destruction.

"At the lava flow, near the base, we saw a literal, actual lake of fire. We stood within twenty feet of this slowly-moving flood of destruction. One of our fellows said, 'Boy, it sure makes a fellow believe in hell, doesn't it!' An American tourist, the wife of a doctor, said she thought so, too. Larry McGuill asked if she knew what the Bible said about hell, and she didn't know it was in the Bible. So Larry read to her from II Peter 3:10-15, and also from Revelation 20, beginning with verse 9. The woman thought it strange a person could find things in the Bible like that. She said that she was a good church member, but felt as far from the things of God as the heathen Indians. We all testified to her of how Christ had saved us, and the importance of salvation. Her son raged against such seeming nonsense. But she quietly accepted an invitation to. receive the Lord Jesus Christ as her Saviour. We found that she had but lately lost another son in the war. It was such a joy to pray with this sincere woman, beside the lake of fire."

The last experience in Mexico was a journey through primitive Sierra Aztec country to the Totonaco Indians. Spending the night in a dungeonlike vault of a medieval *posada* in the town of Zacapoaxtla, the cavalcade set forth on Indian ponies for a remote village named Zapotitlan. The fresh beauty of morning on the trail eased the many bug-bites of the travelers as the group journeyed through villages and terraced farm lands and little changed in the four centuries of Spanish occupation. At nightfall, after passing bowers of bougainvillea and fields of sugar cane and berry-laden coffee bushes, the destination was reached. It was like a page out of George Barrow's *Bible in Spain*.

In Zapotitlan the group met Herman Aschmann, a former Moody student, who was translating Bible passages into the

Totonaco tongue. His body was thin, and he was trembling with the ravages of malaria, but there was a heavenly joy on his face as he worked with the Indian collaborators. And what privilege, short of seeing the Lord Jesus face to face, could surpass this! There was solemn wonder and praise in the hearts of the visitors. That morning gave us memories that would linger always: a lad with a machete in a cane field; a darling little Indian girl with a bashful dimpled smile; a *charro* herding steers across the river. Christ died for them all, but how few even yet have heard the good news of His deliverance from sin unto life eternal!

Glenn Wagner had many opportunities to minister on the visit to Mexico, prophetic of his later long journeys in China with the Pocket Testament League. He introduced the party to his former Dallas Seminary classmates, Arch MacKinlay, translator among the Sierra Aztecs, and George Cowan, Mazateco translator, who kindly served as the party guide to Zapotitlan. Glenn weighed three hundred pounds and had a proportionate sense of humor.

Members of the party testified in the historic Presbyterian church in Mexico City, "Divino Redentor," established in an ancient convent, after the government had shuffled church properties. The church had 1,200 members, hundreds of whom had to stand. The services were long, and Scripture-centered. Bible passages were placed in the niches where idolatrous images had once stood. Testimonies were live and pointed. Here were true believers who had counted the cost of speaking out for Jesus in a land where fanatic religionists killed individual evangelical believers and, occasionally, entire groups of them.

Among many others whom Jack met in Mexico were Dick Pittman, Aztec translator and field director, who arranged the journeys among the Indians; Lydia Zinke, once associated with the Word of Life Fellowship on Long Island; a humble young missionary named Allan Farson, who was soon to be entrusted by the American Bible Society with the difficult composition and printing of the Word of God in all the newly-translated Indian tongues of Mexico; and the English brethren A. W. Webb and Mr. Webberly, godly businessmen whose personal testimony and resources as importers enabled them to spread the Gospel in a gracious apostolic manner throughout the land.

A motto remained dear to Jack, as a consequence of the trip to Mexico. On the island in Lake Patzcuaro is a gigantic statue to the revolutionary hero Morelos. A spiraled stair leads to an inscription in Spanish: "It is nothing to die if for your country you should die." As Jack looked out across the wild beauty of the Tarascan Indian country, he paraphrased the saying, "It is nothing to die if for your Saviour you should die."

At the present writing, 1948, there are twenty-three missionaries, working under mission boards and independently, who receive regular monthly allowances provided by gifts from God's people.

The roll of missionaries with which the Word of Life group has financial fellowship is as follows:

Mr. and Mrs. Ernest Lubkemann, Brazil, South America Indian Mission; Mr. and Mrs. William Wiley, Jr., Brazil, South America Indian Mission; Miss Sunny Soney, Mexico, Wycliffe Bible Translators; Mr. and Mrs. Stanley R. Kline, Africa Inland Mission; Mr. and Mrs. Richard Hightower, Tanganyika, Africa Inland Mission; Hernildo Concha, Yucatan, Pioneer Mission Agency; Mr. Felix Azcorro, Yucatan, Pioneer Mission agency; Glenn Wagner, China, Pocket Testament League; Mr. and Mrs. Clarence Soderberg, Nigeria, Sudan Interior Mission; Mr. and Mrs. Forrest Forbes, Oregon, Independent; Ragnar Bruce, New York, Immanuel Mission to Seamen; Mr. and Mrs. Vincent J. Joy, Alaska, Central Alaskan Missions; Mr. and Mrs. James Savage, Venezuela, Scandinavian Alliance Mission; Mr. and Mrs. Robert Moon, Colombia, independent; Mr. and Mrs. Robert Williams, Borneo, independent.

Chapter 10

JACK AND HIS FAMILY

> I'm a poor sinner, and nothing at all,
> But Jesus Christ is my all in all.

THIS COUPLET FROM the testimony of a poor English tinker is written on the flyleaf of Jack's Bible. The man who wrote the words maintained that it was a good answer to fools and wise men alike. It was a kindly saying of hope to the poor and brokenhearted, but likewise it stood as an immovable rock against the cunning snares of religious Pharisees.

This brings to mind the words of Roland Allen, M.A., of England. In effect, he said, "You can argue against an argument, but you cannot argue against a testimony."

Especially has Jack sensed, while speaking at distinguished and critical gatherings, the necessity of relying solely on the Word of God and the unanswerable force of a personal testimony for Jesus Christ. Well has he known that he would lose great opportunities for God in trying to use "Saul's armor" while fighting with the cynical Goliaths of unbelief.

Also written in his Bible is the saying of a nineteenth-century writer: "Never lay too great stress upon your own

82

usefulness, or perhaps God may show you that He can do without you." There is also a further note: "As my greatest business is for God, to serve Him, so my daily business is with God, to ask Him for strength to do it."

Another flyleaf note shows Jack's great earnestness in appropriating the promises of God: "There are but two reasons why we do not appropriate to ourselves the promises of God: 1. Our faith is weak and our sins are strong. 2. Our self-confidence leads us to trust in ourselves, and our sense of guilt makes us ashamed to claim the help of God."

Another note penned on a much-worn leaf sets forth the prayer: "God, give me a deep spirit of humility and indifference to finance. Lack of these is a rock upon which many of our evangelists have perished." Jack's friends believe that this petition has been truly granted in his life, for he does not even have a personal bank account and has a rare indifference to personal possessions. It is not surprising, therefore, to see in his ministry a rich fulfillment of Matthew 6:33: "Seek ye first the kingdom of God and His righteousness, and all these things shall be added unto you," and the promise "For your heavenly Father knoweth that ye have need of all these things" (Matt. 6:32). And cannot God implement "all these things" without even a hint to influential friends? "Let your conversation be without covetousness; and be content with such things as ye have; for He hath said, I will never leave thee, nor forsake thee" (Heb. 13:5).

No more wonderful illustration of this truth could be given than in the crisis following Jack's return from the Mexican trip.

Marge told him that while he was gone, notice had been given that the family must terminate occupancy of their home in Woodhaven. The housing situation had become desperate. Although their dwelling had been less than adequate because of an ever-expanding Gospel office and headquarters on the porch and in the parlor, it was at least "home," and now whither could they turn?

They agreed that they were too busy in God's work even to worry about it at all, so they left it before the Lord in prayer.

Strange how little things have a great bearing on God's work across the years! As Jack had given out tracts on a Hoboken ferry years before, his testimony had come to the notice of a beloved elder statesman in Gospel work who lived in Maplewood, New Jersey, and Jack had been called upon various times to minister in the midst of this fellowship group.

Now, as if from heaven, without condition or previous intimation, there was made available to the Wyrtzen family a comfortable suburban home. They could use it indefinitely. And housing had been impossible!

Because of a wrong estimate in the remodeling of their previous dwelling, a debt of $250 had followed them. A personal gift from a friend who knew nothing of this burden exactly met the obligation. The new home required redecorating, and, lo, this problem was also solved. The large van of a Christian moving and storage establishment packed and transported all the Wyrtzens' possessions from Long Island to Maplewood, and presented a bill that was already marked "paid."

One gets the impression that Marge's burden as wife and mother in the Wyrtzen home carries no small responsibility. The days when she was free to be piano accompanist in the meetings and early broadcasts now are memories. However, she is no less busy in faithful prayer and helpful planning to free her husband for his round-the-week evangelistic labors. The Wyrtzen home in Maplewood, New Jersey, is a rendezvous for the friends of Mary Ann, Donnie and Betsy. Marge makes them feel welcome and has sponsored a child evangelism class in the home. Those who have known Jack and Marge from early years believe that God has given them unusual gifts as a Gospel team in His great service.

Nowhere have God's overruling providences been more

manifest than in the Wyrtzen family itself. Long was it
thought that children in the home would be an impossibility.
Today there are three healthy children. They are Mary Ann,
born April 17, 1937, Donnie John, born August 17, 1942,
and Betsy Lee, born March 31, 1944.

Jack has frequently expressed his deepest longing for his
children: first, that they should in their earliest years have
a saving knowledge of Jesus Christ, and second, that they
should dedicate their lives completely to His service. "I can
think of no higher joy than the day they may give their
lives to carry the Gospel in the lands that have never heard,"
he has often said.

Mary Ann is a serious little "Goldilocks" who delights in
helping her mother reach neighborhood children in their
home child-evangelism class. Salvation is very dear and real
to Mary Ann and she can tell you when she came to know
the Saviour, at Sunrise Mountain Bible Conference, under
the special leadership of Elizabeth McCall. One of her
favorite pastimes is to play "meeting" with her little friends.
Mary Ann is an able swimmer and at home on the aquaplane
at Schroon Lake.

Donnie John actually dates his salvation experience to one
of Mary Ann's "meetings," when there was a very serious
decision time. He is a likable little fellow, with a thin wisp
of a voice and a shy smile.

One day Donnie asked his kindergarten teacher if she was
going to heaven. The teacher was embarrassed and turned
off the question with the opinion that we could not know
such things.

"But my daddy knows he's going to heaven," Donnie
said. "And my mommie knows she's going to heaven, and
my big sister knows, and I know." When the little fellow
went home that afternoon, he was deeply burdened for
his teacher because he loved her so. He told his daddy,
"We must pray for her until she is saved." "All right, Donnie," said Jack. "Let's read God's Word and pray for her

right now." The Bible passage was Daniel 6, which tells us that the prophet knelt three times a day and prayed and gave thanks before his God. Donnie seemed happy to leave his burden with the Lord.

This was not the end of the story, however. A neighbor came to the Wyrtzen home later and said, "Who is Donnie's friend, Daniel?" Jack said, "I have no idea." "He plays with a Tommy, but I don't know of a Daniel in the block." "Well," said the neighbor, "Donnie tells me that his friend Daniel prays three times a day." "Oh," said Jack, "I know now. He's talking about the prophet Daniel." Donnie had identified himself with God's man in the Bible.

Betsy Lee is a breathless little "bug" whose words tumble all over each other as she tries to explain the latest activities of Buffie the dog and Tippie the cat. Her pretty eyes command all your attention as she tells you a four-year-old's greatest hopes or tries to explain why she meant no harm in pouring cups of water over Mary Ann's dolls.

One gets the impression that the Wyrtzen home is a crossroads of Gospel activity, but there is always time for prayer and praise. The children live as normal Christian youngsters, and receive the proper amount of spankings and loving rewards. They have remained unspoiled.

Jack does not have a study in his home, but there are some splendid books in his office—the worthy works of Spurgeon, Matthew Henry, MacIntosh and also contemporary Fundamental writers. When he consults them, however, he is likely to slip them out of an overcoat pocket and read them while he is hastening to a meeting. You wonder how he obtains his powerful radio and rally messages, but every now and then while he is talking with a friend or reading the Word of God he is also making notes.

It was said of a leading soul-winner in a Philadelphia rescue mission that he didn't know whether one ate homiletics with a spoon or a fork! Jack knows considerable concerning the science of sermon arrangement, even if he is not bound by its traditional canons. One day Jack and Gil Dodds were described by a genial ministerial friend, who introduced them, as men who had preached and run without knowledge of the common human rules of success but were "champions" anyway. After all, champions aren't bound by rules.

Rarely does Jack miss the "morning meeting" in the Plymouth Brethren Assembly in Maplewood. There is a considerable contrast between the Saturday-night rally and the Sunday-morning worship. Both services, however, are directed wholly to God, through Jesus Christ. The Saturday-night rallies are timed to the rapid enthusiasm and energy of young people, and the sole purpose of the meeting is to reach young folk with the Gospel of Christ. In these, Jack, a gifted student and interpreter of Scripture, is an authority. But in the morning meeting he is frequently silent, as his soul feeds on royal fare from the rich expositions, Biblical exhortations and songs by the nineteenth-century English hymn writers.

The quietness of this hour in breaking bread is a tonic to the soul in the speed-madness of our times. No pastor or visible leader directs these seasons of devoted worship. The men who speak are chiefly Christian businessmen who live near by. But one is convinced that no richer interpretation of the Scriptures could be heard from any orthodox pulpit in the land. Moreover, attention is directed to the broken body and shed blood of the Lord Jesus Christ rather than to any of the various gifted expositors of the Word.

A leading international authority on the Bible, such as Northcote Deck, Leland Wang, General Dobbie, or Harry Ironside, may be present at the service and offer rich comment on the timeless theme of redemption. Princely among these speakers was the late Charles Bellinger, who though the head of a New York insurance company, was also thoroughly at home in the Greek New Testament and keenly aware of the problems and victories of God's work the world around.

Jack is well known for his frank co-operation with all individuals who acknowledge the Bible as the Word of God and believe that salvation is through the blood of Jesus Christ. He believes that God looks upon obedient individuals rather than upon organizations, and the success of the latter, he feels, is possible only because of the blessing of individual believers who are living in the will of God.

He sincerely feels that an extra-Scriptural national youth organization, like an over-all governing church federation, carries more liabilities than its well-argued advantages. He feels that the youth revival has swept across the nation primarily because it has from the beginning transcended denominational lines. He says the Gospel message should not be hampered by any human-administered barriers, and places complete confidence in the administration and leadership of the Holy Spirit.

On the subject of preaching, Jack remarks that sermons on hell, far from being out of date, are, as always the most effective in awakening lost multitudes to their peril and need of a Saviour. Hell is Bible truth, affirmed by the same Jesus Christ whom the Modernists pretend to follow and honor. The latter lead in the current ridicule and mockery of it, since in the modern Western world Satan poses chiefly as a benevolent "angel of light," and, through leading liberal pulpits, even as a preacher of morality. (It is interesting to know, at the same time, that Satan is still literally and Scripturally called the "King of Hell" in many pagan lands that have not yet known the Bible, but where his evil sway and powers are well known and feared!)

After all, leading infidels speak of hell, Jack points out. Said Tom Paine, "I would give the worlds, if I had them, if the *Age of Reason* had never been published. O Lord, help me. Christ, help me! Stay with me; it is hell to be left alone!" The celebrated Voltaire declared, "I am abandoned by God and man! I shall go to hell. O Christ! O Jesus Christ!"

Chapter 11

CARL, NORMAN AND HARRY

"For service over and above the call of duty" might well
be the citation given Carlton Booth, Jack Wyrtzen's humble
and greathearted co-worker. To those who do not know him
he may be introduced as perhaps the most outstanding Gospel
tenor soloist and song leader in the United States. And
thousands know him simply as "Carl."

In the fullness of a life set apart for God, he already
had more than he could possibly do in Christian service.
From the time that Jack first met him until the fall of
1942 it was possible to obtain the gifted help of Carlton
only on occasions that meant considerable sacrifice to him.
Thus he gladly participated in a number of banquets, boat
rides and rallies.

Carlton's home is in Providence, Rhode Island. The center
of his life ministry has been the seventeen years of leadership
in the music department of the well-known Providence Bible
Institute. He has sung publicly from the age of three, but
has declined to use his voice except for Christ.

It was from Providence that Carl journeyed to join Jack
Wyrtzen and Glenn Wagner for the Potomac River Boat

Ride, September 6, 1942. Glenn was in charge of this blessed soul-winning occasion on the river vessel *Mount Vernon*. Jack felt that the time had come to ask Carlton a bold question. Would he take over the musical direction of the New York Saturday-night rallies? It reminds you of the time when a man named Moody talked quietly with another man named Sankey. There were higher issues in the conversation than the convenience or plans of either party. It was an impossible request unless God made it possible.

It has often been said that the way to get a job done is to give it to somebody who already has much more than he can do.

"Give me three days to pray about it," Carlton replied quietly.

From a human standpoint, he felt that this added service would be impossible, hardly required by the Lord. Wasn't there something to indicate that one should not neglect one's family and one's health? He wondered if this thought was unworthy. Yet, he was working right around the week, and there was only a little time of rest remaining for home joys with his beloved wife and little daughters. Singing and leading the music in the New York Saturday-night rallies would mean a long round-trip from Providence and the expenditure of much strength. The demands of the week seemed about all he could bear, and early Sunday morning his services were required in Boston, at the Providence Bible Institute broadcast known as the "Mountain Top Hour."

He thought of the experience years ago, too tender to recall often, of the death of his beloved friend, Richard Oliver. They were returning from a Gospel meeting when an automobile accident took Oliver's life. One of the most promising and able spiritual Christian workers had been taken home to glory for reasons beyond human understanding. Carlton meditated on the sovereign ways of God. Why had *he* been spared? Surely for God's best, at any price.

When the three days had passed, the answer was "Yes."

"The way we look at it," Jack says, "the big New York rallies most likely would not have been held had not God raised Carlton Booth to direct the great choir." He has a heaven-given genius for the job. Can you imagine coaching four thousand voices to sing as one glorious human organ with only one rehearsal? With God, this has been possible. Carlton brings something into the meetings which is utterly beyond himself. It is a quality of the Holy Spirit that no man can buy or barter. Carl has it because he lives only to declare his love of the Lord Jesus Christ."

On occasion Carlton has found it possible to accompany Jack on air journeys to such places as Chicago and the West Coast. On such a journey to Seattle he received the degree of Doctor of Music from the Seattle Pacific College, his alma mater. And there was the journey to the British Isles, about which more will be said later. He was with Jack this year in the Moody Founder's Week services in Chicago.

Following is a portion of Carlton Booth's testimony given before he sang *The Stranger of Galilee*:

"I never will forget one rainy, foggy night, as a boy fifteen years of age, attending a Gospel meeting in Seattle, Washington. The message struck home to my heart. I was the only one who responded to the invitation, but, my what a change when the Lord Jesus Christ came into my life! For since that meeting the Lord Jesus has been my nearest and dearest friend, and He's no longer a stranger to me.

"'Not much of a meeting,' someone might have said. 'Just that little towhead at the altar, and he probably didn't know what he was doing.' It was as if I had been going alone down life's pathway pell-mell in the wrong direction, and that night I met the Saviour, and He said 'Now, Carlton, we'll go together, but we'll go in the opposite direction!' Conversion was truly a right-about-face. And Christ is no more a stranger to me."

Carlton was Vermont born, so it was not strange that

after early youth and schooling in the Pacific Northwest his steps were turned again to his native New England.

The joy of Carlton and Ruth Booth in their two lovely daughters, Katherine Ann, twelve, and Miriam, eight, is understandable. At the age of four Katherine truly came to know the Lord Jesus as her Saviour, and has ever clearly testified of this precious relationship. She spends a half-hour each day with her Bible, in prayer. Miriam was saved at the age of five. It came about one day when she was deeply troubled, and asked her mother, "Am I saved?" Her mother knew the Holy Spirit was dealing with Miriam's heart. "I don't think I am," the child added. The Spirit of God broke the heart of the little girl and opened her understanding of the sweet provision of God through Jesus Christ her Saviour.

One thing that impresses you is that Jack Wyrtzen and Carlton Booth have worked together with hundreds of other Christian believers, across the years, without any of the bitter wells of dissension and ugly discord so often seen beneath the most pious claims in Christian work. This is a good testimony of God's appointment. There have been great battles to be won, but they have not been battles among the brethren.

"Two fine things have always impressed me about Carlton Booth," declares Norman Clayton. "I have often given thanks to God for the kind encouragement he has given many of us in our endeavor to develop God's gifts. And then, I have always noticed how he has been able to 'take his burdens to the Lord and leave them there,' an example of living faith."

Everyone who knows Carl delights in his large sense of humor and his immense appreciation of everyone in God's service. "He is doubtless the most appreciative listener in many of the rallies," Jack declares. You see him making notes from the messages, and laughing with highest glee over a good joke.

Top: Charles E. Fuller of the Old Fashioned Revival Hour and Jack Wyrtzen on platform in Madison Square Garden, November 14, 1946

Bottom: Jack broadcasting the Word of Life Hour from hospital bed after suffering a broken hip in July, 1947

Top: Tabernacle boathouse on Schroon Lake. Waterfront and campus at
Word of Life Island
Bottom: Waterfront, speedboat and diving board on Word of Life Island,
Schroon Lake, New York

Carlton's favorite joke about himself concerns a sweet little admirer who came up to him one day and timidly asked, "Mr. Booth, are you a cowboy?"

He found himself embarrassed in that he could not qualify for this exalted position. He was only a doctor of music.

"Anyway, you sing just like a cowboy!" said the little girl helpfully, her face flushed with bashful admiration.

The versatile gifts exercised by Carlton in the rallies and meetings include not only those of song leader, soloist and choir director, but he is also one of the radio announcers and frequently a rally speaker. Many times Jack and Carlton Booth conduct both the radio broadcast and the subsequent rally service.

One of the most pleasant features in the fellowship between Jack and Carl is the weekly exchange of some new glorious morsel of Scripture, too good to keep until they meet at the Saturday-night rally. Sometimes these are exchanged in long-distance telephone conversations between Providence and Maplewood. Jack, Carlton and Norman are especially fond of the Arthur S. Way translation of the Pauline Epistles into modern English.

A favorite rendering of Jeremiah 29:11 was shared with Jack from the Rotherham version: "I know the plans I am planning for you, plans of blessing and not of calamity, to give you a future and a hope." This verse was an anchor of encouragement and strength when their faith met severe testing in the large rallies.

The favorite songs that will ever be associated with Carlton Booth are *The Stranger of Galilee; My Sins Are Gone; Jesus Gives Me a Song; Holy, Holy, Is What the Angels Sing; Living Above; We Shall See His Lovely Face;* and *Singing.*

Whence came these lovely melodies? These choruses in the very phrase of Holy Scripture? They are an ointment to the soul and an earnest of heaven. Thousands of young people are singing them in the rallies, and they have gone by missionary and by radio broadcast to the ends of the earth. We have

heard choruses too light and frothy to live. Others are too
heavy to sing themselves into the needy heart. But we thank
God for the choruses of Norman Clayton, full of the promise
of the "soul's bright home."

Did you hear the choir of four thousand girls in the 1945
Madison Square Garden Rally singing:

> There's a wonderful Name, 'tis Jesus;
> It is ever the same, 'tis Jesus:
> Name that lifts me to heaven, from sin and shame;
> Blessed Jesus, wonderful Name!

There was a solemn purity about it that transcended all the
heartbreak of this earth and transported the soul into the
vestibules of glory. It was not a complicated song, but a
pendulum of slow-burning ardor swinging in a wide arc of
eternal praise. The song exalted the Name above every other
name, on earth and in heaven, as redeemed voices, thousands
of them, sang as one while Carlton Booth led them with
a humble mastery that hid himself.

Before the year 1930 (Norman was twenty-seven then)
there had been no indication that he would be a composer.
He had always liked music, however. His mother had dedicated him to the Lord in earliest infancy. In childhood he
accepted Jesus Christ as his Redeemer. At the age of thirteen
or fourteen he sought to be baptized as a testimony of his
relationship to the crucified and risen Saviour. In childhood
he played on the piano "both hands the same," so he reports.
The playing improved with the years. He apprenticed as a
bricklayer and during the depression years when building
work slackened he found employment in a New York bakery.

After work he was much at the piano and organ. Sometimes he found a new melody for old familiar words. Then,
with this rhythmic base, he found new words for the new
melody! It was a curious process, but it culminated in some
of the loveliest songs and choruses being used today in
youth rallies across the world.

Percy Crawford was among the first to recognize the merit

of these first compositions, now available in *Word of Life Melodies*, and included them in his widely sought "Pinebrook" collections. There were such selections as *I Am the Resurrection and the Life; Walking in the Light; Deep, Down Deep; God So Loved the World; Jesus Saves and Keeps and Satisfies; As Far as the East Is from the West; No Condemnation; Jesus Means More to Me; I Am the Door; and He Holds My Hand.*

Norman and Jack became acquainted in the early "thirties" when Jack appeared with his brass quartet in a Brooklyn meeting where Norman was the pianist. Thus blossomed a friendship and collaboration of many years, a fellowship which began with the early rallies and has continued to the present.

It often remains for the uninitiated, in any field of endeavor, to accomplish the seeming impossible. Norman felt that he should produce a songbook. It is hard to get support for a new publishing project. He had to remember his family, and a living wage would not cover everything.

Could he set the songs in music type? Fantastic! Printers said "No." Music type is as rare as hen's teeth, in the first place . . . hardly shown in any founder's catalog. It costs a great deal. And you would have a world of trouble setting from the music case, even if you were a master printer to begin with!

Against much cold advice in this vein, Norman borrowed a hundred dollars from three kindly Christian ladies and bought a weight font of music type through a doubtful printer. For the entire year it lay unused in the basement darkness of Norman's home!

Then, putting his trust in God for help, Norman began to set the songs that were so dear to his heart. He couldn't do it, but he did it anyway! After the day's work in a bakery he composed the songs in music type.

And that was how *Word of Life Melodies No. 1* came into being. Proofs were made of the hand-set pages, and they were reproduced photographically for the book which Jack desired published for the Word of Life Fellowship. The first edition was ready for the great rallies of 1943. It is now in its fourth edition.

Word of Life Melodies No. 2 came out in 1945. Compilations of songs and choruses by Norman and other composers have been made available in *Melodies of Life* (1946) *Low Voice Melodies No. 1* (1946) and *Word of Life Chorus Melodies* (1947). These are available at the Word of Life Bookstore.

"What do you think is your best song?" the writer asked Norman Clayton.

"*Now I Belong to Jesus,*" he replied. The opinions of other publishers have confirmed the leading place of this hauntingly lovely testimony in melody.

"But songs are unpredictable. What you may think is the best may gain little attention at all." He explained that one of his own favorites, *For All My Sin,* had remained largely overlooked. Only lately had his friend Larry McGuill told him that he could never sing it without a profound breaking within.

We Shall See His Lovely Face is a song that has somehow expressed a great part of the Christian's longing and expectancy for the day we shall meet our Saviour. It is poignant, and in word and melody is an exquisite vehicle for expressing the desire of the redeemed soul.

Norman Clayton's personal preferences in *Word of Life Melodies No. 2* are *Jesus Is All You Need, Christ Jesus Is My Shepherd, My Hope Is In the Lord* and *Long Ago At Calvary.*

There are interesting circumstances associated with the composition of many celebrated Gospel hymns, and the writer thought that Norman could tell of unique Christian experiences which precede his songs. But not so. For example, he says that *We Shall See His Lovely Face* was the result of exploring the melodic possibilities of a borrowed vibraharp!

But that doesn't fool the friends of Norman Clayton. He composes out of a heart supplied with treasured reservoirs of the Word of God. The rare fragrance of the lyrics stems from the metric transliteration of entire Bible passages. Norman, by dint of much study, can repeat more than a thousand Bible verses, with their references. To keep these in mind, he reviews more than sixty of them daily! Thus the songs and choruses are fresh with Scripture, and never labored and stuffy.

Norman Clayton lives at Malverne, Long Island, with his wife, Martha, and his son, Norman, Jr., and daughter, Muriel. He has charge of the music in the Bellerose Baptist Church. Lest the portrait be incomplete, let us add that with his devoted consecration there is a personality that delights in sly, quiet humor, leaving friends with merry memories for years.

Among the lives that touched upon Norman Clayton was that of the aged Christian saint George Stebbins, of Catskill, New York. "Uncle George" Stebbins went to be with the Lord in 1947, at the age of ninety-nine. He had been Moody's "other Sankey" and had not only accompanied the greatly-used evangelist in many of the most fruitful revivals, but had composed the melodies of such undying songs as *Saved By Grace*, *There Is a Green Hill Far Away* and *Evening Prayer*.

In his ninety-sixth year George Stebbins wrote to Jack concerning *Word of Life Melodies*: "There are two remarkable features of the book. The first is that the music of all the songs (and for many, the words also) was written by the author. I have not known of *such* a book—of this size, at least. The author is a musician, and has unquestioned talent as a composer, and what is quite as important in work of this kind, good judgment in the use of 'His gifts.' I hope God will make use of these talents."

Harry Bollback attended the Saturday-night rally, December 6, 1941, the night before Pearl Harbor, at the Gospel

Tabernacle. That night Jack faced an emergency need for a pianist, as Bob Moon would not be able to play the piano for the Ryker's Island Penitentiary service the following morning. So he called for volunteers.

There was no response. But two friends of a third young man pointed him out as being the one to fill the need. Harry grinned bashfully and finally nodded his willingness to help. From the moment he heard him play, Jack knew that Harry Bollback had what youth wanted in Gospel piano-playing. Even the island convicts approved it with wide smiles.

By an interesting coincidence Harry was born in Greenpoint, Brooklyn, in the very neighborhood of Jack's nativity.

From earliest boyhood he played the piano and has been for many years a favorite Christian piano soloist and accompanist in the New York area. His own ingenious arrangements have set forth with much skill the moods of despair and heaviness of heart common to unregenerate man and also the Christian's joyous experience of salvation.

During World War II Harry served with the Marines in several of the most deadly South Pacific campaigns. Though hundreds of his buddies were killed, he escaped injury.

Not only has Harry played on the radio broadcasts, but also, when available, in the largest rallies and meetings. He was with Jack on the trip to the British Isles and to the Pacific Coast. In 1947 he enrolled in the Philadelphia School of the Bible, in preparation for the mission field. (He has a brother serving in China and a sister attending the Missionary Training Institute at Nyack, New York.)

Harry is engaged to marry Mildred Winkler, former Word of Life Fellowship telephone operator, now enrolled at the Providence Bible Institute. She too is preparing for the mission field.

During weekdays, when Harry is in Philadelphia, Bob Post, of Hawthorne Gospel Church, has often accompanied Jack in the meetings. Bob formerly attended Moody Bible Institute and Juilliard School of Music, in New York.

Chapter 12

MARGE'S BRITISH DIARY

MARGE WILL TELL the story of the British Isles. These fruitful weeks of ministry brought out a total of 38,900 people in the United Kingdom, with a total of 890 recorded decisions for the Lord Jesus Christ! During this time the weekly Saturday-night broadcasts were sent from British studios in Glasgow, London, Cardiff and Belfast.

The trip was made possible through the cordial invitation of the British Plymouth Brethren and the loving help of Flight Lieutenant Murray Kendon and many other Christian friends.

Jack set forth on the journey with the commendations of his beloved Christian colleagues Lieut. General Sir William Dobbie, Dr. Harry Ironside, Dr. Donald G. Barnhouse and Charles Bellinger.

May 28, 1946

In the office of the Word of Life Fellowship the council met for a prayer meeting, asking the Lord's blessing and guidance on this new venture of faith. How well each one in this team realized that without Him we "can do nothing"!

May 29, 1946

By noontime the children were all fed and ready to go, and so for our last time together for many weeks, we all got down on our knees, committing each other to Him who is able to keep and guide. He has promised, "I will never leave thee nor forsake thee." What a peace it was to be able to commit our dearest treasures on earth to Christ, who alone is able to keep them, as He has promised to cover them with His wings!

We all got into the car and drove to the airport, where a wonderful group of friends were waiting to see us off. It was such a thrill to see so many, and we thanked the Lord for each one. We were given many parting gifts, such as candy, nylon stockings, a large cake and many gifts of money . . .

The steward told us the plane was N.C. 55 *Clipper Lisbon.* It would take about four hours and forty minutes to reach Newfoundland. At first it was very foggy, but the weather cleared as we flew north. It was beautiful.

All was quiet and semidark on the plane by eleven p.m., and gradually we dropped off to sleep one by one. About six a.m. the hostess told us we were flying at 375 miles per hour. She brought us sandwiches and coffee to hold us over until we reached Ireland. We looked through our tiny porthole window and saw beautiful clouds, and through the clouds, the vast Atlantic Ocean. What a sight! It made one praise and love the Lord for creating all these wonders and then to have us flying through space in this gigantic yet beautiful Constellation plane. Yet, as we marvel at it all, we realize our vast responsibility to these people we are so quickly reaching. We pray at the beginning of this, our first day in England, that God will cleanse us, keep us humble and usable, that we may win young people unto Himself.

May 30, 1946

We arrived in Shannon, Ireland, at eleven a.m. (Ireland time),, after setting a new air-line record for Pan-American Air Lines. We crossed the ocean in six hours and twenty-nine minutes. (The previous record had been six hours and thirty-six minutes.) Also, we covered more mileage in our record than the previous record had done. Breakfast was served in a lovely dining room at the airport in Shannon. We climbed back into the plane after breakfast and left at eleven-forty a.m. for Hurn, England. It took us about one hour and twenty minutes to cover this mileage. With smooth flying, we arrived at Hurn at one-thirty p.m. We went right through the customs (thanks to our British friend, Flight Lieutenant Murray Kendon, who was waiting for us there . . .

We caught a train at ten-fifteen p.m. for Scotland. It was a thirteen-hour ride; since we couldn't get sleepers, we had to sit up all night once more. At seven a.m. we changed trains at Edinburgh.

May, 31, 1946

After getting settled on the train for Aberdeen, we had to wait to be called for breakfast. We were served our meal and were surprised how good it tasted, even the porridge, which was without sugar . . .

Our first meeting of this trip was held in Aberdeen, Scotland. The church was almost filled, and the people were very responsive. Jack started the meeting with Carlton Booth leading the congregation in the *Glory* song. Carl then taught them *Jesus Can Satisfy the Heart*. Harry played his solo, *Onward, Christian Marines*, and gave his testimony. Carl sang *My Sins Are Gone*, *The Ninety and Nine* and *The Stranger of Galilee*. Murray sang, accompanying himself with his banjo, and also gave a word of testimony. Jack's message was taken from Mark 7:20-23. The invitation met with no response at first, but then came a real break, with many decisions. People were slow to respond, but when they did, they really meant it. After the meeting the sexton said it was the largest crowd since the days of D. L. Moody. Moody and Sankey are still dearly loved in this land. The young people stayed to sing around the piano. We left the church at eleven p.m., and some of the young people came back to the hotel with us.

June 1, 1946

Here it is June 1, in Scotland, and the sun is shining brightly for us Yankees. We are quite a spectacle to these people, and they turn around to look us over (especially Harry with his bright tie and socks). Jack wore his plaid shirt to breakfast, which caused much interest. (It seems we are foreigners here in Scotland!) . . .

We arrived in Edinburgh at four-forty p.m. and checked our bags, as we were to leave that night for Glasgow, so that we might broadcast to you friends in America. We were very excited about the broadcast and wished we might have heard you, too, but we had to be satisfied in thinking of you all listening in. We walked to where our meeting was to be held in Edinburgh. While walking along with Jack, I thought of my mother and dad who were born in Edinburgh. It surely was a thrill for me to be walking along the same streets they had walked, especially as they are both home with the Lord now. We arrived at the auditorium and then went out for some "high tea" ("supper" to you Americans). This time we actually found a "wee bit" of steak. When we arrived back at the auditorium, it was filled to overflowing with anxious souls waiting to hear the Gospel. They were a very responsive group . . .

When the meeting was over, we had to rush to catch our train, and crowds of the young people came down to the station to see us off. With much singing and hand-waving we pulled out of the station, so happy over the many who had found Christ as their Saviour and the many new friends we had made in Edinburgh . . .

We had to be up at nine-thirty a.m. so we could attend

Sunday services in Glasgow. After the service we went to dinner with some lovely friends here by the name of Cowan. Expressing our gratitude, we left for our Sunday-night meeting, which was held in "The Picture House." It was a theater and was packed with people. The meeting was similar to the other meetings. Especially did the people enjoy Carl's solos, *My Sins Are Gone, I'd Rather Have Jesus* and then our favorite, *The Stranger of Galilee.* Of course, they were sung as only Carl can sing them. Jack's message was given again on "Sin and Its Cure." Many of the people in the theater had been brought in from the street; just as we give out tickets in New York for our youth rallies on Saturday nights, these people go out into the street where the sinners are and invite them in to the meeting. These are the ones who need the message of God's love for the lost and condemned sinners. As Jack spoke on this theme, some got up and left, as they just couldn't stand the conviction of sin. However, most sat with heads bowed asking Christ to come into their hearts. Immediately a young man in front of me raised his hand. How we thanked the Lord for this life yielded to Him! Many followed. As Jack called them forward, it was such a joy to see the aisle filled, as well as the entire space below the platform.

It was a great evening of blessing, with almost one hundred finding Christ that night.

June 3, 1946

Here it is another lovely day in Scotland. We had a good night's sleep and wandered down to breakfast one by one. After a meal of porridge, toast and coffee, we went to get our train for Inverness . . .

Having dinner at the hotel, we finished in time to get to the Empire Theater where we were to have our meeting. The place was almost filled a half-hour before the time scheduled to start. Jack preached on Psalm 34, giving his testimony. The invitation was given and there was a marvelous response. So many older men and women responded to the invitation to accept Christ, who alone is able to save to the uttermost all that come unto God by Him. After the meeting we again had to catch a train for the night, but this time Mr. MacBeth had gotten us sleepers. Many came from the meeting to see us off, and it was a happy, rejoicing group that waved their farewells to us. We all met in our room for prayer, thanking the Lord for all He had done that night.

June 4, 1946

At six-thirty a.m. there was a knock on our doors, and there was the attendant with our morning tea. We drank it, and then hurriedly got dressed so we could be ready at seven a.m. to meet Jock Troupe of Glasgow. (Many of you remember his visit to America.) After the lovely breakfast we were driven by a Dr. Hendry and his daughter Eileen, also Mr. and Mrs. Jock Troupe, to Edinburgh . . . .

At six-thirty p.m. we were taken to our meeting, which was held in the Brunswick Methodist Church. Carl, as usual, led the song service, and the people sang better than any group has so far in our meetings here in Britain. Jack preached to Christians on I Peter 1:18; 2:9. Jack told the story of the sea captain who found Christ through our broadcast. As this story was told of how the sea captain accepted the Lord as his Saviour and then was killed at sea, many a tear was wiped away. Once more there was a marvelous response to the invitation.

This ends our first week of meetings in Great Britain. Keep praying. "Cheerio!"

June 5, 1946

We start the second week of our visit to the British Isles in Newcastle, England. We have been having such happy and wonderful times in the Lord. So many have been coming to the Lord that we humbly thank Him for His faithfulness.

After our repast we left for our meeting, which was held again in the Brunswick Methodist Church. The church was filled with a wonderful group of young and old. How atten-

tive and interested these English people are . . . So many
older people are coming to the Lord that it makes one wonder
how long it has been since these people heard the simple
Gospel. (Many of these churches have formality, but no
reality.) All those accepting Christ were dealt with by
Murray Kendon. After the service we stayed to have a song
service with the young people around the piano. We left the
church at ten p.m. to get to the hotel to have our supper.
It was a happy day, and one we would long remember for
the many that found eternal life through Christ.

June 6, 1946

We arose once more with a lovely clear day in England.
It is just marvelous the way the sun has been shining, and
we haven't had a wet day as yet. We had breakfast at ten
a.m. and then got on our train for Leeds, Yorkshire. We
arrived there three hours later, and a Mr. Hassum was waiting for us. He is the pastor of the Ventnor Street Methodist
Mission, where we were to have our meeting that night . . .

Our meeting was held at seven-thirty p.m., and we had
a wonderful group of people waiting for us. Many of these
people were from the poorer classes, but how happy and radiant
they were! It seemed that the audience was composed mostly
of Christians; however, the Lord moved and saved many souls.

We went back to our hotel for supper, but could get
only cocoa, tea and a few sandwiches. Each day as we travel
nearer to London we are feeling more the terrible food
shortage. While we were eating, a lady came and asked
us what we were doing in England. We gave her an
announcement of our meetings, and then as Jack, Murray,
Harry and I were leaving the lounge, we saw a group of six
men and women sitting around reading our pamphlet. We
recognized the same lady, so Jack was able to talk to them
for about an hour. He gave his testimony, and then Murray
testified, sang and played his banjo. They were very interested.

June 7, 1946

Once again we awakened to the sun shining in our rooms in the dreary city of Leeds. Murray had left us to go to London to get ready for our arrival there on Saturday. It is "Whit Holiday" here in England, and the people are celebrating V-E Day along with Whit Week End . . .

We got our train for Nottingham at one p.m. What a mob! Everyone was on his way to see the King.

We arrived for our meeting which was scheduled for seven-thirty p.m. (two-thirty p.m. your time). We often try to visualize what our dear ones are doing at home and compare their activities with what we are doing. We are so very far away from all those we love, but we think constantly of you and thank you for your prayers. This was a very difficult meeting, as it was held in an old dilapidated building. It is owned by the Baptist church, but they rent it out for anything and even have seances in it of late.

We had a good crowd, but the building wasn't full as so many had left for a holiday in London. Harry and Carl played and sang, and it was very much enjoyed . . .

What a blessed hope for each one of us who have named the Name of Christ! Many hands were raised, and these, too, entered into the joy of the Lord. After arriving at our hotel, we put a long-distance call overseas and heard the sweet little voices of Mary Ann and Donnie John, along with Grandma Wyrtzen. What a peace of mind to know all is well! Good night! And so to bed.

June 8, 1946

At last we are having real English weather. We awakened this morning to the patter of rain on our windows. This is V-E Day here in England, and it is hard to get even a taxi. One came along finally, and we got to the station in time, with all our luggage. It seemed to us that everyone in Nottingham was getting on that train. We were very fortunate to get seats at all. We arrived in London at two p.m., spent the rest of the afternoon at Murray's, and then waited a half-hour for a trolley to take us to our meeting in Kingsway Hall. This place held 2,500 people, and it was packed with a happy group, singing choruses, most of which are well-known in America. It certainly is true that God has His people everywhere! Many wonderful testimonies were given by servicemen. Jack gave his testimony after Carl and Harry sang and played many solos. Many were at the altar-rail at the close of the service. Individual workers dealt with each convert. After the meeting we met many servicemen and others who had attended our broadcast in New York City. We left for the broadcast in a big Buick which belonged to a Christian doctor. When we reached the studio, it was packed with young people wanting to sing on our program. I am sure you were all thrilled as you heard these Londoners sing for you. Broadcasting here is very different from that in the States, and most of these young people had never been to a broadcast. They were an eager group, and we surely enjoyed working with them . . .

After the broadcast it was quite a problem how to get everyone home, as all the buses and trolleys had stopped running for the night. We put eight people into the Buick; Harry rode on the running board, and we put a great big policeman ("Bobbies" they are called here) who had testified in the meeting, in the trunk of the car. What a sight we made rolling down the streets of London! Once again we crawled into bed at three a.m. . . .

June 9, 1946

It is Monday morning in London. Ruth and Carl went to get pictures of Buckingham Palace, Westminster Abbey and St. Paul's Cathedral, along with many other historical places. It is a miracle that St. Paul's Cathedral stands amidst the ruins. For blocks around there is nothing but bombed buildings, but the Cathedral stands untouched.

Jack, Harry and I had to leave at ten-thirty a.m. for a Bible conference where Jack spoke to about thirty young people. He challenged them for the mission field, and four young fellows stood to their feet accepting the call of Christ to give up all and follow Him to the ends of the earth, to the thousand tribes that have never heard the Name of Jesus. We had lunch with these young people, and then were driven to a train which would take us out in the country where we would meet Tom Rees, one of Great Britain's leading evangelists. We took a taxi from the station, as Tom's conference was seven miles away. When we arrived at the conference, Tom Rees and his wife, Jean, were there to give us a warm welcome. Right away we loved this couple who are leading the youth of Britain into the knowledge of the truth. Tom has held rallies like ours in the Royal Albert Hall, which holds ten thousand. (This is the largest auditorium in Britain, and it has been filled several times.) In all our meetings here in Great Britain we have met many young people who have accepted Christ in Tom's meetings. God's hand is upon this man . . .

June 11, 1946

Jack had an appointment with J. Edwin Orr, and Carl had an engagement with another friend, so Ruth and I stayed at home and did some much-needed washing and ironing. It is quite a problem over here keeping your clothes washed and pressed.

Our friend with the Buick had kindly consented to drive us to Dereham for our meeting, which was held in a picture house 110 miles east of London. We had a good responsive group, and we enjoyed ministering to them. These Britishers, after all, are no different from our own people. They have the same problems and sorrows, and so often they are much easier to talk to than the people are back home. They seem hungry for the Gospel. I wish you could see the eager faces watching Jack when he is giving them the message from the Lord—souls needing and seeking a Saviour! When the invitation was given, there were so many who responded that they were lined up two and three deep across the front of the theater. Among those who gave their hearts to Christ was the husband of a Christian lady who had prayed for him for forty-five years. His heart was overflowing with joy. He asked one of the leaders from one of the local Plymouth Brethren assemblies if he could break bread with them on Sunday morning, and, of course, he was accepted with open arms . . .

As we go through city after city and see such awful destruction here in the British Isles, we hate to think what the cities on the Continent look like. Oh, how we long for the day when Jesus will come to rule and to reign in righteousness here on earth, for not until that day will there be any peace on earth or good will toward men, and the prayer of our hearts is "Even so, come, Lord Jesus."

June 12, 1946

We found our train was leaving for Bristol at one-fifteen p.m., so we had to pack our bags hurriedly and get moving again. A few hours later we arrived in Bristol, and what a bombed-out city this was! I have never seen anything quite so bad (yet each city we come to seems worse than the last). The hotel we were in had been bombed, and the two top floors were gone completely. It seems that half of Bristol is gone. At least two thousand of its people were killed, and some of the bodies have never been recovered from the wreckage.

After refreshing ourselves, we took a bus to our meeting. There was a large crowd, with people sitting in the aisles and in the choir loft. It was a very easy meeting, for these people had been praying for this meeting for many weeks prior to our visit. We know the Lord will work miracles when a meeting is bathed in prayer. At the close there were many decisions for Christ.

June 13, 1946

As I write my notes on today's happenings, I look back to the happy day we have spent. We were invited to visit the great orphanage which was started by George Muller, that faith warrior of God. He was a man who believed God's promises, and he founded these great orphanages on faith. At one time they cared for two thousand children. The younger girls were leaving for a day at the seashore, and as they were all lined up to get their train, they sang a few songs for us. It was great! They looked so nice in navy blue dresses with white polka dots, navy blue reefers and hats. After leaving the orphanage, we got on the train at two-fifteen p.m., which was to take us to Newport, Wales . . . We walked to the church where our service was to be held. The building held two thousand people, and it was filled "to the rafters." They were singing when we came in, and you should have heard these Welshmen sing. It was wonderful! We had a good meeting, for these people also had been praying for weeks for God to bless our visit to Newport . . .

June 14, 1946

Stephen Olford, who is one of the young men with real vision here in Newport, joined us for our morning devotions. After lunch we got into a seven-passenger "Austin" which was owned by a Mr. James. He had offered to drive us to Swansea. It was raining hard and the day was terribly dreary, but thank God, there was plenty of sunshine in our hearts. When we arrived in Swansea, we found that the whole center of town had been bombed away. The only building standing was a Gospel mission. Yet, in the midst of this awful ruin, a great tent had been pitched and the glorious Gospel is going out each evening to over one thousand people.

When we arrived at the meeting, it was a thrilling sight, for the street was filled with hundreds of people who couldn't get into the building. In fact, we wondered how we'd get in ourselves. The police finally persuaded the people to go to the tent, and the American Team (as they called us) would hold a special overflow service there later on in the evening.

We started the meeting in the large building, with songs and choruses. The Welsh are noted for their good singing, and this is the town which was in the heart of the famous Welsh Revival. We have never heard such Spirit-filled, four-part-harmony Gospel singing before in our lives. It was truly magnificent! After singing *Guide Me, O Thou Great Jehovah* in English, they sang it in Welsh . . .

Many people were unable to get into this meeting, so we had an overflow meeting in the big tent. At the close of the first service we hurried over to the tent, and on the way we could hear these hundreds of people singing. The tent was packed to capacity, so that meant there were some one thousand people waiting to hear a message from the Lord. We had a great after-meeting with these people, and then drove back to Newport, which was about fifty miles away.

June 15, 1946

This is Saturday again, and we are looking forward with great anticipation to the broadcast from Cardiff, Wales, back to the States. We put in a busy day getting all the testimonies and scripts ready. By four o'clock we were ready to roll along to our meeting, which was scheduled in Cardiff at six-thirty p.m. . . .

After the broadcast the chief engineer of B.B.C. here in Wales spoke to Carlton Booth and begged him to write to him after we get back to America. We found that years ago he had accepted Christ as his Saviour and then dedicated his life to be a missionary in Africa. Until last Saturday night he was a first-class backslider. Little did we realize as we were broadcasting to you in America that the Lord was speaking to the engineer in the control room here in Wales. As far as we know, these broadcasts are making church history, as this is the first time a Gospel program has gone back to the States and has been released over a network of stations.

June 16, 1946

. . . All afternoon, groups were meeting for special prayer for the evening rally here in Newport. After the wondrous outbreak of blessing last night in Cardiff, everyone is believing the Lord has prepared for a real victory tonight. We arrived at the great Central Hall long before meeting time, and the crowds were already lined up waiting for the doors to open at seven-thirty p.m. By seven-forty-five p.m. the Hall was filled to capacity (about two thousand), and young people were seated on the stairs; the platform and every other available space was also filled with people. There was great expectancy in the meeting, and at the close more than eighty gave their hearts to the Saviour.

June 17, 1946

This morning we were up early, for the train from Newport, Wales, to Manchester, England, left at eight-forty a.m. When we arrived at the station, a large group of young people were there to sing and to say good-bye. As we leave Wales, we will always remember Stephen Olford, the keen young evangelist who met us four days before, when we arrived. There he was at the station shouting "Hallelujah!" at the top of his lungs. Steve is a spirit-filled enthusiastic preacher of the Gospel. His exclamations, "Amazing! Tremendous! Terrific! Marvelous! Massive!" will not soon be forgotten. We can hear him yet.

After a four-hour train ride on their little wooden trains, we arrived in Manchester in the rain (as usual). We were taken to a Christian guest house, where we were made very comfortable. We were served a nice lunch which tasted especially good after our long train ride. The meeting was not scheduled until seven-thirty p.m., so we had an hour's rest. The service was held in the Albert Hall (which is the largest building in Manchester) and we found it filled with about nineteen hundred people. As the invitation was given to accept Christ as Saviour, between fifty and sixty responded.

June 18, 1946

Dr. and Mrs. Wyse invited us to their beautiful home and served us a delicious meal. They have a delightful little baby named Sheena, which is Scotch (Gaelic) for "Jean." We had "tea" with a large group of Christians at five p.m., and enjoyed a nice time of fellowship, leaving afterward for our meeting which was held in the Albert Hall again. The place was filled long before starting time, and we had a fine hymn-sing together. Carl and Harry sang and played as well as usual, and Jack's message was "Sin and Its Cure." At the close of the rally another great number came forward to give their hearts to Christ. In the two nights of meetings in Manchester, 127 people signed the decision cards in the inquiry room. Among those who accepted Christ tonight was one man seventy years old. He told us that he had put off making this decision for years, but finally he gave in. He had been in England for only two weeks, having just come from Canada. Praise God, He is always on time. Thank God, whosoever will may come—young and old alike.

June 19, 1946

We start the last week of our British tour in Liverpool, England. We have had thrilling experiences as we have traveled through England, Scotland and Wales; now we leave for Ireland, which will end our trip.

Well, to continue with my story, we arrived in Liverpool at about one p.m., whereupon we were taken to a lovely hotel. The Central Hall was near the hotel, so we had a short walk and were ready to start our first meeting here in Liverpool. We had a fine meeting, but we thought the audience was composed mostly of Christians, so Jack spoke on the joy of the Lord, which is our strength. "Joy unspeakable and full of glory" (I Pet. 1:8) and "Thou hast put gladness in my heart . . ." (Ps. 4:7). Even so, there were many conversions at the close of this meeting . . .

June 20, 1946

When we arrived at the Central Hall for our meeting, it was packed to the doors, and we had an inspiring service as Christ was preached in His fullness. A young couple sitting near us caught our eye during the invitation. They were jeering and laughing at everything that was said and done. How tragic it is to see young people going merrily on their way to hell! How we prayed that the Lord would break them down and convict them of sin in their own lives! Blind and stubborn youth of England—no different from our own young people in America; in fact, no different than we ourselves were a few years ago when Christ was just a name to us.

As we turned in for the night, our hearts were overflowing with joy when we recalled the glorious victories of the last six days alone, for in these last six days there have been more than 11,000 people in our rallies and more than 350 decisions for Christ.

June 21, 1946

We flew from Liverpool to Belfast, Ireland. It was so very interesting crossing the Irish Sea and entering Ireland. Belfast is still in the United Kingdom, but Sunday we leave for the Irish Free State and will finish our campaign in Dublin . . .

A great crowd was packed into the Wellington Hall of the Belfast Y.M.C.A., and we had a fine time of fellowship with them. Again at the invitation many came forward to trust the Saviour.

June 22, 1946

Our last day in Belfast turned out to be a very warm one This is the first time we have felt warm since we arrived in the British Isles. We all met for dinner and then went to Wellington Hall for our last service here in Belfast. Once again the place was packed. We met many friends who had been in New York or who had relatives living there. It was very warm, especially for these people who are not used to this kind of weather, but they were all most attentive as Carl and Harry sang and played, and then as Jack broke the Bread of Life to them . . .

June 26, 1946

This morning we awakened early, all excited over the thought that this time tomorrow morning we would be, the Lord willing, in New York. We were taken to the Dublin airport by bus, and then we flew from Dublin to Shannon airport to await our check-ups on tickets, reservations and all the necessary details in leaving a foreign country. We finally boarded our plane Tuesday night at eight p.m. and headed out over the Atlantic. As we traveled farther out over the ocean it became quite foggy and cloudy, but as the plane climbed higher and higher, we broke through the clouds. We will never forget the magnificent sight of the sun shining on the beautiful cloud formations. We were certainly reminded of what the Psalmist meant when he said, "The heavens declare the glory of God, and the firmament sheweth his handiwork" . . .

June 27, 1946

At six forty-five a.m. today we made a three point landing at La Guardia Field. What a joy it was to see our loved ones and friends who had gathered at such an early hour in the morning to greet us! After clearing through customs, we headed for home, praising the Lord for victories won in His precious Name.

As we look back on Great Britain, we feel that there is a real turning to God in many places . . . Certainly the only hope for Great Britain, America or any other country is to get back to a simple New Testament witness for Jesus Christ. Even as of old, they overcame Satan "by the blood of the Lamb, and by the word of their testimony."

Chapter 13

"WORD OF LIFE" ISLAND

AFTER RETURNING FROM great Gospel victories in the British Isles, Jack wondered where God would lead next. He hoped there would be some way to share the new blessings and lessons that had come out of this international ministry.

Surely there were plenty of battles to be won. Never had American youth been more needy; never were foreign fields calling more desperately for Gospel workers. Never had there been more open doors. But again they needed God's direction.

Jack had been studying a folder printed by his friend, Tom Rees, in England. It told of salvation and blessing that had come to hundreds through the ministry and fellowship of a summer youth conference. He recalled what a summer camp had meant to Marge and to him, bringing her to a knowledge of salvation, then both of them to a consecration of their lives to Jesus Christ.

"Pinebrook" had been the place, and there were like centers of blessing such as "Sunrise," "Rumney" and "Harvey Cedars." Yet there were too few camps to meet the needs of

America's fun-loving and impressionable youngsters. This opportunity was great and yet neglected.

Even as Jack was thinking of these things, he was approached by a real-estate representative. A sure-enough island was for sale—more than eighty acres of glorious woodland on a hilly islet in the midst of Schroon Lake. The location was in the beautiful Adirondacks, not far from Lake Champlain and Lake George. It was described as a goodly place, and well favored with buildings and accommodations maintained by its former wealthy owners.

"If this thing is of God," Jack said to himself, "it will still be there after we have prayed about it." With the council, he was inclined to take a conservative view of this island offer, unless the Lord should make it plain beyond any possible mistake that this was His will for a Christian summer camp.

"What is the price?" he inquired, with no little misgivings. "Well, the place is really worth $125,000," said the land merchant, "but we are prepared to let it go at a very special price of $70,000." Jack gulped to hear such an astronomical figure, and he said there was no possibility of considering the purchase.

The real-estate agent suggested a plane ride to the Schroon Lake area. This offer was politely declined, but a group from the Word of Life headquarters thought a car trip to the island might be made without obligation, and would enable them to satisfy themselves concerning the situation and appearance of the place. As they rode northward, they reviewed the description of the agent: "This island was built as an estate for a private family in 1928. No expense was spared. It became a home of luxury and distinction, having every comfort that a million-dollar income could afford. No other family has lived there, nor has it been used by any organization. The buildings are in good condition, with excellent floors, ceilings and walls. There are ten permanent buildings, surrounded by richly timbered woods, lawns and flower gardens." Other merits were described in additional paragraphs. It had been a guest spot for such families as the Franklin Roosevelts. The lake was mentioned in aristocratic land-holdings as early as the French and Indian wars.

When the party arrived at Schroon Village, looking out on the "Lake Como" of America, they were much pleased by the lovely view of the timbered island and shores, surrounded by the highest peaks of the Adirondacks. A former care-taker remembered offers of $250,000 to $500,000 for the the place! The visitors engaged a rowboat and went out to the island. It had been, obviously enough, a millionaire's estate, but now it was grown over with thick underbrush and there were many signs of vandalism. The state troopers had been guarding the island, unoccupied for several years, against trespassers. Despite this, intruders had invaded the buildings, blowing up a safe and damaging other property.

Still, the possibilities of the place for a Christian youth camp seemed tremendous to Jack and Marge, who were accompanied by Fred Scharmann, business manager of the Word of Life Fellowship, Harry Bollback and Mrs. Gaylord Barclay, wife of a member of the council.

If God wanted them to have the island as a vacation center for soul-winning and the deepening of Christian experience, then He would perform a miracle. It entered into the minds of the group to offer the owner $25,000 cash. Of course, they did not have the $25,000, but if the sum were accept-able, it would indeed be as a sign from God. And also, perhaps the equally great miracle of the $25,000 would appear! Having reached this conclusion, they returned home to report to the council and to lay the question before the Lord in prayer.

After prayer, the council thought it wise to approach the real-estate representative. Jack borrowed $1,000 to make a legal offer on a $25,000 purchase. The real-estate firm, made indignant by the impossible offer, several times refused even to

submit it to the owner. Eventually the offer was made, only
to bring an immediate rejection. Now, however, the price
was down to $50,000! The Gospel group stood flatly on its
first offer. They believed that only by doing this could
they know the will of God. They also pointed out that large
expenditures would be needed to make the island serve its
purpose.

At long last the owner came to a decision of her own. She
looked sympathetically on the Christian project that would
benefit so many thousands of young people. To the astonishment of the real-estate agent, she agreed to sell the island and
its equipment for the unchanged first offer of the Gospel
group!

There was much thanksgiving on the part of the Word of
Life Fellowship for answered prayer to know the will of
God, but now—where was this vast sum of money coming
from? Only God knew. It is thrilling to add that the
entire sum of money came in within one month, from
forty-seven Christian friends who somehow heard of this great
new opportunity for ministry and wanted a part in it.

It took most of the year to get the place ready for a
summer camp. Many volunteer groups and crews, with thousands of dollars' worth of repair equipment, transformed the
island into something that resembles the real-estate description. The list of the equipment needed reads like the in-
ventory of a hardware and dry-goods store. It was a terrific
job of supply, transport and labor. God also brought to pass
a series of miracles to provide every needful thing, even
including two splendid speedboats for the island connection.

What a lovely spot Word of Life Island proved to be. Just
far enough from shore to be mysterious, no traffic but
the camp jeep and the saddle horses walking along the
two and-a-half-mile road encircling the wooded vacation re-
treat; the gentle slope of a hillside for a campus; towering
trees, breaking the brightness of the summer sun into shadowy
patterns; eighteen square miles of crystal-clear Alpine lake for

rowing, canoeing and water sports, such as water skiing, speedboating, water polo, fishing and "drifting and dreaming"; ideal conditions for hiking, riding, ball games, horseshoe, volleyball, badminton and tennis; and should it rain, ample provisions for ping-pong and other indoor games.

The great week finally came. Word of Life Camp on Word of Life Island opened for the first week of its first summer season, June 21, 1947. Every helpful idea that could be gained from the pooled experience of Christian summer camps in various parts of the world was utilized in the program and arrangements for the youthful guests. It was determined, for example, that there would be definite value in keeping the age limit beneath the age of thirty except for leaders escorting groups. Costs were kept to the lowest operating figure possible. The food was excellent. Water and land sports lured scores of young people who would not otherwise have been interested in a Christian camp. A capable staff of some twenty-five young men and women assisted as counselors and instructors. Personnel was chosen through prayerful guidance and because of an evident personal salvation experience and a spirit of willingness to reach others for Jesus Christ.

Concerning the speakers, Jack called upon twenty-nine of his fellow Gospel workers, some of whom had aided in the early Woodhaven meetings, and all of whom he felt had some particular Scriptural contribution or challenge for the throng of promising fellows and girls who would be on the island from June 21 to September 1. There were from two to four speakers taking part in the three daily services, and the speakers changed each week end. These were leading youth workers, evangelists, teachers, pastors, missionaries and song leaders.

The speakers for the first summer were Tommy Steele, Arthur Bowen, Don Robertson, Stephen Olford, James E. Bennet, Don Moffat, Beverly Shea, Walter MacDonald, Clarence Jones, Brandt Reed, Herrmann Braunlin, Dawson

Trotman, Forrest Forbes, Carlton Booth, Ralph Davis, Dick Robinson, Charles Woodbridge, Alfred Smith, Glenn Wagner, Jimmie Johnson, Bob Sutte, Ed Christensen, Clifford Lewis, Harold Martin, Donald MacKay, Leon Sullivan and Larry McGuill.

Those who were at the camp recall joyfully the almost unbelievable series of conversions resulting from the ringing testimonies and Scriptural challenges of the Christian young people and the Bible teachers. A considerable number of the new believers from the Word of Life Camp are in Bible schools, and not a few of them are in preparation for service in the mission field because they yielded to the Bible claims on their lives.

Perhaps one of the most outstanding conversions was that of a husky state trooper named Jack Holtz. Jack had been well acquainted with the world of sin. He was not only arresting criminal offenders in the line of his duty, but from time to time he felt within his own life the condemnation of sin common to the entire family of Adam.

His younger brother, Chuck, came to the camp. There he found salvation and had such a good time of fellowship on Word of Life Island that he put out the bait for his trooper brother. Big Jack was immensely interested. The cost fit his pocketbook, and the sports promised him a week of tremendous fun.

Jack Holtz participated easily in the island sports but found himself confused and ill at ease at the obligatory meetings. Yet he couldn't condemn them because, believe it or not, these young people were plainly the happiest people he had ever seen, and their happiness did not come from any of the common vicious habits that bound him and all his friends.

When the trooper believed in the Lord Jesus Christ, an entire new world of blessed new relationships came into his heart with the Saviour. Returning to his job seemed intolerable, so he stayed on, full of wide-mouthed wonder at the Word of God and the plans and hopes of Christians.

Camp plans for the second summer seek to include even larger numbers of young people between the ages of twelve and thirty and a rich expectancy in a harvest of souls.

At the very height of the summer camp season, Jack Wyrtzen was seriously hurt when waves from a speedboat overturned his aquaplane. His hip was broken. After he was rescued from the lake and taken to the Ticonderoga Hospital, it was said that he would be in bed from four to six months. This seemed to be the hardest blow that could come to the camp which had just launched such a successful season of soul-winning. "Happy Mac" did much to stand in the gap. Jack's staff assistant, Bob Mehorter, a former marine officer converted in a youth meeting on Guam, carried on ably in the absence of the leader. Everyone knew that the gravest problem would be the New York broadcast and youth rally.

Since no special care was available in the north, arrangements were made to bring Jack to a hospital near his New Jersey home. The only transportation that could be found was a hearse!

The grave diagnosis was confirmed in the Summit Hospital when a leading New Jersey specialist examined the fracture. But this surgeon had the advantage of a special technique learned in the last war. He offered the hope that Jack would be on crutches within two weeks! Here was an answer to prayer.

However, a serious operation was first needed. This took two and a half hours, and when it was finished, a four-inch vitallium pin was driven through the joined fracture. Jack broadcast two Saturday-night messages from the hospital cot. The hospital room took on the apperance of an evangelistic meeting, to the marked interest of the medical staff and the patients. Jack was trying out his crutches a week after the accident!

But the great reward and meaning of the trial seemed

wonderfully revealed after the bedside broadcast, even before Jack was able to return to camp. (Jack's recovery was so complete that his pace of travel, involving much rapid walking, shows no change, and there was no semblance of a limp after the first few months.) A letter came to Jack from another young man who had a similar trial. It reads as follows:

Dear Mr. Wyrtzen,

I must write and tell you what happened when I accidentally heard your broadcast last Saturday night.

My story starts back two and a half years ago. I had been brought up in a wonderful Christian home and was at that time preparing to go to Bible school in order to study to go out as a missionary, as I believed that was where the Lord was leading. The day before I was to leave for school I was horseback riding. I was alone and was considered a fairly good rider. However, when I was riding along my horse threw me and I landed on a rock. When the next riding party came by and found me I was taken to a hospital where I was told I had a broken hip. For six weeks I lay flat on my back and I had to remain in the hospital for three months. During this time I was allowed no visitors except my family who were allowed to come only once a week. I was in a room with three others and as time went on they kept asking me that if there was a God, why would He let me be so injured just as I was preparing to serve Him.

The dreary days and restless nights got me down and soon I, too, was asking these questions. I thought at first that the Lord didn't want me to go to school, but my call had been so plain that I abandoned that reason. I could see no reason why God should be letting me suffer so when I could have been studying His Word. Then and there I decided there was no God, and I was even more bitter when I came out of the hospital with a slight limp. I had not had Christian fellowship but I no longer wanted it: I withdrew my membership from my church, canceled my reservations at Bible school and renounced anything having to do with Christianity.

I said good-bye to my family and came here to New York to live. I never wrote to my family or old friends except to a beautiful Christian girl to break our engagement. Since coming to New York I have lived a life of sin. I can't say I hated it all, for at times Satan can give us a good time. However, back in my room, away from new-found worldly friends, I was sad and lonely, but I still did not know the reason for my accident and refused to go back to my home, no matter how lonely I was, until I knew the reason.

My life went on like this, making merry till early morning and then returning home to a sleepless night thinking of home and loved ones, until last week my doctor said I could stand it no longer and insisted that I stay in bed all week end. Being completely exhausted, I followed his advice. So it was that on Saturday night while I was lying in bed the fellow in the next room had his radio on very loud. It was turned to your program. At first when I heard the singing I wanted to turn it off but, of course, I could not do so. Later when I heard it announced that you would be speaking from a hospital bed because of a broken hip I became very interested in what you would have to say.

As I listened to you speak I realized how foolish I had been to question God's way. After your program went off the air I knelt down and thanked God for permitting me to hear your program, and asked forgiveness. Thank God, He has lifted my burden! I called my family and will go home this week end to be reunited with them. The lovely girl whose heart I broke has once again become my fiancée. This fall we both expect to go to Bible school, and from there to Japan as missionaries. Now once again, at twenty-four, I have begun living the only worth-while life. I still do not know why I was laid up, but I now can say, "God's way is the best way."

I'm ashamed of the life I have been leading the past two and a half years, Jack, but truly I thank God on every remembrance of you.

In Him,
LAWRENCE

Chapter 14

YALE AND WEST POINT

GREAT OPPORTUNITIES FOR Bible ministry have come to
Jack Wyrtzen in special services at leading Christian colleges
in our land, among these being Dallas Seminary, Wheaton
College, Eastern Baptist Seminary, Bob Jones University, Gordon College, King's College and Houghton College. Besides
these, there have been many opportunities to give a practical
testimony of home and foreign missionary work in the no less
important Bible colleges and institutes across the United
States. Among these were Providence Bible Institute, Provi-
dence; National Bible Institute, New York; Philadelphia
School of the Bible; Pennsylvania Bible Institute; Columbia
Bible College; Washington D.C. Bible Institute; Baltimore
Bible Institute; Moody Bible Institute; Bible Institute of Los
Angeles; and London Bible Institute, Ontario.

Of added interest is the entrance that God gave into our
leading universities which have for some generations disavowed
the Scriptures and the Christ of the Bible. It is remarkable
that Christian believers in special courses necessary for their
teaching credentials have been able to invite into chapel
services and special meetings an uncompromising Bible testi-

mony from an evangelist like Jack Wyrtzen. Here follows Jack's report of such an experience:

"This past week a group of Christians now attending Yale University invited me to speak in the Dwight Memorial Chapel, right in the very heart of Yale campus.

"The fellows told me afterward that it was one of the biggest crowds that ever attended a religious service there in the chapel, and what a joy it was right there, in the center of all the learning and wisdom of this world, to give an invitation and invite men and women to take Jesus Christ as Saviour. And what a thrill it was to our hearts to see young people walking down the aisle giving their hearts and surrendering their lives to the Lord.

"After the service was over, we looked around the campus at some of the buildings and some of the memorials, and how thrilled we were as we realized that even in this day when the Bible is being denied and laughed and mocked at, that right in the center of all this infidelity we found testimonies engraved right in the wall. And there above one of the drinking fountains was engraved an inscription to William Borden of Yale, a graduate of 1909, a young fellow who, when he attended Yale University, started Bible-study groups. He started the Yale Hope Mission right there in New Haven. This plaque was erected by his classmates as a tribute to his marvelous character, and around the water fountain I read these words: 'Let him that is athirst come.'

"And I found another plaque, and it was dedicated to Timothy Dwight (son-in-law of Jonathan Edwards), one of the greatest presidents Yale University ever knew. And on the plaque was a quotation from the baccalaureate address of the President of Yale University. Here's what Timothy Dwight said: 'Christ is the only true way, the living way of access to God. Give up yourselves, therefore, to Him with a cordial confidence, and the great work of life is done.'

"You know, as I read that, I was thrilled, for I had just been speaking to the students on John 14:6 where Jesus said, 'I am the way, the truth, and the life: no man cometh unto the Father, but by me.' How thrilling to find that years before, the president of Yale University had said, 'Christ is the only true way, the living way of access to God'!"

Entrance into the United States Military Academy at West Point and the privilege of speaking twenty-five minutes to the flower of young American manhood in training for tomorrow's leadership in the armed forces came about purely by God's providence.

Gideon workers had obtained the privilege of distributing New Testaments to the officers and cadets of West Point. The Academy chaplain had approved a five-minute service of dedication. He had no marked interest in this activity, much less was he seeking a speaker whose desire was to win souls.

The report got around that Jack Wyrtzen was going to speak at West Point. Many friends began to call the chaplain's office, much to his annoyance. No one knew how the report had become exaggerated, and there was certainly no expectation that it would be possible except for the limited time.

When the day of the exceedingly formal presentation service came, the chaplain fell ill and could not take charge of the chapel period, so he decided to give the entire time to the young youth evangelist.

From cavalry trombone player to guest speaker at one of the most august and formal gatherings in the world—that was a tremendous distance. Jack tells how the sea of faces swam before his eyes and how he was bewildered by a series of three ascending altars, the escort of top-flight generals and the snappy attention of two-thousand meticulously uniformed cadets.

But he remembered that the problem was no different from preaching on the street, in rescue missions, state reformatories and leading prisons. Men were alike, lost, despite their breeding. Culture was but a veneer to cover a sepulcher of death and sorrow.

I am not ashamed of the gospel of Christ, thought Jack. He remembered that he was invincible so long as he stood behind the Word of God, and he knew also that the testimony of a born-again believer is without possible refutal by any man born of Adam's stock.

The story of Joshua came into Jack's mind. Here was a mighty five-star general whose military career was unique in the history of God's ancient people. His very name was the Hebrew form of the name "Jesus," meaning "God is our salvation."

"Who created us? Why are we here, and where are we going?" was the electric query which Jack hurled straight to the cadets. He pointed out that the only answer was in Jesus Christ who made us, who died for us and who wants to have our lives now and to take us to live with Him forever in heaven. "Choose you this day whom ye will serve" was the challenge. Jesus Christ alone can deliver us from the certainty of hell, Jack declared. It was old-fashioned preaching, but as sure as mathematics, and it was the only deliverance from the curse of old-fashioned sin. Consequence of a wrong choice was exemplified even physically and morally in the descendants of the Jukes family, rejecters of God, who not only committed virtually every form of crime but were a public charge of millions of dollars. In contrast to this was the family of Jonathan Edwards, whose descendants occupied places of trust and usefulness and cost the public nothing. It is not likely that Jack's message was forgotten.

Climaxing the privileges of many years was the invitation to speak in the two closing services of Founder's Week of the Moody Bible Institute, at the Moody Memorial Church, Chicago, on February 8, 1948. Carlton Booth accompanied Jack, leading the song service and presenting solos. The meetings were a fitting conclusion to a week of soul-stirring revival in which many noted Gospel leaders were instrumental.

Chapter 15

OFFICE, SCHOOL AND STORE

"IT'S GREAT TO HAVE an office staff that goes right on with full responsibility in God's work whether you can be there or not," Jack declares heartily.

And to see *how* it goes on, you join the staff prayer meeting from nine to nine-thirty in the morning, feasting on God's Word, observing its message for the day, and then bringing every burden of prayer in grateful acknowledgment before the Lord in praise. There are always broadcasts, rallies, missionary advance and many special requests that call for intercession. No radio request for prayer is ever neglected. Many have been the définite answers to these faithful petitions.

When Jack is not in New York, Fred Scharmann, business manager, conducts the staff prayer meeting. With Jack, he feels that no decision of any sort should be made without prayer. This emphasis on God's Word and the guidance of the Holy Spirit has doubtless saved the group irreparable blunders and thousands of dollars of God's money.

For example, pencils—six thousand of them—were needed for the Christian workers at the Yankee Stadium Rally. Fred did not take the first bid that came along, but found a much better price on a discontinued line of bridge pencils. He's that way—extremely practical—in everything. The money saved has helped to bring the Gospel to many unreached places at home and abroad. And prayer about little things has meant much in the greatest decisions.

Fred Scharmann lives in Woodhaven, Long Island. He was led to the Lord in Jack's home one night in 1938, in a meeting attended by eighty young people. (Saturday-night "Youth for Christ" meetings were held in the Wyrtzen home as early as thirteen years ago, Jack reports.) With the neighborhood Christian fellows, Fred entered into Gospel opportunities that now touch the entire world. He continued in a responsible business post until the war, when he went overseas. Upon his return from England in 1944, he was employed by the Fire Department, but gave his spare time to help Jack with the business problems of an activity that covered radio broadcasts, rally arrangements and weekly meetings. It was another obvious case of "a man's gift making room for him," and like every other personnel appointment, it was obvious before it was made official. There was an equally heavy inducement for him to work elsewhere, but God made the decision plain to Fred. The Word of Life Fellowship advisory council has often thanked God for this humble and gifted young business executive whose dealings for the Lord in the heart of New York City have worked out the arrangements for the super-rallies, radio broadcasts and meetings.

There have been twenty-eight staff workers since it was found necessary to establish a central office for the Gospel work. Most of these have continued their witness by attending Bible schools, preparing for the mission fields or establishing Christian homes in their neighborhoods.

The first secretary to the Gospel group was Janet Hobley, who left the staff late in 1943 to marry Henry Kelley, a government employee and Gospel worker.

Anne Lubkemann, one of the original members of the Woodhaven group, has been the office secretary since that time. Upon her has fallen a large responsibility in conducting personal correspondence with Gospel leaders in many places. Not only has she been concerned about multitudinous details of the Fellowship work in the homeland, but she has maintained a living bond of prayer with the foreign fields. Her brother, Ernie, saved through her instrumentality in the earliest Woodhaven meetings, is laboring with his wife and two little sons in the heart of Brazil's Matto Grosso, and they are thrusting forward to the unreached Xingu Indians.

Staff members who have entered Bible-school training are Agnes Michaelsen, Columbia Bible College; Eleanor Adolph, Columbia Bible College; Eleanor Rowe, Providence Bible Institute; Talbot McNutt, Gordon College; Patricia Marquardt, Philadelpia School of the Bible; and Mildred Winkler, Providence Bible Institute.

Others formerly of the office staff and now married are Gladys Schneider Hawley, Virginia Sloat Davison and Mary Johnson Catchpole.

Sophie Gerdes, who helped prepare the radio scripts until December, 1943, left for missionary preparation with the New Tribes Mission in California, and field service in Mexico. She married Frank Jenista, and both of them have taken advanced training for entry into the tribal area of southwest China, under the sponsorship of Word of Life Fellowship. They have two little children.

With Fred Scharmann and Anne Lubkemann in the present office staff at 140 Nassau Street, New York City, are the following members: Florence Otterbeck, Martha Stumpf, Mildred Wolfertz, Ardelle Armstrong, Betty Jane Harris and Anne Lindle.

Many are interested in knowing about the thorough help which the Word of Life Fellowship has felt led to give the new believers in Jesus Christ. The follow-up with the new

Christian begins at the inquiry room where the person who has made his decision is shown from God's Word the meaning of the step and the promises and provisions of God, through Jesus Christ. The next step is the signing of a decision card which is an open confession of faith and a means of future contact with the individual. Each new believer is sent a letter of encouragement with which is included *The Christian's Guide*, by Alfred P. Gibbs. Also made available on request is a free Scripture memory course. The same letter contains an offer of *The Young Believer's Bible Work*, by Keith L. Brooks. Advanced Bible memory work under Dawson Trotman's supervision is offered, as well as further doctrinal teaching by Dr. Brooks.

Whenever possible the new converts are commended to the care of pastors in their neighborhoods who have an interest in deepening the young convert's Scriptural knowledge and offering them Christian fellowship. However, this co-operation has often been lacking in regions where there have been no Bible pastors; thus the necessity of providing the helps by correspondence and urging attendance at the Word of Life Bible School when possible.

Remembering the unspeakable value of the kindly Scriptural teaching given to the young believers in Woodhaven, the Word of Life Fellowship was concerned about providing basic Bible helps for those hundreds of radio and rally converts who desired them. This follow-up work was aimed at directing the new Christian to a Bible-centered life, essential for spiritual growth and service for Christ.

The thorough teaching in the inquiry room, immediately following the evangelistic rally, and the providing of such valued exhortations and outlines as shown in Captain Reginald Wallis' books *The New Man*, *The New Boy* and *The New Girl*, were attempts to achieve this objective. Follow-up work on behalf of every individual was felt to be a blessed responsibility whether the confession of faith came by radio, meeting, tract or personal contact. This concern has made a difference, for thousands of new believers have been directed to sound churches, and many have completed courses at Bible schools and entered the ministry or missionary service.

For this reason also came into being the Word of Life Bible School. Beginning in October, 1942, the school met one night a week, from six-thirty to nine-thirty. It follows without apology the tried outlines of the Hawthorne Evening Bible School, in New Jersey. Outward credentials are confessedly not the aim of the school, but the students indicate that the courses are filled with the most practical helps for victorious and fruitful Christian living. The students become "workmen that need not to be ashamed."

Meeting only one night a week, and since 1945, at the National Bible Institute building, 340 West 55th Street, New York, with a staff of gifted Bible teachers drawn from the New York and New England area, the school has given large service to many business employees and housewives who could not spare further time. Those going on to full-time Bible training institutes and colleges have reported that their way has been greatly aided. Cost of the school is borne in part by free-will offerings. There is no enrollment fee. At the end of three years of training a certificate is given for completed work. It is gratifying to know that the school is more concerned about evidences of fruitful living and soul-winning than the mere gain of outward knowledge. Horace Klenk, popular Bible teacher of Glenhead, Long Island, will serve as dean of the enlarged school, in 1949.

The teachers and subjects as of 1948 are as follows: Studies in Daniel, by Thomas Lawrence; Child Evangelism, by Betty Worrall; Practical Christian Living, by Theodore Hummel; Gospel of John, James E. Bennet; Great Words of Scripture, Horace Klenk; Personal Evangelism, John Duchardt; God's Plan for the Ages, Arnold C. Borgman; Book of Acts, Horace Klenk; Christian Character Course and Memory Work, John Duchardt; Missions, John Duchardt, and outstanding missionaries; James, and First and Second Peter, Horace Klenk; Studies on the Tabernacle, Arnold C. Borgman.

Of no small importance in the ministry of making known the "Word of Life" has been the contribution of John Sidebotham, talented Christian commercial artist. He has aided all the great rallies by providing posters, advertising cards, letterheads and stationery. He also designed the attractive covers of the songbooks compiled by Norman Clayton, Carlton Booth and Beverly Shea.

The Word of Life Bookstore, 140 Nassau Street, New York, was established after the office was moved from Woodhaven to its present address in Manhattan. The first director of the store was Horace Davies, a present member of the radio staff.

Opportunity to minister by providing sound Bible helps and Fundamental Christian literature was long seen by the group in consequence of its radio ministry and meetings held in churches, prisons, camps and institutions. New converts needed the best guidance available from orthodox Bible teachers and leaders past and present.

The bookstore has been one of the most popular activities of the entire Fellowship and has supplied the texts of the Word of Life Bible School and hundreds of choice doctrinal and biographical books for the radio audience. At the Word of Life Island Summer Camp it has been as popular as the soft-drink stand.

Though she modestly depreciates her ministry, many Christian friends know that the devotion of Florence Otterbeck to the work of making Bibles and valuable Christian helps available has been the reason for an ever-widening blessing on the bookstore. With the office staff, Florence has a night and day concern for the Gospel testimony by way of the printed page.

Chapter 16

THREE SUPER-RALLIES

GOD WILLING, by the time this book appears, in 1948, three of the greatest youth rallies ever conducted by the Word of Life Hour will have taken place. These will have been preceded by months of prayerful preparation, through the godly intercession of hundreds of thousands of Christians on the Eastern seaboard, as well as around the world.

The first of the three super-rallies to be conducted by the Word of Life Hour during the spring of 1948 took place on Saturday, April 3, at Convention Hall in Philadelphia. After the hymn sing in the Pennsylvania Station in New York, 1,000 young people boarded the train headed for the Philadelphia rally where they were met by 5,000 Philadelphia young people. Six thousand strong, led by forty mounted policemen and the Kallman Home Band, they paraded to Convention Hall. The police estimated that by seven o'clock, when the rally started, there were 15,000 seated and about 3,000 standing. Another 1,500 left because no seats were available. At the invitation about 250 came forward for salvation, hundreds offered their lives for the foreign field, and between three and four thousand others dedicated their lives to the Lord according to Romans 12:1. The rally was sponsored by the Christian Business Men's Committee of Philadelphia, under the chairmanship of Leon Sullivan, with local churches and youth groups co-operating. Carlton Booth, Beverly Shea, the Evangel Trumpet Trio of Toronto and others took part. Jack Wyrtzen led the rally and brought the main message of the evening.

The Boston super-rally will feature a similar program at the Boston Garden on May 8. The rally will be sponsored by a special committee, representative of all the evangelical groups of New England and headed by Allan C. Emery, Jr., and Gordon MacKerron, Word of Life council members.

Possibly one of the greatest Gospel rallies in history is that prayerfully scheduled for June 19 at New York's Yankee Stadium which has a seating capacity of 75,000. For this, as for the other rallies, round-the-world prayer groups have been formed.

Noteworthy in the large rallies is the simplicity of program, devoid of all pageantry and sensationalism. Jack believes that the views of the Word of Life Fellowship have been vindicated by the immense fruitfulness of the meetings kept to a plain, Spirit-filled, Bible-loving testimony of Jesus Christ. It is his conviction also that soul-winning is possible without perilous experiments in drawing crowds by means of dramatic entertainment features.

The large rallies have never been conceived for the boast of numbers, but they have been recognized as a peculiarly effective means of bringing thousands of unconverted persons into the hearing of the Gospel. During the four previous Madison Square Garden rallies, nearly four thousand persons accepted the Lord Jesus Christ. In all these rallies the tremendous expenses have been met by the gifts of Christians, mostly of humble financial means.

As in the Acts of the Apostles, these young men and women whom "God hath chosen" are continuing to move outward to the ends of the earth with the Gospel of Christ. They are part of that throng of today's valiant young people, who, having found reality in Jesus Christ, are seeking by all means to bring others to Him. Through the toil and the heat of the day, their witness has been heard in home, school and factory. Beyond the beachheads and railheads of the unevangelized lands they have gone to give forth the Gospel testimony and commit it to able native colleagues. The laborers are yet few, and the harvest is great in a world that is suffering the unhealed agonies of the greatest wars in history.

What part will you have in this task? Are you saved? Are you yielded to the Saviour's last command, "Go ye into all the world and preach the gospel"?

Bob Moon writes the following note from South America:

No one serves the Lord out-and-out in this life without tribulation. That was guaranteed by the Lord, but what have we to fear, for He has overcome the world . . . Already there has been much bloodshed and stoning here in this country, and from now on we will never know when it may cost us our all to name the Name of Christ. But name His precious Name we will! And if we should ever have the supreme privilege of 'being made conformable to His death,' then what greater privilege could we have . . . On this last trip I nearly lost my life, for I was surrounded by I don't know how many hundred people with big rocks in their hands ready to stone me and crying for my blood, but the Lord must have had further use for me.

The challenge is to you. For all who know Him there are ever the ministries of giving, praying and going. And the task remains unfinished until the golden daybreak when we shall see His lovely face!

To God be all the glory for His moving in the hearts of men, and the revealing of His Son, Jesus Christ, the only Saviour.

Printed in the U.S.A.

Portrait sketch of Tommy McFarland, done by Charles Templeton, director of the Toronto Youth for Christ. This sketch was made in the presence of 1500 young people at Chicagoland Youth for Christ Banquet held at the Stevens Hotel.

Young Man on Fire

The Story of Torrey Johnson
and Youth for Christ

By MEL LARSON

CHICAGO
YOUTH PUBLICATIONS

Dedicated to

YOUTH FOR CHRIST

the world around.

Might God Use the Movement

to

His Greatest Glory

Published August, 1945
Composed and printed
in the United States of America by
Good News Press   •   Chicago 6

CONTENTS

FOREWORD

IT HAS been a real privilege to be permitted to read the proof
sheets of this book. Again and again, my heart has welled
up with thanksgiving to the God of all grace, who delights to
manifest His power and goodness through any one who is
willing to be subject to His will. Someway, it has seemed to me
as though I were reading of a modern Gideon as the life story
of Torrey Johnson unfolded before my mind's eye. I do not even
now understand why I was chosen to write these introductory
paragraphs. There are many others far more suited to do so,
both because of greater literary ability and fuller acquaintance
with the subject of this biography, but I truly appreciate the
privilege thus conferred upon me.

I have watched the progress of this devoted pastor-evangelist
for the last ten years and I rejoice in all that God has wrought
through his instrumentality. I feel sure that the perusal of this
book will bring blessing to many more young men and to many
young women who have not yet come to the place where they
are willing to say from the heart, "Lord, what wilt thou have
me to do?" But as they see what life-surrender has meant for
Torrey, I am sure many will be encouraged to yield themselves
wholly to the Lord, that they too may be instruments of blessing in His hand.

But I must not keep the reader standing at the door. These
words of mine are simply intended to be as an earnest invitation
to enter the portals of this volume and become acquainted with
one of God's chosen instruments for the blessing of old and
young in these stirring times.

(Signed) H. A. IRONSIDE

PREFACE

Winning the youth of our nation to a saving knowledge of Jesus Christ truly is one of the most stirring challenges of this fifth decade of our fast-moving twentieth century. God is using young people to influence young people, and God is using Torrey M. Johnson as perhaps no other young man in North America to win souls for His kingdom and to throw out the resounding need for fully consecrated and yielded lives both at home and on foreign mission fields.

With those thoughts in mind we give you the story of Torrey M. Johnson. Might God use it to inspire thousands of young people toward the only heart-satisfying things in our materialistic age—salvation through the blood of Jesus Christ and a willingness to say, "I'll go where you want me to go, dear Lord."

Chicago, Illinois
1945

YOUNG MAN ON FIRE

CHAPTER ONE

"For Me to Live . . ."

IT WAS Thanksgiving day in 1928. Autumn had come with its raw chill and Chicago's famous lake Michigan shore was being swept by one of the winds which justly have tacked onto this giant hub of the United States middlewest the tag, "The Windy City." Only a few people were strolling on that beautiful lake front on this night. The warmth of Thanksgiving was threading its way through millions of hearts as home after home found loved ones gathered from near and far.

This was pre-depression Chicago—and pre-war Chicago. Everything· was "rosy" as far as material needs were concerned. The post-war sag after World War I had been straightened out; things apparently were under control and a new era of prosperity was "here to stay."

Along the lake front that Thanksgiving night walked a young lad of 19. He looked like the athlete which he was as he moved along. He wasn't big—and he wasn't small. Just comfortably between. Blond, curly hair proved the top piece for a face clearly Scandinavian and a body which seemed to exude energy even on this cold night.

From the outside he appeared calm, but on the inside of that young fellow's being there was raging a tumult and storm such as often was seen on the lake by which he walked. His mind and heart were in constant conflict as he drifted aim-

1

lessly along. For a moment all would be clear as he unfolded dream upon dream and plan upon plan. College . . . medical school . . . hard work . . . and finally, the best eye, ear and nose specialist the world ever has known!

But then came the clash, and it came hard!

"Torrey, will you go to Africa?"

That question maddened him . . . and because it did he was walking along the lake front that chilly night. Without being dramatic about it, he was ready to commit suicide. The internal battle between the two opposing pulls in his life was getting to be too much for him. He was ready to call it quits.

"Africa, God? Lord, I'm not fit to go to Africa. I'm not qualified for that type of work. I'd never make a good missionary. Lord, I'll send someone else in my place. Lord, if you prosper me in my profession I'll send two. Lord, I'll give ever so much for the work of the gospel."

The question persisted.

"Will *you* go to Africa?"

One thing kept that 19-year old Northwestern university sophomore from drowning himself in lake Michigan that night. He knew he could swim! Moment after moment of decision worked through his mind, but . . . he just kept on walking, kept on thinking, kept on refusing to meet God face to face. After a few more blocks he veered away from the lake front; God still had the upper hand—at least the fellow was still alive.

An hour or so later that same night the fellow was sitting with his sweetheart on a davenport in her home on the northwest side of Chicago. He had been there often, both before and since the night he had slipped a diamond engagement ring on the proper finger on her left hand. This wasn't the first time, either, that their conversation swung to the inward struggle through which he was going. That lovely Christian girl knew of the conflict going on in the husky, athletic body of the man she loved. She helped him most in the best way she knew how, by praying . . . much.

2

She had much for which to be thankful this Thanksgiving day, and his love for her was high on the list. Nineteen months previous he had accepted Jesus Christ as his personal Saviour; a few days after that they were "going together for keeps." They had known each other before that time and had dated often in a casual way, but their feeling for each other never had gotten past the "casual" stage; she was a Christian and he wasn't. Only once did she step down from her high standards to please him—and that involved going to a dance. She knew in her heart that she was falling in love with him and that he was "tops." But . . . he wasn't a Christian.

Salvation had changed that—changed it in one glorious night in Wheaton college's sacred chapel when yet one more college student got right with God. Following that experience the young fellow still felt that he wanted to continue with his medical training. For a while things went along all right, but during this present semester he started to lose weight, became nervous and fidgety. His Christian mother had thought it was the confining nature of his school work. She knew nothing of the inward spiritual struggle and the obedient son felt that this was something he had to battle out alone.

This night was due to have its heartaches. He and his sweetheart talked at length, and then prayed to God for help and guidance. They rose from their knees, and sat solemnly on the edge of the davenport. The burning question was still there, and it kept him in misery.

"Will you go to Africa . . . Will you go to Africa . . . Will you go to Africa . . . Will you go to Africa . . . " and over and over again.

They talked some more—and prayed some more. Then they stood up. He had made up his mind.

"Evelyn, I won't go to Africa . . . and you'll never see me again."

The wet-eyed girl slowly slipped the diamond ring from her finger, handed it to the man she loved, and said softly,

"Here's your ring then, sweetheart. I don't want to be engaged to a dead man."

If this were fiction we might insert at this point that he drew himself to his full length, gave her a farewell kiss, and went out of her life forever. We don't know if he kissed her or not.

But we do know that he walked out of the front door, down the steps and toward the corner. She walked back to the davenport, dropped on her knees, and prayed.

He got as far as the corner—and stopped! He couldn't move another step—except back! He turned around and in a few moments was knocking at the door. One look at his face was all she needed.

God had won!

They knelt to pray together, and as he prayed he told the Lord,

"Lord, I'll go to Africa. I'll be the doormat of the church. I'll do anything you want me to do." As he prayed that prayer, waves of joy, peace, love and blessing flowed through his heart and mind.

When they stood up and smiled at each other through their tears, another miracle had happened.

"Honey," he said, "I don't feel at all now that I should go to Africa. It's gone . . . that feeling and burning question is gone . . . all gone . . . and I've got peace."

The "fellow" in our story is Torrey M. Johnson.

The girl is now his wife.

Every detail is true. Why we pick it to open the amazing story of Torrey M. Johnson is hard to say. Surely it is one of the most dramatic and touching instances of God's dealing with a man that it has been our fortune to read. Unless God had had His way that night there would be no Torrey M. Johnson today, and without Torrey M. Johnson there would be many things missing in this year 1945 A.D. which God is using mightily to His honor and glory.

The life of 36-year old Torrey M. Johnson presents a maze of experiences which at times startle you. We find at the core "just another son of just another Norwegian immigrant," full of life and bothersome pranks as any young fellow ever

4

was. Nothing stamped him as unusual and sensational as he moved from school to school, place to place and church to church. Until the time he accepted Christ as his personal Saviour he was definitely a "problem child." His Christian dad had shipped him off to Wheaton college in 1926 in the hope that he would find Christ as his personal Saviour while on that godly campus.

He did just that.

After that event he didn't immediately proceed to astound either the Christian or secular world. As our story opens we almost find Torrey M. Johnson as the name on a tombstone rather than among the living. However, God had His way that night and a human ball of fire was started on its way.

Within two months he was back at Wheaton college. In June of 1930 he was graduated. The same month he accepted the call to serve as pastor of a Baptist church in Chicago. He stayed there one year and then went on the road for two years as an evangelist. The urge for more schooling bubbled over in 1933 and he enrolled at the Northern Baptist seminary in Chicago, at the same time serving as pastor of a little church on the Chicago northwest, called the Midwest Bible church.

As he grew in book learning, the Midwest Bible church grew spiritually. After graduation from the Seminary he stayed on to teach Greek part time along with serving his church. In 1940 a decision had to be made—should he be a pastor or a professor?

The "pastor" got the decision. He'd rather preach than teach, and the members of the Midwest Bible church—one of the fastest growing churches in the land—were happy.

"Youth for Christ" appeared on the scene. It didn't start in Chicago, nor did it start in the idea-filled brain of Torrey M. Johnson. But it started, and Torrey feels that God started it. Today as that God-given and God-guided movement sweeps the North American continent and threatens to cross the many oceans and win thousands of souls to the Lord Jesus Christ, the man behind the scenes as God's human

5

instrument in working out His program through it is the man of our book.

His yet-young wife readily admits these days, "I can't keep up with him anymore."

His church looks at him with awe and love as it tells him to spend as much time as he desires in spreading Youth for Christ; one associate and one assistant pastor now assist him at Midwest Bible church in carrying on one of the most effective church ministries on the North American continent as property after property is acquired to handle the increasing crowds and membership.

He's "on the go" from morning until night, excluding a private nap right after dinner . . . when he's home for dinner. He's no "great preacher"—even he himself readily admits that—but God has used him to win many to a saving knowledge of Jesus Christ. He has but one hobby, as he told a lady on a streamliner one day, and that is to win souls for the Lord Jesus Christ. To that end he works tirelessly. He feels that he is no great organizer, but he has a wonderful ability to get things done and get them done in tiptop fashion . . . to the salvation of souls.

Were you to spend a day with him you might well wonder where he gets the energy and strength to carry on the tremendous work which is his. If you asked him about it, he perhaps would tell you this story.

In April of 1933 he was holding a series of evangelistic meetings in Duluth, Minn. While there, word came that his brother, Arling, two years younger than he, had passed away after an illness of fourteen months. He had taken sick while on a tour of Europe and after being returned to America he lingered on for five months before God called him home. Arling had the "brains and everything else" in the family. Torrey's mother and father and his brothers and sisters admitted that, and they looked to him to accomplish much in this world.

But, God saw fit to take him home, with these last, closing words,

"Dad, I'd like to be able to see those jonquils in the front

6

yard, but . . . there are more beautiful flowers in heaven."
With that he was gone.

Torrey came home for the funeral. In his finite mind he had a hard time figuring out why Arling had had to die. While on his back Arling had promised the Lord that if He raised him up again that he would go into the ministry or wherever God wanted him to be. Torrey had prayed to God endlessly that Arling's body would be healed; he felt so deeply that his younger brother's personality, intellectual power and dependence on God could be used greatly to win souls for Him.

"But," as Torrey explained, "God didn't see fit to heal his body. As I stood by his casket at the funeral I promised the Lord at that moment that if He would give me the strength that was intended for my brother that I would do his work and mine, too. That realization has spurred me on in everything I do. I'm not only doing the work which God has for me to do, but I'm doing my brother's work, too."

The aged and well-worn feeling of never being able to put into writing the warmth of a personality alive and on fire for Jesus Christ seems unusually pertinent as these words are being written. It is hard to picture for you the Torrey Johnson *exuberance* for *anything* which tastes of the furthering of God's kingdom here on earth. It'll be hard to describe for you the Holy Spirit power behind the pointed gospel messages which he preaches from Sunday to Sunday in the Midwest Bible church and in Youth for Christ meetings through out the week. It'll be difficult to open up for you the great organizational mind of this man of God as he keeps things on an even keel in the great Youth for Christ movement; the God-given results and the facts will be there, but the prayerful touch of the leader in the background will be hard to see. It'll be hard to show you on paper the tremendous amount of time he spends in prayer . . . but here again the results are proof of his constant communion with God.

Truly, a "Man on Fire." But it's a clean, crisp, crackling, healthy fire. God has taken away the smoke and smudge as Torrey M. Johnson lets his light shine before men.

7

CHAPTER TWO

"... You Must Move."

JACOB MARTIN JOHNSON, a pleasant piece of Norwegian
personality, walked cheerfully into his humble home in
Chicago after a hard day's work on March 15, 1909. The
day had been an unusual one in many ways. Early that morning at 5 o'clock he had become a proud father for the third
time. The first time it had been a boy, the second time a girl.
Now it was a boy again and even though the day had been
long and he hadn't had much sleep for quite a stretch, he
wasn't tired. Fathers seldom are at that stage of the game.
All day long he had been "extra pleasant" to the many people
who boarded his street car. And, like most new fathers, he
didn't have to be coaxed very long to explain the reason for
the extra inch of smile on his face.

As he walked into the house he noticed a small note stuck
into the icebox next to the door. He opened it up, expecting
to find in it a note of congratulations from some kind neighbor
and perhaps an invitation out for dinner. Instead to his surprise he found a few words scrawled in a firm German hand-
writing. After rounding up an interpreter he read these words
on that note:

"Two children are enough for any family. Three are too
many. You must move."

Such was the situation which Torrey Maynard Johnson
put his God-fearing parents in when he came into this world
on March 15, 1909, in the city of Chicago. They talked to

8

the landlady, but she was not to be persuaded. Two children were enough, and three were too many, so plans soon were underway for the moving.

The cause of the exodus, squalling, yelping Torrey Maynard Johnson, had caused a little excitement even before he officially made his arrival on what now has become known to most Americans as "Income Tax day." The usual discussion about his (or her) name had come up frequently. Torrey's dad thought it should be Torrey Moody Alexander Johnson in honor of the two great evangelists, R. A. Torrey and Dwight L. Moody, and the great song leader, Charles Alexander. His mother thought that it would be a great enough order if he could measure up to any *one* of them.

Mother won and it was Torrey Maynard. "Papa Johnson" didn't mind so much; he had wanted another boy, and he had one.

The home into which Torrey made his entrance was Christian to the core. His mother, Thora Mathilda Evensen Johnson, the youngest of 10 children, was born and reared on a farm in Lister Farsund, Norway. Her ambitious father worked for the Norwegian government along with his farming as he helped in the construction of bridges and docks.

Torrey's father was the sixth of ten children and was born in Lyngdal, near Mandal, in Norway. His father was a sailor and also managed the farm on which his children were reared. The towns in which Torrey's mother and father lived were but 75 miles apart but they never met each other while living in Norway. It took the emigrating spirit and the desire for adventure to bring both of them to America and ultimately to Chicago. Here they met, promptly fell in love as immigrants and non-immigrants have a habit of doing, and were married in due time on September 2, 1904. Both of them previous to this time had accepted the Lord Jesus Christ as their personal Saviour and when the knot was tied another fine Christian home was established.

They possessed two distinct personalities which combined perfectly to create an ideal home. Mrs. Johnson is quiet, un-

9

assuming, never active in church work due to the needs of bringing up six children. As a worker in the home she was tireless. She was up early in the morning, and generally was the last to retire at night. She sewed most of the clothing for the family and Torrey, along with the other boys, didn't own a complete suit of clothes, ready-made, until he was ready for confirmation; all of the others were either sewed by his mother or hand-me-downs from his brother.

She was always busy. As she worked she would sing her loved gospel hymns in Norwegian. She prayed much, and her prayer sessions alone made a deep imprint on each of the children. Mother wasn't to be disturbed during those times. As her husband was away most of the day the religious instruction in the home fell largely to her and the excellence of that instruction is shown today in that all of her children are born again Christians. She never prayed in public, but in the home her prayers never will be forgotten by any of the children. They were filled to overflowing with feeling, Christian love and tears. Along with the prayers there was plenty of exhortation; she was kept constantly busy "preaching" to her little congregation of six. As Torrey explained it, "We needed it, too."

The cheerful father of our story had gone to sea at the age of thirteen. After he took unto himself a wife, however, he thought that the life of a sailor with its long periods of absence wasn't just the thing for him so he obtained a job as a streetcar conductor. Later he switched to the painting business, then to a job as a coffee salesman and finally, when Torrey was 10 years old, to the real estate and building line in which he now is engaged. The Lord gave him a ringing testimony when he was saved and he has been using it ever since. He is very active in church work, and his sociable nature and pleasant personality have won for him personal friends which number into the hundreds. He has a great memory and doesn't forget names, places, dates or people.

It wasn't long before Torrey knew who was boss in the Johnson home. In the kitchen hung a fine picture, and whenever the children would act up a bit Mr. Johnson would casually look up at the picture. The children would follow his look, but instead of stopping at the picture their eyes would pass an inch or two higher. There hung a razor strap, with its end cut into strips. It was used often—when the look didn't suffice—and as often as not the pair of pants on the receiving end were owned, or at least worn, by a boy named Torrey.

With these fine Christian parents as guardians of the home into which he was born, Torrey was certain of being well taken care of. Both of his parents were sturdy and staunch Norwegians, sincere and sweet to the innermost parts. They had moved much since leaving Norway, and now that Torrey had arrived they were due to move again. So it was, with Torrey in tow, that two weeks after he arrived the family packed up and moved from 1830 N. Washtenaw in Chicago to 2645 Homer street, in the Humboldt park district. Someone said about Torrey that he started to move when he was two weeks old and has been moving ever since. They lived for two years in that home and one day the landlord knocked on the door and said, "The house has been sold, and you'll have to get out."

In looking for a place to move to this time, Torrey's mother and father decided that now was the time to buy the home that both of them had been dreaming about. After searching the area they found what they wanted at 2848 North California avenue. It was ideal for several reasons, but the most attractive was its being located only two doors from the Salem Evangelical Free church. The parents were counting heavily on their children being brought up the right way and the nearness to the church would help a good deal in keeping the youngsters interested in going consistently.

It was in that home that the family circle was completed, as far as additions were concerned. When it was finished it looked like this:

| Marshall. | Torrey. | Clifford. |
| Lillian. | Arling. | Eugene. |

Five boys and one girl. That meant a riotous home, full of fun, but through it all moved the sweet Christian love of the parents to such a resounding depth that all six of the children found Jesus Christ as personal Saviour. Along with that, all of them except the one now home in heaven are active in church work.

Marshall lives in La Grange, Ill., with his wife and two children and is a member of the Evangelical Mission church there. He owns his own coal business.

Lillian is married to Stanley Berntsen, secretary of the Belmont-Central Savings and Loan association in Chicago. They are the parents of one girl and are members of the Midwest Bible church.

Arling went home to be with the Lord on April 4, 1933.

Clifford is president of the Belmont-Central Savings and Loan association and junior member, with his father, of the Mars Realty company. He is married and has two children; he and his wife are members of the Midwest Bible church.

Eugene, born in 1919, is a full lieutenant in the United States navy and last was stationed at the Midway islands in the South Pacific.

There always has been a family altar in the Johnson home. The Bible was always open in the home and the children were taught to revere it, learn to study from it and regard it as the true Word of God. From that initial training in the home the children were taken to Sunday school as soon as they were able to toddle there, and even before. The children attended Sunday school at the Salem church and all six rolled up perfect attendance records ranging from 10 to 15 years. As soon as the Sunday school habit was firmly imbedded into them they were taught to "stay for church" or have some explaining to do at the Sunday dinner table.

The Johnson home was a haven for visiting pastors and students. Hospitable Mr. Johnson always was walking in the front door with a pastor or two or a Bible school student or two, either for dinner or for a night or a week. This meant more work for Mrs. Johnson but she was as eager and happy as he was in having friends visiting in the home. The Salem church of which they were members was known throughout the North American continent and Norway as one of the greatest Bible-teaching, evangelistic and missionary centers of the time. Venerable Dr. Christian Dyrness was its pastor from its founding until he passed away 43 years later. His great Christian life has formed and shaped thousands of Norwegian young people and sent them out as missionaries and preachers to all parts of the globe. Two of his sons now are in full-time Christian service: Professor Enock Dyrness is vice president and registrar of Wheaton college at Wheaton, Illinois, and Rev. Franklin Dyrness is pastor of the Orthodox Presbyterian church of Quarryville, Pa.

The Salem parsonage was next to the church and so the "preacher's kids" and Torrey soon became fast friends. They together with the son of an elder who lived across the alley—now Lt. Franklin Olson, M.D.—ran around together and kept three sets of parents on edge wondering what was coming next. Between Torrey and Franklin there grew an especially deep bond of friendship which was to ripen many years later. One of the cementing ties was the fun they had together as boys.

One day Torrey's father wanted to re-decorate his basement and as the first step he had Torrey and his pals sponge off the calcimine. All the boys were enthusiastic about it at first, but as the novelty wore off they started to wrestle and fight on the basement floor. Before they knew it sponging of calcimine was a thing of the past as they had a good, friendly free-for-all in the Johnson basement. Result: Mr. Johnson sponged the walls himself.

When Torrey's dad was away on his coffee-selling route he often took his second son and his pals along with him. Torrey, Franklin and the Dyrness boys thought they were going along to "protect" Mr. Johnson. On one of his trips he had been held up by a man who had answered to the description of the gangster, Tommy O'Connor, and when on later trips he took the kids along they were sure that he wanted them there to help him in case he was held up again.

13

In his early days Torrey caused concern among many people. His wilful disposition and his uncanny ability to get into mischief led many to warn his parents that they would have many problems with "that boy." Torrey knew at an early age what sin was all about, but he rebelled against restraint and regulation. As such he was the cause of many parental tears and periods of prayer before God.

Torrey's dad believed it a good thing for boys to start earning a few pennies for themselves at an early age so when Torrey reached the ripe old age of nine he went scouting for a job. He found it—in a Chinese laundry. He wrapped collars and shirts at first, and later learned to iron collars and shirt cuffs. For working before school, after school and all day Saturday he earned fifty cents a week! Boy, he was rich!

But one day he came running home to dad, badly frightened, and announced that he was quitting that place! When his father got the story out of him he discovered that the owner had taken Torrey to the back of the store that afternoon to show him a few things he had brought with him from China. Among them was a gun, and when Torrey saw it he became so frightened that he bolted for the door, hurried through it and ran all of the way home. He wouldn't even go back to collect his pay, but sent his father for it. His dad collected the money, gave it to Torrey, who promptly went out in search of another job.

This time he landed in a printing shop where he served as a printer's devil and distributed handbills. He didn't like this, however, so was off again in search of another job. A glove factory looked inviting, so he started to work there, turning out newly-sewed gloves. The owners didn't ask Torrey how old he was when he started and so he didn't tell them. In a short while, however, they found out that he wasn't as old as he looked—they thought he was 14 and he was only 12—and so he was dismissed because of the child labor laws.

Next he worked at a grocery store, delivering food and doing some counter work. When high school days rolled around he was "grown up" and so applied for and received a

14

job working in a tin shop. This job he held all four years in high school; he learned how to solder, make gutters, pipes for furnaces, install furnaces, etc. The two partners who owned the tin shop were out-and-out evolutionists—one a socialist and one an atheist! Torrey heard their philosophy for over four years, but God spared him from allowing their ideas to take root in his young mind. Had his parents known the philosophies of those two men they would immediately have stopped his working there. God and the Bible were ridiculed almost as often as a rivet was pounded in, but God preserved Torrey from absorbing their thoughts and words. Once more prayer was working.

Confirmation came along when he was thirteen. Out of the class of 30 confirmands, Torrey was the only one to take the examinations in Norwegian. He knew the Norwegian language from hearing it so often at home. His parents spoke English well, but in the home his mother generally asked the questions in Norwegian and the children answered in English. As a boy of thirteen he believed the Bible as the Word of God, knew all of its truths in all clarity, but he wasn't saved and he knew it! It was all in his head and not in his heart.

In 1922 he finished the Thomas J. Water grammar school and started the Carl Schurz high school. He had been anything but the "ideal child." He had started attending the movies in grammar school, without the knowledge of his parents. They believed strongly in separation from the world and would not condone dancing, card playing, movie going, smoking, etc. Torrey did a little smoking on the side, but not too often after his mother had detected it on him on two occasions and had seen the razor strap applied in its proper place. He liked to get into anything and everything that was exciting and everything into which he put his boyish energy found him in it 100 per cent.

Take marbles, for example. The city of Chicago playgrounds held a marbles contest and little Torrey walked off with the north side title. In the city playoffs, however, he lost out. He was disappointed when he lost in the finals and to add sores

15

to the wound they misspelled his name when it was printed in the paper. They called him "Tony" instead of Torrey.

High school days arrived. Torrey knew he wasn't a Christian and he kept on his own way, living the "fast" life into which so many of his pals and himself fell. He learned to dance in classes held after regular school hours and taught by the regular teachers. Eighteen years later he paused to ask himself, "Isn't it strange that in those days they taught us how to dance but wouldn't have a thing to do with a Bible club?"

As a member of the "athletic crowd," he was popular. As a swimmer he specialized in the breast stroke and during his senior year he placed fifth in the breast stroke in the national interscholastic meet held at the university of Chicago, at that time the outstanding prep swimming meet in the country. That same summer—1926—he won the *Chicago Daily News* national breast stroke title in the meet held at Jackson park in Chicago.

He warmed the bench occasionally for the Schurz football team and on Saturdays and Sundays he played football with a corner lot team called the "All Pals," a group of fellows—including his pal Franklin Olson—who were more interested in the things of the world than the things of God. All of this time Torrey knew that he wasn't a Christian and he knew that he wasn't happy. He had been raised in a Christian home, two doors from one of the country's greatest churches, under the ministry of one of the great pastors of the day, possessing a perfect Sunday school attendance record of 10 years, going to church every Sunday without fail, sitting in on revival meeting after revival meeting—but yet not a Christian! In his own words, "I loved sin. I loved the ways of the world, with its worldly pleasures. My companions were the same way, so it would not have been easy to become a Christian."

He had the light . . . but did not receive THE LIGHT. He knew of the Saviour but did not know Him. It is because of those days spent in high school when the real joy of salvation was not his that Torrey Johnson today has the tremendous burden for young people which he has. He knows from bitter personal experience what a Christ-less high school career can mean to a young fellow and in his little yet big way he is doing everything he can to win the high school youth to a saving knowledge of Jesus Christ.

In his days—not too long ago, either—there was no such thing as high school Bible clubs such as the Miracle Book club or Young Life. He spent much of his time in community centers and community houses and although he admits today that there is much about such places that is wholesome and body building, in the way of sports, etc., he feels definitely that they do not produce Christian character. To him, salvation comes not from environment, but only through faith in the shed blood of Jesus Christ.

But if high school days didn't bring Torrey into a saving knowledge of Jesus Christ they at least gave him the chance to meet the girl who was to have much to do with bringing that decision about. Torrey didn't go around much with girls in high school—he liked them, as did just about every other fellow in school—but he never went "steady" with any of them. Six months after Torrey enrolled at Schurz high school a little blonde, sweet and pleasant girl named Evelyn Nilsen also enrolled. Although in the same school they had little to do with each other in high school days; about the only direct thing which Torrey can remember is that he held the door shut on her once when she wanted to get off the streetcar on the way home, thus forcing her to go an extra block. Thus through three and a half years in the same school they knew of each other's existence, but not much more.

Graduation day came and the worlds to conquer loomed up before each student that day. Franklin Olson was graduated from Oak Park high school the same spring in which Torrey finished at Schurz, and during their senior years and immediately after graduation they worked frequently as laborers in the building boom which then was on. During those high school days they often made as much as 87½ cents an hour. Torrey helped as a brick layer and also as a helper in making cement. Between the two of them they became "Building and

17

Excavating Contractors." After the foundations were laid they would hire themselves out to fill in the wall with dirt, filling, etc., then leveling the lot and covering it with black dirt. They purchased a motorcycle in order to get around better and find the houses which needed the type of work in which they were "specializing."

One incident which happened just before school was out carries an indelible impression on the mind of Torrey's father. Torrey and Franklin had hired out to finish a certain job at 87½ cents an hour, but school work interfered so they hired a Negro laborer named Wallace to do the work for 75 cents an hour while they went to school. But when they came back after school one day they found that Wallace had pulled a fast one on them. He had hired a Norwegian fellow to do the work for 50 cents an hour while he sat in the shade of a nearby tree!

Later that summer Torrey and Franklin found themselves at the Wheaton college football camp at Williams Bay, Wisconsin. As far as a desire to attend Wheaton college, famed center of Christian education, was concerned, Torrey and Franklin were decidedly against it. But the hands that earned the bread for each of them decided that Wheaton was their school, so during the summer they made their way to the football camp as both intended to go out for the grid sport.

Being freshmen, and "smart ones," too, many tricks were pulled on the two of them that summer by the older players. The one which they never will forget is the much-used "snipe hunting" trick. Torrey and Franklin went with the other members on the squad to the middle of a dark forest nearby and were given the "snipe bag" and told to hold it while the others supposedly rounded up the snipe in a large circle and drove them into the large bag held by Torrey and Franklin. A few hours later the sheepish duo walked back into town to find the rest of the snipe hunters sound asleep! Torrey still insists, however, that he "almost caught" two snipes as they went past his bag!

Spending the summer at Williams Bay was convenient for

Torrey in several ways. His parents had a cottage there and so the entire family usually spent some parts of the summer away from the heat of Chicago at that well known summer resort. One night Torrey and his brother Arling were listening to a band concert. They saw two girls nearby; they knew one of the girls but not the other. They slipped over to say hello to the one they knew and then were introduced to "the other one." This was the girl whom Torrey had spied and whom he was anxious to meet. "The other one" was one of the girls with whom Torrey had gone through high school, but he didn't know her out there. They went for a little walk that night and from then on through the remainder of the summer they saw each other frequently, as Evelyn was working part time in a tourist home at Williams Bay.

There was just one hitch. Evelyn was a Christian ... and Torrey wasn't. That made all of the difference in the world to her. During those courting days she never would go anywhere with Torrey except for a walk, a rowboat ride or to church. It was especially to church that she pulled him. One night she told a girl friend that if Torrey would get saved and give a testimony in church as such and such a person had done that she would feel completely at ease in keeping steady company with him.

Torrey, on the other hand, was deeply interested in her but not interested in becoming a Christian. Because of that she kept him at his distance—and prayed! On only one occasion did she flinch—when she went to a dance with him. She was a Sunday school teacher, a young people's leader and devoted to her Master. Outside of that one time when she went to a dance with Torrey she had lived a separated life from the things of the world, with one other exception—when she went to a movie with a fellow before she met Torrey. She had been saved when seven years of age and had been baptized and joined the Logan Square Baptist church in Chicago when eight years old. Her parents, even as Torrey's, had been born in Norway; her dad was a sailmaker there

19

and an awning manufacturer here. The only other child in her family was a younger sister, Coreen.

She believed God's Word that Christians should not be unequally yoked together with unbelievers and she held her ground against Torrey until that day in January 1927, when he accepted the Lord as his personal Saviour while going to Wheaton college. They became engaged on July 16, 1928, after things had been "settled" at a Memorial day weekend picnic of the Evangelical Free churches at Madison, Wis. Soon after that trip, according to roommate Franklin Olson, Torrey was working especially hard to raise cash, and lived quite frugally. The sparkling diamond which blossomed on July 16 was the answer to that.

They were married on October 30, 1930, (the day before Hallowe'en, by intention) after he had earned his B.S. degree at Wheaton and she had finished her education at the Chicago Teacher's college. She then agreed wholeheartedly with what his high school annual had said about him:

> "A boy with spirit, a boy with pep,
> A finer boy has not been known yet."

And, according to him, her high school annual wasn't far wrong either when it said, "She has that rare quality—charm."

Three children have come into their home. Ruth Evelyn was born on December 4, 1934, Torrey Maynard, Jr. on August 5, 1938, and Arlene Coreen on April 23, 1941. And as is the case with Torrey any place, there's never a dull moment around the house—except when they're sleeping.

They were married by Dr. Peter Stiansen, pastor of Evelyn's church, spent the Sunday of their honeymoon in Paul Rader's tabernacle listening to a missionary challenge and on the following Monday morning Torrey was back at work with $2.00 in his pocket (and hers now, too) to start their married life together.

When Torrey's dad shipped him off to Wheaton college he prayed that his "problem child," as Torrey was termed, would change. Torrey, on the other hand, had an agreement

20

Upper left: Young Torrey at age two with his sister Lillian and brother Marshall. *Upper right:* At three years of age, with his sister and two brothers. *Center:* Torrey at extreme right, age eight. *Lower left:* At four years, Torrey sits astride a pet donkey. *Lower right:* Confirmation picture.

Above: High school graduation time in 1926.
Lower left: As a college freshman at Wheaton.
Lower right: Summers spent at Williams Bay, as ice man.

At 21, young Torrey was displaying attributes that were to bear fruitfulness in days to follow at Northern Baptist Theological Seminary, Midwest Church and Youth for Christ: unbounded energy, the faculty of organizing people and keeping them busy, and keenness to devise new ideas.

Upper left: At Williams bay in 1928, Torrey and his girl friend, later to become his sweetheart and his wife. *Upper right:* Torrey, in football togs, with his daughter Ruth. *Center:* Schulenberg, Christensen and Johnson and the car they used in evangelistic tours. *Lower left:* Just after ordination in 1930. *Lower right:* A Wheaton graduate in 1930.

Upper left: At college graduation time. *Upper right:* Torrey the preacher 11 years later. *Center:* The first daily vacation Bible school teachers in 1933 at the old store-church. *Lower left:* The Johnson family in 1942. *Lower right:* Two years later.

Upper left: Torrey the soul-winner, direct, appealing, and all business. *Upper right:* Before the "mike." *Center:* Charter members of Midwest Bible Church. *Below:* Two characteristic poses.

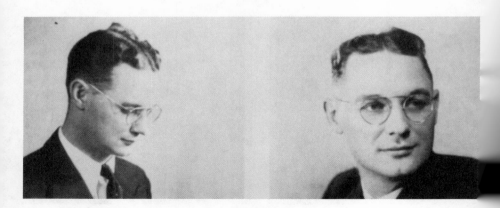

with Franklin Olson that they would perform just as much mischief as humanly possible.

Both Torrey and his dad saw their wishes fulfilled. Torrey had his fun for a period, but one day he met Jesus Christ face to face on the Wheaton campus.

He never was the same after that.

CHAPTER THREE

"Come on, Torrey!"

WHEATON COLLEGE nestles quietly on the fringe of the town of Wheaton, Illinois, population of slightly over 7,000 and a typical college town. It has been turning out Christian leaders ever since 1860 and today ranks as one of the best Christian colleges on the North American continent. Ever since its beginning it has adhered strictly to the fundamental truths of of the Bible and its value and reputation is such that it is clearly one of the top interdenominational schools of our land and accepted and revered by those many denominational groups.

Located twenty-five miles west of Chicago, Wheaton college has derived the benefits of that great metropolis and at the same time has been far enough away to feel itself a separate, independent and untouched entity. Its scholastic standards are high and it intends to keep them there. Were you to pause on a quiet afternoon or early evening stroll through the campus and think of the many Christian leaders who received their college training on these grounds you would be amazed. Should you be on the campus at five o'clock any afternoon you would step with some 1,200 students and utter a silent prayer for the many Wheaton graduates and former students now in the service of the country . . . praying to the background of chimes from the campus tower. Wheaton is proud of the fact that out of every 100 chaplains in the armed forces today, one received his training at Wheaton college.

When Torrey Johnson had his mind made up for him that he was going to Wheaton he resolved that as far as possible he would work his way through. His father agreed to that, with the provision that he would help his son whenever he needed help. With those facts in mind, Torrey went searching for work soon after he found himself at Williams Bay, Wis., in the summer of 1926 after graduation from high school. He went up to Mike Ambrose, owner of an ice company bearing that name, and asked for a job peddling ice for the summer. Ambrose looked at him once . . . and said no, but to "come back in a few days." Torrey returned, and Ambrose said he'd give him a chance. Torrey was looking for some heavy and hard work; he had his heart set on making the Wheaton football team that fall and he wanted to be in tip top shape when the season rolled around.

After one week at the job he not only convinced Ambrose that he could handle it all right but he also took over the route handled by a brother of the owner. But this wasn't enough work for Torrey, and in his odd moments he shoveled coal to "stay in shape." When the summer was over and Torrey was ready to leave for Wheaton, Ambrose offered to sell him entire rights to the route for $900. That was a lot of money to this high school graduate, but after a conference with his dad he agreed to buy it. Mr. Johnson made the first down payment of $500 and at the end of the 1927 summer season Torrey was able to pay off the remaining $400 and still have a sizeable chunk of money on which to start his second year of school. Torrey wasn't out to make his fortune in the ice business, but he did all right for himself. In three months in the ice business during the summer he made more than he did his entire first year of preaching the gospel. Very often he made more in a week peddling ice than he did in a month preaching; those facts have stuck with Torrey, and they give him a feeling of knowing that had he gone into a business or a profession that he could have been able to make a success of it.

Thus it was that with enough money on hand to get started

23

at Wheaton, Torrey and Franklin Olson gingerly made their way to the campus when the fall term started. Neither of them were "sold" on the idea of going to Wheaton ("not enough fun,") but they decided to make the best of it and make their own fun. They "holed up" in Blanchard hall's famous fourth floor and proceeded to have their fun.

They had a "suite" of three rooms between them. They painted the woodwork and calcimined the walls so that they had a red, white and blue color scheme. One room had the two cots where they slept. The second, or "large room," was for study and for company. The third was the dressing room and the closet.

One of the first persons to greet Torrey and Franklin when they reached the campus was Evan Welsh, captain of the football team, leader of the debating team and president of the Excelsior Literary Society (Celts). Torrey admired Evan Welsh from the first meeting, not only for his football brilliance but for the out-and-out Christian life he was leading. This thing called "salvation" was real to Evan Welsh, and in his tactful and intelligent way he went about winning his schoolmates to the Lord Jesus Christ. Also on the welcoming committee as Torrey and Franklin arrived was Torrey's chemistry teacher in his senior year in high school, Mr. DeVelde, who made his home in Wheaton. DeVelde also was a Christian and saw something in his former pupil and so went out of the way to make him feel at home in his new surroundings.

Football practice came along and Torrey was right in the middle of it. Although only a freshman he made the team very quickly, playing an end position opposite Evan Welsh, and also at guard. He enjoyed playing in the line and especially at end in order to get plenty of the bruising contact which falls to that position both on offense and defense. His wife-to-be came out to see him play on several occasions, but she never could tell what position he played.

"All I know," she said, "was that he had the job of knocking the other men down as soon as someone passed the ball to someone else."

24

Torrey won his varsity letter in his first term and felt good about it. Things were working out according to his plans. He was in school to have a good time, and he was having it. The Sunday nights at Blanchard hall were nights to celebrate, especially when one of the fellows returned home with a box or package of cookies or candy. They didn't do anything excessively bad, but they had their fun. He wasn't a "rounder" in the real sense of the word. He had learned to play cards and was becoming known as somewhat of a card shark. He liked to dance, so he danced. He liked to go to movies, so he went to movies. As an athlete he felt that he shouldn't smoke and he rigidly stayed away from that habit. He felt the same way about drinking and to this day he is thankful that neither of those habits came his way to mar his body and hamper it for future use to the glory of God.

Although surrounded by a godly atmosphere on all sides, under the splendid Christian leadership of President James Oliver Buswell, Jr., with praying parents, a praying sweetheart, reared in a godly home and now enrolled in a truly Christian school—all of these; and yet Torrey persisted in living in sin. There were plenty of topnotch Christian fellows on the campus, and it must be said that Torrey watched them like a hawk, as he not infrequently found himself under conviction. Men like Dr. Paul S. James, now pastor of the Baptist tabernacle of Atlanta, Ga., Stephen Paine, now president of Houghton college in New York, Percy Crawford, widely-known Young People's Church of the Air evangelist, and many others were at Wheaton at that time. Yet Torrey persisted in fighting off the decision to accept Christ as his personal Saviour. He had no logical reasons for doing so, as he now admits; he just didn't want to give up the worldly pleasures in which he was sunning himself.

But God was working.

Christmas vacation came and Torrey took a job sorting mail on a railway mail car operating between Chicago and Des Moines, Iowa. It was a good job and paid him good money, but in the opening and closing of the doors at the various stops he caught a severe cold. He didn't feel like quitting in the middle of the mail rush then as every man was needed so he hung on until Christmas eve. Then he quit and went home to bed. He thought he would be up in a day or so, but those few days lengthened into two full weeks.

Those fourteen days were the longest through which he ever has gone. To be shut in a room and forced to lie still for two weeks was the hardest thing he ever had done. But God was working and Torrey was doing a deal of thinking. But all he did was think; he did no acting on his thoughts and so when he returned to school on Sunday afternoon, January 16, 1927, he was still unsaved.

There was nothing to do that evening. Torrey hadn't been in the habit of going to church on Sunday nights, but inasmuch as the gang wasn't back yet he decided to go to pass the time away. He was lonely and not a little discouraged as he thought back on the siege of illness which had bedded him.

As he recalls it now, the meeting was not particularly interesting. From his seat in the balcony—"second row, second seat from the aisle"—he had a hard time keeping his mind on the singing or preaching. The crowd wasn't too big and Torrey was the only person in the balcony beside the usher, who happened to be Evan Welsh. Torrey doesn't remember anything that Rev. Joseph C. Ludgate, the evangelist, said, but he does know that at the end of the service an invitation was given to any who might wish to accept Christ as personal Saviour.

Welsh knew Torrey well and Torrey knew him well. A spirit of brotherliness always exists between members of an athletic team, and Torrey admired and loved Evan Welsh as an athlete—and as a Christian. Many times that previous season Welsh deftly had slipped in a word for Christ, and it always made Torrey think. What Torrey didn't know was that he was one of several fellows being remembered in prayer by a faithful prayer band which had been formed the fall before. An evangelist who had held meetings on the campus had urged the students to band together to pray for

26

the salvation of their fellow students. Stephen Paine was another member of that prayer band, and before school was out that year *every single person* on that list had made a confession of Christ, and every profession was the real thing.

Welsh felt spirit-impelled to go and talk to Torrey. When he got there he noticed that there were tears in his eyes. Welsh took hold of his arm and said, "Come on, Torrey. Tonight's the night for you to give your heart to Christ."

Torrey pulled back, and, feeling that he was under conviction, Welsh got hold of his arm and gave it a little pull. Torrey pulled it back, and Welsh gave another tug. As Welsh, now pastor of the College Church of Christ in Wheaton, explained it,

"It was the most unorthodox type of personal work—this tug of war act—but I think God was in it and I just kept pulling. I could see that Torrey did not resent it and that he was struggling. I do not remember exactly what words were spoken during this physical encounter, for I only know that he was pulling back as I held his arm. All of a sudden, without a word, he ceased struggling and, arm in arm, we went downstairs to the front of the church."

By the time the football captain and the fellow with whom he had played all season reached the front of the church Mr. Ludgate had closed the service and was giving the closing prayer and benediction. He was standing on a chair down in front and Welsh pulled on his coat tail and said,

"Brother Ludgate, here's a boy who wants to get saved."

Torrey lifted his tear-heavy face toward the speaker of the evening and gave him his hand. At the same moment he threw open the door of his heart and received the Lord Jesus Christ. Then he knelt to pray with Welsh and Evangelist Ludgate.

Something happened! The verse in II Corinthians 5:17 became a reality in his heart: "Therefore if any man be in Christ, he is a new creature; old things are passed away; behold, all things are become new." In a flash Torrey saw that a host of things previous to this moment had worked to make it possible. Praying parents, a praying sweetheart, a devoted

27

pastor, the great concern of a Sunday school teacher, the atmosphere of a genuinely Christian college—all these and many more contributed their bit to bring Torrey to the foot of the cross, "tackled" and led there by his football team's captain.

Only one person accepted Christ that night. Perhaps the heart of the speaker might have been a bit sad as he left the Wheaton college chapel that wintry Sunday in the middle of January. Only one, and yet, as Dr. V. Raymond Edman, present head of the college, said in a Chicago church on the night following a mass meeting sponsored by Chicagoland Youth for Christ, guided by Torrey Johnson and drawing 30,000 people to the Chicago stadium, "That one person that night was Torrey Johnson, and you've seen what has happened since."

Torrey went to his room and slept the sleep of the born again Christian. He was at peace with the world, and he knew it! No more beating around the bush; no more living half in the church and half in the world. No more of the unpleasantness which is present in every person, young or old who has not found Christ as personal Saviour.

But it wasn't going to be easy. He had slept only a few hours when in bounced his roommate. In some way he had learned that Torrey had accepted Christ and he woke him up and met him with these words,

"Got religion, have you? I suppose it's the Billy Sunday type. It'll last about six months. Pal, we'll get that out of you in a hurry."

The old "gang" did try to knock it out of him—using that word in the physical sense, too—but Torrey stuck to his guns every time. The more they rocked him with criticisms and flailings the deeper he became imbedded in the Lord Jesus Christ. He had something now, and he knew it. He wasn't afraid to tell others about it, either, and perhaps the happiest person to hear the news was his girl friend. God had answered her prayers—her sweetheart now was a Christian and although it wasn't quite spring then, love did all right in the middle of the winter on this occasion.

Not long after this Torrey came face to face with another problem. This revolved around his work in life. He was taking pre-medical work at Wheaton and intended to become a doctor. This had been on his mind and heart since a young lad and he had hoped to be able to follow it through, together with his roommate. Keeping his eyes on that goal he finished his second semester at Wheaton, worked on his ice route at Williams Bay that summer and in the fall enrolled at Northwestern university, taking his courses on the McClintock campus in Chicago. He had been able, during the summer, not only to make enough money to get himself started toward his medical degree but in Williams Bay he had been able to grow spiritually under the counsel and help of Mike Peterson, town mayor, leading grocer and lay preacher of the Williams Bay Gospel tabernacle. This church and its pastor had a deepening effect on him that summer and in succeeding summers as he drank in the words of the country's leading evangelists and Bible teachers there and at other places on Lake Geneva, termed "America's Galilee."

As he started his studies at Northwestern he continued to be active in the Salem Norwegian Free church to which his parents belonged. When Harry Vom Bruch held special meetings at the Salem church in 1927 a large group of young men in the church found Christ as personal Saviour. Torrey was active in and among these fellows, and as the glow and the glory of salvation came upon them they felt immediately that they wanted to "evangelize the world" and go out preaching every night.

But in stepped a wise and intelligent Sunday school teacher. He asked the fellows, "What are you going to preach about when you get through giving your testimonies?" They didn't quite know for sure, but they were positive that they would have something. But Oscar Larsen, the teacher, convinced them that what they needed was a more thorough knowledge of the Bible before they went all over holding meetings.

29

Thus came into existence the Christian Crusaders class, and landing on top as president was Torrey Johnson. For three years they met every Thursday night and studied the book of Acts; many of those sessions broke up in the wee hours of the morning. The fellows were eager to learn and in Oscar Larsen they had a man just as eager and anxious to teach. Even at that, he says, "They taught me more than I ever gave them."

It wasn't all study, however. Street meetings were held, services in missions conducted and work among young people's groups undertaken. But when they did go out they had much more of an idea where they were going, why they were going and how they expected to get there. Torrey never has been able to get away from those three years spent in the book of Acts. They grounded him for life and to Oscar Larsen he owes a debt of gratitude for molding his thinking and studying, in those formative days and months.

Then started the "Will you go to Africa" struggle. It was minor at first and didn't affect him and his medical studies at Northwestern. He finished the 1928 school year and was off to Williams Bay again to throw the ice chunks around. The summer was another pleasant one—plenty of hard work, which he enjoyed, a chance to be with his sweetheart, which he also enjoyed, and a chance to get himself straightened out on the Africa problem. On July 16, 1928, when he was 19 and Evelyn was 18, Torrey slipped the engagement ring on her finger. He had been saved for 17 months at that time and even though he was bothered about going to Africa and his testimony didn't have the ring of a truly victorious life, she knew that he was the man for her.

The summer ended, and soon it was Thanksgiving. The fact that his parents were on vacation in Norway at this time didn't help Torrey, although the spiritual struggle through which he was passing was mainly an individual one, in which even his sweetheart had a hard time in advising or helping him.

But Thanksgiving day came, and when it had passed Torrey Johnson was, to all outward appearances, a new man. He began to speak here, there and everywhere as the occasions presented themselves. He knew that he wasn't slated to be a doctor then, and so in December of 1928 he completed his quarter's work at Northwestern, waited a month for a new semester to start at Wheaton, and re-enrolled there.

Things were different now in another way. When Torrey left Wheaton, his roommate had taken up a single room on the same floor. Franklin wasn't a Christian then, but when Torrey came back he found that meantime he had accepted Christ, and they ended up as roommates again. Things were on a new plane now and together they feasted on the Word of God, attended the early morning prayer meetings together and were with each other constantly as they grew up as Christians together. The nightly devotions and discussions were a source of mutual blessings; discussions often led them to other Christians and the "bull sessions" were numerous and long.

They went together when they both tried out for the debating team . . . and they went home together after a few visits. Once they challenged the football coach and the gym caretaker to a tennis match. They walked home from that one with a trouncing defeat on their racquets. From that day until now, although Lt. Franklin Olson, M.D., is serving with the United States navy, they have been as close as any two college roommates ever were.

But graduation time was bound to come, and in the spring of 1930 Torrey Maynard Johnson had his name inscribed on a Bachelor of Science diploma from Wheaton college . . . and out into the world he went.

College years were over. Young Torrey, just 21 years of age, was eager to preach the Gospel anywhere and everywhere. His own desire as regarding college had been fulfilled—he had had a "lot of fun," both in his pre-conversion days but especially after he was saved; then it was that his humor and wit hit its all-time peak. Even during the "Will you go to Africa" battle he was able to keep up his spirits to a certain degree; after that internal struggle was over he was

31

more than ever his usual jovial and fun-loving self. A good student, he had acquired much from Wheaton college, both scholastically and otherwise. He had excelled in athletics and was extremely popular on the campus. Although he had spent a year and a half of his four years on another campus he was one of the best known persons in the senior class.

Now, out to preach the gospel! His parents had known soon after they arrived home from Norway that Torrey was going into the ministry. One day soon after their return, Torrey was out riding with his father. While going along he said, "Dad, I'd like to talk to you about something."

"Okay," his father replied, "go ahead."

"No," answered Torrey, "I'd like to talk to you in your office."

So up to the office they went. Mr. Johnson was a little concerned, but his main thought was that Torrey had been married while they were gone and now wanted to tell his dad about it. When Torrey told him, however, that he had decided to go into the ministry his dad looked him straight in the eye, shook his boy's hand and said,

"I'm for you one thousand per cent. But you know what I thought you were going to tell me? That you had run away and been married while we were gone."

With mother it was a little different. When Torrey told her she said frankly and simply,

"But you can't talk, Torrey. You're like your mother and you just can't talk."

"But mom," Torrey replied, "God has called me, and He can loosen my tongue." The Lord has done that very thing, according to people who heard Torrey talk as a youngster, as a youth and now as a young man.

And so mother and son knelt to pray. She prayed first, in Norwegian, and asked the Lord to make Torrey true to the gospel at all times and make him a simple preacher so that people like herself, without much formal education, might understand and receive the Word.

Torrey never has forgotten that prayer. His aim continually since he has been in the ministry is to make the gospel story so simple that even the most unlearned could and would understand and accept its message.

During collegiate days a church in Chicago had had its eye on Torrey. With sheepskin in one hand, and the tried-and-true Word of God in the other, he accepted the call extended him and started his first pastorate.

CHAPTER FOUR

"J'm Not . . . But J Could Be."

A RE you married, Mr. Johnson?"
"No, I'm not, but . . . I could be."

Those last three words, "I could be," were important in this conversation. They meant, in a way, the difference between the Messiah Baptist church at 2930 Flournoy street in Chicago having Torrey Johnson as pastor or scouting around for someone else to fill· the pulpit.

The Messiah Baptist church contacted Torrey a month before he was scheduled to be graduated from Wheaton college. Harold Ward, one of the leading members, called Torrey one day and asked him if he could preach there the next Sunday, as the candidate who was scheduled to preach couldn't come. Torrey accepted. The people liked him in the morning service and asked him back for the evening service. He was there that night, and after that message was asked to come the next Sunday. After the fourth straight Sunday they issued a formal call to him to become pastor.

Besides the problem of his single bliss there was much other to consider. His only preparation for a pastorate was the fact that he knew he was saved, knew that his life had been surrendered to God, knew the book of Acts thoroughly thanks to Oscar Larsen, knew the person of the Holy Spirit, knew God's plan of salvation, *What the Bible Teaches*, by R. A. Torrey, plus much experience in speaking in missions, street meetings, Sunday school classes and young people's gatherings.

He liked the Messiah church for one other reason—there were no steps there to keep the sinners out! In riding past the church on one occasion he said that he had liked it because there were no steps. That little detail is a hobby which he has, and in the Midwest Bible church which he now serves the entrance is on a level with the street. He feels definitely that very often sinners will not climb a flight of stairs to get into a church whereas they will slide in if they can do so without much effort.

On June 15, 1930, Torrey was baptized in the Messiah church by Rev. Elmer Hutchinson and the same day the church voted unanimously to call him as pastor. On July 29, 1930, he was ordained into the Baptist ministry by a regularly called council of pastors and laymen of the Chicago area, becoming at that time the youngest minister in the city's denominational association. At the ordination examination one of the older pastors wanted to have a little fun with Torrey and so asked him the definition of a bishop.

Torrey replied, "A shepherd of the flock."

"Well," the pastor queried, "then you're a bishop."

"Well, . . . yes." Torrey answered.

"It says here, too," he went on, "that the bishop shall be the husband of one wife. What does that mean?"

"It means that he shouldn't have more than one wife," he replied.

"But don't you think, too, that it means that he should have at least one?" the veteran of Christian service asked.

"Why, yes," answered Torrey, laughing, "and maybe I can do something to 'alter' that situation."

The church took on new life when Torrey took over. Prayer meetings became a living thing again, attended by both young and old. Souls were saved even at the midweek prayer services. It wasn't long after Torrey came that people began to note his peculiar ability to gather young people about him and put them to work. The Messiah church was, and is, hardly the easiest place in the world to preach the gospel and build a church. The area is predominantly Catholic—more than 90 per cent so—and largely foreign born. Within a radius of one mile of the church it has been said that hardly a week goes by when there is not a murder committed. It was not unusual on a Sunday night to come out of church and find your car possessed of only enough gas to take you to the corner. One fine Christian lady whose husband was unsaved and opposed to her church-going came out one Sunday evening after an especially blessed meeting to find the rear end of her car sitting on a box and the two rear wheels missing. A watchman soon was posted outside to watch the cars, but during the week the boys in the neighborhood had their fun . . . and plunder!

Soon after Torrey arrived he gathered to him two young men who were full of the gospel and eager to let it bubble over. One of his first needs was a choir director. One day he mentioned that need to Dr. Harry McCormick Lintz, nationally known evangelist, who replied, "Say, I think I can help you. Go over to that garage over there and you'll find a young fellow under a car. He should be the fellow you need."

Torrey went. When he got there he saw a pair of feet pointing heaven-ward as the owner thereof stretched out unseen under the car. Torrey kicked the soles and said, "Say there, can you lead a choir?"

The "voice" from under the car chirped, "I guess so."

"Well come on," Torrey replied, "I've got a job for you."

The man scrambled out from under the car, stood up and Bob Cook, later to become Torrey's associate pastor at the Midwest Bible church and co-worker in Youth for Christ, shook hands with Torrey M. Johnson.

That settled one problem, but what about the song leader?

This also solved itself in short order and here is how it came about.

Ray Schulenburg, an easy-going and pleasant-voiced young fellow with a lot of pep, ability and vision, was working at the Chicago Board of Trade during the week and serving as Sunday school superintendent in a church which had a trend toward modernism. Schulenburg stayed for three years in the hope that he could do a bit to swing it the other

36

way. It became too discouraging, however, and so he felt led to pray to God that if He didn't want him there that another door would open up somewhere. He had faith to believe that someone would open the door, but he didn't know it would be Torrey M. Johnson, a fellow he had known since grade school days but with whom he hadn't been in direct contact for some time.

One Sunday night Schulenburg was waiting for a bus on a forlorn corner in the city of Chicago. It was 1:30 a.m. and the bus was late. In the distance he saw an automobile approaching, but he didn't take notice of it as is didn't look like the bus whose face he was anxious to see. When the car neared the corner it prepared to stop for the stop sign on the corner. Suddenly it emitted a loud noise and ground to a complete stop. The door popped open and the driver jumped out to see what had hit him. The driver was Torrey Johnson. He started to look at the back of the car and then spied Schulenburg—now more than casually interested—standing on the corner. He recognized him, stopped looking at the car and walked over to Schulenburg and said, "Hello, Ray, what are you doing here," and before waiting for an answer kept on, "By the way, what are you doing these Sunday nights?"

Schulenburg told him that he was working in a certain church but that he felt his work was finished there. Torrey grabbed his arm and cried, "You're just the fellow I'm looking for to lead singing at the church I'm now serving. Will you come?"

"Well, I guess I will . . ." Schulenburg replied.

Then, with that settled, they decided to look at the car! The axle had broken completely off! Torrey has felt ever since that night that the Lord had His hand in that accident; how else could it gauge its breaking point in front of a far off corner in the city of Chicago under whose arc light was standing a man whom Torrey needed in his church, and who himself felt that he needed a change?

So the three of them went to work—Johnson, Cook and Schulenburg. None of them thought that years later they still would be together, only under a different organization. In 1945 it was Youth for Christ, with Torrey and Bob active in the Chicagoland Youth for Christ group and Ray leading the Mississippi valley Youth for Christ meetings at Moline, Ill.

God blessed that trio in a remarkable way in the Messiah church. Souls were constantly at the altar seeking salvation, and it seemed as though they often had to ask God to withhold the blessings as they were being filled too much. Many a night found Torrey either in the church or in some home, sitting with open Bible until the wee hours of the morning, if need be, in opening the way of salvation. The neighborhood was hard, but God was working. Cook had a couple of cars stolen, but souls were being saved. People talked about the church on the corner, became curious, came over, went inside ... and were saved! Many of them were mocked at by their Catholic neighbors but most of them stood true.

Street meetings were held regularly and were interesting if nothing else. As one of the members wrote,

"We surely had things 'coming our way' then. The fruit was plenty ... and fresh, too, especially the tomatoes. But we were dressed for it. What sights we were when the tomatoes and eggs had done their jobs. No wonder we got the crowds!"

But the meetings were more than interesting. Flying wedges often threatened to break the meeting up, but the fellows and girls held their ground. Souls were saved in those meetings and many were attracted to the church because of the services on the corners. Perhaps the brightest jewel salvaged from the street gatherings was Fred Jarvis, a brilliant young fellow who was converted after one meeting, and who now has achieved his doctor's degree and is an outstanding figure in Christian education while preparing to go out as a missionary to China. When the Lord came into his heart, He went deep and the fruit has been coming ever since.

In the fall of 1930 Torrey thought it about time he fulfilled his pledge to the church to do something about his bachelor state. Evelyn was willing, and so on October 30, 1930, they were married. Torrey was making $20 a week at this time, and after the wedding the bride continued to teach in the public schools as they sought to make both ends meet. It soon became apparent that Bob Cook would be a frequent visitor at the Torrey Johnson home. The new Mrs. Johnson had a younger sister, Coreen, and after a few looks Bob became more interested in her than in Torrey. She later became Mrs. Robert Cook. As Torrey explained it, "I got there first and took Evelyn. Then Bob came along and picked Coreen."

Torrey will have a hard time forgetting the first wedding ceremony he performed. One Saturday night, just as the group was about to go out and hold a street meeting a young fellow walked into the church and asked to see the pastor. When told he was talking to the pastor he looked surprised and said he expected to see someone much older. Anyway, he asked Torrey if he would perform the ceremony and Torrey said, "Yes, bring in the bride and witnesses."

While the groom went to get them, Torrey slipped into another room to study his minister's manual. He knew nothing of the form. The main thing, he thought, was the part that followed—the kiss. ("I was to learn better in later years.") When the couple came in Torrey had them kneel for almost the entire ceremony and while they were on their knees he preached a straight, hard-hitting gospel sermon to them. For almost 20 minutes they stayed on their knees as Torrey preached his heart out and, incidentally, married them.

His first funeral message also was unusual, perhaps because it never was delivered. A Mrs. O'Leary of his congregation lay dying in the county hospital. Torrey was notified and plans were tentatively made for the funeral. He called a neighboring pastor to check on the details of a funeral and then went to work on his message. But ... the patient recovered and the message never was delivered. When she died years later Torrey was not serving the church.

Experiences those early months were thrilling as well as unusual. The fact that the neighborhood was hostile to the gospel made the work all the more challenging. One Sunday afternoon a baptismal service was scheduled. One of the ladies to be baptized had to devise a way to get out of the house without her husband, an unbeliever, knowing where she was going. So she hid her clothes behind the house in an alley. Then when she went to church she walked into the alley, picked them up, went to church, was baptized, came on home, replaced the clothes and took them up the next day. Had her husband known that she was going to be baptized that afternoon she never would have reached the church, she later revealed.

One evening Torrey and Schulenburg asked the Lord to give them some especially challenging experience as they prepared to go out and make pastoral calls. They felt a need to be allowed to witness in some special way this night. They knocked on the door of a west side home in Chicago and were met by a man who hesitated to allow them in. Finally he did open the door, and as Torrey and Ray walked into the room a number of men slid toward the rear door. In a few minutes the "visiting brethren" found out that they were paying a pastoral call on hardened jail birds. Each one had a court record, with safe cracking their "specialties." They flashed rolls of bills which made the young visitors gulp. Before they left, however, Torrey and his song leader left those hardened men with a ringing and true gospel message and a personal request to each of them to accept Christ as personal Saviour.

During these months Torrey accepted each and every speaking engagement offered him. He loved to preach and he preached his head and heart out every time he had a chance. Finally the deacons at Messiah called him in and asked him what he was going to be—an evangelist or a pastor. To be frank about it, and Torrey admits it now, he hardly knew the difference between the two. When he got things straightened out, however, a decision had to be made and he was in a quandary.

It was solved for him, however, by circumstances. Schulenburg at this time had quit his promising job in the Chicago Board of Trade to go on tour as song leader for an evangelist. At the last moment, however, the evangelist decided to cancel his entire schedule. Schulenburg was left high and dry, and that proved to be Torrey's answer to prayer. He decided to go with Schulenburg and on July 20, 1931—after serving exactly one year as pastor—he resigned. He left in a spirit of deep Christian love. The church could agree heartily with his desire to go into evangelistic work; in his one year at Messiah his calls for meetings had increased so rapidly that it was a question of being one or the other. When he left he left behind a work that was lasting and its effects still are being felt in the church through the lives of the members who were saved when he was there and others who are working to carry on the work. As Torrey left the congregation called Bob Cook to serve as interim pastor and he filled the bill nobly until a permanent pastor was called.

The next two years were eventful ones for Torrey and Schulenburg. Some of their experiences read almost like fiction, but God was with these two consecrated youths and used them mightily. They held hundreds of meetings together, in campaigns ranging from one to four weeks. They were privileged to pray with hundreds of souls in their services, and God seemed to bless their every effort from the very beginning. They had the fire of youth, two winning personalities and an unbounding zeal and passion to see souls won to the Lord Jesus Christ. As a team they fitted like a new suit; they were serious and in dead earnest about this business of winning souls to Christ but on the other side they both enjoyed having a good time; were sold on the idea of being happy and cheerful Christians. So things clicked.

Their first campaign was the hardest . . . and yet one of the most blessed of God. They had been called to a town to hold union meetings sponsored by seven co-operating churches. When they arrived they found after a meeting or two that the "co-operation" was all on the surface, the churches were having a very hard time getting along with each other. It showed on the meetings only too readily. The two evangelists prayed night after night until two and three o'clock in the morning that God would straighten His people out so that He could do His work in that vicinity.

Finally the gates were loosed and the blessings came. Sores were healed, hearts were warmed ... and over 150 people accepted Christ publicly during the campaign. That series of meetings was all that Torrey needed to let him know that he had made the right decision in resigning his church and going out as an evangelist.

Souls were won to the Lord in every campaign they held together. Some of the towns and cities visited were Marinette, Wis.; Minominee, Iron River, Iron Mountain and Watersmeet in Michigan; Grinnell and Victor, Iowa; Duluth, Minnesota; and Chicago, to name a few. At Iron Mountain they were having breakfast one morning with the pastor of the Swedish Baptist church when suddenly someone came running up to the back door and shouted, "The church is on fire! The church is on fire!"

From the table Torrey cried back, "Praise the Lord! That's what we've been praying for!"

But this was wood fire, not Holy Ghost fire, and after a few more words from the fire-spotter they hastily moved outside to see sparks pouring from the chimney of the Mission Covenant church in which the meetings were being held. Someone hurriedly scrambled up and the blaze was extinguished before too much damage was done.

Following a very successful campaign in Iron River, Michigan, they were called to Duluth, Minn. The Iron River people heard about this and asked them if they wouldn't stop over in Iron River for one meeting on the way to Duluth. They agreed and as they were on their way that day they realized that they might be late for the service because of a delay in leaving Chicago. The meeting was scheduled at 7:30, and at 7:15 there still was no sign of Johnson and Schulenburg.

A minute or two before the start of the service they rolled in. The meeting was held in the town hall, and a good publicity job had filled it to the rafters. There was no time to change clothes, so onto the platform they went in the sport clothes in which they had been riding all day—old knickers and polo shirts with short sleeves. No one seemed to mind,

42

however, and a great meeting was held and a number of souls sought the Lord for salvation.

On another occasion the young people in the church in which the meetings were being held wanted to take them along on a swimming party in Lake Michigan. Torrey and Schulenburg weren't quite in a mood to go swimming that day—which is something for Torrey, who, it is safe to say, is one of the best swimmers among pastors in the entire world—but they agreed to go along and paddled in a boat as the others swam. While they were in the boat, Torrey got the brilliant idea, according to Schulenburg, to tip his song leader into the lake. He broached the idea to the swimmers and they agreed in a hurry. As Torrey started to rock the boat the young people headed for Schulenburg's end. In a moment or two he was in the water—clothes and all.

But he was to have his revenge. He cornered a pail on the beach, dashed back out and sprayed Torrey with water as the others stood by and howled. Finally Torrey was so wet that he might just as well have been in the water—so he stood in the middle of the boat and dove in head first.

They didn't wear those clothes that night.

Those two years were fruitful ones, for God was using them to bring blessings to others. Every place in which they served they kept their eyes and ears open, acquiring education in how to be successful pastors by watching the men in whose churches they were serving. Their own hearts constantly were being filled and re-filled with spiritual blessing which flowed over onto their listeners, but even as God used them mightily on those trips He also was allowing them to pick up valuable information as they went from church to church. They were young, they had ideas, they thought they knew what they wanted to do and how they wanted to hold their meetings, but on the other hand they were ever eager and willing to listen . . . and learn.

Perhaps the best example of that involves an 85-year old florist in Grinnell, Iowa. This old man, truly a saint of God, had but one arm; the other was just a stub protruding from his shoulder. He had a long, white beard and for his age was extremely alert and keen of mind and heart. He had been to two of their meetings and one afternoon Torrey and Schulenburg stopped in to see him. There in his greenhouse that day the two young servants of God heard a message from a heart full of Christian love and experience which they never will forget. He looked them straight in the eye, put his one good arm on their shoulders as they stood side by side, and said, "Boys, book knowledge is important, and training is essential, but *never* lose sight of the fact that it is the Spirit that does God's work through human vessels. And oh, boys, seek the Spirit's infilling in your lives if you would be used of God. Don't *ever* try to do God's work in the energy of the flesh, but rely wholly on Him."

Somehow those words struck home. When the old man had finished his eyes were moist and he pounded home every word with what it seemed was a year of constant communion with God. They walked from that florist shop with the feeling that they had talked to one of God's choicest flowers and the fragrance of those few minutes together has been with them to this day.

As they traveled extensively, hard and often, they were learning another lesson. It started to come to them not long after they had been out; as they moved from place to place it grew in depth. Both were well-versed in the Scripture from their years of being Christians and through definite, well-developed systems of Bible study, but soon the thoughts were being expressed that they needed more schooling. Torrey often said when this point came up that he would like to acquire an education which would enable him to stand up against anyone in the country, from the scholastic point of view, and meet their arguments against the Bible and salvation through the blood of Jesus Christ. Schulenburg felt the same way; his main duty in their travels was song leading and singing solos and he felt the need to go deeper into God's Word so that he, too, might some day be a successful minister of the gospel (He now is one, at the Evangelical Free church in Moline, Ill.)

But there were problems. Torrey had a wife, no church in Chicago to serve (he wanted to attend Northern Baptist seminary there), and he didn't feel as though he should take up secular work while going to school, unless he had to, and they had to have some financial help in going to school. Finally one day he and his wife made a covenant—if no calls for meetings came for one entire week they would settle in Chicago and go to school, depending on the Lord to work out the details.

Not a single call came that entire week—an unusual thing inasmuch as the calls for meetings had flowed in regularly for two years! That was all they needed, and so plans were made to start school in the fall of 1933.

The Lord then undertook to work out further details. Shortly after he had started attending classes at Northern Baptist he received a call to serve the Midwest Bible church, a small group meeting in a remodeled store building on the northwest side of Chicago. During the previous summer he had made the contact with the Midwest people; he had spoken in and near Chicago in tent meetings sponsored by the newly-formed Christian Business Men's committee headed by C. B. Hedstrom; to that organization and to Mr. Hedstrom, one of its original founders, Torrey owes much, and not the least of which is the initial contact with the Midwest Bible church members.

Northern Baptist seminary was to do much to mold Torrey Johnson. He was to remain there seven years—three as student and four as teacher and student combined. From its professors and from his fellow students he was to acquire the Bible training which has stamped him as one of the top men ever to be graduated from the seminary. Northern Baptist was founded in 1913, with initial classes in the Second Baptist church of Chicago. In 1920 it moved to its present grounds at 3026-3060 West Washington, and since then has grown to be one of the top fundamental seminaries in the United States, and known throughout the world by the achievements of its graduates.

Soon after Torrey had enrolled at Northern he was making himself felt. He was elected president of the freshman class of

45

80 students, was one of 36 students in the entire student body who was serving a church while going to school, was rated first as "The man most likely to succeed" and rated second as the "Most handsome man in college."

As a junior he again was elected class president. One of the snapshots in the 1935 *The Northern*, school yearbook, shows Torrey, wife and first child, born in December of the 1934-35 school year. In the "best" voting that year Torrey rated first as having the "best drag with the faculty" and pulling into second place as the "best dresser in school."

As a senior he established a record at Northern when he again was elected president, becoming the only student in Northern's history to be elected to presidency of his class for three straight years. He was a speaker at commencement, associate editor of *The Northern*, and during his last semester as an undergraduate, taught church history to the first and second year students. The senior class motto as Torrey graduated was this: "That in all things He might have preeminence."

Below Torrey's picture in the senior section of the yearbook were these words: "No really great man ever thought himself so."

Torrey's scholastic record was one of the best in school. In the 38 courses in which he was given grades he had an average of 94.1 per cent. Of those 38, only two were under 90—one an 85 and one an 84, both in the same term. Moreover, as he was attending school those three years he was doing the foundation work at the Midwest Bible church together with other activities in Christian circles and channels. His soul-winning zeal never flagged for a moment during those classroom days. One of the most gripping incidents of his years at Northern came when he was called to preach the funeral message of one of his fellow students, Charles E. Baird. Charles was killed by an automobile one Sunday night on the way home from preaching in a Chicago church. When his body was shipped home to Bowling Green, Ohio, and funeral arrangements were being made, Torrey was asked to go along and conduct the funeral.

46

God used the funeral to the salvation of souls. Torrey preached from an outline of a message prepared by the deceased student. At the end of the service over 20 people gripped the hands of pastors on the way out and in that way indicated that they that afternoon had accepted Christ as personal Saviour.

Some of his schoolmates were as brilliant as he. Included in his class roll were such men as Dr. T. Leonard Lewis, now president of Gordon School of Theology and Missions in Boston, Mass.; Dr. Carl Henry, professor at Northern Baptist and nationally known author; Dr. George M. Johnson, professor of theology at Central Baptist Theological seminary in Kansas City, Missouri, and many others. Included among his professors was one of America's outstanding Greek scholars— Dr. Julius R. Mantey—and from him Torrey absorbed much as he "ate up" everything he could get along that line. Included in his seminary honors was election to Pi Gamma Mu, national social science honor society, and membership in the honor society at Northern.

Torrey's primary object in going to Northern was to acquire a more thorough knowledge of the Bible, especially the New Testament. So fully was that goal reached in the eyes of his professors and administrative officials of the school that in the spring of 1936, upon his graduation, he was offered a teaching position, not in world history which he had been teaching, but in Greek. He accepted the offer after much prayer and when the 1936-37 school year came by he was teaching "baby Greek" to the first and second year students and "getting more out of it than they were." This arrangement, too, enabled him to continue with his work toward his doctor's degree. He has finished all of his classwork toward that doctor's degree, and has only the thesis to write before it will be his.

As he "taught and was taught" those years he took some 22 more courses. In checking his classroom average during his entire seven years at Northern we find that in 60 subjects his average stands at 93 and 59/60, or practically 94. This also rates as one of the highest averages at Northern.

47

For four years Torrey taught Greek, studied for his doctor's degree and served as pastor of the Midwest Bible church. Any one of those three might have been enough in itself, but Torrey was able to handle all three in an effective and efficient manner. In the spring of 1940, however, a decision had to be made and once more he looked to God to guidance in making the right choice.

The Midwest Bible church was growing and growing, and the congregation had felt for some time that it would like to have its pastor working full time for them. At the same time he was proving to be one of the most popular professors at Northern and "baby Greek" was becoming less of "Greek" to the students as they started to say, "It's all Greek to me now." Years before, when he had started his evangelistic work, one member in his audience had described him as "talking unintelligibly fast and blinking his eyes as he talked." Now he had slowed down, and possessed a fine classroom style and an equally effective platform composure and speech. In either of the two spots in which he was serving the Lord—the classroom or the pulpit—he was successfully at home, but he realized, as did his church and the seminary, that a choice had to be made. Which would it be . . . a pastor or a teacher?

The church won.

The evangelistic fervor triumphed over the desire to mold the lives of future ministers and leaders. In the spring of 1940 he severed his teaching connection with Northern Baptist seminary, finished his work as president of the Wheaton College Alumni association, which he had served for four years, and went to work on the Christian project closest to his heart—the Midwest Bible church, "fastest growing church in Chicago" and in itself one of the miracles of the middlewest.

That moves us into another phase of Torrey Johnson's life—his relationship to the Midwest Bible church and the story behind its growth. That story cannot he covered adequately in one chapter; God's working through that faithful group seems worthy almost of a book in itself.

48

CHAPTER FIVE

"God Answers Prayer, Mister . . ."

A REAL estate man was talking to Torrey M. Johnson early in 1945. "You know," he said, "something amazes me about you and your church."

"And what's that?" asked Torrey.

"Well, you see all of this property in this block? Over a period of years I've wanted *every single piece* of it at some time or other. But I haven't been able to acquire even one foot of it, and here you come along and get all of it. I just can't figure it out," he replied.

"Want me to tell you," Torrey queried, "how we happen to have it and you don't?"

"I sure would," he answered.

"It's simple," said Torrey, "God answers prayer, mister."

"I think He must," was the unsaved man's reply as he walked away.

That little conversation seems adequate to use as a key to open the door to the Midwest Bible church of Chicago, Illinois, one of the most unusual works of God in the land in this day of sinking churches and decreasing memberships and attendances. Until a year or two ago the growth of the Midwest Bible church had not attracted much more than local attention. Non-residents of Chicago perhaps had heard of it occasionally, but now its fame and the story of its God-guided progress has become widely known as its pastor has "spread his wings" and people have come to see what the home nest is like.

There is something vital, challenging and inspiring about the Midwest Bible church. It's not so much the building; there are and will be finer buildings than that which houses it. It's not so much the members, although you'll have a hard time finding better ones than exist at Midwest. It's not so much the leaders of the various departments—Chester J. Scholl, Joe Gunderson, Mrs. Percy Moore, Doug Fisher, Merwin Webster, Dimmock Steeves and a host more—although you will have to admit that they are using their God-given talents completely to His glory. And it's not so much the pastor, Torrey M. Johnson, nor his associate, Robert Cook, nor his assistant, John De Saegher, although all three of them are as consecrated servants of God as you can find anywhere.

Buildings, members, leaders, pastors—then where lies the key?

Perhaps the words of Pastor Torrey Johnson explain it best. He said on one occasion when being interviewed for a national magazine, "We believe in mixing large measures of both faith and hard work and then in a spirit of cooperation asking God's blessing on our efforts. What has been accomplished here can be accomplished anywhere if people meet the divine conditions."

When you find yourself at 3469 North Cicero avenue in Chicago you find no massive building which astonishes you and draws from you deep sighs of admiration. The church is built in the tabernacle style, with no balcony other than a sound proof, glassed-in mother's room in which both mother and child can listen to the services, and make as much noise as they want without disturbing anyone in the meeting. Construction of the church was started in the fall of 1939 and it was dedicated on May 5, 1940; it cost $40,000 to erect.

The inside is modern and attractive. Curtains along the 4 sides of the main auditorium allow for Sunday school rooms to be set up. The only permanent seats in the church are the two sections down the middle, and the choir seats. When movable chairs on the sides are put in place the auditorium will seat 900 persons.

Slip from the main auditorium through a side door and you find yourself in a combination kitchen and Sunday school classroom. Through another swinging door and you're in Maranatha hall, used by the young people for one of their meetings as well as for smaller meetings when the church auditorium is not needed. Through another swinging door you find yourself in the third Sunday school classroom and young people's room. On Sunday evenings at 6:15 three young people's groups thus are able to meet simultaneously, each in a modern, up-to-date room of its own.

Outside you see what now is a parking lot, part of which is a filling station which is being razed. Alongside that is a garage recently purchased, which is being remodeled to seat 1,200 people.

To the rear of the front lots is a converted garage (most everything and everybody is converted at Midwest) which now serves as the radio studio for the Chapel Hour heard each Sunday from 5 to 6 p.m. over station WAIT in Chicago. Directly behind the church is a neat, well kept-up yard and across the alley is the home of the sexton.

On the west side of Cicero avenue—across the street from the above mentioned properties—are three store buildings which are rented for Sunday school classrooms. When the new church is ready it is believed that the rental of these will not be necessary.

It took vision, faith, prayer and plenty of work to develop that church layout in the short span of 12 years. In the early spring of 1933 there was no Midwest Bible church in existence; six years later the group still was meeting in a remodeled store a few steps away. But all along the way they kept plugging and praying even in the midst of discouragements which would have stopped many others. Today God has answered their prayers and rewarded their faith and His Spirit is continuing to work among them as in few churches in the land. That is why on even a hot summer night you might

51

step into the Midwest church a minute or two after the 7:30 starting time and hear these words from a well-groomed usher, "There's not another seat in the house. Over 900 are in now and we're packed to the doors."

Midwest Bible church actually began in the hearts of a few men and women in the spring of 1933. A series of weekly prayer meetings was held by this group; the men especially had a deep love for God and a burden for the salvation of souls. The meetings went on for some time and on May 7, 1933, the first public service was held in the home of Mr. and Mrs. Peter Kjelstad. There were 41 present. The following Wednesday a prayer meeting was held in the home of Mr. and Mrs. Chester Scholl. On Sunday, May 14, a morning service was held at the home of Mr. and Mrs. Otto Schlonga and the young people's and evening services in the home of Mr. and Mrs. Arthur Lukey. Rev. Norman Camp preached morning and evening at these services.

Within a month a meeting place was needed and the hall of the Columbia Business college at Cicero and Irving Park avenue was rented. This served excellently as a temporary place of worship. During the summer the members scoured the neighborhood in search for a more desirable building. They finally found it—at 3509-11 North Cicero avenue. When the details were arranged, Peter Hansen and a group of men working under him went to work on the re-modeling task and on September 10, 1933, the first service was held in it. No chairs of their own were available so the group rented 160 of them from the Columbia Business college, where they had been meeting.

Two weeks later the "church" was dedicated. Dr. Wm. McCarrell of the Cicero Bible church delivered the dedicatory address in the afternoon and in the evening Rev. William F. Rawlins, who had served the church at various times during the summer, came to start two weeks of evangelistic meetings. Other men who had come along in those early days to preach the Word and lend encouragement included Rev. A. H. Lehman, Rev. Isaac Page, Rev. Arthur J. Bowen, Rev. Vincent

Upper left: At the Stadium rally, with Gil Dodds, world champion indoor miler. *Upper right:* Invitation time at Youth for Christ. *Center:* The new building that houses Midwest Bible Church. *Lower left:* Doug Fisher directs the girls' chorus. *Lower right:* Talmage Bittikofer leads the massed choir at the stadium.

Upper left: Master of ceremonies at the Stadium. *Upper right:* "Make a note of this," says Torrey to his secretary, Amy Anderson, at the Soldier Field rehearsal. *Center spread:* The crowd of 30,000 who attended the stadium rally. *Lower left:* With Dr. V. R. Edman, president of Wheaton College. *Lower right:* Doctor of Divinity, Wheaton, 1945.

Upper left: Opening moment of the Soldier Field Memorial Day rally, 1945. *Upper right:* Torrey and Gil Dodds talk it over. *Below:* At Soldier Field, Torrey makes a prophecy: "This gathering of 70,000 is not the climax, but the beginning of a great crusade for the salvation of this generation of American youth."

Still young, still confident, Torrey has plans for many
a revolutionary project in the interest of reaching young
people for the Lord Jesus Christ.

Brushwyler, John Duff and others. To these men of God and especially to Rev. Charles P. Meeker, another saint of God, the Midwest Bible church owes much for help and guidance in those early years of life.

One evening in August of 1933 Vincent Brushwyler came up to a youthful evangelist after a tent meeting at 5416 West Chicago avenue, and said, "Torrey, I understand you're interested in going to school."

"Why, yes, that's right," Torrey replied. He knew Vincent Brushwyler well from Wheaton college days together.

"Well," Brushwyler went on, "my father-in-law, Peter Kjelstad, is meeting with a group of people on north Cicero avenue and they're looking for a pastor. Think you might be interested?"

"It sounds good to me," Torrey said, and on September 3, 1933, he visited the church at the request of its members. He preached for them and they liked the young, wavy-haired Norwegian who talked pretty fast but who seemed to have the spark their church needed.

A call to become pastor for one year was extended. The salary was $20 a week, which, incidentally, was more than twice what they previously had been paying.

The next days were prayer-filled and prayerful ones in the Torrey Johnson home. Torrey liked the people in the church, and they liked him. Still, he felt that God wanted him to go to seminary and he realized that that took more than peanuts to pay the expenses.

But God prevailed, and looking to Him to take care of any and all expenses above that which they were planning on, the Johnsons accepted the call. Torrey had a little money saved, and his wife intended to keep on with her teaching in order to help make both ends meet.

Thus it was that Rev. Torrey M. Johnson stepped into the pulpit of the "converted" store at 3509-11 North Cicero on October 1, 1933, read his text from Acts 2 and preached to his new members a message titled, "The Ideal Church." Following that message he, together with his members, set about

53

trying to build the church which he had outlined in his sermon of the morning. And, from outward appearances, they have succeeded admirably in putting into practical usage the message sent from God on that first Sunday.

As with most of the things in which Torrey has become interested, things perked up right away. It wasn't long before the store building was too small for the group. By 1934 there were 82 enrolled members—exactly twice as many as in the previous year and showing an increase of 100 per cent. Sunday school children literally were falling all over each other soon after the church was formally organized. Under Torrey's leadership the group then purchased a double portable schoolhouse from the city of Chicago for $50. This was placed on the rear of the property and used conveniently as a Sunday school annex in the mornings, and as a young people's meeting place in the afternoons and following the evening services.

That solved the space situation temporarily, although most services continued to find the members sitting in all parts of the church, and extra seats being brought in often to accommodate the crowds. God seemed to bless the work in every way. The prayer meeting continued to be the most important service of the week and people crowded to it. Even as they prayed, they worked, too.

On the first Sunday of 1936, tragedy seemed to hit the church!

During the evening service, Torrey's wife was standing in the rear of the church with their first child when looking past her husband's head she saw flames leaping from the annex. She interrupted Torrey's message and told him what was happening. Torrey did the sensible thing. He wanted to keep on preaching, as he usually does, and in order to keep the people from being upset he dispatched the deacons to take care of the fire. Then he went on with the service. After he finished his message he gave an invitation and once again souls came to seek the Lord as their Saviour. It was another glorious service. After it was all over and the last soul had been dealt with, they slipped out of the back door to see what had become of their annex.

It had burned to the ground. There just wasn't anything left of it. They searched everywhere to find where it had started and what had started it, but to no avail. Members of the church have felt somewhat that it was started by someone in the neighborhood who didn't like the church for its preaching the old-fashioned gospel and for its forthright stand against sin. Fire had started all along one side of the annex, much as though gasoline or kerosene had been poured on it. Be that as it may, all that was left was ashes.

It had been insured, however, and the $800 insurance money was placed into a building fund and furnished the inspiration for a drive to build up a larger fund for a new church building. It was probably right there that the germ of the idea to expand and expand as much as possible was started; ever since then the church constantly has been on the lookout for new outlets and new ways to develop its work both in and around the Midwest property and throughout the world by way of missions.

With the inspiration for the building fund created and the money starting to come in the problem of "where to build" was faced. After full consideration it was deemed inadvisable to enlarge the quarters in which they were at that time. The frontage on Cicero was small. It was in the middle of the block. All agreed that the corner lot on Cornelia and Cicero was the ideal spot, but there were hindrances popping up every time they made a move to acquire it. It was hopelessly tangled up in litigation and red tape and presented a tangled mess which seemingly could not be straightened out.

But Torrey and many others of the church had the faith to believe that if God wanted them to have that lot that they would have it. In the spring of 1937, after all else had failed, Torrey stood on the lot one afternoon, leaned against a tree during a conversation with Carl Dahlin of Duluth, Minn., and lifted his voice to God in a two-man prayer meeting. He asked

Him simply to somehow give them the lot if it was in His will.

God answered!

On Thanksgiving day, 1939, the ground was broken on the lot, which measured 75 by 180 feet. In God's own way, the tangled red tape on the property had been cut and Midwest Bible church was able to pay for it in cash. When it came to financing the new building and $40,000 was needed, the members chipped in to buy enough bonds over a ten-year period so that they did not have to go outside of the church to finance the building program. On May 5, 1940, the new church building officially was dedicated to the glory of the Lord and to the preaching of the gospel.

That acquisition served merely to whet the appetites of the Midwest members. The desire to expand even more and set up a physical plant which would be adequate to handle the many people and the heavy program burned within the hearts of many. Persons from all over flocked to this gospel lighthouse because they knew they would find a church where the gospel was preached in its entirety.

Thus it was in 1942 that four stores to the south of the church were purchased and remodeled into three fine young people's rooms and Sunday school meeting places. As the Sunday school grew, more space was needed and they crossed the street to the west side of Cicero Avenue and rented three stores there. The Lord continued to bless, and the next step found the garage in the rear of the property being converted into the radio chapel. For years the elders had tried to purchase the home just east of the church for its sexton; finally that, too, opened up and it was purchased.

Parking space wasn't needed so much during gas rationing days, but it was convenient to those people who could drive. To that end a parking lot was developed behind the three young people's rooms and on over toward the opposite end of the block. Next to the parking lot stood a filling station which filled cars, not souls, as its next door neighbor. When the owner of the station signed the papers yielding the lot to the Midwest Bible church he said, "I don't know just why I'm selling this to you people. I've been offered $500 more by another party, and he still wants it right now. But, well, I like you people over there, and I know you'll use it to a good end."

Those words came from a non-Christian but from one who had been able to see that the gospel preached at Midwest was worthy even of his co-operation and help.

Last but not least of the physical properties is the recently purchased garage which soon will be remade into an auditorium which will seat 1,200 people. It isn't exactly what the members at Midwest had in mind for their new church, but due to war conditions the members realized that they could not expect to build very soon. In the visionary mind of Torrey Johnson, however, the new acquisition easily can be switched into an effective unit in the Christian high school he has in mind some day to establish, D.V.

Tables of figures in books are welcomed by most readers as portions which easily can be skipped, but in the hope that some of you will read the table below we print it. It gives you a year by year picture of the way in which the church has grown.

	SUMMARY OF GROWTH			AVERAGE ATTENDANCE			
Year.	Members.	Baptism.	Income.	S.S.	Sun. a.m.	Sun. p.m.	Wed.
1934	82	13	$2,221.23				
1935	91	9	3,213.99				
1936	93	5	3,777.96	146	93	105	32
1937	103	7	4,980.75	149	97	102	47
1938	133	21	5,706.65	157	126	138	59
1939	150	7	8,008.87	161	131	151	70
1940	170		9,281.37	163	139	148	72
1941	191		21,748.38	238	207	292	119
1942*	263		23,506.00	324	306	395	131
1943**	306		40,393.82	397	384	536	163
1944	349		51,448.47	504	462	668	171
1945	378		115,042.23	...	...	...	...

* 1942 radio funds—$11,900.00
** 1943 radio funds—$13,950.00

It is thrilling to wade back into the figures at Midwest and see how God has blessed the church. In 1933 there were 41 members—in 1943 there were 308 and today that number

57

has jumped to 378. At the end of the 1934 fiscal year (April to April) the church had handled $2,221.23. During the tenth year it handled $40,393.82 exclusive of some $13,950.00 which went into radio work, and was not on the church budget. In 1945 it had skyrocketed to $115,042.23.

That table looks good and those figures thrill you as you note how God has progressed the work. You see those indications of growth and visualize with your eyes the buildings and the physical setup and you might tend to feel that perhaps all they are interested in is a "building program."

But that is far, far from the case.

In October of 1943 the church celebrated its tenth anniversary with a fine banquet in the parlors of the First Baptist church of North Austin. Included in the fine anniversary booklet were greetings from Rev. Vincent Brushwyler, Dr. V. Raymond Edman, Dr. Will H. Houghton, H. A. Ironside, Dr. Charles Koller, Dr. T. Leonard Lewis, Frank Sheriff, Rev. A. W. Tozer and a host of others, but the most challenging words in the booklet were these written by Torrey M. Johnson and giving you a true picture of the goals at Midwest:

"Let us in the days to come not minimize the importance of material facilities and advantages, but let us remember that they are only the scaffolding to be used in winning and building of immortal souls in the kingdom of our Lord and Saviour Jesus Christ. Let us always put first things first, and eternal things are the first things."

To emphasize that love for putting "first things first," that annual banquet ended up in an old-fashioned prayer meeting when everyone at the banquet knelt to ask God's continued guidance on the work at Midwest.

In its organization, the Midwest Bible church is much like any other church. The church is the main body and the other groups all stem out from it as they seek to meet some special need.

The Sunday school always has been one of the outstanding features and marks in the growth at Midwest. Cheerful and happy Chester J. Scholl, one of the original charter members, has been superintendent for over nine years. When he started out he was alone; now he has an assistant, six department heads and a registrar. His has been the vision, in part, which has found for the growing Sunday school enough spaces for the classes to meet; he realized early that there is nothing like a little privacy to make classrooms and meeting places attractive. With Torrey he has worked hand in hand in building the Midwest Bible church from the recruits of the Sunday school. Both of them feel definitely that in the Sunday school exists the future church—and it is from a small Sunday school in 1933 that the present Midwest Bible church has come.

Children are brought to a saving knowledge of Jesus Christ right along during the Sunday school hour. Only on rare occasions does the entire Sunday school meet together. The separate departments meet together and then split up into classes. Many thrilling experiences of children accepting Christ during the Sunday school periods have cheered the workers at Midwest but perhaps none as warmly as the story of nine-year old Georgia Severance.

On Sunday, October 15, 1944, little Georgia accepted Christ as her personal Saviour at the Sunday school hour. A day or so later she said she wasn't feeling so well, and on Thursday afternoon she was dead. She went that fast when a dread disease killed her. The following Monday she was buried, just eight days after her soul had been redeemed for eternity through the effective work of a Spirit-filled and Spirit-guided Sunday school. So deep an impression did that incident make on Torrey that he used it as his main thought in talking to the 30,000 people in Chicago Stadium two days after little Georgia passed away.

Superintendent Scholl believes in contests and during one which lasted six weeks the Sunday school jumped 40 per cent as it added 175 members. In October of 1933 there were 40 in the Sunday school; today there are 915 enrolled.

Filling in during the week are boys' and girls' clubs which do much to keep up the interest among the pupils during the week and letting them realize that they can make the church their home during the week as well as on Sunday. These efforts also have been deeply blessed of God in pointing young, energy-filled lives to the Lord Jesus Christ.

Completing the work with the young people are three young people's groups—Ambassadors, Pioneers and Live Wires. These are divided according to ages and meet every Sunday night from 6:15 to 7:15. Competent leaders and counsellors keep these groups moving and interesting. Torrey generally sees to it, too, that they have something to do in serving the Lord so they won't just receive the blessings and let none out. The trade mark on the young people's work is vitality; they realize that young people won't hang around unless things happen—so things happen!

A men's fellowship meets on Monday nights and draws all of the men of the church into an active, working group. The ladies missionary society, led by Mrs. Percy Moore at present, meets twice monthly. The first is for an all-day work session in sewing for missionaries, etc., and the other is for prayer, a luncheon and a devotional message. At present there are 150 members in the group. A kitchen plays an important part in any church and Midwest has a "Scripture-quoting kitchen" with Bible verses on all walls.

A choir of 50 voices led by Douglas Fisher and a band of 30 pieces directed by Merwin Webster provides the main musical part of the church services. As far as music is concerned, Midwest has been extremely fortunate and favored of God in having some of the top Christian talent in the country on its platform. Fisher is known nationwide as a musical specialist on the organ, the piano and in directing choral groups. Webster received much excellent training in conducting gospel music when he worked under Paul Rader and Richard Oliver. Down through the twelve years of existence the church has seen such excellent musical men as Peter Kjelstad, Don DeVoss, Cornelius Keer, Norman Voss, Marvin Matson, Bob Cook and many others leading the singing or the choir. The reasoning in reaching for the best has been that good music will help to draw people to the church; once they get in they will have to listen to the gospel as it is preached.

Wednesday evening prayer meetings are the high spots of the weeks. On a recent Wednesday night we slipped into a Midwest prayer meeting. Had we come an hour earlier we could have had our choice of attending a class on soul-winning led by Floyd Gephart or a teacher's training class taught by Robert Cook. Promptly at 8 o'clock the service started. When we walked in we were met by five or six rows in the back of the church which were roped off. "Everyone up front," the usher said. So we went up toward the front and slipped into a pew alongside a couple who sang out of the same song book and thus appeared to be man and wife.

We looked up toward the platform during the opening song and saw this painted Bible verse above the baptistry:

Magnify the Lord with me
And let us exalt His Name together.

In front of the pulpit and being emphasized by a hidden light is this motto cut out of wood:

Jesus Saves
To the Uttermost.

The young people are in abundance. Bob Cook calls for verses of promise from the Scripture in between the opening songs, and they flow out like springs from hearts full of testing of those promises. A member is called up from the audience to lead the testimony meeting—"eight minutes of it," he is cautioned. He gives his own testimony first and then calls for others. After a three-second wait a young businessman pops up. He is followed by a cadet nurse who praises God for trials as she "has seen His face in them."

Then come these in rapid succession:

FINE-LOOKING LADY: "My best friend was buried today, but I couldn't stand to go to the funeral. I had tried so many times to win her to the Lord, but I had failed. And I knew there was no hope at her funeral."

HOUSEWIFE: "I've been on a mountain top all day. My soldier son wrote from the South Pacific that he is completely well now and that he was able to give his testimony at a servicemen's league meeting the other day. And then God was so near at our servicemen's prayer meeting this morning."

BUSINESS MAN: "Romans 1:16 tells us, 'For I am not ashamed of the Gospel of Christ, for it is the power of God unto salvation, to the Jew first and also to the Greek.' He keeps me and He answers prayer. In the last two weeks I've had two particular answers to prayer. Some of you might think that one of them is sort of small, but I believe in asking the Lord for small things, too. Last January I lost my spring coat at the cleaners—just couldn't be found anywhere. The cleaner looked everywhere. Finally I asked the Lord to find it . . . and it showed up the other day!"

STENOGRAPHER: "Jesus is truly the sweetest name I know. He leads constantly. Tomorrow I leave for home and from there for Missouri for a full time job in His service. I'd appreciate your prayers for me as I go."

HIGH SCHOOL GIRL: "One and a half years ago I was saved right here in this building, and I'm so happy about it yet tonight."

BUSINESS MAN: "A few Sunday nights ago the pastor asked us to raise our hands if we ever had led anyone to Christ. I couldn't do it then, but last Sunday night a fellow in our office was saved and it was so real that he told everyone in the office about it the next morning."

GIRL WITH PIG TAILS: "I was saved right here and you don't know how happy I am tonight."

YOUNG LADY: "I've got a request to put before you. I wish you'd remember especially a girl with whom I talked today at the Victory Center. She was so discouraged about everything."

YOUNG LADY: "I've had an experience which is so new that it's still warm. On the way here tonight a Jewish lady asked me where I was going as we stood waiting for the streetcar. I told her, and she wanted to know just what we did up here nights when the lights were on so much. Did we dance, or hold parties, etc? I just told her that we loved the Lord and enjoyed being in His house. We got on the car together and I had a further chance to stand by her and talk. I gave her the tract, 'Which

62

Church Saves,' and I wish you'd pray for her. I had been downhearted a bit when I left home tonight, but that's all gone now."

That ended the testimonies, and each one had brought a little warmth into the service. After a few announcements and an offering, Torrey Johnson brought a short, pointed message on the Holy Spirit. Then the entire group of some 225 persons knelt to pray. The prayer meeting is supposed to be over by 9 p. m., but when we got up from our knees on this night it was 9:20. We see people around us who haven't missed a prayer meeting for three years, others who hadn't missed for two and quite a number who hadn't been away from a prayer meeting for an entire year. Then we realize once more why this church is moving ahead for the Lord.

But it's still not time to go home. In a new "Accent on the Bible" series, which started the first Sunday after New Year and ran through Easter, Torrey at 9:05 (if on schedule) each Wednesday night teaches a class on prophecy and Bob Cook handles one on the Gospel of John. Because of the late start the session runs until 10:15 instead of 9:45, and everyone stays until the end. We sat in on the class on prophecy taught by Torrey Johnson and got a fine glimpse into his great teaching ability and why it was that students at Northern Baptist seminary liked him as a professor.

But Wednesday isn't the only prayer meeting night at Midwest. Every Saturday night a Revival Hour prayer band meets in the pastor's study to pray for a heaven-sent revival. This group has been meeting for years. One Saturday a young couple walked into the meeting and a bit later were asked to join in prayer.

"We don't know how," they said in unison. "We came here to get saved."

Needless to say that meeting was a heart-warming one to both God and man.

Each Sunday evening just before the evening service the usher band gathers for special prayer for the service to follow and Pastor Johnson has said more than once that much of the

God-given results of the evangelistic services come from those moments spent in prayer before the service gets under way.

Several gospel teams from the church operate in various missions, holding street meetings, handing out tracts, etc. In 1942 alone over a third of a million tracts were handed out, many of them by red, white and blue uniformed girls who passed them out on the beaches. Hardly a night of the week or month passes when some one of these gospel teams is not holding a service in a jail, hospital, street corner or mission.

And God is using those efforts to win souls. One of the tracts handed out is a small booklet titled, "The Four Calls." It gives the life story of Earnest Anderson, one of the Midwest boys in the service and a brother of Torrey's "a smile for every-one" secretary, Amy Marie Anderson. Earnie had said before leaving for a naval flying school for training, "If ever I get into the thick of the battle and the Lord says, 'Earnie, your time is up, I need a sailor in heaven,' say, that'll be the best thing that ever could happen to this sailor lad." God took him home at the naval air station in Jacksonville, Fla., but his testimony through that tract has lived on and on and has been used to win many souls to the Lord.

Once a month—usually—the *Midwest Messenger*, an extremely attractive and capably edited magazine—finds its way into your home if you're a member at Midwest or a listener to the radio broadcast. When started it was edited by Helen Needham, a teacher of English at the Moody Bible institute. Its appearance is definitely eye-appealing and it serves as an excellent medium of co-ordinating and bringing into eight or twelve pages the many activities of the church and bringing in printed form many of the fine messages preached from the pulpit. It also serves to keep the 163 servicemen on the Midwest flag informed of what is going on at the home front.

In the winter of 1940 God put Torrey flat on his back with sickness on two different occasions. Each time he promised God, "Lord, if you raise me up I'll start a radio broadcast."

But when he was well his faith wasn't quite up to his vision and he lost his courage. He looked at the amount of money needed—$10,000—and decided to table the thought for a while.

In February of 1941 he was down in bed again. Again the vision of the radio work came, and this time he determined to go through with it when he was well again. Along came William Erny, owner of a manufacturing company and a member at Midwest, and his vision, too, was kindled as Torrey talked to him. All during the spring and summer of 1941 they worked on the idea and on October 1, 1941, the eighth anniversary of Torrey's coming to the church they went on the air for a full hour on station WAIT in Chicago from 5 to 6 each Sunday afternoon. Torrey took full responsibility for the program—the church was not financially responsible at all—and if it failed it would be "his neck" and no one else's. As he told his members, "If this thing doesn't go you can come down to the jail and make pastoral calls on me there."

But God honored that step of faith, too. It wasn't long before he was itching to expand to another program, so he went on another station each Thursday night from 8:05 to 8:30. This was discontinued after a period because it necessitated his staying home every week and forced him to pass up too many invitations to hold meetings in other churches. Instead of Thursday night it was moved to Sunday night and the title changed to "Songs in the Night." This arrangement held for a long period, with the radio time each Sunday thus coming to an hour and forty five minutes. This proved to be a bit too tiring, physically, and so "Songs in the Night" was turned over to Billy Graham, young pastor of the Village church in Western Springs, Ill., 15 miles from Chicago. The contract, however, still remains in Torrey's name. When the programs were first put on the air the auditorium of the church served as the studio but one day Torrey took a good look at a garage in the rear of the property, visioned it as a radio studio and today it is just that. Seating 150 people comfortably, it is the spot from which the Sunday afternoon program now is aired.

The radio work has been one of the potent factors in building the Midwest church to its present stature. At present the work is carried on in the name of the church. Even as the regular church services have been blessed of God to the salvation of souls, so too have the radio broadcasts. One Sunday a Midwest member tuned the program in while recuperating in a hospital on Chicago's north side. A lady in the same room also listened to the program and became interested and under conviction. After the program was over the Midwest member was able to lead her to a saving knowledge of Jesus Christ through conversations between their two beds.

One day the phone rang at Midwest and a lady on the other end told this story: "I know that your church is interested in seeing others find the Lord as their Saviour because you sound like it over the radio. I wish you'd pray for a man in the Covenant hospital in Chicago. And if Pastor Johnson or someone could go and visit him, why, that'd be fine."

Torrey couldn't go this time, but one of the soul-winning members of the church was dispatched. The result: an ailing man was led to the Lord and the man who led him to the Lord was bubbling over with joy as he told the details at the prayer meeting the following week.

One Sunday afternoon a Jewish lady tuned into the Chapel Hour. God spoke to her through the program and that night found her in a pew at the Midwest Bible church. When the invitation was given, she was one of the first to go forward and give her heart to the Lord.

Summertime in most city churches generally means a slackening of the ropes, but not so at Midwest. In 1943, following the customary two weeks of Daily Vacation Bible school, the church decided to hold a summer Bible conference right in its own church in the middle of August. The speakers included Rev. R. R. Brown of Omaha, Nebraska, Bob Jones, Sr. of Cleveland, Tennessee, Dr. H. W. Bieber and Rev. Robert Cook, then pastor at La Salle, Illinois.

The idea clicked, a fine conference was held and souls found the Lord. It was tried again in 1944 with Dr. Harry Rimmer of New York, Rev. H. B. Prince of Minneapolis and Dr. William Ward Ayer of New York as the speakers. It's on the docket for 1945, too, D.V., with Rev. Charles Templeton of Toronto, Canada, Dr. Paul Bauman of Los Angeles and Dr. Walter Kallenback, blind evangelist, as the speakers.

The spirit of progress at the Midwest Bible church seeps into your blood after you've been there only a few minutes. Someone else has rightly said, "A spirit of evangelism is present in every meeting too, with the anticipation that souls can and will be saved in any meeting, no matter what its size, what time of the day or night it is or what night it is." As you check back through the table on a previous page you'll note that the Sunday evening attendances are the biggest of the week. You'll note, too, that the attendance far surpasses the regular membership. That perhaps can best be explained by the 12-point doctrinal statement of the church which states clearly what type of a church Midwest is going to be if the constitution is going to be followed. And followed it is, to a letter. These points give the reader an excellent look into the makeup of the group, so we list them:

1. We believe in the Scriptures of the Old and New Testaments as inspired of God and inerrant in the original writings and that they are of supreme and final authority in faith and life.

2. We believe in one God, eternally existing in three Persons, Father, Son and Holy Spirit.

3. We believe that Jesus Christ was begotten by the Holy Spirit, and born of the Virgin Mary and is true God and true Man.

4. We believe that man was created in the image of God; that he sinned and thereby incurred not only physical death but also that spiritual death which is separation from God; and all who reach moral responsibility become sinners in thought, word and deed.

5. We believe that the Lord Jesus Christ died for our sins according to the Scriptures as a representative and substitutionary sacrifice, and that all that believe in Him are justified on the ground of His shed blood and resurrection.

6. We believe in the resurrection of the crucified body of

our Lord, in His ascension into Heaven, and in His present life there for us, as High Priest and Advocate.

7. We believe in the "blessed hope," the personal, pre-millenial and imminent return of our Lord and Saviour Jesus Christ.

8. We believe that all who receive by faith the Lord Jesus Christ are born again of the Holy Spirit and thereby become children of God.

9. We believe in separation from all worldly practices and in wholehearted devotion to the cause of Christ as the only scriptural basis for a happy and useful Christian life. For this reason we oppose all indulgences in intoxicating liquors, in dancing, card playing, the narcotic use of tobacco in any form, theatre going, membership in secret societies, and all similar practices which detract from a separated life.

10. We believe in the bodily resurrection of the just and of the unjust, in the everlasting felicity of the saved, and the everlasting conscious suffering of the lost.

11. We believe that Christian baptism is the immersion in water of a believer "in the name of the Father and of the Son and of the Holy Ghost," to show forth in a solemn and beautiful emblem our faith in the crucified, buried and risen Saviour, with its effect, our death to sin and a resurrection to a new life.

12. We believe that the Lord's supper is a memorial service and is the setting forth in a sacred and symbolic manner the death of the Lord Jesus Christ on our behalf. The emblems of the communion service are not literally the body and blood of Christ, nor do they contain His flesh and blood. The service is for believers only, and to partake has value only as it is mingled with faith and repentance upon the part of the communicant.

The ninth point especially has kept many from becoming members at Midwest but it has cleanly culled out the un-desirables and left in the church the many who are deeply rooted and desirous of serving the Lord with all of their hearts and lives. As a result, the church finds practically every member doing something, be it ever so little. One of the points in Torrey's philosophy on church members is that everyone can do something and it's the job of the pastor and other leaders to find out what that person can do and put him to work doing it.

To say that all has been roses in the growth of the church would be to present an error. There have been plenty of discouragements along the line. For instance, people criticized the new neon sign when first it was placed in front of the church. It has a clock in the middle and around it these words, "Now is the time to seek the Lord."

Other little and big things have come up from time to time but God has miraculously guided the church through its deep waters and has put His stamp of approval on its efforts time and time again.

Thus far we've given you a picture of the Midwest Bible church and its many activities. This picture has been but a hurried glimpse as it would take much space and many more illustrations to bring into true focus the immense work revolving around the building at 3469 North Cicero avenue. But this is mainly a story about a man and not about a church, and so we next try to place that man—Torrey Johnson— in his proper position in the picture.

A few moments with him and you'll find out that he has the "greatest church in the world" and that the members deserve all of the credit for anything that has been done to His honor and glory. Follow that trail to the members and you wind up with the other view—"Torrey is the one who has had most of the push and vision."

But no matter what the proportion might have been, and still is, Torrey truly is the leader of the church, as all pastors should be. Ideas pop out of his head at all times. The latest is to hold his evening services in the summer of 1945, and thereafter, in an outdoor stadium to be constructed in the parking lot owned by the church.

"If it rains," he explained, "we'll go inside. If the mosquitoes are bad, we'll go inside. Otherwise we'll stay out there and preach the gospel. We feel definitely that more sinners will come to the outdoor meetings."

Torrey's first call to the church was for one year. After that period the call was made for another year. This happened again the third year and following his graduation from Northern Baptist seminary they made the call a permanent one—and he accepted.

He started his ministry in the depression, having nothing, and therefore had nothing to lose. When you talk to him now you will hear him tell you that he personally has accumulated very much, spiritually, from the Midwest church. On the heels of the depression came the war so Torrey really hasn't been pastor of the church during a very lengthy period of normal times. The church has been able to see him mature into full stature as a pastor and in so doing the members have come to love him even as parents love their children as they see them grow up.

When ideas crowd into his mind and his vision hits a new peak he prays much about them before he broaches them to his members. When he does bring the ideas up he generally has had the God-given ability to "sell" the thought to the church board and congregation. After he has convinced them that God will honor their steps of faith he proceeds to go ahead and do everything he can to bring that new venture to a successful end. Although you don't see his hand in the many organizations in the church you soon realize that it is there nonetheless. He holds true to his philosophy of never doing himself what someone else can do for him, and once he puts his confidence in a man or woman that confidence holds true until he either has proved himself or failed. Until that time is reached, however, he keeps his hands off.

The three-fold program which the church attempts to carry out involves these factors:

Evangelism—putting out every effort to reach the lost.

Exposition—to feed new born babes and strengthen the Christians.

Extensive missions—to reach the whole world with the Gospel.

Into each of these three efforts Torrey puts his every ounce of energy. He's a soulwinner, first, last and always, yet he realizes that Christians must be strengthened and he knows that missions are dear to the heart of the Lord. Midwest itself has fourteen missionaries serving in six different countries—China, India, Central America, Guatemala, Alaska and Africa.

His relations with the church and the church board always have been mutually healthy. Many of his activities take him away from the church, but the church board's action when Youth for Christ came up is an example of the way it has been all along as he has followed through on his ideas. When the question of Chicagoland Youth for Christ and Youth for Christ International came up the board gave him a blanket vote to spend as much time as he wished to on those efforts. In various things he has had to prove to his members that his visions and plans would work out, but he has done so in each case and blessings have been the result. When the church grew so large that he could not handle it alone, the congregation called Robert A. Cook as associate pastor. Now he has been accepted with as much love and respect as is given Torrey. The most recent move has been the calling of an assistant pastor, a former Midwest member who moved to Hollywood, California, a few years ago. He is John De Saegher and he will handle much of the visitation and personal work. When Torrey was on the West coast in January of 1945 De Saegher made an appointment with him and tried to induce him to come out to the West Coast to live. Instead, Torrey talked him into coming back to work at the Midwest Bible church.

Without wasting words it can be rightfully said that Torrey Johnson has been and is God's man for the Midwest Bible church. He has had many, many opportunities to leave for other churches and perhaps bigger congregations but he has preferred to stay with the group of Christians who mean so very much to him. Between a pastor and a church there generally grows a love which avoids proper description. It's that way between Torrey and Midwest. He is so vitally a part of Midwest that he would have a hard time becoming adjusted elsewhere

71

and it is saying nothing against the church to state that it would find itself in the same position, should he leave.

Torrey's study in the church is alongside the platform. It's open at all times to the members, with the possible exceptions when prayer meetings are going on or Torrey is dealing with someone about salvation. It's a quiet room, well-filled with books and having on one wall one of his prized keepsakes—a picture of the 41 members who comprised the charter members of the church. The desk is clean and well kept; everything is in order, even as God expects to find it in His places of worship.

Thus we see it—a great church, a devoted pastor and a great God. Mix well together, add the sweetness of Christian love and you have the recipe behind the unusual growth of the Midwest Bible church. Each and every member at Midwest feels definitely that every penny put into the offering plate at any time is an investment in the work of the Lord. It never has been necessary to plead or "bleed" for special offerings; God has paid rich dividends at this investment house in the past and the people at Midwest are beginning to feel, and rightly so, that God never will fail them as long as they trust in Him.

To the four corners of the earth the Midwest Bible church now is becoming known. Its reputation seems based fundamentally on one thing—its unflagging zeal and its burning passion for the winning of souls to the Lord Jesus Christ.

Soulwinner number one, in all humility and unselfish feeling, is the bespectacled human dynamo of a pastor, Torrey Maynard Johnson.

CHAPTER SIX

Extra Curricular Activities

F AR from shore on the dark waters of lake Michigan the S.S.
City of Grand Rapids plowed its way along. The crowd on
board was a "different" type of crowd, the crew readily admitted. Not a drop of liquor was being consumed; instead of
the raspy tunes of a dance band the sweet music of the gospel
hymns and choruses filled every corner and oval of the boat
as it slithered along.

Fully 2,200 young people were on the City of Grand Rapids
this night. The occasion was another moonlight cruise sponsored by Torrey Johnson's Midwest Bible church and God in
His goodness was making it a night not soon to be forgotten
by those on board.

On the boat Torrey started up a ladder to another deck.
On the way up he met a man who seemed as though he wanted
to talk to him. As Torrey stepped aside the man came up and
said, "Are you Torrey Johnson?"

"Yes, I am," was Torrey's reply.

"I've been waiting to talk to you for a long time," the
man answered, "when do you think we could get together."

"No time like the present," said Torrey, and they crowded
off into a corner where it was somewhat quiet.

The man was Walter Block, president of the Quaker Stretcher
corporation of Kenosha, Wisconsin, manufacturer of curtain
stretchers in peace time and army cots in war time. Mr. Block
unburdened himself in a hurry. He had a heavy burden on his

heart for the salvation of his employees and wanted to know how to go about reaching them with the gospel.

"That's strange," said Torrey, "but I've felt that same burden for the men and women in industry. I've felt all along that differences between management and labor never could be solved sufficiently apart from the gospel of Jesus Christ, and I've been praying to the Lord that He might allow me to have a little part in doing that very thing."

They talked for a few more minutes and then agreed to meet the next Tuesday noon for lunch at the Gospel Fellowship club, headed by Vaughn Shoemaker, chief cartoonist for the *Chicago Daily News,* in downtown Chicago. After the luncheon Torrey and Mr. Block had a conference which lasted late into the afternoon. The result: a gospel shop meeting with a radio broadcast so that people listening in could share the novel witness of the gospel being preached in a factory, to men in working clothes.

The plans were culminated on the third Monday of September in 1943. The meetings originated in the Quaker recreation hall at Kenosha, Wisconsin, and were broadcast five days a week over station WJJD in Chicago. They proved to be a success from the very beginning. After Torrey had been used in getting them off to a successful start, Mr. Block felt led to call Charles J. Anderson, who had been employed by the Arma corporation in Brooklyn as an industrial chaplain, to work full time with his men. Anderson came and today he is carrying on the program from day to day. Torrey received a tremendous personal blessing from being able to help bring the gospel to a portion of our American population which he feels is being missed by the churches. It thrilled him, too, to see how God worked to bring it about, and especially the initial contact on the boat. Who else but God would think to bring two men interested in the same thing into each other's way on a boat in the middle of lake Michigan on a dark night. To him it is just one more example of the mystery and marvel of God.

Torrey's part in starting those gospel shop meetings is but one example of the "extra curricular activities" which he has found time to participate in along with his serving as pastor at Midwest. One might wonder if such activities would not hurt the church because of his absence, but the contrary has been the result. The zeal and enthusiasm of the various ventures carried right over into his work in the church and the blessings which came Torrey's way overflowed into the hearts of the members at Midwest.

A few years back it was the Christian Youth Week which he sponsored in Chicago and which proved to be an outstanding success. He didn't know it then, but those meetings gave him valuable experience and contacts for the greater Chicagoland Youth for Christ organization which was to develop later.

For four years—1936 through 1940—he served as president of the Wheaton College Alumni association, no small task in itself at that growing and healthy institution. Starting in 1942 he served as president of the Chicago Hebrew mission board and still is head of that board. When the National Association of Evangelicals came onto the scene he became one of the strongest boosters for it in the middlewest, serving as treasurer of the Chicago regional district and as a member of the board of administration. Much of the work on the 1945 convention in Chicago fell upon his shoulders as he served as local chairman for the sessions.

These and many other activities tended to bring him into wider usefulness in the Christian world as he let his talents be used to further the gospel in many places. As early as 1938 he was tabbed as "someone to keep an eye on" when he was listed with 6,000 others in "Who's Who Among America's Young Men." This included men under 40 years of age, and Torrey at that time was only 28 years of age.

One of the things which proved to be such an outstanding success was the moonlight cruise idea. It wasn't original with him as it had been tried in Detroit with success, and the Moody Memorial church in Chicago, also, had held one previous to the time he took it up. It can be said, however, that when he took hold it reached a group of people until then unreached and proved to be a spiritual and Christian testimony not only to those on board but to many who were on hand to see the boat leave.

The first cruise sponsored by Midwest was held in the summer of 1943. There was trepidation as to the possibility of 2,200 Christian young people being interested enough in such an idea as to buy a ticket, but when sailing time arrived it was a sellout. Included on that first cruise were 500 servicemen, guests of the Midwest Bible church. Torrey has a great heart for servicemen and he has done his bit to make Chicago known as one of the best cities in the nation in hospitality and friendliness.

Five services were held simultaneously on the boat. Speakers were the best. So successful did it prove to be, and so many requests for tickets had been turned down in the days preceding the event that another cruise was held later in the summer when 2,200 more young people crowded on board for the trip. Never to miss an opportunity to spread the gospel, Torrey arranged for a meeting at the pier at 8 p. m., thus reaching the many thousands who line the bridge and docks to see the boats take off. Speakers that summer included Robert Van Kampen, president of the Hitchcock Publishing company; Al Conn, director of the radio program called "The Old Sunday School"; Billy Graham, southern evangelist serving as pastor of the Village church in Western Springs, Illinois; Don Hoke, religious reporter for the *Chicago Tribune*, Wilbur Westerdahl of Belvidere, Illinois, and Reamer Loomis, outstanding businessman in Chicago. Music was the best and included Beverly Shea, noted gospel baritone and radio singer, Miss Winifred Larson, contralto, Marvin Matson, Don DeVoss and many others. A radio broadcast was arranged for the second trip, being short waved to the station on shore. There it was picked up and rebroadcast and as it went out portable radios on the decks of the ship picked up the program, and let the participants know how they sounded even before the cruise was finished.

In 1944 two more cruises were sponsored by the Midwest Church of the Air. Once more street services were held before going on board and again thousands of gospel tracts were

76

handed out to people lining the bridges and on the streets as the "songs of the saved" proved to the listeners that there is joy in salvation. And once again the musical and preaching programs were geared to youth; five meetings were held at the same time and God spoke through each one of them. The idea still is alive in Torrey's mind and to date one is definitely planned for the summer of 1945 with the possibility of another to be added later. He feels that it should be used just as long as God continues to use it to reach souls.

These specific activities mentioned have been but a part of the outside efforts in which Torrey has been interested. As stated previously, from 1933 through 1940 the church was forced to share his time with the seminary, first as a student and then as an instructor. Even that "share the man" plan did not hamper or hinder the growth at Midwest. Though he was not able to put his entire time into the church, he nonetheless kept it going as fast as God seemed to desire it to move. When he started to give it his main attention in 1940 it took a definite swing upward.

Along with other executive and administrative positions held were the many calls for special meetings in churches and for appearances at youth conferences. They flooded his desk; many he accepted but he was forced to turn many away, too. In the summer of 1944 he was preaching in Dr. William Ward Ayer's Calvary Baptist church in New York city; six months later he was moving up and down California with Gil Dodds, the Christian athlete, at the famed Torrey conference sponsored by the Bible institute of Los Angeles. In between those appearances he had tried to take a month's vacation in Florida but ended by working with youth leaders in Orlando, Tampa and Miami in getting Youth for Christ started there.

Wherever he has gone, the church has let him go. The members feel that God has complete control of his life and although Midwest is the focal point of his activities they realize that his sphere of spiritual influence must of necessity spread farther than the area around 3469 North Cicero avenue in Chicago. Wherever he has gone he has brought a blessing with his challenging, clearcut gospel messages. When he comes "back home," the overflow from his heart reaches the members.

One of his extra curricular activities is too big to be incorporated with others in one chapter. Back in 1942 Torrey was thinking and praying about Youth for Christ; at that time the general plan of the movement which now is sweeping the United States and crossing oceans to foreign lands existed hardly at all in the minds of its leaders. Torrey let the challenge boil and simmer in his own mind until the spring of 1944. Then the necessary faith and vision combined with many years of praying and waiting on God to bring into existence "Chicagoland Youth for Christ" and its God-directed result, Youth for Christ International. The Youth for Christ movement is hard to classify at this moment, as it continues to spread out like wildfire, but from all indications it rightfully has been called "The Wonder of the Twentieth Century," as far as the spiritual world is concerned. Day by day and week by week it continues to reach out, out, and out into town after town, city after city and now nation after nation. Where it will stop no one knows but God. Where it started is also hard to say, too, although through Jack Wyrtzen's fine "Word of Life Hour" in New York Times Square the movement was given its greatest national publicity in its early stages.

Since formation of Youth for Christ International, however, the "man behind the movement" perhaps rightfully can be said to be Torrey M. Johnson, a "youth on fire" for Christ.

CHAPTER SEVEN

"Youth on Fire for Christ."

ONE thousand souls in twenty-one weeks! Twenty-eight thousand people in one meeting!

Visionary and day dreaming, you might say, but to a prayer-bound, sincere, and energetic group of young men in Chicago in the spring of 1944 they were challenges given to them by God, and in which they had the utmost confidence that God would complete for them if they but stepped out in faith.

Thus it was that Chicagoland Youth for Christ came into being. As its organization and plans unfolded and developed, the miraculous way in which the Lord was with it gave calm assurance to its workers that "God was in it."

After years of planning, waiting on God and feeling out the pulse of Chicagoland young people to such a movement, Torrey Johnson felt that on the night of April 13, 1944, he had received God's "Go" sign. It came to him in a hotel room in Columbus, Ohio, where he was attending the annual convention of the National Association of Evangelicals. A series of conferences at that time with other Youth for Christ leaders had given Torrey the "convincing" he needed and the feeling that the time was spiritually ripe to launch Chicagoland Youth for Christ. From that hotel room went a long distance call to Douglas Fisher in Chicago; Fisher slid out of bed, forgot to put on his slippers, and went to answer the phone. He got the message and the next day went down to his work at the Moody Bible institute radio station, WMBI, and gave them two weeks' notice that he was resigning to start full time as managing director of Chicagoland Youth for Christ.

79

Chicago had the men it needed to start the movement in that great city. One of the nation's top vocalists, Beverly Shea, was eager to see it start after having seen how the idea had worked in New York under Jack Wyrtzen. Lacy Hall, a student at the Moody Bible institute, brought valuable experience with him from working with Glenn Wagner in Washington, D. C. Bob Cook had come to Chicago that very spring from LaSalle, Illinois, and God was using his editorial ability along with his song leading and preaching. Doug Fisher had come a round-about way from Toronto's Canadian Broadcasting company to Chicago and radio station WMBI. Businessmen with ferver for serving Christ with their means as well as their abilities—such as William Erny, Floyd Gephart and Robert Wyatt—were more than willing to lend their talents to see Youth for Christ blossom in Chicago.

Things looked rosy for a while. What a talent array! What possibilities for speakers when you thought of Chicago's central location and its central advantages as a transportation hub. These and many other factors kept the organizers cheerful for quite a period.

But suddenly they were faced with the problem of a place to meet. This was thought to be one of the solved questions, but all at once it stuck itself out like a sore thumb. The staff combed downtown Chicago for a place which would seat from 1,000 to 1,500 people. Nothing was available. Opening after opening closed up even as fast as the contacts were made.

Then Orchestra hall, acoustically the most perfect auditorium in Chicago, opened up like a flash! Twenty-one weeks for $5,000! The faith wavered momentarily, but on the following Monday morning Torrey Johnson was in the office of the Orchestra hall management with the necessary check in down payment, signed by him personally. Once more, he was putting no one else on the spot, financially, but himself; it was his check and if anything flopped he alone would be the loser and no one else would be out a penny of money, at least.

The next problem was radio. The religious broadcasting situation in Chicago is much the same as in most cities and towns in our nations—not too favorable. Torrey tried every major station in Chicago trying to line up a Saturday night broadcast. Each time he met with the same answer—no time available.

But through the help of Herbert J. Taylor, president of Club Aluminum company of America and sponsors of Beverly Shea's afternoon hymn program, the door to WCFL, the Voice of Labor station in Chicago, swung open. Six times previously the group had contacted WCFL, and six times it had been turned down. On the seventh try it opened and Chicagoland Youth for Christ became the only gospel broadcast on any Chicago station on Saturday night.

Two dinner meetings brought the backing of some 25 youth organizations in Chicago and some 100 businessmen. Through four weeks of planning, promotion, advertising and work, Chicagoland Youth for Christ made its unknowing way. Each time something was done, it was done for the first time, and they had not much to fall back on for advice and help.

Finally on May 27, 1944, the opening night arrived. The feelings of doubt and wonder were heavy as the group gathered for its final touching up work. Would any people come? How would things turn out? Would souls be reached for Christ?

The answers came fast. Following the final prayer meeting in the lower rooms of Orchestra hall they moved to the platform to be greeted by . . . 2,000 people! That crowd itself almost knocked them over as they gazed on it from the platform. Once again God had answered prayer, and people were on hand. A few hours later God answered the prayer closest to their hearts when, after the evening message by Rev. Billy Graham of the Western Springs, Illinois, Village church, forty hands were raised and almost as many came forward to seek Christ as Saviour. What a thrill it was to see God's sanction on their efforts and how precious were those souls, the "first fruits" of their prayers and work.

The offering? Just enough to cover the expenses and give them enough to get started on the second week.

From that first night on Chicagoland Youth for Christ moved

81

steadily on, Saturday night after Saturday night, toward its goal of winning 1,000 souls for Christ during the summer months. The second and third Saturday nights proved to be "trial nights," too, as the leaders felt that perhaps people might stop coming after the newness of the thing wore off. But God was working and the opposite proved to be the case. From May 27 through October 14, when the last meeting of 1944 was held in Orchestra hall, over 2,000 young people attended the rallies each Saturday night and the average ran to 2,500, with several nights finding thousands being turned away.

The ways in which God used the meetings to bring salvation to souls are enough almost to require a book in themselves. On one night a Japanese girl, two Navajo Indians and a separated sailor and his wife were saved. People were brought in from the streets through an intensive program of tract and plugger distribution on Saturday afternoon and early evening. These brought hundreds of young people, and especially servicemen, to the meetings. One evening a sailor was saved and in giving his testimony after he had been dealt with he said, "Someone gave me a tract and told me this was a good place to go, so I came. Believe me, they didn't tell half the truth. It's more than a good place; it's the best place on earth."

On one occasion a girl phoned Torrey Johnson three times in two days, each time being unable to reach him. Finally she was persuaded to talk to Bob Cook and there over the telephone he was able to lead this 15-year old high school girl to the Lord Jesus Christ. Another time a young fellow went forward to yield his life completely to the Lord for His service. When he was through praying he told the person praying with him his name and it developed that the lad was the son of a leading pastor in Chicago. The father happened to be in the service that night and they met and had a glorious after meeting all by themselves.

The meetings were definitely evangelistic from start to finish. No expense was spared in obtaining the best in gospel music and musical numbers. Men of God with a definite appeal for young people were scheduled months in advance and without exception brought messages direct from God and aimed to win the hearts of young people to Christ. Included among the speakers for the first year of meetings were the following: Billy Graham, Jim Rayburn, Wendell Loveless, Mervin Rosell, Harold Erickson, Dr. Paul Rood, Dr. Harry Rimmer, Dr. Henry Savage, Dr. Harry Ironside, Dr. Louis Talbot, Dr. William Culbertson, Dr. Martin DeHaan, Dr. B. Lakin, Dr. Merrill MacPherson, Richard Harvey, Dr. Walter Wilson, John Zoller, Jack Schuler, Dr. V. R. Edman, Walter (Happy) MacDonald, Robert Murphin, Dr. Bob Jones, Jr., Dr. Isaac Page, Jimmie Johnson, Vincent Brushwyler, Dr. Walter Kallenbach, Clifford Lewis, R. G. LeTourneau, Wilbur Westerdahl, Theodore Anderson, Bob Cook, Mun Hope, Charles Templeton and Hyman Appelman.

An all-girl choir was organized, directed by Doug Fisher and featuring the solo work of Rose Arzoomanian. Dressed in white, they brought a definite youth appeal to the meetings. Time after time they found themselves hemmed in on the platform by the overflow crowds, but they didn't mind that as they kept right on singing. During the hot summer months the crowds continued to come, aided by the "air conditioned appeal" of Orchestra hall.

But contracts have a way of running out, and when the prospect of leaving Orchestra hall for the winter months loomed up there was much praying and thinking to be done. One group, definitely in the minority, thought of stopping the meetings for the winter months and then resuming in the spring. The majority felt that it was God's will that they keep going and so they set out in another search for a downtown hall. But again there just wasn't any available downtown and to the rescue came the members of world famous Moody Memorial church with an offer to throw their church open for the meetings if the organization wanted it. The invitation was graciously accepted, and plans were made to start the services there on October 28.

The Orchestra hall contract expired October 14. The meetings at Moody church were to start October 28.

In between lay October 21 . . . and out of that night developed one of the greatest one night evangelistic efforts in the history of Chicago.

This was the plan. To work up to a climax and tide over the swing from Orchestra hall to Moody church a "Victory Rally" was planned for the Chicago stadium. The stadium seats 28,000 people and faith-heavy Torrey told the management that he wanted every available seat in the house set up. They agreed to do it, although they told him behind his back, and to his face, too, that there just wouldn't be any 28,000 people in the stadium on the night of October 21 for a "religious meeting." They told him he'd be lucky to get from 10,000 to 15,000 there.

Torrey didn't say anything—much—but went his way of making plans for the rally. A 2,500-voice choir was to be led by Professor T. J. Bittikofer of the Moody Bible institute. A Salvation army band was to provide the opening music. The speaking lineup was the best—keyed to youth and aimed at youth. They came from all over, and included Gil Dodds, world indoor mile champion, Bob Finley, national collegiate boxing titleholder, Mervin Rosell, youth evangelist from Rochester, Minn., Robert Nelson of the Arma corporation of Brooklyn, N. Y., Herbert Taylor of the Club Aluminum corporation of America, Chaplain William Conley of the paratroopers at Fort Benning, Ga., Philip A. Benson, president of the Dimes Savings Bank of Brooklyn, N. Y., Freelin Carlton, manager of the Sears State street store in Chicago, Clarence Jones, director of radio station HCJB in Quito, Ecuador, Peter Stam III, member of a famous missionary family and headed for Africa himself and Lt. Col. Erwin Stoll, home alive after five years in the South Pacific amidst disease, and near death.

Singers and musicians besides the giant choir and the band included Beverly Shea, Rose Arzoomanian and Clarence and Howard Jones. The program had been worked on for months and had something going on every minute and everything keyed to the presentation of the blessed gospel story.

84

October 21 arrived. In the afternoon the choir was on hand for a two-hour rehearsal. After the practice, in true Torrey Johnson method, an invitation for salvation or dedication of lives was extended to that great singing group. Torrey believed in having his singers singing out of saved hearts and he took that final opportunity to reach them.

The doors opened at 6 p. m. and the hundreds of people who had been waiting rushed for the choice seats. At 6:30 the auditorium was over three fourths full. At 6:45 the last remaining seats were being snatched up—or sat upon. One thousand students came from Wheaton college, 25 miles away, on a special train. At 7 o'clock, when the program started, the people were starting to line the walls where it was legally possible under fire ordinances. Reports from downtown Chicago said that fully 5,000 people were snarled in a traffic jam and could not reach the stadium because of inadequate facilities. Torrey had informed the street car and bus line officials that a great crowd was coming, but they tended to disbelieve him.

God blessed every part of the meeting from the time of the posting of the American and Christian flags until the benediction was pronounced almost three hours later. Even since then He has been making it a blessing to the 30,000 who were there as it has been re-lived and thought about. Thousands of people since have seen the movies taken of it and other thousands have been blessed by hearing it over the air, including the round-the-world airing of it by HCJB in Quito, Ecuador. The meeting presented a stirring Christian challenge to the city of Chicago, to the great middlewest and to the nation as a whole. Christians everywhere were encouraged and inside of the stadium that night hundreds of hands were lifted and names signed to salvation cards as the Holy Spirit worked His way into the hearts and minds of the listeners.

The following week Chicagoland Youth for Christ moved to Moody Memorial church where the meetings continued to be held until the first Saturday night in April, 1945, when

85

they switched back to Orchestra hall for the next seven months, D.V. With the move into the church came an opportunity to allow two servicemen to phone home from the platform at each meeting. It also allowed the formation of a great drive among the youth of the Chicago area to send used clothing overseas to the needy born again Christians in war torn Europe. As of May 1, 1945, fully seven tons—14,000 pounds—had been collected and shipped overseas through Chicagoland Youth for Christ.

As the meetings went on in Moody church, the benefits from the stadium rally continued to flow in. Whereas letters of inquiry regarding Youth for Christ had been trickling in on the order of a trout stream before, they now came with the rush of a waterfall and literally swamped the offices of Chicagoland Youth for Christ. Echoes of the rally brought a personal note of thanks and congratulations from Andy Frain, handler of the crowds at the stadium, who said it was the best crowd he had ever handled in his 17 years at the stadium and at other places. Arthur Wirtz, manager of the stadium, was so impressed by the meeting that he presented Chicagoland Youth for Christ with a check for $500 to help meet its expenses. The offering of the evening totalled $7,600 and the expenses ran to something over $9,000. This difference between the receipts and the expenses was made up through a profit on the program bulletin and through Christians who were interested in it.

Night after night, through the chilly winter season in Chicago the meetings continued on at the same pace. Torrey felt that he could use a little rest after a strenuous year and so took off for Florida for four weeks. Even while he was gone the movement kept steaming ahead. At times during the winter the crowds were down, but God didn't bother about the size of the crowds as He used the speakers to preach the Word and sinners were saved and Christian young people brought to a point where they yielded their lives completely to Him.

Highlights popped in constantly. On February 9, 1945, the staff tried something new—a Chicagoland Youth for Christ banquet.

The result: 1,500 young people crowded into the Stevens hotel main ballroom for an evening of sweet Christian fellowship and a challenging message, among others, from Charles Templeton of Toronto, Canada. It was more than "just another banquet."—God used it to speak to many present about the "first things" in our lives here below.

Ever pushing ahead, Chicagoland wanted to do something big for its first anniversary celebration. The date coincided with Memorial Day—Wednesday, May 30—so a great patriotic Christian demonstration was planned.

A typical Saturday night meeting of Chicagoland Youth for Christ finds Doug Fisher starting his organ prelude at 7 p. m. At 7:15 Bob Cook starts the congregational singing and from then until the main speaker of the evening a steady—fast-moving parade of musical and spoken talent moves before your eyes and ears.

Testimony time over the radio is generally one of the highlights, with experiences of servicemen some of the best features. The half hour radio program is transcribed from 7:45 to 8:15 and is re-played a half hour later over WCFL—from 8:45 to 9:15. The servicemen never are forgotten. After they are recognized from the platform and asked to stand, Rose Arzoomanian, Beverly Shea or Ray McAfee alternate in singing *God Bless our Boys* as the audience bows in prayer and someone leads in oral prayer for the "boys at the front."

The radio time includes an eight-minute message given usually by Torrey himself and is a definite, stirring appeal to the radio audience. To the tune of "I Surrender All," the program goes off the air along with a gospel invitation.

Following the broadcast a report generally is given on the growth of Youth for Christ throughout the country and across the waters. Songs, instrumental numbers, recognition of servicemen and then the speaker of the evening. As the entire program is "geared to youth" the speakers generally limit themselves to 22 minutes, or longer as the Lord leads. Somewhere between 9:10 and 9:25 the closing song is announced and the invitation given. Promptly at 9:30, in accordance with the "Code of

Success" which the organization follows in order to allow the young people to get home on time, the benediction is pronounced and only those who have answered the invitation and are kneeling in prayer stay. As the organ softly plays *God Be With You 'Til We Meet Again,* the crowd slowly wends its way home.

Without exception, there has been some visible response each Saturday night in which a service has been held. The staff meets several times during the week for prayer and each weekend gathering is fortified solidly by the backing of many prayer warriors. Chicagoland Youth for Christ has been built on prayer and its backers feel that any success which God has bestowed on it has come because of the complete dependence on Him for all help and guidance and results.

As news of the success of Chicagoland Youth for Christ began to spread, and be seen throughout the nation, inquiries for help began to pour in. For a long time, Torrey and the staff answered every inquiry and gave them the full benefit of the experience which had been theirs. In the early fall of 1944 God laid it on the hearts of Torrey and Bob Cook to write a book for the Moody press in Chicago, titled, *Reaching Youth for Christ.* It is the story of the growth of Chicagoland Youth for Christ from the very beginning, how it progressed and with a chapter or two on hints to those who might wish to start a Youth for Christ meeting in their locality. The book first was presented at the Victory rally in the Chicago stadium. To date over 15,000 copies of the book have been sold and it is being used everywhere as an inspiration and a guide book to potential leaders of similar organizations. Written in a simple, clearcut and fast-moving style, it has reached the hearts of young people and has been a blessing and an inspiration to thousands. Ten points of definite, pointed advice serve to make the book well worth the dollar it costs.

With the inquiries flowing in so fast that it was hard to keep pace with them, something had to be done. As the letters came for help, Torrey, Bob Cook and the others working with the group often left on Saturday evenings to speak in other spots and help others get started. On one Saturday night the only staff member left was Doug Fisher—Torrey and Bob were both away speaking at meetings and the song leading job fell to Al Smith and in charge of the service was Billy Graham. Some might have felt that such a move would weaken Chicagoland Youth for Christ, but even while they were gone the blessings continued and some other place was off to a good start.

The fall of 1944 found God blessing Youth for Christ in a marvelous way all over the land. At that time there was a feeling going around among several Youth for Christ leaders that a national organization should be formed. To this end a group of leaders met at Detroit late in November and set up a temporary national committee, with Torrey as chairman. The main task on hand was to arrange the week of meetings that Youth for Christ was sponsoring through the world-famous Winona lake, Indiana, conference grounds on July 22-29, 1945. With Arthur W. McKee, executive manager of Winona lake on hand together with Dr. W. Raymond Edman, president of Wheaton college, Bob Parsons, assistant director of radio station WMBI in Chicago, the directors from several midwest cities and areas met to see what could be done. Nothing definite was organized until a meeting in Chicago in January 1945, when, after three months of waiting on the Lord to ascertain His will in the matter, "Youth for Christ International" was organized during a meeting which lasted for two full days.

Something had to be done. Chicagoland Youth for Christ, as efficient and as capably run as it is, was finding it humanly impossible to keep up with the growth of the movement. The requests to "come over and help us" just couldn't be filled with any degree of regularity. A flying trip to the west coast by Torrey, with mile champion Gil Dodds in tow, gave Los Angeles and other cities in that area a great help in starting their meetings there.

Billy Graham, known throughout radio-land as the director of "Songs in the Night," was granted a year's leave of absence by his church and accepted a call to become the first field man for the Youth for Christ International movement. An office was set up on February 1, 1945, at 130 North Wells street in

89

Chicago. Capable Clyde Dennis, founder of Good News publishers, world-known tract specialists, answered God's call and came to edit *Youth*, and the *Youth for Christ* magazine.

Slowly the number crept up. First it was fifty cities holding Youth for Christ meetings; then it was 100. Soon it reached 200 . . . then 300. At this writing the total is 400 cities or towns holding Youth for Christ meetings of some sort, either on every Saturday night or on alternate Saturday nights. God is blessing the movement in such a remarkable way that many Christians feel that it is in the early stages of a great, sweeping revival, at least, to Torrey M. Johnson, the leader, the movement stands on this footing. He explained it in a statement for an article in the *Protestant Voice* of March 2, 1945: "Youth for Christ must be of God. It has come in the most unusual way and is moving in the most unpredictable way. All we know is that God is in it and is blessing it. We believe that it is God's answer to the sin and unbelief of the present day."

The goal stands at 1,000 cities and one million young people every Saturday night in a Youth for Christ meeting! Whether it reaches that goal or not is in the hands of God, the same place it has been ever since it started. Improper leadership and unwise planning have caused some of the attempts in various places to miss the mark, but these have been few and far between. It is to help avoid these failures that Youth for Christ International was formed and it is safe to say that the organization has more than proved its worth in the few short months it has been operating.

The second full-time field man for Youth for Christ International started working on May 1, 1945. He is Bob Finley, a fine young man who was graduated from the university of Virginia in 1944 as the president of the student body along with his prowess as a boxer. Others are expected to be out on the field in the near future as the Lord leads. The demand for help has been so heavy that more and more field men are becoming a necessity.

The nation is beginning to take note of this "Twentieth Century Wonder." Practically every religious magazine in the country has had an article on it at some time or other. *Colliers*, the national weekly, had an article on it in the May 26, 1945 number, authored by William McDermott, one of the nation's top free lancers and himself a truly born again Christian. The Chicago *Daily News* recently devoted five pages to it in its roto section. Here, there and everywhere the movement and its impact slips into someone's home and lets him know that God still is working among our young people, even if the devil is also. On a recent morning Torrey received a letter from Dwight H. Green, governor of the state of Illinois, and wondered to himself, "Oh, oh, what did I do now." But the letter thrilled him and gave him the encouragement he needed for that specific day.

It read, "I have recently been advised of the splendid meetings of young people which are being held under the auspices of your Youth for Christ organization each Saturday evening, and of the fine response you have received.

"During this period when so much is said about juvenile delinquency and so many plans are offered to combat the problem, I want you to know that I feel that your Saturday night meetings are tremendous forces for alleviating the situation.

"With kind regards and best wishes for the continued success of your movement, I am,

Sincerely,"

etc.

It is hard to appraise rightfully and correctly Youth for Christ at this moment. No one is more optimistic and idealistic about it than its energy-filled leader, Torrey Johnson. And yet, no one is more realistic about it than this same Torrey Johnson.

Criticism has been leveled at Youth for Christ in increasing volume as it has picked up its momentum. The devil is working against it as hard as he can. Along that line, opposition to the movement went so far that a private in the army of the United

States was faced with court martial if he didn't desist from trying to start a Youth for Christ meeting in the town in which he was stationed, and whose young people's sinful living had burdened his Christ-filled heart. Many pastors not only have failed to cooperate in the soul-winning movement when it has come to their areas but have openly opposed the instigation of such a movement.

God, however, seems clearly to be having His way in the spread of the movement. There seems to be but one answer to its amazing growth—God must be in it. Working with God and for Him are hosts of young men like Torrey Johnson who with him feel that they must do everything they can to bring the young people of today under the power of salvation if there is to be an America of tomorrow worth living in. The average Youth for Christ meeting today is more than a gathering for Christian fellowship—that end is achieved, to be sure—but in almost every case the sought-after goal is the salvation of precious souls. If that goal is held uppermost and primary, it is bound to meet with the continued favor of God.

Where does Torrey M. Johnson fit into this picture?

The board of the Midwest Bible church told him one night, "Spend just as much time as you want to spend on Chicagoland Youth for Christ," and they hired an associate pastor to help him out.

Youth for Christ International arrived on the scene. Once more the board acted, and its chairman said, "Spend just as much time as you want to spend on Youth for Christ International," and within a few months they had hired another man to act as an assistant to his associate.

There was a period when Torrey thought he would resign from his church and go into Youth for Christ work full time But God decided otherwise for him and so he continues to serve as a pastor and still be the guiding light and steadying hand in the great youth movement which seems destined to be one of the things on the home front for which returning servicemen will thank the Lord.

It's been said that an organization moves about as far as its leader. If such be the case, Youth for Christ International has endless possibilities because Torrey M. Johnson has endless possibilities. Tie those endless possibilities onto the Hand of God and you have . . . a revival in the making.

CHAPTER EIGHT

Torrey M. Johnson—Soul Winner

FOUR thousand feet above the ground the airplane churned its steady way toward Tulsa, Oklahoma. The trip had not been one of the easiest nor one of the smoothest; weather conditions were not ideal for flying, but as is true in the vast majority of our commercial flying today, the trip was being made in safety.

Among the passengers were two men who had boarded the plane at Chicago. One was a businessman. The other was a young preacher. As they took their seats they had taken note of the stewardess, had made themselves acquainted and had exchanged with her a few words of everyday conversation and humor. Once in the air they found occasion to swing the conversation to spiritual things, but her duties had called her away before they could "close the deal."

Now Tulsa was nearing. Suddenly the young preacher excused himself and said,

"I'm going back to talk to the stewardess again."

He moved back to where she was sitting. She smiled as he sat down, and they started to talk. Slowly he drew from her a tragic story. Her fiance had been due home from overseas after his next flying mission; she had asked to be transferred to the middlewest so as to be near him when he would be visiting with his family on the expected leave. Her request had been granted, but just as she was being transferred she received the news. He hadn't returned alive from his last mission.

94

There was a well of sadness in each of her eyes. All hopes were shattered. Everything on which she had counted was gone; all for which she had hoped was suddenly not hers. She unashamedly let a tear drop as she showed the diamond ring which she still wore on her left hand.

The young preacher had listened with a heart full of Christian love. He could know the feeling of losing a dearly beloved friend because he had gone through such a siege when his brother had died. But he had a message for this girl. He had felt burdened about her soul ever since he had stepped onto the plane. Now, knowing her story, he unfolded to her the remedy for her sorrow as he told her about Jesus Christ, the One who gives joy which is unshakable even by the heartaches of this world. The way of salvation came from his lips in a simple and clearly understandable way as his Bible opened now and then to let her read for herself what God said about certain things.

The motors of the big plane hummed and hummed on through the night as they neared Tulsa. As they approached that city, God once more worked the miracle of salvation in the heart of a human being. She accepted Christ as her personal Saviour and when the plane came to the ground the air stewardess who had boarded the plane sad-eyed and heavy hearted stepped out with a new-found joy in her heart.

The man who had talked to her gave her a New Testament and shook her hand warmly as they separated. She was a different girl now. Utter despair and a dark outlook on life suddenly had been changed. Her sweetheart still wasn't coming back, but she had Christ in her heart now, and in some way, the ache was gone and peace was in her heart.

Two young fellows were visiting the Mexican district in Los Angeles. One of them, known to the sports world as Gil Dodds, holder of the mile indoor record in track, wanted to buy some perfumed candles to take home to his wife in Boston. The other fellow thought that maybe it'd be a good idea if he did the same.

A charming black-haired and dark-eyed Mexican girl waited on them. In a few moments the candles had been bought, but the men lingered on. They had started a conversation and it had to be finished. As they had talked to her they mentioned the Lord Jesus Christ and it wasn't long before they inquired of her as to how she stood with Him. A tract then went into her hand and the way of salvation was made clear to her. Then followed a prayer meeting right across the counter, as the men prayed to God for her salvation. That was all they could do as business then called her away. Whether she accepted Christ only God knows today, but whether she had or not she had had a chance because two of God's children once more had been faithful in witnessing to those with whom they came in contact.

As the train sped its way back to Chicago three people from three different walks in life moved into the dining car to find themselves at the same table. As is true so often in traveling, dining car conversations generally bring out much information from the various people involved. Everyone seems eager to talk, either to help pass the time or to suppress a feeling of excitement which often comes when a trip is necessary.

It wasn't long before the conversation started among these three people. In due time the most adept at making conversation had the talk going his way. The starter was this:

"What's your hobby?"

The elderly lady promptly replied,

"Making of fine perfumes."

The businessman said,

"Barber shop quartets."

The young fellow with the wavy hair and the twinkling eyes who had started the question on its way then answered,

"The winning of souls to the Lord Jesus Christ," and before they had a chance to change the conversation he was dealing with them about their personal relationship to the Lord Jesus Christ.

Those three incidents perhaps give you the best description which could be given of Torrey M. Johnson.

First, last and always he is a soul-winner, from the time he wakes up on Monday morning through the late hours of Sunday night when he either finishes preaching his regular message or spends the hours following his evening service in dealing with souls about the Lord Jesus Christ.

You can't be near Torrey very long without knowing that he practices what he preaches when he says, "Soul winning should be both our vocation and our avocation." He is evangelistic from top to toe and he believes sincerely, deeply and definitely that the one main function of any church should be the clear-cut, persistent and concentrated effort to win souls for the Lord Jesus Christ. He never misses a chance to put the salvation challenge to anyone, no matter how small the group, how large the group, where they might be gathered or where they might not be gathered, what they're doing or what they might be refraining from doing. He believes with all his heart that "Now is the appointed time . . . " and he doesn't wait for the possibility that might open up at a future meeting when he has an opportunity open in front of him at that moment.

To him there is nothing more important than a soul seeking salvation. If you talk to him after a Sunday evening service at the Midwest Bible church he will talk to you just as long as there is no one around whom he can help with their spiritual problems. One Sunday night he stood in front of his church talking to a young evangelistic singer about his future plans when a fellow who had walked out of the church after the service was brought by two of his friends because he wanted to get right with God. Torrey quickly excused himself and as he headed for his study he said, "That's the greatest work in the world," and he pointed at his study and the group entering it for a prayer meeting. Minutes later a young man walked out of that study a born again Christian.

To his office staff he has one standing rule which must never be broken. He must not be interrupted for anything when

97

he is talking to someone about salvation. Those occasions happen very often during the week as unsaved people come in to see him about getting peace of mind and heart. His study always is open to the sinner—and to the saint, too—and he pushes aside everything else in order to talk to them about salvation.

This deep and burning desire for souls is the keynote of Torrey's personality. Until you realize how deep it goes you cannot come to know him with any degree of completeness. One afternoon he finished giving dictation to his secretary, Amy Anderson, and as she opened the door to cross through the church to her own office she found a man sitting in the front pew of the church. He had just one thing in mind—he was miserable about the condition of his soul and he felt that Torrey Johnson, though he never had met him, would be able to help him. Torrey was more than willing. He talked to him and prayed with him for a long time and finally the man yielded. One habit had held him back—drinking—but God took that away that afternoon.

Torrey believes that invitations to sinners to accept Christ should be given at any time the Lord prompts him to do so and he feels that the Lord is ever and always prompting him. Thus it is that following his radio broadcasts on Sunday afternoon he will give a special invitation to the studio audience after they have gone off the air. Thus it is that he'll sometimes give two invitations a night during a Youth for Christ meeting. Thus it is, as mentioned previously, that he will follow up a lengthy two-hour choir drill in the Chicago stadium by giving an invitation for salvation and consecration to the 2,500 men and women in that choir. And thus it is, too, that he will prolong the invitation as long as God tells him to, feeling that perhaps in the heart of someone another verse of yet another song might shake him loose and set him free.

A soul winner—first, last and always.

The second thing you'll run into when you start rummaging around in the recesses of Torrey's personality and life is a deep and vital dependence on the power of prayer for *everything* which he does. It's been said that the Midwest Bible church is the most prayer-saturated church in Chicago, and that might well be true. Even as the church is saturated with prayer, so is its leader and pastor.

He never will make any decision without first talking to God about it. He prays much—much more than even his office associates and closest personal friends realize. Before every service at Midwest, and anyplace else, you'll find him on his knees asking God's blessing on him and on the audience that night. He is vitally conscious of the unsaved people in every service, no matter what type it may be, and he asks God's help in leading him to say the right words to reach their hearts and win them to the Lord Jesus Christ.

Every Tuesday morning he calls in his secretary and the other co-workers in the church for an all-morning prayer meeting and conference. During that time a girl who is a member of the church comes in to answer the phone and meet the requests of anyone who might call in person. Prayer requests for the work are made known by each of those working there; plans and projects are discussed, too, but most important is the prayer meeting part of it. The "batteries are being charged" for the week ahead.

Very often Torrey feels a burden which he cannot bear alone. At those times he will tell his secretary that he doesn't want any phone calls or messages for the next half hour.

"I'm going to pray," he usually says. "I'm burdened and must talk to my Heavenly Father."

Then he'll stop by the office of associate Bob Cook and call to him, "Come on up, Bob, let's pray."

A short while later God has the burden and Torrey is free to once more do His work.

He'll talk over plans with someone for 10 minutes and then hold a prayer meeting asking God's guidance on those plans for the next 15 minutes. Time and time again the secretaries get the inter-office messages from Torrey or Bob, "No calls for the next 15 minutes. We're praying."

You can't be near Torrey very long nor be associated with

him in his work for the Lord without absorbing some of the tremendous vision and energy which he has. His vision sometimes makes his fellow workers gasp! Amy puts it this way, "His faith in Jesus Christ and what He can do through His children is astounding. At times it seems truthfully that 'The Sky is the Limit.'"

He has vision to burn and the needed energy to carry out those visions, and yet, he never goes off half cocked about anything. Youth for Christ is an example. The idea behind that had been growing for years in his mind as he carefully worked out all of the pros and cons. When it reached time for starting it he put everything he had into it. It might have sounded radical and out of the ordinary to most Christians, but to him it was just the culmination of a long series of plannings and ideas.

The Bible tells us, "Where there is no vision, the people perish."

If such be the case, no church or organization which Torrey Johnson ever serves need fear perishing if his vision is used. His ideas for the future are farfetched to some people, but not to him. Some of them include a Christian high school in the Midwest district, a week of meetings in the Chicago stadium (striving to reach 28,000 people every night for one week straight), 1,000 cities and towns in the nation and world holding Youth for Christ meetings on Saturday nights, and others too numerous to mention.

In carrying out those visions he is exceedingly practical. He has said often that 100 people banded together under God can do *anything* they want if they set their hearts on that goal and act accordingly. He also feels that God will do anything for the man who loves Him with all his heart. In carrying out those visions Torrey never will ask anyone to do anything which he · himself would not do. He'll pitch in and paint, dig or lay cement just as the other men in the church or stuff letters or address cards with the office girl next to him.

It's that vision plus the driving energy that is his which gets things done in the many things into which he puts his

100

efforts. Once the ball starts rolling on any project or plan, he puts his every energy into it. He runs things on a high business plane and he has a keen mind for business. He has no tolerance or sympathy for inefficiency or laziness. He is a hard worker himself and he feels that he has a right to expect others to work just as hard as he is working. For a man with as many ideas as he has had and still is having he is extremely considerate and co-operative to all suggestions which come from others. His mind is always wide open for a better way in which to do a thing. He has much in common with that great British soldier, Field Marshal Sir Bernard L. Montgomery. In getting a thing done he will lay out the general plan of attack and then leave it to the men and women with whom he is working to use their own initiative in getting the details carried out in the most efficient way.

Many people have wondered, aloud and otherwise, how he manages to keep going as strongly and as energetically as he does. His personal answer to that is two-fold. First, he feels that he is doing the Lord's work and that He will give to him the strength he needs to carry out each and every task that comes up. Secondly, he has the solid conviction and vision which stands before him in everything he does that he is doing two men's work, his own and that of his deceased brother. Ever since Arling died in 1933 Torrey has felt that he always will have all of the energy and strength he will need to carry out the tasks which might have been handled by both of them, had Arling lived.

Add to that another little bit of his philosophy and you see that he gets things done. That is this: "never do anything yourself that you can get someone else to do for you." Torrey doesn't shunt work which rightfully is his off onto other people, but if he feels those people can do the job as good if not better than he can, he asks them to do it while he goes ahead on another plan.

It is hard to find a man—preacher or otherwise—who is enjoying life more than Torrey Johnson. He has a smile which is contagious and a laugh which lets itself go frequently. His

solid, healthy and much used humor and wit flows over endlessly into the hearts and minds of his listeners and co-workers.
The humor has a peculiar way of working its way into the
hearts of the young people. He bubbles over with it almost
every time he is on the platform and his ability to "make
people feel good and at home" does much to prepare their
hearts for the piercing messages of salvation which later come
from his mouth. He is public exhibit No. 1 of the happy and
joyous Christian and he constantly passes that idea on that
Christians need not be long faced about anything in this world
if their faith is in Jesus Christ and His power is working in
their lives.

He can "dish it out" to people when introducing them but
he can just as easily take it when they turn the humor wheel
toward him. One night he was telling his congregation at Midwest that after the war is over and people start flying all
over that the members will have a harder time holding onto
him than they ever did before.

"Why," he said, "We'll be able to be in London for a
Sunday morning service, in Shanghai for the afternoon and
maybe in the Congo for the evening."

Behind him associate Bob Cook let out an enthusiastic
"Amen!"

"Oh, no," Torrey spun around to say, "you stay back here
and take care of the congregation!"

One time he came home from a meeting in another town and
described his conversation in the railroad car in the following
words: "We were sitting there, talking and minding our own
business so that everyone in the whole car could hear us talk
about the Lord."

He rates highly as a toastmaster. In his pre-college days he
was asked to be toastmaster at a father and son banquet in
the Salem Norwegian Free church in Chicago, his home church.
During the course of the evening it fell to his lot to present the
need for money for a certain project. He did it so effectively
and so well that the men on hand came across with more
than enough. Then to get on the good side of the ladies he

102

promptly took the surplus and gave it to them to buy a new stove! It always has been his strategy to be on the good side of the women in the church.

One night in Orchestra hall he somewhat seriously asked if any of the servicemen standing could give him a hog call. Suddenly from the top "peanut gallery" the sweetest hog call ever heard by Torrey or the 2,500 young people on hand floated down ... and set the crowd roaring.

You've read about his ability as a student and as a Bible scholar. His grades at Wheaton college and at Northern Baptist seminary attest to the fact that he knows his way through a textbook. As a preacher he has more than fulfilled the prediction made when he and his mother had that prayer meeting after he had informed her that he was going into the ministry, that is, that God would loosen his tongue. When he was on the road as an evangelist he talked extremely fast; now he has slowed down and puts thought, weight and power into every word. His messages have a simplicity and a straightforwardness that makes them vitally real to every listener. When asked to speak at the Wheaton college evangelistic meetings in the winter of 1945 he told a reporter for the college paper, the *Wheaton Record*, that "I promise not to be profound." Those meetings, incidentally, were reported to be some of the best held on the Wheaton campus in several years.

Standing in his pulpit he preaches often with his left hand in his side pocket and his right hand and fingers turning the pages of his Bible and being used to emphasize his points. The next moments might find the hands reversed, with his left hand turning the pages of the Book and his right hand doing the emphasizing. Often he will look to the side when he preaches, talking directly to one portion of his audience for perhaps a minute straight. He doesn't sing during the congregational numbers, although on occasion, if needed, he will lead singing and even do a good job of it.

On the platform he is completely at ease. He knows psychology of people and how to reach them, but his main psychology is to reach them with the old-fashioned gospel message which he preaches endlessly to his own people and to anyone else who will listen to him. His messages are sprinkled heavily with Scripture—that message has been left indelibly on more than one out of town visitor who has stopped in at the Midwest Bible church to see what was making that church known even in towns thousands of miles away. The strangers usually find out the reason and go away with a blessing through the Word of God preached in all simplicity and sincerity.

His secretary, Amy Anderson, once brought out another point about Torrey which is another reason why the Lord is using him. She knows from contact with him seven days a week that he lives his Christian testimony every minute of the week. As she pointed out, "I can get a blessing out of every message from him as I know that the messenger is true."

She should know. For several years she worked with the government and enjoyed her work as much as she ever thought she could enjoy anything. When the door suddenly opened for her to serve as church secretary at Midwest she stepped into a new and even more thrilling field of service. Now, she says, "I'm working for one of God's generals and my hours are counting for eternity."

When Torrey is through with his work at the church or finished with his other duties and his athlete's appetite tells him that it's time to eat dinner, he finds his way to an upstairs apartment on Chicago's northwest side to be with the family which God has given him. When he steps inside the door he's another man. Cares and plans of the day are forgotten as he plays with his three children and listens to the "important" things that have happened to them during the day. Most of the time they make a straight line for the davenport. That tried and true piece of furniture then goes into service as a "pier." Torrey lays on his back and represents the diving board. The rug is the water. Then one after another in quick and unending stream the three children jump first from the "pier" to the "diving board" and then into the "water." That process goes on endlessly until they're too tired to keep it up or the dinner bell rings.

On the way to the supper table 10-year old Ruth might show him the pocketbook she "made all herself." Torrey Junior, called Timmy, might drag him into his room to show him the gold fish swimming around in a three-gallon jug of water, or pull him over to his turtles. Or little Arlene, the "sweetheart of them all," will insist on singing a chorus for him.

Torrey's home life is a happy one. His lovely wife has submerged her talents of teaching into the joy of bringing up their three children. On one occasion Timmy became sick and was forced to stay home from school for months. Rather than see him lose his class, Mrs. Johnson lined up his work for him and taught him herself. She had been a schoolteacher before Torrey came along and she brought that training and experience into use once more. When the regular teacher stopped by to test little Timmy she found that not only was he up to his class but that he was many steps ahead of them.

Immediately after dinner, the house becomes quiet for a few minutes. Without fail, Torrey takes a five minute nap right after he finishes eating, and the children realize that there's no playing or noise allowed during that time. Once that "snooze" is over, however, they get together for another time of play before they go to bed. After they're all tucked in Torrey and his wife have a chance to talk things over and outline their plans—immediate and distant—for the future. God has been good to both of them. In many, many ways they are an ideal American couple. They met when young and there wasn't any doubt as to their ultimately being married once Torrey accepted the Lord as his Saviour. They have a good time together, no matter where they are. One night when they were young—at least younger than they are now—they drove their parents frantic when they failed to come home. The two mothers phoned each other to compare notes, and soon the fathers were awakened, too, to see what could be done.

But everything solved itself when they walked in. Their explanation? They had fallen asleep on a swing where they had been sitting and had slept there for hours. This happened while both of them were working at Williams Bay during the summer.

105

Mrs. Johnson now remarks that Torrey often went to sleep in her company that summer after his rigorous days of throwing ice around on his route.

They were married when quite young, but Torrey feels and has told others as much that "the time to get married is when God has brought the right man into the abiding love of the right young lady and He provides the circumstances for their marriage. It may be early, and it may be late. God's time is the best time. It is never God's will for unsaved to marry saved people."

Their life to date has been a struggle to make all ends meet. When Torrey went back to school in 1933 they realized that not too easy financial days were ahead. As the children came the burdens became a little heavier, but God always has provided their every need. The children have been blessings in themselves. Although all three of them carry almost as much energy as their illustrious father they have a hard time tiring him out as they play.

Once the children are in bed and Torrey and his wife have talked over the happenings of the day he as likely as not will spend the remainder of the evening reading or studying. He likes to read and most nights find him reading himself to sleep about 12 or 1 o'clock. When phone calls come at home, as they often do, he likely as not will sit himself down on the floor to carry on the conversation. When that happens, it isn't long before his good wife slips over to him and insists that if he is to sit on the floor he at least can sit on a pillow. So, like all good and obedient husbands, he sits on a pillow for the rest of the conversation!

In all of his work, Torrey carries a spirit of humility and utter dependence on God. One day he received a bitter letter from a friend, raking him over the coals for some matter. His secretary could see that the reading of it hurt him. When he finished reading it he bowed his head for a moment of prayer and then dictated a sweet and gracious letter to the friend, not in one word mentioning the letter received. The gist of the letter exalted the Lord and urged his friend to go on serving the Lord in all his power.

He is 100 per cent for his fellow pastors and discourages wrongful remarks about them. As long as a preacher is true to the Word of God he will get full and complete co-operation from Torrey Johnson. He believes in co-operating fully with any program which is basic and fundamental and whether such programs stem from himself or others makes no difference. He will go along with as much aid and help as he can give.

The love which he shows at all times for his fellow men often comes back to him in double and triple measure. When the Midwest church celebrated its 10th anniversary in 1943 the congregation showed its appreciation to him by giving him $1,200 in war bonds, enough to finance his dreamed-of trip to Palestine after the war. The gift came in 12 different packages during the evening's program as people popped up all over the church by pre-arrangement and said, "Say, I've got something here for the pastor."

Each time that somebody had a $100 war bond on his person and thereupon transferred it to the Torrey Johnson pocketbook.

Wherever he is and whatever he is doing, Torrey does it to the hilt. Before he was saved he did a good job of being a sinner. Since he became a Christian and especially since the Lord took complete control of his life he has done a good job of being a Christian. He is decidedly human and as a human is making decisions which have a far-reaching effect on the lives of an increasing number of people. Through all of the varied interests in his life into which we have sketchily looked in previous pages, we find that over and above all stands one life-consuming drive that makes him what he is today.

That is his desire to win souls to the Lord Jesus Christ. Family, friends and fortune fade into insignificance when he goes out "fishing for men."

CHAPTER NINE

It Could Happen to You

IT WAS John Wesley who said, "Get on fire for God and people will come to watch you burn."

In this year 1945 A.D. Torrey Johnson is on fire for God and people are coming to watch him burn. But even as they watch him "burn" they are finding that as they go away they are carrying with them a bit of the fire which he has in him. Contrary to the natural fire, however, the more of the fire in Torrey Johnson which is passed on to others, the more he seems to have. That is one of God's truest laws when it comes to serving Him. The more you give the more you get. The more you let your light shine for Him the greater it becomes even though people from here, there and everywhere absorb some of that light and take it into their own hearts and minds.

The tremendous challenge which the life of Torrey Johnson presents is two-fold:

First, it opens the way of salvation to the millions of young people who today might be in the same position as he was when he was an unsaved, unhappy and unwilling youth in his teens.

Secondly, it shows, to use his own words, "That God can use even the simplest of vessels to bring a blessing if only He can have complete control of the life and of the living."

In using him as He has, God has been able to keep Torrey humble, and it is because of that humility and dependence on

108

God that he perhaps is being used as much as he is. Full of confidence in everything he attempts, Torrey makes sure beforehand that God is with him and close by him before he ventures into anything new. With his hand in God's, he feels that he can attempt the biggest things in the world because he knows that even should he fail—humanly speaking—it will have been to His honor and glory.

To the unsaved young people of today, Torrey's life and experience present a testimony that there is no lasting happiness in living as an unsaved person. His miserable years in high school and the first few months in college have so stirred him that he wants to do his best to prove to young people in that age classification that "living without Jesus Christ just doesn't work." Because he was unhappy he wants to keep others from going through that same experience.

To the Christian young people his life stands as a challenge of the way in which God can use a man if *everything* is only turned over to Him to use as He sees fit to use.

God has had to deal with him in dramatic ways. On several occasions he has been close to death but God had a purpose in keeping him alive. Once as a small boy he fell under a train. He feels to this day that God helped him to remain completely still and calm until it had passed over. When it had gone by there was not a scratch on his body. In other ways and at other times He has had to put Torrey aside or put him through a severe trial in order to prove his steadiness under fire. Each time Torrey has stood the test and when it was over he was more fitted to serve the Lord better.

At 36 his life stands out to the millions of American young people with one ringing sound. As it is heard the first time and echoed back through various channels it brings this clear-cut and simple message *It could happen to you, too.*

With that challenge resounding every time we care to listen, we leave Torrey Johnson. To his thousands of followers he is just plain "Torrey." Their love for him is deep, because God has made him lovable. We know not what the future may hold for Torrey, as he labors hard until Jesus comes, or he passes on to wait for the trumpet call, but we do know that God will continue to use him in a mighty way as long as he stays close to his one primary rule in his personal code of success.

It reads, "Success? I have only one gospel to preach, and that is the old-fashioned gospel as we find it in the Word of God. As long as God gives me strength I will preach that gospel story with all the energy and strength which He gives to me. Everything I have belongs to Him to use as He sees fit."

He can do the same through you.

The Challenge of the Future for Youth for Christ

This message was given by Torrey M. Johnson in Orchestra Hall, Saturday evening, June 16, 1945, and was broadcast over radio stations WDLM and WMBI, Moody Bible Institute, and WCFL, Blue Network.

AFTER our great Soldier Field Rally on Memorial Day, when more than 65,000 young people and their friends gathered together in that great testimony to the Saving Grace of Jesus Christ, friends in Canada and across America, began to ask, "What's next? What's on the program?"

Tonight I want to answer those questions, and I choose two verses of Scripture in connection with my answer . . . first the words of Jesus, the last words before He left this world and went to heaven. He turned toward twelve young men who had caught the vision, whose hearts had been touched, who had been led to loyalty to Him, to receive Him as their Saviour. He said unto them, "Go ye into all the world and preach the gospel to every creature." The second passage is the word of obedience, as we find it in Acts 8:4, " . . . they that were scattered abroad went everywhere preaching the word."

What about this thing called, "Youth for Christ"? What is the future? What are the plans? What is the job toward which we roll up our sleeves and to which we look forward, and upon bended knee ask God, by the power of the Holy Spirit, to enable us to press on until Victory has come?

We have, it seems to me, young people, a four-fold job, and I want you to get it tonight. The first big job which you and I have is to reach into every city, every town, every village, and every rural community on the North American continent and in the English speaking world with the good news that Jesus Saves!

Young people are ready.

Young people are hungry.

Young people are responsive.

They are sick and tired of all this "boogie-woogie" that has been going on, and all this "jitterbugging"—they want something that is REAL! They want something that challenges the heroic. They want something that demands sacrifice. They want something that appeals to the highest and the holiest. They want something that is worth living for and dying for, if necessary. They have found, as we have found, that the gospel of Jesus Christ is the only thing that is ultimately worth living for and dying by. It is their job and it is my job to pray workers into all of these communities until all of the thirty-six million and more young people in the United States, together with our brothers and sisters across the border in Canada, in Great Britain, Australia, New Zealand, and other English speaking countries, shall have heard the good news that the Lord Jesus Christ is able to save from sin.

The second great job that we have in these days is to promote and encourage great city-wide revival meetings. I believe that God has raised up "Youth for Christ"—a most unique ministry of the Holy Spirit—to bring together churches and people who otherwise couldn't get together. Here we are tonight—Baptists, Presbyterians, Methodists, Congregationalists, Lutherans, Free Church people, folk who belong to independent churches, and folk who gather in assemblies of one kind or another—and we love each other! We feel that there are no differences between us that would bar fellowship and co-operation. Bless your heart, you do not know anything about the person seated next to you, except that he is a nice looking fellow or that she is an attractive looking girl, and that they have lovely voices. Otherwise you do not know a thing about them, but here it is—God has brought us together.

Young people, we must not fail God in this way. We must do all we can in every way we can to bring about, under God, revival in the cities of America. I am trusting God, and I know you are praying—listen, get this tonight—I am hoping that one year from now, in the providence of Almighty God, we will move into the great Chicago Stadium seating 30,000 people,

112

and that we will have a revival, the like of which this city has not known for decades of time.

You have it within your power, under God, to bring about in this city a movement of God by the Holy Spirit—a movement that will shake our city and will move beyond our city to other portions of this land until the thing for which our fathers prayed and about which our mothers cried shall have come and America shall have moved back once again to Almighty God.

A third thing lies before us. It is this: We must lift up our eyes, not only to the hills, but also beyond the hills, and we must see a whole world that needs the gospel of Jesus Christ today. We must not be satisfied with America, Canada, Great Britain, Australia, New Zealand ... we must pray to God that the gospel of Jesus Christ shall penetrate the lands of the Reformation once again.

I know what higher criticism can do. You have heard what infidelity can bring about. Germany today is in disgrace—a nation that has rejected the Word of God and has turned its back upon Jesus Christ and cast aside Martin Luther and the message of the Reformation. They have said, "We have a culture that is *beyond* the culture of the Bible ... We have education that is *beyond* that which Martin Luther taught us." They have thus brought about Dachau and Buchenwald, and the concentration camps of the present day. We don't want any repetition of what is taking place in Germany! If we are going to save our time from a repetition of that same thing, we must go into Germany with the gospel of Jesus Christ.

We may have to *smuggle* the gospel of Jesus Christ into Russia, but in one way or another we are going to get in to the land of Russia with the glorious good news that Jesus saves.

Japan needs Jesus Christ. Oh, I sometimes pity Japan more than Germany. Germany is the story of a land that had the truth but rejected it. Japan is the story of a land that *never* had the truth of the gospel of Jesus Christ. My heart goes out to that nation.

I see you scores of Servicemen in this audience—you have been out over the world. You have seen what Christianity can do, and you have seen the lands which Christianity has never

113

touched. You fellows know more than any other people in the world, that the gospel of Jesus Christ is the thing; it's the only thing; it's the thing that has brought *all* of the blessings of western civilization to us.

In these days that lie ahead, as we penetrate every part of the English world and as we ask God to give us the spirit of co-operation and good-will with churches, schools, and leaders here and there, we must press the battle on the mission field. That leads me to the fourth word that I have tonight.

It is possible in your generation and in my generation, in our time, to reach the last person on earth with the gospel of Jesus Christ. Will we do it? Will you accept the challenge? Are there young men in this audience tonight, who, if I gave the call, would stand to your feet and would say, "Torrey, by the grace of God, my hand is linked with yours. My shoulders rub shoulders with yours. By the grace of God we'll see to it, if it is humanly possible, to bring the gospel of Jesus Christ to the ends of the earth, until the last one shall have heard, everyone shall have had an opportunity, and those souls for whom Jesus died shall have come weeping their way to the foot of the Cross of Calvary."

I do not challenge you to something soft. I do not challenge you to something easy. I do not challenge you to something that has comforts and luxury. I challenge you to something that involves all that you have, but Jesus gave his all for you, when He died on Calvary's Cross.

If you have never trusted Him as your Saviour, will you not do it tonight and then with that, give Him your life and say, "Jesus, Thou art the only one that is fully worthy of my all, and I now surrender all to Thee!"

REACHING YOUTH
for CHRIST

by
TORREY JOHNSON

and
ROBERT COOK

MOODY PRESS
153 INSTITUTE PLACE
CHICAGO, ILLINOIS

PREFACE

It had to be done.

This book was a compulsion—Spirit-impelled.

Here's how it came about:

"Chicagoland Youth for Christ," as you will read in these pages, was launched amid fears and prayers—fears lest we had bitten off more than we could chew, and prayers of desperate longing that the rich blessing of God might be upon the venture.

Then . . . God worked, banishing our fears and answering our prayers so marvelously that the only possible reaction was a consuming desire to give Him all the glory. If only we could tell all the world how wonderfully God had met every need!

Co-incident with the apparent success of this child of faith, there came a flood of inquiries from people who wanted to start a similar ministry in their own towns and cities

"How did you get started?"

"How much does it cost?"

"Must we have a broadcast?"

"How did you get everybody to work with you?"

"Can you come over and help us get started?"

There we were, mired down in a flood of work ourselves, unable to give help to others—help they deserved, and help they needed if their work were to be launched profitably and successfully. If only we had some way of putting out some helpful suggestions to these inquiring folk—if only we could take off a few weeks and travel about helping others to get started! But we couldn't!

Then came Mr. Don Norman, of Moody Press, with a suggestion. How about a book on the "Youth for Christ" movement? Could we, would we, put such a book together?

Humbly we bowed and said, "Thank you, Lord, for hearing our heart's cry. We desire to give Thee all the glory, and to help others along the way of a successful ministry to young people."

And it is with this prayer that this book, "REACHING YOUTH FOR CHRIST," is sent forth.

TORREY JOHNSON
ROBERT COOK

CONTENTS

Illustrations between pages 32 and 33

—5—

INTRODUCTION

OF these last days it was prophesied long ago, "I will pour out of my Spirit upon all flesh: and your sons and your daughters shall prophesy, and your young men shall see visions" (Acts 2:17).

Today is distinctly a day of youth, in the roll of drums and the roar of battle, in the realm of government and the region of business, and especially in the religious light of America. Young people have found Jesus Christ as a sufficient Saviour from the penalty and power of sin, and with vision, enthusiasm and compassion are presenting Him to those who know Him not. Their faith is unbounded, their courage unafraid, their zeal unflagging; and their effectiveness is tremendous. They are crusaders for the Crucified, Risen, and Coming Christ.

REACHING YOUTH FOR CHRIST tells the story.

Dr. V. Raymond Edman,
President of Wheaton College

CHAPTER ONE

HOW THINGS BEGIN

"HELLO! Doug? This is Torrey. Did I get you out of bed?"

"That's O K, Pal. What's on your heart?"

"We just had a prayer meeting and have come to our decision. We are ready to go ahead with 'Youth for Christ' in Chicago and want you to be free to begin to work two weeks from tomorrow, if you feel so led. How do you feel about it?"

"That's swell! You fellows know that I've been praying for something like this to happen for a long time, and I'll be ready—April 28."

After a little further conversation, the telephone receivers clicked on both ends of the line, and Doug Fisher—turning to his wife, Betty—shouted gleefully, " 'Youth for Christ' is going ahead, and I'm to begin two weeks from tomorrow."

That midnight call from Columbus, Ohio to Chicago on the evening of April 13, 1944 was the culmination of many months of prayer and thoughtful consideration as to the possibility of a "Youth for Christ" movement in Chicago. Among those who had been spending much time in prayer concerning this matter were Beverly Shea, formerly of New York City and then on the staff of the Moody Bible Institute; Lacy Hall, formerly with Glenn Wagner and his "Youth for Christ" movement in Washington, D. C.; Robert Cook of LaSalle, Illinois; Douglas Fisher of WMBI; William Erny of the Mid-West Church of the Air; and Torrey Johnson.

God used Beverly Shea. He and Jack Wyrtzen had worked in the same insurance office in New York City for about eight years and had been intimately associated in the work of the Lord throughout all that time. Beverly was with Jack when he started his "Word of Life" Hour and "Youth for Christ" meeting held at Times Square each Saturday night. He shared with Jack, Carlton Booth, and others the prayer and burdens of those early days. He had also been presented at rallies in the various parts of the country with Jack, and spent three months, June 15 to September 15, 1943, in continuous work in the interest of the "Word of Life" Hour.

Beverly had seen "Youth for Christ" in New York City grow from a small gathering into a movement large enough to pack Madison Square Garden with 20,000 people on April 1, 1944, with more than ten thousand turned away. He had seen hundreds won to the saving knowledge of the Lord Jesus Christ and had witnessed the radio development of the "Word of Life" Hour until it spread over more than twenty stations, and around the world by short wave.

When Shea first came to work for the Moody Bible Institute in Chicago, he became burdened for the same kind of youth work in Chicago as that carried on in New York. Often when we would meet or work together in meetings, he would say, "Torrey, there should be a 'Youth for Christ' meeting in Chicago every Saturday night. You're the man to get it started." Repeatedly we brushed him off with the remark that we had all we could do with a growing church, the work of the Mid-West Church of the Air, and other obligations that rested upon us. All the time, however, God kept speaking to our hearts, and we became increasingly burdened and interested. Often in secret prayer we would cry out, "O, God, if you want this work done and if you want us to do it, lead us definitely by Thy Holy Spirit."

God always answers such a prayer if it is presented in humility and in faith. Surely, regarding "Chicagoland Youth for Christ," He looked down with compassion and shaped the course of events so that finally there was no uncertainty in our hearts as to His will.

One day after Beverly Shea had returned from New York in the fall of 1942, he called and said, "There's a fellow who has just enrolled at the Moody Bible Institute, whom I would like you to meet. He has just come from Washington, D. C., where he was associated with Glenn Wagner in his 'Youth for Christ' movement in the nation's capital." Glenn Wagner was a former University of Illinois athlete in the days of "Red" Grange. God has graciously saved him and is mightily using him in Washington, D. C., to win many precious souls for the Lord Jesus Christ.

A few days later we met Lacy Hall. Again the same challenge came—this time it was from Lacy. He said, "Chicago ought to have a 'Youth for Christ' and while I have never met you before, Beverly says that you're the man God would have to get it started. Others have told me the same thing. I know what is going on in Washington and in New York, and I am sure that God would bless a similar effort in Chicago. Why don't you try it?"

We smiled again, shrugged our shoulders, and said, "But we have more than we can handle now. Surely someone else ought to get this thing under way. We will be glad to help in any way that we can."

When God wants you to do a job, however, He is not satisfied to have you pass it off on someone else. God is not looking for your *assistance*. He is looking for your *allegiance*. He wants a complete surrender of your entire will to Him. If He is calling you for a particular job, like Jonah of old, it is not easy to turn Him aside.

Such was God's call concerning "Chicagoland Youth for Christ." He was working, and He was answering prayer. He was using both men and circumstances to bring to pass His purpose. During 1943 we had the opportunity of speaking or participating in meetings for the "Voice of Christian Youth" in Detroit and in the newly begun "Youth for Christ" movement in Indianapolis, Indiana. In

— 11 —

both of these meetings, God blessed and through these meetings, He spoke to our hearts. We knew the job could be done in Chicago and believed that God wanted the job done in Chicago, but we were hesitant to believe that we were chosen of the Lord for such a task as this.

The Spirit kept prompting, however, and dealing: "God wants YOU to get this job started."

"The Voice of Christian Youth" in Detroit is carried on by young men and young women who are occupied during the day with school and secular employment. God has marvelously blessed them throughout the years. In Indianapolis God used a young pastor of the Christian Missionary Alliance Church, Roger Malsbary, to get the work under way there. We preached at one of his opening rallies in June, 1943. It was a hot night, and there were about seven hundred present. After the meeting, on the way home to Chicago, we said, "Malsbary is sunk with a budget of more than six hundred dollars; he will never make the grade in the heat of July and August." But God rebuked our unbelief and during July and August, "Youth for Christ" in Indianapolis went forward increasingly and has flourished ever since.

God seemed to say, "If I can bless and use a young insurance clerk in New York, a former athlete in Washington, a group of young people not especially trained for Christian work in Detroit, and bring a young pastor from a nearby village into Indianapolis, don't you think I am sufficient for Chicago?" It was the old story that all of us know and yet few experience—it was that which the prophet was thinking when he said, "Not by might, nor by power, but by my spirit saith the Lord." It was Paul who said, "Not many mighty—but God hath chosen the foolish things of the world to confound the wise."

During Founder's Week Conference in February 1944, we received a telephone call from Richard Harvey, pastor of the Christian Missionary Alliance Church of St. Louis. He was in Chicago not only for Moody Bible Institute's annual conference, but also to contact speakers for his

"Youth for Christ" in St. Louis—a work which was to begin in March. Harvey called us and asked whether we'd come. We said we would. After having accepted his invitation, we said, "Dick, come over and speak at our prayer meeting on Wednesday, and tell us more about your 'Youth for Christ' movement." He came.

After the prayer meeting, we ate together in the railroad station while waiting for his train. When we had finished, we said, "Tell us now, Dick, all about your plans for St. Louis."

"Well," he replied, "I am sinking everything that I have into it. I have only been in St. Louis for a short while, and I have a very small congregation. If 'Greater St. Louis Youth for Christ' fails, people will lose confidence in me, and I will have to start somewhere else, but I can't get away from this thing. God wants this youth movement for St. Louis. I have laid the whole matter out before Mrs. Harvey; she is with me, and we are putting every cent that we have into the venture. We have rented Kiel Auditorium, the civic auditorium of St. Louis. It has three halls, one seating seven hundred, one four thousand, and the large one seating fifteen thousand, and we will not be satisfied until the largest one is filled."

"What's your budget for this program, Dick?"

"It will cost conservatively about six hundred dollars each week, and everyone participating is donating his services, including myself."

It was about time now for Dick to board the train, and after having bid him "good-bye," as we were returning to our car, we said, "Surely hope he makes it. It's a big load, but he has great faith."

Two months passed by, and from April 12 to 17, the National Association of Evangelicals held their annual conference in Columbus, Ohio. We were there. One day we saw Dick Harvey on the conference floor and inquired, "How is the 'Greater St. Louis Youth for Christ' movement going?"

"Wonderful!" was his reply. "The crowds are running

—13—

well over two thousand and souls are being saved and every need is being met."

"Dick, come over to our hotel room and tell us more about it. We're interested."

He came. We sat down and he explained all the details of God's working in St. Louis. All the time Dick was giving his account, the Spirit of God was saying, "It's working in New York City. God is blessing in Washington. It's going in Detroit. Souls are being saved in Indianapolis. Now Dick Harvey, a comparative stranger to that city, has been blessed of the Lord in St. Louis. Can you not trust God to meet your need in Chicago?" Looking up into His face, we said, "Yes, by the grace of God, we will." That night after prayer, at the midnight hour, a long distance call was put in for Doug Fisher, and "Chicagoland Youth for Christ" was launched.

CHAPTER TWO

LET'S KEEP IT ON A MIRACLE BASIS

O GOD, we want this kept on a miracle basis. We want everyone to know that God's hand is on this movement. We want folks to see that this is too big and too great for any man or group of men to accomplish by themselves. We want folks to say, 'GOD DID IT!' "

When we had finished our season of prayer, Bob Cook repeated, "Let's keep this thing on a miracle basis from beginning to end all the way through." "Amen, Brother!" chimed in the rest of those who had been praying, as they contemplated securing a hall for "Chicagoland Youth for Christ," a radio outlet, the financial support, and the backing of interested young people and business men.

God had seemed to bring the original group of workers together miraculously. He had brought Beverly Shea from New York City to the Moody Bible Institute where his favor and influence had grown by leaps and bounds. He had led Douglas Fisher by a round-about way from Toronto's Canadian Broadcasting Company to Chicago. Doug had for some time been in evangelistic work with Douglas Roe and now was on the staff of WMBI. Lacy Hall came to us by the Holy Spirit all the way from Washington, D. C. Robert Cook, who had been editor of the magazine, "Young People Today" and a youth leader, both in Philadelphia as well as in the Middle West; also Robert Wyatt, Floyd Gephart, and Bill Erny— all these men had been miraculously brought together with Torrey Johnson in the early days of planning and preparation for "Chicagoland Youth for Christ."

Who could say anything else but that this was of the Lord? Surely bringing men from Toronto, New York, Washington, and LaSalle, as well as Chicago, and equipping those men with talents that dove-tailed so well, could have been the work of none but the Holy Spirit.

We say, then, this was a miracle of God.

The prospect of a meeting place for "Chicagoland Youth for Christ," as the work began, was very discouraging. Some wanted a hall that was acoustically perfect in order to produce the best program possible. Others wanted a theatre building where the unsaved would be willing to come. No one even dreamed of the possibility of Orchestra Hall, acoustically the most perfect auditorium in Chicago, centrally located, and a place where both saved and unsaved gather upon different occasions—but God is abundantly greater than both our fears and our faith.

The only other suitable auditorium in down-town Chicago seated but five hundred people, and the theaters of Chicago, with the Republican and Democratic Conventions going on, were not going to close for the summer of 1944. The situation looked very discouraging on Saturday, April 29. The opening date of "Chicagoland Youth for Christ," May 27, was only four weeks away, and there was as yet—no auditorium!

Having to leave the office for some hours in the early afternoon on that never-to-be-forgotten April Saturday, we turned to Einar Christianssen and said, "Einar, there is the telephone. Call up anywhere you can and see what you can find out about an auditorium. We seem to be getting nowhere." After several hours, we returned to the office. There were seated Douglas Fisher, Bob Cook, and Einar Christianssen. They all chimed in together saying, "We've got the place! It's Orchestra Hall—twenty-one weeks for five thousand dollars." We replied, "You fellows are crazy. Orchestra Hall seats three thousand, and we want a place seating about one thousand, and five thousand dollars—who is going to pay for it? We haven't a dime between us!"

At the same time we heard the still small voice of the Holy Spirit saying, "Is anything too hard for the Lord?" We replied, "No, nothing is too hard for Him."

—16—

That same evening we had dinner with "Pop" Cook, Bob's father. During the course of our conversation we said, "Look, Pop, if there were one wealthy man behind this work, there would be nothing to worry about, but five thousand dollars for an auditorium, the cost of a radio broadcast, the advertising, the help, and all the other expenses—who is going to pay them?" Mr. Cook replied, "If you had a millionaire behind you, you would be happy, but you have more than a millionaire, you have God! I think you fellows need to determine first whether God wants this job done, and then whether He wants you to do it. If you feel that God wants the job done and that He wants you to do it, you have nothing to worry about. He will see you through and meet your every need."

The following Monday morning we signed the contract for twenty-one weeks in Orchestra Hall, seating three thousand people. We had wanted a place for one thousand. Would God fill *this place?* He did, and we say that the securing of Orchestra Hall as the place where "Chicagoland Youth for Christ" began was a miracle of God's grace and power, far beyond the faith or plan of any one man or group of men.

Having now personnel and a hall, the next thing that we felt to be needful was a radio broadcast. How to get one—that was the question.

Newspapers and magazines, because of the paper shortage, had to cut down on advertising, and this drove many who would otherwise advertise in print to use the radio. Business everywhere was picking up and more money was being spent on radio advertising than ever before. More than that, many station owners did not want the gospel on the air.

We tried every major station in Chicago and were met with the same answer, "We already have more religion on the air than we want. In the future we expect to cut off some that we now have. There is no place for you." The situation seemed quite hopeless, but we wanted to be "geared to the times and anchored to the Rock." How could we be "geared to the times" without a broadcast? Jack Wyrtzen had one; Roger Malsbary had one; Dick Harvey in St. Louis had one, and we felt that we also needed the lengthened reach that only radio can give.

About this time Beverly Shea was to start his program, "Hymns from the Chapel," over the Blue Network station, WCFL, under the sponsorship of Club Aluminum Corporation—a great business with a consecrated Christian president, Herbert J. Taylor. We felt led of the Holy Spirit to speak to Mr. Taylor about our problem and solicit his help. God again marvelously undertook and, through the gracious co-operation of Mr. Taylor, we were able to secure one half hour on the Voice of Labor Station, WCFL . . . *after* we had already been turned down by that station on six previous occasions! "Chicagoland Youth for Christ" is the only Saturday evening gospel broadcast in Chicago. Again we lifted our hearts and said, "This is of the Lord. This is another miracle from above." God had now undertaken to bring together the personnel, to provide Chicago's finest Loop auditorium, and time on a very valuable network station.

We were ready now to present the work to Christian business men for their consideration and to outstanding youth leaders for their co-operation. Two banquets were held, the first for a group of about fifty business men, and the second for a group of about fifty Chicago young people's leaders. At both these banquets, we outlined to these friends, God's gracious dealings thus far, and how the Holy Spirit seemed to bring together these men for this job at this particular time. We wanted the favor of these influential people, but scarcely knew what their reaction would be. How little we sometimes trust the Lord!

No suggestion of any kind was made regarding financial support or any other obligation that these leaders might assume. We wanted their prayers and their good-will. God gave us that and more. At the close of each banquet, these business men and young people's leaders volunteered their prayerful co-operation, influence and support. In addition they also suggested that they wanted a part immediately underwriting some of the expenses of "Chicagoland Youth for Christ." It was thought that the first twenty-one weeks would cost about fifteen thousand dollars (since that time it has proved to cost even more than that) and these gracious Christian business men and leaders of young people's organizations kindly volunteered to support the work to the extent of more than three thousand dollars.

We could hardly keep back the tears as we thought of how wonderfully the Lord was working. "He which hath begun a good work . . . will perform it," and He who had begun "Chicagoland Youth for Christ" in the preparation of many hearts in different places was now bringing to pass the development of the program, and the time was approaching for the first meeting in Orchestra Hall. The personnel was ready; the hall had been secured; radio time had been contracted for; the backing of business and youth leaders and the good-will of pastors had been solicited.

Now . . . was God going to meet the challenge of filling an auditorium three times as large as we had at first contemplated? That is the story of Chapter Three.

CHAPTER THREE

GREATER THAN OUR FAITH

EVERYONE is alive to the problem of delinquency. There is delinquency among parents. There is delinquency among youth. The fact is that our whole nation has been negligent, disobedient and delinquent for many years. The tragedy is that very few know how to cope with this growing menace. One prominent social worker described the pitiable attempt at meeting the delinquency problem by saying, "There is nothing that we can do about a delinquent until after the case is brought into court."

Every true child of God says and repeats a thousand times over, "There are a multitude of things that can be done before a child is brought into court, and there are a multitude of things which, if done, will keep that child from ever getting into court." Thank God, "the gospel of Christ . . . is the power of God unto salvation to everyone that believeth."

Our hope from the very beginning of "Chicagoland Youth for Christ" was to help meet the challenge of a day of constantly increasing sinfulness. We believed with all our hearts that God was leading in this matter and were leaving no stone unturned, either by advertising, by the arrangement of an attractive musical program, or by the preparation of ushers, personal counselors, and speakers, to present God's very best to Chicago's youth.

Busy days—those four weeks between April 28, 1944, when Doug Fisher began working full time for "Chicagoland Youth for Christ" and Saturday, May 27, when the opening rally was held in Orchestra Hall. During that time the type of program to be followed had to be well thought out and prepared. The advertising material had to be printed and circulated throughout the city; help had to be secured for the usher band, for the personal workers, and for the All Girl Choir; and the entire personnel had to be thoroughly trained for their part in the work.

During those four weeks of final preparation, much prayer was going up, and prayer meetings were permitted to interrupt the work whenever anyone felt so led. The constant cry of every heart unto the Lord was, "O God, our supreme desire is that Thou mightest be glorified to the salvation of many, many precious souls."

Yes, we dared to ask God to give us in twenty-one weeks of the summer season, one thousand souls for Christ. We also cried out unto the Lord, "O, God, if it pleases Thee, fill Orchestra Hall!" Then, too, there was the financial load, and we had laughingly said, "If this thing fails, you friends will have to make pastoral calls on us in jail." The financial responsibility, however, was more than a bit of humor. It was something that would have to be met, and we prayed that God would meet the financial need each week, just as He provided manna for the children of Israel while they journeyed through the wilderness country.

We prayed that, from the beginning to the end, each program might be definitely under the guidance of the Holy Spirit. We prayed that each speaker, each musician, each testimony might present only a God-given message. In the midst of all our prayers we were glad that "the Spirit itself maketh intercession for us" because we found often that "we know not what we should pray for as we ought."

The work of promotion and advertising for "Chicagoland Youth for Christ" was placed in the hands of Robert Cook. His was the task of preparing the publicity so that insofar as our means would allow, everyone would know about "Chicagoland Youth for Christ." Those who appreciate the presentation of the printed page in the best form have said that Bob has "geared his advertising to the times, but has anchored the message to the Rock."

The music, with responsibility for what is called "good

production," was assigned to Douglas Fisher and Beverly Shea. They immediately secured two grand pianos for use with the four-manual concert organ of Orchestra Hall. What a musical team! There would be Douglas Fisher at the console of the organ; LaVerne Christiansen, an accomplished pianist and well acquainted with evangelistic work; and Blanchard Leightner of Radio Station WMBI. Fisher also had the responsibility of organizing the All Girl Choir; and Shea, in addition to his solo work, was given the radio "commercial," introducing and closing the broadcast. Robert Cook assumed the task of leading congregational singing. With this nucleus, and with the added help of scores of talented young people, the musical program "sparked" from the very beginning.

The "mechanics" of a service are important and God gave us the right folk to make the wheels go 'round. Lacy Hall, with a background of experience in "Youth for Christ" at Washington, D. C., organized a band of young ladies to do the work of ushering. Floyd Gephart, with his wide experience of handling personal workers at the Chicago Easter Sunrise Service each year, rallied together an efficient corps of personal workers, whom we call "Counselors." Robert Wyatt took charge of circulating advertising material, and William Erny, with a rich background of business experience as a manufacturer, negotiated the contracts. In addition to these already mentioned, there were also scores of others, both on the committee of recommendation and otherwise, who lent a ready and willing hand during that busy month of preparation preceding the opening rally on Saturday, May 27.

The responsibility commissioned to Torrey Johnson was to organize the various committees into units and to take charge of the rally from week to week. The meetings would be evangelistic throughout. They must be slanted directly toward youth. There must be life in the program, and yet it must be spiritual. There must be spontaneity, yet dignity. There must be liberty, yet the program must be on the highest possible level. Our aim was to present the gospel in as attractive a form as anything presented by the world.

We hoped, as a friend stated after one of the rallies, that young people would say, "The quality of this program is as good as anything the world has to offer." At the same time, we were also praying that there would be *conviction* and as a result, salvation, consecration and revival in all of these meetings.

Throughout the days of that month preceding the opening rally of Chicagoland, doubts often came to our minds, "Orchestra Hall is too large. You wanted a place seating one thousand. Now you have one seating three thousand. It will never be filled. Summer is coming on, and the vacation season is also at hand. You will never make the grade." The die was already cast, however, and so we had to look up continually and say, "O, God, increase our faith! O, God, do more than we ask or even think! O, God, in the name of Christ, we pray for at least one thousand souls to be won this summer season!"

Finally, May 27 arrived. It was the day toward which God had been planning and preparing our hearts. He had called together a group from various parts of America. He had raised up scores of fellow-helpers. He was now about to answer the prayers that had gone up from hundreds of hearts, many of whom we shall never know until we stand in the Presence of Christ. It was the day of our opening rally. Could God, would God, give us a gracious start in "Chicagoland Youth for Christ"? We didn't know. We scarcely dared to hope. We felt something like one of old who said, "Lord, I believe. Help Thou my unbelief."

The last thing that was done before the beginning of the meeting was to hold one further prayer huddle in the West Room of the basement of Orchestra Hall. Once more, those who were most interested, gathered together and cried unto the Lord. Present in that group were a large number of our committee of recommendation and other interested friends.

Finally the big moment came. Who would lead the

way up to the platform of Orchestra Hall? Who would dare to look in and give the rest of us a report as to the crowd? We hoped that the main floor seating one thousand would be filled and that no one would look up into the balconies and see the empty chairs. We do not remember who did go out on the platform first, but we know that before we went, *God was there*.

That evening for the opening rally God sent more than two thousand. Billy Graham, pastor of the Village Church of Western Springs, was the speaker. At the close of the meeting, more than forty hands were lifted, indicating a desire to accept the Lord Jesus Christ as their personal Saviour. When the offering was received, God had sent in enough to take care of the expenses of the following Saturday.

And then, suddenly, the meeting was over. We wept, shouted, and praised the Lord. He had given us an audience twice as large as our original expectation. He had given us more than two score souls for Christ, and expenses for the following week were met. "Chicagoland Youth for Christ" was now on the way with twenty weeks yet in Orchestra Hall. After that, what might our God yet have in store?

CHAPTER FOUR

THE WORK GOES ON

I HOPE we have as many as seven or eight hundred next Saturday. It would be too bad if we should fall very far below that mark on the second week," said Jim.
"What do you mean—seven hundred?"

"Well, after a big opening night with all the publicity and prayer and emphasis put upon it, we are bound to fall back—I hope not so far as to make it too discouraging for the future of the work."

That doubt seemed to be in many minds as we looked forward to the second "Chicagoland Youth for Christ" rally in Orchestra Hall. After all, maybe it wasn't too much in expect, that with all the effort put forth for the opening night and the curiosity of many who might attend once, there should be more than two thousand present. The second and third weeks were felt to bo the acid test as to whether God was in this program or whether it was just a flash to die out as quickly as it arose.

You may be sure that much prayer went up throughout the days of that second week. We cried unto the Lord day by day privately, and in smaller and larger groups as well: "O, God, rebuke our unbelief, rebuke what otherwise might be the ridicule of the enemy, and give to us Thy blessings for the second meeting."

The speaker for the second rally was Dr. Peter Rees Joshua, Pastor of the First Presbyterian Church of Aurora, Illinois, and a Captain in the British Army in World War I. In music the program was well planned, and all was in readiness. After a season of prayer in the basement room of Orchestra Hall, it was time to approach the platform and begin the second meeting.

Once again, fear and anxiety mingled with faith gripped our hearts as we contemplated what the crowd might be. Who was first on the platform, we do not remember. But again we found that *God was there* before any of us arrived. When we lifted our eyes slowly from the main floor to the balcony, our hearts rejoiced to see more than two thousand gathered again for the second evening. At the close of the meeting a large response to the offer of salvation, and once again when the offering was received, there was just sufficient to carry on for the third rally of the following week. God had once more proved Himself faithful.

No sooner was the second meeting over and our thoughts directed toward the third meeting, but the same doubts crept in once again—"The people will get tired of this program. They will not stick to it week after week throughout the summer, and you will find a slump coming one of these times." All we could do was to pray and with our prayers seek the guidance of God. We can testify now that, as we labored and prayed, God continued to work with us and to pour out His blessings.

The attendance throughout the summer in Orchestra Hall has continuously exceeded two thousand, and the rallies have been averaging about twenty-five hundred each week. On numerous occasions Orchestra Hall has been filled and hundreds have been turned away. On the Saturday before Labor Day, every available corner was occupied and one thousand were estimated to have been turned away from the service. In all of these meetings scores of young people have been won to a saving knowledge of the Lord Jesus Christ and hundreds have been encouraged and inspired to go forth and serve Christ as never before.

On one particular Saturday in the middle of the summer two Navajo Indian boys came into the meeting and surrendered completely to Christ. A Japanese girl, who supposed that when she was baptized she became a Christian, saw her need of Christ and accepted Him as her

— 26 —

Saviour; a young sailor and his wife from Kokomo, Indiana, who had been backsliders, were restored to Jesus Christ, and a large company of civilian young fellows and girls, as well as servicemen, gave their hearts to Jesus Christ.

A Sunday school teacher had a class of ten boys, all of whom lived in a home for children of delinquents and unfortunates. Four of these boys had been professing Christians but six were unsaved. As a result of attending "Chicagoland Youth for Christ," on two successive Saturday nights, all ten came out and out for the Lord Jesus Christ, four to be restored and six others to accept Him as their personal Saviour. What a joy to realize that these who have had such a handicap at the start of life should now be given an opportunity to accept the Lord Jesus Christ!

A nurse had been a Christian but one evening, in response to the message, stepped out and yielded herself completely to the Lord Jesus Christ. The result is that in her hospital and among her friends, she has now organized a class for instruction in soul-winning. These young people are going forth and winning others to Him.

"That was the greatest experience of my entire life!" said one of the young lady ushers at the close of a meeting, after she had spoken with an elderly woman and led her to a saving knowledge of the Lord Jesus Christ. Yes, "Chicagoland Youth for Christ" has done a great deal for these girls who usher from week to week. They not only usher but also help in bringing souls to the Cross.

One evening a sailor responded to the invitation at the close of the meeting, and when asked how it was that he came to "Chicagoland Youth for Christ" rally replied, "Someone gave me a tract and told me that this was a good place. Believe me, they didn't tell half the truth. It's more than a good place. It's the best place on earth." That sailor that night met another fellow from the place where he was stationed, and he continued from that time to attend the meetings, together with the Christian friend that he had met in Orchestra Hall. What a joy to work with parents and loved ones of these in the Service, to bring their own to Christ!

On another occasion, a young man came forward to surrender for full time Christian work. After he had been dealt with and had filled out a card, giving us his name and address, so that we might keep in touch with him, we said, "Aren't you the son of an evangelist?"

"Yes," he replied, "I am, and my Dad is here tonight."

In a few minutes father met son—what a joyful meeting that was, as the father in full time Christian work welcomed his boy to the joyful fellowship of service for our Lord Jesus Christ.

One day a call came into the office. "I have to see Torrey Johnson. I am not saved. I have been under conviction since last Saturday, and I can't sleep. I'll go crazy if I am not saved soon." An appointment was made for the girl to see Torrey Johnson, but he was not able to keep the appointment. Without telling those in the office what was on her heart, she went on her way, even more sorrowfully than when she came.

She called again the next day.

"This thing is getting worse and worse. I am *so* under conviction! I have thought I was a Christian, but after last Saturday, I know I am not. I have to be saved."

"Won't you talk with Bob Cook? I know he will be very happy to help you," said the young lady who answered the telephone.

"Yes, I will. I will talk with anyone that can help me."

Over the telephone that day, Robert Cook led the fifteen-year-old girl to a saving knowledge of our Lord and Saviour, Jesus Christ.

These stories could be repeated in dozens of instances. Souls have been saved. Back-sliders have been reclaimed. Christian young people have dedicated their lives for full time Christian work. Others have come out into a clear-cut testimony and separation from the world. Of the fruit of this labor, it is impossible to tell fully. One pastor said,

" 'Youth for Christ' has meant more to my church and young people than anything else I could speak of. Our whole Sunday is transformed because our young people have attended 'Youth for Christ' on Saturday nights."

The encouragement given by "Chicagoland Youth for Christ" together with other Youth for Christ movements have stimulated the development of similar testimonies all over America. Inquiries have come to "Chicagoland Youth for Christ" from Tampa and Miami, Florida; Atlanta, Ga.; Augusta, Ga.; Columbus, Ohio; Toledo, Ohio; LaCrosse, Milwaukee, Kenosha, and Racine, Wisconsin; Rockford, Belvidere, and Chicago Heights, Illinois; Gary, Indiana; Sunnyside, Washington; Los Angeles, California; and even from as far away as Hamilton, Bermuda, where two Chicago sailor lads have started a "Youth for Christ" in the city hall! We can only pray and hope that this may be one channel, under God, of bringing about revival in these days.

The question is often asked, "What about the future of 'Youth for Christ,' both in Chicago and elsewhere?" This is a difficult question to answer. We can only reply, "It seems quite evident that God is in this movement."

If "Youth for Christ" took root in only one or two places, it could be attributed to unusual leadership or to especially providential circumstances. But "Youth for Christ" has taken root all over America, wherever it has been prayerfully and carefully launched. For that reason it seems evident that this movement is of the Lord and as long as He sees fit, it will continue.

In that spirit of faith, "Chicagoland Youth for Christ" presses on, trusting Him for guidance week by week. He who began the work by His Holy Spirit and raised up every provision will lead on so long as it suits His purpose.

The leaders of "Chicagoland Youth for Christ" felt that a fitting climax to the twenty-one weeks in Orchestra Hall would be a Victory Rally. Where could it be held? Where *should* it be held? The largest indoor stadium in America is the Chicago Stadium, seating upwards of twenty thousand people. Here have been held the Republican and Democratic National Conventions of 1944. What a place to have a "Youth for Christ" Victory Rally! What a testimony it might be to the entire nation, whose eyes have been focused upon that building and the candidates there selected to run for President of the United States.

Would the Chicago Stadium be open for that evening? Would those in authority rent it to "Youth for Christ"? The answer to both questions was "YES!" At this writing prayerful planning is being made for this rally in anticipation of a packed auditorium with multiplied thousands listening over the air and hundreds won to a saving knowledge of the Lord Jesus Christ. For the Victory Rally, T. J. Bittikofer has been selected to direct the 2,500 voice Youth Choir, and the Salvation Army is to provide a band, representative of all their corps in the Chicago area. In addition the support and encouragement of hundreds of churches and pastors in Chicago, as well as Bible-loving schools and colleges, have been given.

Growing out of the Chicago Stadium Rally will be the winter work of "Chicagoland Youth for Christ." The center of winter activities will be world-famous Moody Memorial Church, whose founder, D. L. Moody, was mightily used of God in bringing revival during the last half of the nineteenth century. Will God again awaken the spirit of D. L. Moody and move in Chicago, beyond Chicago, and throughout the length and breadth of America, to the salvation of another generation? Let us pray to that end!

The Moody Memorial Church seats four thousand people, and we are trusting that it will be filled every Saturday and that multiplied hundreds will be won to Christ throughout the coming winter. In the Spring—back to Orchestra Hall for the summer to follow and then . . . "the Spirit knoweth where it listeth and thou hearest the sound thereof and canst not tell whence it cometh or whither it goeth . . ."

We purpose to follow the Spirit of God.

CHAPTER FIVE

"BY MY SPIRIT"

THERE is a great deal of difference between a composite scene and a true pictorial. The one is made up of several pictures mounted together and then photographed—always artificial. The other, showing some impressive sweep of nature's handiwork, includes several possible "scenes"—but merges them all into one refreshing, harmonious whole.

Human reporting, because it *is* human, necessarily shares the musty flavor of the composite. But one has the feeling that if we were to view the "Youth for Christ" movement as God sees it, there would emerge the unified beauty of a great, sweeping horizon, on which God is working in several places at the same time.

Actually, the "Youth for Christ" movement has sprung up spontaneously throughout the United States. Times differ, as do methods and personnel structures, but underlying the entire movement is the unmistakable sign of God's handiwork. "Not by might, nor by power, but by my spirit, saith the Lord."

Take the matter of origins, for instance. All of the vigorous youth ministries we see today started with a conviction in the heart of a man—a conviction that God wanted something done.

Jack Wyrtzen, insurance company employee by day, preacher by night, would stand in Times Square on a Saturday night, his heart bleeding for the thousands there —unsaved and unreached. When he prayed for them, there came the conviction that God wanted him to do something about it. Out of that vision in the 1930's grew the great work of today, which has for more than three years weekly packed the Gospel Tabernacle auditorium at 8th Avenue and 44th Street in Times Square, New York City, broadcasting over more than a score of radio stations here and abroad, gospel messages slanted for young people.

Roger Malsbary, college-town preacher just outside of Indianapolis, felt a burden for the hundreds of young people within his reach, and yet unreached by the churches. Earnest prayer, the enlisting of cooperation from interested individuals, and the "Youth for Christ" movement was launched May 27, 1943 at the English Theater in Indianapolis. Interest has remained at a high peak, and God has blessed that venture since its inception. But again, God spoke to a man.

Glenn Wagner, former All-American football star, and now president of the Washington Bible Institute in Washington, D. C., felt a burden for the thousands of service men and the other young folk who throng the streets of our nation's capital. Growing out of this exercise of heart, there came the "Christian Youth and Service Men's Campaign." Saturday night youth rallies were the backbone of the work, with a radio broadcast, a free canteen for service men and women, and a program that would gain and hold the interest of young folk. The work goes on, with two full years of blessing behind them, and a future bright with the promises of the Lord. God found Glenn Wagner, a man who would listen to Him.

It was the same in St. Louis. Richard Harvey, pastor of the Christian and Missionary Alliance Church there, became burdened over the condition of young people in his city. Harvey, now in his thirties, had come to St. Louis to find a city packed with worldly amusements, but with no place where Christian young people could go for fellowship and service. Fervent prayer only served to increase the conviction that God had something for him to do.

A few "feeler" meetings with influential Christians finally resulted in a nucleus of a half-dozen conscientious Christian men, and the movement was on. A constitution

John Huffman, director of Boston "Youth for Christ."

Torrey Johnson, director of "Chicagoland Youth for Christ."

Roger Malsbary, founder-director of Indianapolis "Youth for Christ."

Jack Wyrtzen, dynamic leader of the New York group.

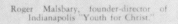

Jack Wyrtzen, director of "Word of Life" Hour and New York "Youth for Christ."

Glenn Wagner, former All-American football star, now directs a thriving youth program in Washington, D. C.

Johnson: "Let's put the punch in it!" Doug Fisher, Rose Arzoomanian, Beverly Shea and Bob Cook seem to be in agreement.

Part of the crowd of five thousand that gathered for Boston's initial "Youth for Christ" rally.

Full house at Orchestra Hall — a weekly miracle of God's grace!

Walter H. Smyth, director of Philadelphia
Youth Center.

Song leader Bob Cook reaches for a
high note on his trombone.

Philadelphia Youth Center with Walter H. Smyth.

Richard Harvey, director of St. Louis "Youth for Christ."

Radio Bible Quiz—a highlight of the St. Louis youth rallies. Richard Harvey in the pulpit.

Servicemen are ushers at Kiel Hall in the St. Louis "Youth for Christ" rallies.

Hatch Memorial Shell on Boston's Esplanade—scene of Boston's first "Youth for Christ" rally.

Carlton Booth, soloist of Jack Wyrtzen's "Word of Life" Hour.

Youth For Christ . . . the American flag. Young Americans are finding that patriotism and the gospel go well together.

Posters, circulars and mailing cards were distributed to pastors
churches and key youth centers.

Ads in leading newspapers carried a "different" kind of appeal
to attract attention.

was drawn, committees on prayer, finance, publicity, etc., were appointed, and on February 26, 1944, there were more than 1,000 persons in the Municipal Auditorium for the first "St. Louis Youth for Christ" rally! God "sought for a man among them" in St. Louis, and He found Dick Harvey.

So it goes throughout the movement. There was Oscar Gillan in Detroit, back in 1938, first founder and director of the "Voice of Christian Youth," succeeded today by the vigorous leadership of Edward Darling, and his competent staff. There was Theodore Elsner, whose Philadelphia Youth Center started eleven years ago with fourteen young people gathered in a back room of his church on a Saturday night. Today Walt Smyth packs in 750 to 1,000 each week with a live-wire program. And in April of '44 there was Torrey Johnson, who said, "Lord, I believe you want me to start this thing. I don't know where the staff or the place or the program or the money are coming from, but I'll trust you for it all." George Wilson, with his staff, has found that thousands in Minneapolis were ready for "Youth for Christ," too.

Even as late as September 9, 1944, "Youth for Christ" started in Boston, with an estimated 5,000 on the esplanade in front of Hatch Memorial Shell. Moving later into Dr. Harold Ockenga's Park Street Church, the meeting filled the auditorium to capacity. John Huffman, director of the movement, announced that hundreds who had come out to hear Carlton Booth and Dr. Howard Ferrin were turned away.

God has been working among young people, wherever He could find a man who would listen!

Methods are strikingly similar. Over all, the list would be something like this:

A co-operative approach
Testimonies from two or three born-again Christians
A radio broadcast in connection with the service
Good music—the best available
A definite gospel invitation.

Innovations growing out of this basic technique depend upon the personality of the leaders. Dick Harvey has a radio quiz for St. Louis boys and girls. Glenn Wagner has a free canteen for service men, set up each Saturday night prior to the meetings. The Detroit "Voice of Christian Youth" features annual boat cruises on Lake St. Clair, banquets, and a Gospel Team ministry. Interesting advertising angle is their Sales Promotion Group, with district managers in the various churches, serving under a regional manager, who in turn reports directly to the promotional chairman. Mailing groups, prayer groups, and personal workers are all handled under volunteer leadership. Philadelphia Youth Center allows two or three service men to call their homes—or sweethearts!—during the rally, telephoning directly from the platform.

The unifying factor of the entire movement, however, is the pull for souls. Every one of these groups is out for the salvation of the thousands who are tagged with the dreadful word, "delinquency." It is the passion for souls that is uniting American youth today. One doubts that there ever will be a highly complex, nationally organized "Youth for Christ." Who knows? One thing we do know, however, when we look at what the Holy Spirit is doing in scores of cities today, that Christian young people are already united in a fresh realization that "now is the accepted time; behold, now is the day of salvation!"

CHAPTER SIX

GETTING STARTED IN YOUR TOWN

THE first, second, and third things to do in getting started are, in order of their importance:

1. Pray. 2. Pray. 3. Pray.

Organization is not the prime factor, as you might suppose. It *is* important, but more well-intentioned schemes have gone adrift upon the rocks of organizational prayerlessness than anywhere else!

We found it so in Chicago. Actually, our progress could have been charted in exact ratio to the intensity of our prayers. We moved well for a time, and all the machinery seemed to be functioning smoothly, when some unforeseen difficulty would show up, threatening the very life of the venture. Then, down on our knees we went, a little band of men who had asked God to keep their work on a miracle basis, and who were being reminded that miracles are God's methods—but that they depend on prayer!

There was prayer in Columbus the night of April 13, 1944, when "Chicagoland Youth for Christ" was born. There was earnest prayer in Chicago later on, when the first meeting of the staff was held. There was beseeching prayer when we were faced with the prospect of having a meeting—and no place to hold it. There was desperate prayer when radio channels all seemed to be blocked. And in all the turnings of everyday corners, prayer seemed to be the only way to get things done. God's expediters were forced to God's expedients—and how glad we are now that it was so!

Granted, then, that God has given you a vision for the work, and that you are definitely committed to a policy of prayer and faith, start working and praying for a staff adequate for the task.

It is a mistake to try to sell the idea to the community until you have something to sell. Organizations and individuals will co-operate more readily if they can see behind your plans and promotion some solid thinking and the presence of a competent staff to head up the work.

You need, for instance, good music. The old cliché, "special music," no longer holds an appeal for today's young people. They still thrill to good gospel melodies and messages, but they want the best.

Oddly, radio has spoiled things for the careless gospel musician; for your young folk can hear, if they wish, worldly music, *perfectly produced,* any hour of the day or night. It is not that they appreciate the gospel less, but that they have found out what good production is, and, brother, they'll hold you to it. Dare to offer them something shoddy, and they'll shun your meeting.

So, look for God's choice of musicians for your program. You need a pianist (or organist) with enough background to accompany well, and enough imagination to improvise upon familiar gospel themes. Nobody temperamental, please! You need a competent song leader who knows God. Bad song leading, or even good song leading with the flesh in it, can kill your meeting. For all your soloists and musical groups, emphasize high quality and spiritual sincerity. And always—rehearse, rehearse, rehearse! If someone wants to put on his number without rehearsal, tell him to take it elsewhere—you don't want it. Set this standard at the very start, and it will save you untold embarrassment later.

You'll need some one who knows publicity. Many good ideas die for lack of proper promotion. "Chicagoland Youth for Christ" was launched at the beginning of summer—what most Christians call the slack season—and in the face of such odds as that, good publicity helped a lot.

Now, find a place where the meeting can be held. It

ought to be a neutral spot, one that will appeal alike to saints and sinners, with equal attraction for members of various denominations. Some "Youth for Christ" movements are housed in large church auditoriums. This is good, but many feel that a large secular hall (like Kiel Hall, Orchestra Hall, or a Civic Auditorium, for instance) is better. Suit yourself, and ask God for His direct guidance in the matter. If God laid the work on your heart, He will tell you where to hold the meeting.

This word about size: Humanly speaking, you should select an auditorium that is just a little smaller than the crowd you anticipate. The world would class this as smart showmanship. Spiritually speaking, you ought to pray thoroughly enough to secure God's guidance, for He alone knows the size of the crowd He will send you. What if "Chicagoland Youth for Christ" had been launched in an auditorium seating only five hundred?

Some one asks: "What about radio? Must we have a broadcast?" The answer to that one would be this: In a youth program, dare we neglect the one thing which (with the possible exception of aviation) more nearly typifies the spirit of young people than anything else? Can you visualize the millions of G. I. Joes and G. I. Janes without including a mental image of their use of radio—both on and off the field of battle? Isn't radio a part of every youngster's environment today? Furthermore, doesn't the world present its best via radio? Then how can you conceive of a Christian youth program that does not include some broadcast in which the young people themselves can take part?

Now you begin to understand the persistence with which we prayed and worked to secure a broadcast for that first Saturday at Orchestra Hall. The radio period helps the people who listen to it—undoubtedly—but it helps the youngsters in the meeting even more, for they feel they are part of something big, and alive, and vital—and so they are!

If you can't get a "live" broadcast (direct from the place

of meeting), make a transcription. If you can't air the transcription that same night, take what time you can get, and pray for a better one. And if you can't get radio time at all, pray and work harder, and . . . God bless you!

Over the long pull, a "Youth for Christ" movement cannot be a one-man or one-church set-up. It must be co-operative and interdenominational, or fail of a truly great and representative ministry. Temporarily, any good promoter can "sell" himself and his program to a large following. But—we repeat it—over the *long* pull, he is dependent upon pastors, churches, city-wide youth organizations, and Christian leaders from all groups.

We faced that problem frankly and prayerfully. After we had sought the Lord's will in the matter, the answer seemed to be, "Ask, and ye shall receive." Ask we did, at two supper meetings in a down-town restaurant. The vision that God had given the founders was shared with groups of business people, and youth leaders. The present set-up was laid before them—Orchestra Hall, radio broadcast, a Spirit-sent personnel, a great heart burden for the lost. Then the blunt question: "What do you think of it? Do you want to help?" In every case, the answer was "Yes."

By "co-operation" we mean active help. Names on a letter-head in connection with the movement are all well and good—and we have them—but it was clearly understood from the beginning that those who were "in" were all the way in—to work! Accordingly, we put them on various jobs that ranged from distribution to personal work, from ushering to the provision of musical numbers from city-wide groups. Of course, everyone was supplied with "ammunition"—promotional literature of all kinds—and it must be said here to their credit that the people whose names appear on our advisory council and committee of recommendation have done a wonderful job. From the very start, and on through preparations for the Victory Rally at Chicago Stadium, we have received the finest kind of co-operation and practical help—this, from upwards of eighty people representing nearly a score of different denominations and twenty-five city-wide groups.

Co-operation involves problems immediately. We listed as many as we could think of, and faced them frankly. "Why not come out in the open with a declaration about some of these matters, instead of trying to dodge them?" we said. The result of this observation was our "Code for Success," a little document that was circulated in the audience during our first rallies, later printed and pasted in the back of our song books.

We faced the question of late hours, and said, "Get home before midnight—earlier teens by eleven."

We considered what a big Saturday night meeting might do to a Sunday school and church.

We realized the danger of criticism concerning proselyting, and we admonished, "Be loyal to your pastor, your church, and your city-wide young people's organization."

We know the tendency of all flesh to avoid work, so we urged, "There is work here for hundreds of consecrated young people. Find a place, and fill it."

Publicity and promotion was a big job in itself. Here is the way things shaped up in those early days:

1. City-wide distribution of hand cards, mailing cards, and posters. We circularized the pastors and churches, and loaded each of our committee members with "ammunition."

2. Adequate newspaper advertising, with pre-rally announcements three weeks before we started. News stories to fit each occasion were given to city and religious editors.

3. Ads in the leading evening newspapers of Chicago, with emphasis on a "different" kind of ad that would both attract attention and say something worth while.

4. Just before each rally, volunteer workers ranged through the Loop of Chicago, armed with tickets,

"Admit Two—Free" and tracts (donated 10,000 a week by one tract house) inviting strangers into the rallies. This procedure has paid out in the salvation of souls in several instances.

After a few weeks, we followed through with a couple of descriptive folders, and another poster, which advertised not only Orchestra Hall, but "plugged" our Victory Rally as well.

For the Victory Rally, through the excellent help of members of the committee, free advertising space on elevated platforms was secured, besides the regular routine of news stories, ads, and printed "pluggers."

It will pay you to spend money on good advertising. Remember, Jesus said, "The children of this world are in their generation wiser than the children of light" (Luke 16:8). Watch the clever advertisers in the world; they don't throw money away, but they are willing to invest heavily in something that will *pay*.

Here, then, is the set-up:

Pray

Get a staff

Find a place

Schedule a broadcast

Secure co-operation from pastors, laymen, city-wide youth groups.

Put people to work

Face problems frankly and fairly

Do a good job of advertising

Incidentally, here are some "don'ts" for those who contemplate trying a "Youth for Christ" in your community:

1. Don't alienate pastors and churches. You need them and they need you. Cultivate their confidence and support. Over the long pull, you succeed or fail in exact proportion as you have the good will of pastors and churches.

2. Don't make a typical adult gospel meeting out of it. Remember that this is YOUTH for Christ, and plan your program with teen age young people in mind.

3. Don't use the language of theology, nor the language of the street, but typical, wholesome, youth expressions. You are not addressing men and women, you're speaking to fellows and girls.

4. Don't let your program lag. Have well-planned variety, directed to a definitely evangelistic and missionary goal.

5. Don't build a Saturday night church. Plan to reach as many *new* people from week to week as possible. Remember, "Youth for Christ" means you have failed until you reach ALL the youth of your community for Him.

6. Don't ever try to put over an unprepared program. Young people can get what the world has to offer—perfectly prepared. If you have less, they'll leave you in a hurry.

7. Don't let your offerings degenerate to the level of a funny story and a specious plea for money. Keep your offerings on a high spiritual level, and God will bless you with sufficient funds.

8. Don't drag out your invitations. Young people are quick to resent the "tear-jerker" appeal, the "be-a-man" kind of challenge, the blunderbuss offer that gets anyone and everyone to the front. They want a straight-forward, hard-hitting gospel invitation—honest and fair.

9. Don't neglect to tell *all* your personnel exactly what is expected of them. Ushers should know where their place is, and what the planned procedure will be; personal workers should be coached in the matter of their approach to seekers, their routine in dealing with souls. Every person who has any part in the program should have a mimeographed copy of the program, timed to the second, so there will be no possible chance for mis-cues.

10. Don't be lax in your timing: start and stop your meeting on time.

A word about speakers: Get the very best available, even

if it involves bringing them from some distance. Make use of what you have in town, visiting evangelists, and such, ONLY if they qualify as young people's speakers. Many a good brother who can give out the Word to people in his certain bracket may go flat in a youth meeting.

Be sure your speaker understands what you are after. His twenty-two minutes are not to be spent in joking around and telling anecdotes, but in a straight-from-the-shoulder gospel message that has some "hooks" in it. Tell him to start preaching as soon as he has been introduced, and to fill every minute with the Word of God, given in power.

Unless you broadcast your entire rally, you may want to follow the two-message technique. This procedure involves a five to seven minute message on the air, and a longer (22-25 min.) message off the air, to wind up the meeting. Ordinarily we do not ask the visiting preacher to speak on the air, because the average person finds it impossible to say anything connected in such a short time—he generally compromises on a greeting and testimony. We must have a genuine gospel message on the air, therefore we have standardized on one speaker for the broadcast (Torrey Johnson almost always handles this work) and the visiting speaker for the closing message.

Much the same comment applies to the invitation. Not everyone knows how to give a gospel invitation—be sure you do before you try! If the leader of your "Youth for Christ" has had outstanding success in giving a gospel appeal, then it would probably be better to let him take the invitation after the main message. A smooth transition from speaker to leader can easily be effected, in prayer, or by some other device.

None of these directions is "sure-fire." You will have to work out your own routine, through prayer and thought and counsel together. Neither the means or methods used in Chicago, St. Louis, or New York, can be absolutely guaranteed to work, say, in Fresno or in Tallahassee. You might not want a meeting *every* Saturday night—alternate weeks might be better. Your budget might be more modest, or more lavish, depending on your local needs.

In any case, this movement is of the Holy Spirit. Take every problem to Him, and secure His infallible guidance. There is no failing, no missing the mark, with God.

CHAPTER SEVEN

RADIO—"THE LENGTHENED REACH"

FROM Orchestra Hall . . . CHICAGOLAND YOUTH FOR CHRIST!"

This "punchy" announcement by Torrey Johnson introduces the half-hour broadcast from Orchestra Hall every Saturday night. During the seconds before we go on the air, the pitch has been given from the organ, the audience has been rehearsed in their part, and now, the moment Johnson has given his announcement, the audience—three thousand strong—joins in singing,

"Christ lifted me, Christ lifted me!
When no one else could help, Christ lifted me."

The familiar theme with the words of "Love Lifted Me" continues through a verse and two choruses, and the broadcast is on its way. Beverly Shea, announcer and soloist extraordinary, gives the "commercial" while the audience is singing our sign-on theme.

The "flavor" of "Chicagoland Youth for Christ" broadcast comes not only from the personality of Master-of-Ceremonies Torrey Johnson, but also from the timing and pacing of the entire period. For instance, no time lag is allowed between numbers. The moment one is finished the next one is announced with very little unnecessary wordage. Emphasis is laid on *more* numbers with *fewer* stanzas, rather than more stanzas and fewer numbers.

Every announcement is "punchy" and has to do with the *significance* of the item to which it applies, as well as the *title*. This puts meaning and force in all that is said.

Highlight of the first part of the broadcast is the section given over to testimonies, where two or three outstanding young Christians are invited to give their personal witness for Christ. These testimonies are limited to forty-five seconds, and must be written out beforehand. This is a wise expedient because of the fact that in forty-five seconds, *ad lib*, the average person gets precisely nowhere. Testimonies written out in full insure accuracy and a minimum of stumbling.

Care is exercised to make these testimonies outstanding in every way. For instance, the testimony of a service man must come from one who has seen some special service or experience; the testimony of a medical man must represent noteworthy medical achievement; and the testimony of some person in ordinary life must represent one whose work as a layman has been characterized by unusual achievement for the Lord Jesus Christ. This precaution takes the testimonies out of the realm of mere talky-talk and insures listener interest.

Another musical number or two follows, then a five to seven-minute message by Director Torrey Johnson. His messages very frequently use some event of the day as a springboard. One of the most successful radio talks that Johnson ever gave, many think, was his message based on the "Red Cross." It starts by citing the experience that eight German Red Cross nurses had when, after their capture by the Allies, they were carted back across No Man's Land in an ambulance and returned to the German lines. Meanwhile, all shell fire ceased and the entire progress of the war waited upon the delivery of these Red Cross nurses safely back to their base. The similarity between the Red Cross and the Cross of the Lord Jesus Christ was graphically and forcefully presented that night. Other messages follow different leads, but every one of them has a true-to-life approach and a tremendous gospel appeal. Very frequently the gospel invitation is extended after one of these radio messages.

Sign-off chorus is the tender refrain of "I Surrender All." Many have said that it leaves the listener with the sustained impression of the pleading of the Holy Spirit.

If there is any secret of success in the radio portion of

"Chicagoland Youth for Christ," it is that every split second of the time is made significant in the light of a ministry to souls. Songs are "blood-gospel" songs, testimonies are strictly salvation testimonies, the message is a salvation message, everything is keyed to a salvation standard, and the appeal is straight-forward and direct.

This word about "commercials": They ought to be written so that the reader of the announcement will find no hissing sibilants or awkward phrasing, and they ought to be commercial in the best sense of the word; that is, that they help to "sell" the broadcast and the ministry to the radio audience.

The following radio messages by Torrey Johnson demonstrate the kind of impact your unseen audience must receive: brief, simple, direct, and always, crystal-clear gospel.

PROBLEMS NOT SOLVED BY SCIENCE
JUNE 3, 1944

One hundred years ago Samuel Morse sent the first message by telegraph. We celebrated the anniversary a few days ago. This was the first message—"WHAT HATH GOD WROUGHT."

I wish it were possible tonight to bring Samuel Morse to Chicago and have him with us on the platform of Orchestra Hall. I would like to have him look at the amplification system we have for this auditorium. I would like to have him speak into this microphone that carries my voice across the hundreds of miles and into the thousands of homes where people are listening tonight.

I wish he might hear the ring of a telephone, pick up the receiver, and hear a message from someone aboard ship at sea, someone in a plane in the air, someone in a submarine under the sea, someone from some other part of the world. I would like him to step down a few doors into the lobby of a hotel and put ten cents into a box. He would see before him marvelous things on the screen. While he looked, and listened and took in all of those things, I would like to ask, "Samuel Morse, what do you think about all that has been wrought in these one hundred years since that day you first sent that message across a few miles of these United States?"

Having presented to him that picture, I would take him across the avenues of Chicago to the courts of our city, to the courts of our county, and even to the Federal Court that is here in Chicago. As he stands there in those court rooms, I would have him listen to the description of the crimes that are being committed every day by teen age young people. I would take him into a divorce court and explain to him how during the month of May there were three divorces for every seven marriages here in the City of Chicago—three out of every seven marriages at the present time going on the rocks! I would take him into the Federal Court, and I would have him listen to the record of crimes and offenses that are being committed against the finest government in all the world.

Having first seen all the marvel of this mechanical age and then having gone into the court room to hear the categories of crime that have been committed, I would ask, "Samuel Morse, what do you think about all of this?" He would come to the same conclusions that every thinking man in our day comes to, and it is this:

While we are living in the most marvelous mechanical age, such as this world never before has known, at the same time we are living in the midst of sin, of trespasses, and of offenses of every kind, never before catalogued in all the ages of human history.

There are still three problems today that are not solved by science. The first is the problem of SIN, the second is the problem of the SOUL, and the third is the problem of ETERNAL DESTINY.

I am glad that I can say that the problem of sin was settled nineteen hundred years ago when Jesus Christ died for sin upon the Cross of Calvary. With outstretched hands, He says tonight, "Him that cometh unto me, I will in no wise cast out." "I am the way, the truth, and the life: no man cometh unto the Father but by me." The second problem is the problem of the soul. I testify to you that all the research and all the good things that science has brought to us can never satisfy the soul of man. But Jesus Christ *can* satisfy the soul, as you heard from the testimonies of these three young friends a few moments ago.

Then I think of the problems that come to us day by day. I am glad that Jesus not only saves, He not only satisfies, but He also solves all the problems that we meet along life's way.

A young woman several weeks ago gave her heart to Jesus Christ. She took her engagement ring from her finger and laid it on the altar of the church and said within her heart, "I cannot marry that man. He is not a Christian. I will not marry him until he puts his trust in Jesus Christ." She wrote him a letter that she had accepted Jesus Christ and also told of her decision about their engagement. He came to the city of Chicago to see what was wrong. He saw her on Saturday. They were up late into the night. The following morning he continued again and throughout the day—he was going to straighten that girl out—but it was to no avail. She had found that Jesus Christ, when she placed her trust in Him, settled the question of sin in her life. She had found that Jesus Christ satisfied her soul as nothing else in all the world. She had found that Jesus Christ could solve all the problems that she met on life's way.

Toward the evening of Sunday, the young man was giving up, more or less, being discouraged and disgusted. The young woman said to him, "Come to the church where I was, listen to the man to whom I listened, and see if he has not something for you." They went into a certain church and there heard a young man preach. At the close of the message that night, her friend lifted his hand and said, "I want to take Jesus Christ into my heart and into my life. If Jesus Christ can take away the sin out of a life of the girl who has been my companion, if Jesus Christ can satisfy the longings of her soul, and if she has found in Him a friend that never fails, I too want Jesus Christ."

Several weeks went by, and there came a letter to the pastor of that church. In the letter was a sum of money, and also a notice that the man and this young woman had been united in marriage as a Christian young man and as a Christian young woman, establishing a Christian home. They also wrote, "We are sending this gift along, and we want you to know that this thing worked for one, and now it has worked for the other. We believe it is going to be good for our home in the days that lie ahead."

I wonder, my friend, in the midst of all the scientific inventions and all of these conveniences that we have today, whether you have settled the sin question. I wonder whether your soul is satisfied. I wonder about all your problems of life. Let me say to you tonight that Jesus Christ is adequate to meet every need for time and for eternity. While this company of friends blend their voices in singing, will you not trust yourself to Jesus Christ and accept Him as your personal Saviour from sin?

"D" DAY—DAY OF DESTINY

JUNE 10, 1944

It was midnight between June 5th and June 6th. The minute hand on Big Ben was making its way around to the midnight hour. That great clock, overlooking the Thames River in London, sounded out one, two, three, four, five, six, seven, eight, nine, ten, eleven and finally the midnight hour.

Out to the south of England, in the stealth of the darkness, there were 4,000 ships moving out to sea. They crossed about one hundred miles at the longest point of the English Channel, wending their way upon the greatest invasion that the world has ever known. Overhead,

as these 4,000 ships pushed their way into the channel
and across the sea, there were 11,000 planes, like an um-
brella. The human eye can see in the skies overhead
at one time about 1,000 planes. Here were 11 times more
planes in the air than any man could see at one time.
The planes dropped their cargo—paratroopers—inland on
the invasion coast. The barges moved upon the beachheads, and out from the barges jumped large groups of
young American, British, and Canadian soldiers, together
with some French, and others of the Allies. They were
moving in on one of the greatest battles, one of the most
important events in all history.

As light dawned on June 6, the word was flashed around
the world that it was "D" Day. It was the day of destiny. It was the day when the destiny of our Western
civilization was hanging in the balance. It was the day
of defeat for our enemies of many months' standing. It
was the day of deliverance for those who had been cap-
tive in the hands of the oppressors in all the lands of
Europe.

It was the day of devotion for young Americans, young
British, young Canadians, and others of our Allies. What
a day that was! We are still thinking now of that day.
We are still praying now for those same young men and
for that same cause.

As I think of "D" Day, the day of destiny, I think of
another "D" day, another day of destiny—when an only
Son slipped out of the portals of His Father's house and
into the darkness of night. Far off from His Father's
home into a little place that is called the world. In that
world, the only begotten Son was born of a virgin in
a manger in the little town of Bethlehem. After thirty
years, having been reared in the town of Nazareth, He
began his public ministry. He ministered for three years,
teaching, preaching, and performing all kinds of miracles,
even to the raising of the dead. When He was thirty-
three years of age, they took Him one morning, as the
light of a new day was breaking, from the garden where

He had been praying, to court for trial. From that court to another court, and then out beyond the gates of what they then called the Holy City, to be crucified upon a tree. That was a "D" Day that far exceeds what took place a few days ago. That was a day of destiny, the greatest of all days of destiny, because on that day Jesus Christ, the only begotten Son of God, died on the Cross of Calvary.

He brought defeat, not only to a temporal enemy, but He brought defeat to the eternal enemy of my soul. He brought defeat to Satan himself. When Jesus died upon the Cross of Calvary and cried, "IT IS FINISHED," He brought deliverance for every last man of Adam's race that was under the oppression of sin, that was shackled by the habits of evil, and under the dominion of the enemy of his soul. From that day to this, throughout nineteen hundred years, young men and young women, older men and older women have been devoted to the cause of Jesus Christ and have gone forth to the ends of the earth to testify to the saving grace, keeping power, and the satisfying power of this same blessed Lord and Saviour, Jesus Christ.

June 6th was the day of destiny for our Western civilization, but back yonder nineteen hundred years ago on a certain day, that has since become known as Good Friday, there was a day of destiny for all the human family. On that day Jesus Christ, God's Son, defeated Satan, brought deliverance for the human family. Around that same Saviour multitudes have followed in devotion, who have tasted to see that the Lord is good.

I am not interested today primarily in Good Friday. I am not interested alone in June 6. I am interested in this tenth day of June 1944, because this day can be the day of decision for many young men and young women. This can be a day when you decide to put your trust in Jesus Christ as your personal Saviour from sin. Scripture says, "As many as received him, to them gave he power to become the sons of God." "The wages of sin is death; but the gift of God is eternal life through Jesus Christ our Lord."

The day of destiny—June 6, 1944. It was a greater day of destiny when Jesus Christ died upon the Cross of Calvary. But may the day of decision, I pray, be today when you, just as you are, will thrown open your heart's door and let Jesus Christ come in and save your precious soul from sin. Do it now, out yonder as you listen and here in this auditorioum. Let Jesus come into your heart.

THINGS YOU CAN COUNT ON

JUNE 17, 1944

It was "D" Day. The word had gone around among the troops of the Allies that the hour had arrived for the invasion of Europe. Out from one of the secret hangars built into the side of a hill in the south of England, a crew wheeled their plane, ready to take off. Someone gave the order, and a group of about twenty paratroopers filed silently into that plane. They were huddled together in a group as the plane crossed those few miles across the channel to the Normandy coast of France. They looked at one another. They looked at their officers. Finally the word came. A door opened and in less time than it takes for me to tell you, those young men filed out into the darkness of that sky, one after another until all were gone. One of them descended into an open place, another near the bank of a stream, another in the edge of the woods, and so on—twenty different places.

Shortly after they had descended, they found their way to one another and then to the place that was their spot to hold while the troops came across in barges and otherwise, to invade the camp of the enemy and bring deliverance to those that were in bondage and in tyranny.

Every one of the paratroopers, every one of those fellows that rushed out from the barges, and the young women that were there to assist the wounded, were counting on certain things in those early days of that invasion. They are still counting on certain things today. One of the things those young men were counting upon was the supply of every need that might arise in the course of the conflict. Another thing that they were counting upon was the co-operation of their officers, and the co-operation of all their buddies, that they might be one unit in facing a common foe. They also were counting upon directions, for one of the things that every one of those soldiers had was a map of the lands and terrain of Normandy, every creek, every road, every bridge, and every gun emplacement, as far as they knew it.

They were also counting upon enemy action. They knew it was not a Sunday school picnic to which they were going. They knew they were going to face the most terrific fire that the enemy could put together in one place at one time. But all those fellows were counting also on the fact that, at the close of those days of invasion, there would come a glorious victory. The people of the continent of Europe, who had been held in bondage, in suppression, and in tyranny, would once again be liberated.

I am telling you all of that this evening hour for this reason: When a young person receives the Lord Jesus Christ as his personal Saviour from sin, and he steps out into life with his new found friend and Saviour, there are certain things he too may count upon.

That young person who receives Christ as his personal Saviour may count upon the supply of every need through faith in Jesus Christ. Paul the Apostle said, "My God shall supply all your need according to his riches in glory by Christ Jesus." Young fellow in uniform in this company tonight, let me tell you without reservation, you will find that Jesus Christ never fails the young man. He never fails the young woman who puts her trust in Him as Saviour and embraces Him as Lord.

Again, just as those who invaded the coast of Normandy were counting upon the co-operation of their officers and buddies, so you can count on the co-operation of the Captain of your Salvation. Paul said, "I can do all things through Christ which strengtheneth me." We sometimes hear in a humorous vein of officers being in the rear lines. I am glad that in this conflict in which we are now engaged, the generals of the United States Army and the leading officers have been out in the front with the men. I tell you tonight that Jesus Christ goes out into the front WITH every man and FOR every man that puts his trust in Jesus Christ as his personal Saviour. You can count on the Captain of your Salvation.

Furthermore, just as those fellows had a map that outlined for them all of the land, so you can find direction for your life in the blessed Holy Spirit who comes to take His abode in your heart. The moment you receive Christ as your Saviour, you will hear a voice behind you saying, "This is the way, walk ye in it."

Just as every one of those young men were counting upon the enemy action, so you can count upon every kind of evil force to work in opposition to you when you put your trust in Jesus Christ as your Saviour. But let me say this: "Greater is he that is in you, than he that is in the world."

Just as the boys out there on the invasion coast are counting on victory, so we have the assurance of victory over sin, over the grave, and over the enemy of our souls, through faith in Jesus Christ our blessed Saviour.

Have you trusted in Christ? One young man said that it was harder for him to open his heart to Jesus Christ than it was for him to crawl across those front lines in the face of enemy gun fire. I know that the hardest thing any man or woman, young fellow or girl ever did was to throw open the heart and let Jesus come in. Young fellow, I challenge you to let Jesus come in as your Saviour. Young woman, I challenge you to throw open the the door of your heart and let Jesus Christ demonstrate just what He can mean in your life.

THE CHRISTIAN: HIS PLATFORM
AND CANDIDATE

JUNE 24, 1944

Chicago this year once again welcomes two great national conventions, the convention of the Republican party which opens on Monday evening of next week, and then in the month of July, Chicago welcomes the Democratic party. They will convene in our great city to select their candidates to run for president, and for vice president. They will establish a platform on which they are to operate and prosecute the plans for which they hope to be successful in the November elections.

I have been thinking during these days about the platform. I have been thinking also about the party candidates. My mind has been thinking again of the plan of campaign.

I am so glad I am a Christian tonight and that the Christian has a platform that is absolutely incomparable. These conventions and these men, as they gather from the forty-eight states of the Union and the various territories, are to develop, submit, and adopt a platform for the four years to come. The platform that I find in this Book which I hold in my hand, God's Holy Word, is a platform not only for time but for all eternity. The platform that these men are to adopt for four years to follow has to do with the temporal and material needs of men. The platform that I find in this Book has to do with the eternal and spiritual needs of men. As I compare the two platforms, each with the other, I find in the Bible so much more than the very best that the political parties of our country or of the world could possibly offer. These platforms deal with the needs and problems of your life. This Book deals with the needs and problems not only for this life, but also for the life that is to come.

I think not only of the platform, but I think also of

the party candidates. I do not know tonight whom the Republicans will select. I am quite confident I know whom the Democrats will select. But be that as it may, no matter whom these men may select to run for president of the United States in the November election, these things are true of both of those men: First, that whoever it may be who runs for president, he is a man of imperfect character. No matter how good a man he may be— "All have sinned, and come short of the glory of God." "There is no difference." Paul said, "I know that in me (that is, in my flesh,) dwelleth no good thing." The second thing about these candidates who will be elected next week end and in the month of July is that they are imperfect in their knowledge. They do not know it all. In fact they know very little about what is going to transpire in the next four years. They know very little what may transpire in the next twelve months. The third thing about these candidates is that they are imperfect in their ability to fulfill the promises that their party may make. They are imperfect in character. They are imperfect in knowledge. They are imperfect in ability.

Now I turn from these candidates who are to run for the high office of president of the United States, and I read of that Man concerning whom all of the twenty-seven books of the New Testament speak and the thirty-nine books of the Old Testament foretell. I find One who is perfect in His character, perfect in His knowledge and perfect in His ability.

I am so glad for that because there are four things that I am especially concerned about. I am concerned about the answer to life's greatest question, and the White House does not have the answer to life's greatest question. Life's greatest question is sin, and Jesus Christ, God's only Son, has the answer to the sin question. "He who knew no sin was made to be sin for us that we might be made the righteousness of God in Him." Jesus Christ is my candidate for time and for eternity. Our lieutenant friend of the U. S. Marines said a few moments ago that he

— 56 —

salutes Jesus Christ. I say with him that I also salute Him, not only salute Him but embrace Him as my Saviour and as my Lord. He is the One in whom I have confidence both for this life and for that which lies beyond.

Again, Jesus Christ has the answer to life's greatest fear—death. No young man in the Army, Navy, or Marines; no young woman in any of the branches of the Service need have any fear of any kind if he or she has Christ in his heart. Jesus Christ takes the fear of death *out* of their hearts and brings the assurance of life eternal to their soul.

Jesus Christ has the answer to life's greatest quest— the quest for life itself. Jesus Christ said, "I am come that they might have life, and that they might have it more abundantly." Jesus Christ is my candidate tonight. God's Word is my platform tonight, and I am voting a straight ticket in that direction.

Again, Jesus Christ has the answer to life's greatest question, "Where are we going from here?" He said, "I go to prepare a place for you. And if I go and prepare a place for you, I will come again, and receive you unto myself; that where I am, there ye may be also."

I do not know tonight whether you are a Republican or a Democrat. I am not so concerned about those things. But I am vitally concerned about your attitude toward you and your personal relationship to Jesus Christ, God's candidate, the one whom God presents as the Saviour from sin, the one who can give you life eternal, if you will trust in Him as your all.

If you have never embraced the Lord Jesus Christ as your Saviour, as you listen to my voice here in the auditorium, and in your homes, will you not throw open the door of your heart and say, "Yes, I have been interested in the political candidate. I have been interested in things of this life, but the things that are eternal are of vital consequence. I will put my trust in Jesus Christ as my personal Saviour."

— 57 —

THE RED CROSS AND THE CROSS
OF CHRIST
JULY 8, 1944

In Galatians 6:14 we read—"But God forbid that I should glory, save in the cross of our Lord Jesus Christ, by whom the world is crucified unto me and I unto the world."

This afternoon there stepped into my study a young woman with her fiance. He was a sergeant in the United States Army. They said, "Let's get it over with in a hurry." The young man looked at me and said, "This uniform is awfully hot. Make it as short as you can." I did exactly what they wanted me to do, but, nevertheless, I packed in a lot of the truth of God's word. Immediately after the ceremony we were talking a little bit about his going back to Camp Shelby, Miss., and their future in these days of the war. Among other things that we talked about was the allotment that would come to his new bride. I said, "I do not know much about allotments. I always turned over all of my check to my wife. I am sure of this, however, that if you go to the Red Cross, they can help you out."

You know the Red Cross is a marvelous institution, not only here in America but among all the nations of the world, in Japan, Germany, and Italy as well as in France, England and the United States. The Red Cross is here to help. Not only does the Red Cross help those who are in difficulty, but I know that many of you have sent and received messages, through this great international organization, from people in other parts of the world.

In addition, there is protection in the Red Cross. Let a Red Cross be painted on the roof of a hospital, school, or some other institution, and by international law and the observation of the international law, that school or hospital is to be protected because of one thing and one thing only—the RED CROSS.

Again, the Red Cross guarantees safety in transit. There

are many people traveling the high seas or the oceans to-day in perfect safety because of the Red Cross flags, because of the Red Cross emblem painted on the roof of the deck and upon the sides of those ships.

This account was interesting to me as I read it in the paper a few days ago. Among those who were captured on the Normandy beachhead were eight Red Cross nurses associated in the German Army. A time was arranged when the firing of American and German guns would cease. An ambulance left the American lines with these eight German Red Cross nurses in it. At the same time from the German lines there left another automobile. They met in no man's land, between the two front lines. There in that place these eight Red Cross nurses were exchanged and moved from the ambulance of the Americans to the German automobile and were whisked back of the German lines in safety. After that the gunfire began once more.

Now, why was it that when thousands of German prisoners were sent across the channel to prisoner camps in Britain and in America, these eight nurses were permitted to go free? Because they were members of the Red Cross.

I have told you these five tremendous truths about the Red Cross tonight for this reason: I find those things true not only in relationship to the Red Cross, but I find those things eternally and spiritually true in the Cross of our Lord and Saviour Jesus Christ. There is protection according to the will of God for those who put their faith and trust in Jesus Christ as their Saviour. It is by the blood of Jesus that we have access into the presence of God with all the messages, petitions, and the burdens of our hearts. There is help through the medium of the Cross of Christ, for we read, "Let us therefore come boldly unto the throne of grace, that we may . . . find place to help in time of need." There is safety from this world for those who have trusted in Jesus Christ. The man who has trusted in Christ is never any longer a prisoner to Satan or to sin for "if the

Son therefore shall make you free, ye shall be free indeed."

I have been a member of the Red Cross for many years, and I have received benefits from many sources. Among all the benefits I have ever received, the greatest of them all is salvation, full and free, through the Cross of my blessed Lord and Saviour Jesus Christ.

My friend, if you have never trusted in the Cross of Christ and in the Christ of the Cross, if you have never received Him as your personal Saviour from sin, I would encourage you and I would challenge you to throw open the door of your heart and let Jesus Christ come in and save your precious soul tonight. "God forbid that I should glory, save in the cross of our Lord Jesus Christ, by whom the world is crucified unto me, and I unto the wórld."

THE ONLY INDISPENSABLE MAN

JULY 22, 1944

In recent years we have been hearing a great deal about the "indispensable man." I propose to speak to you tonight about that man.

A few days ago a doctor recommended that I call on a certain man that had become enslaved to the evil habit of drink. The call was made, and after the call, he responded to the invitation to come to church. At the close of the evening service last Sunday night, that man came forward indicating he would receive Jesus Christ into his heart. He was dealt with afterwards; he was prayed with, and went on his way, we trust, with Christ in his heart and a new power in his life.

That man needed two things especially. The first thing he needed was a power that would liberate him from the enslavement of sin. The second thing he needed at that moment was a cleansing of his heart and life from the guilt of sin. That Sunday evening as he knelt with others and prayed, "God be merciful to me a sinner, and save me now for Jesus' sake," he found that this One who was absolutely indispensable to him did those two things for him. He found that by faith first of all Jesus Christ could cleanse his heart from sin. He found also that the same faith which led him to trust Christ, released for him a power that enabled him to have victory over all sin.

The man, the only man, the man who can truthfully say he is the "Indispensable Man" is Jesus Christ, and He said it in John 14:6—"Jesus saith unto him, I am the way, the truth, and the life: no man cometh unto the Father, but by me." Again in John 10:9 He said, "I am the door: by me if any man enter in, he shall be saved."

Peter found that Jesus Christ was indispensable in his life, for Peter said in Acts 4:12, "Neither is there salvation in any other: for there is none other name under heaven given among men, whereby we must be saved." The great Apostle Paul found that Jesus Christ was the Indispensable Man, for in I Timothy 2:5, Paul said, "For there is one God, and one mediator between God and men, the man Christ Jesus." And for nineteen hundred years men and women that have trusted in Jesus Christ as their personal Saviour from sin have testified to the fact that He is the one pre-eminently indispensable man for any man and any woman, and He is indispensable for these reasons:

First, because He alone can cleanse from the guilt of sin. Second, because He alone can liberate from the power of sin. Third, because He alone can fully satisfy, and fourth, because He alone can give me perfect assurance.

We have been hearing in recent days about the "abundant life." Jesus Christ first pronounced those words when He said, "I am come that they might have life, and that they might have it more abundantly." I tell you tonight that the more abundant life is found not in some political theory or philosophy of government, it is found in Jesus Christ. Here are multiplied hundreds that would stand out and testify to the fact that Jesus Christ was indispensable, because when they tried everything and everyone else, they found that Jesus alone could satisfy.

Again, He is the Indispensable Man because He alone can open Heaven's doors. He didn't say, "I am *a* door." There isn't a Christian way, a Buddhist way, a Unitarian way, a Humanitarian way—there is only one way, and Jesus Christ is that Indispensable way, for He said, "I am *the* door."

I say to you tonight that it is not only a good thing, but it is an absolute necessity to put your trust in the Lord Jesus Christ if you are to be saved for time and for eternity. I know that in this vast audience there are hundreds and thousands who have never bowed the knee and by simple faith received Christ into your heart as your own personal Saviour from sin. You think you need this person or that person; there are voices clamoring for certain ones that are indispensable for a period of time, but . . . they may die one of these days! I'm so glad that the Scripture tells us "he is able also to save them to the uttermost that come unto God by him, seeing *he ever liveth* to make intercession for them."

I have found that Jesus is the indispensable man, and I've found that Jesus satisfied my soul. He liberated me from the enslavement of sin; He pardoned me from the guilt of my sin; He cleansed my heart; and He gave me the assurance that when I shove off from here, I'm going where the gates swing outward never, where there's a welcome for all who come.

If you have never yielded to Christ, may I encourage you to throw open the door of your heart and say, "Jesus, I've tried others, now I'm willing to take Thee as my personal Saviour from sin. . . . God's Indispensable Man."

CHAPTER EIGHT

MESSAGES GOD USED IN WINNING SOULS AT ORCHESTRA HALL

FROM the outset, it was plain that the meetings at Orchestra Hall demanded a certain type of message. It must be slanted for young people, to gain and hold inter; est; clear gospel and helpful Christian life truth must be packed into those brief 22 minutes; and, above all, the messages must lead naturally into a definite invitation to receive Christ.

The messages in this chapter are representative of the kind that "got results."

FOUR LOOKS AT CHRIST

*Message delivered by Wendell P. Loveless, Director,
Radio Department, the Moody Bible Institute, Chicago,
June 10, 1944*

Recently, while reading some excerpts from a very old book, I found the words of a distinguished theologian of another day. They were his expression of that which he conceived to be the message of the gospel of the grace of God.

The words are these:

"Christ, absolutely necessary,
Christ, instantly accessible,
Christ, exclusively sufficient,
Christ, perennially satisfying."

As one meditates upon those words, he feels that they

epitomize the very heart of the good news concerning
eternal salvation in Christ.

The Scriptures tell us of at least four views of Christ
which are possible to the eye of faith, which parallel these
four statements by our old theologian concerning Him.

The true believer, through the eye of faith, sees the Lord
Jesus

On the cross,
In the glory,
Indwelling the Christian,
Coming again.

First we look at Christ *on the cross*.

Here, the view reveals "Christ, absolutely necessary."
Paul the Apostle, in Romans 3:10, declares, "There is none
righteous, no, not one," and Romans 3:23, ". . . for there
is no difference: for all have sinned, and come short of
the glory of God."

God Himself has met the eternal need of sinful man.
God has demanded perfect righteousness from man.
Man cannot give God any righteousness acceptable unto
Him. What is God's remedy? The Cross of our Lord
Jesus Christ, the shed blood of God the Son.

Listen to the words of II Corinthians 5:21, "For he
(God) hath made him (Christ) to be sin for us, who
knew no sin; that *we might be made the righteousness
of God in him.*"

God has required *of* man perfect righteousness. God
has supplied *to* man perfect righteousness. That perfect
righteousness is not merely an attitude; it is a Person—
the person of our Lord Jesus Christ.

An old Puritan gave a definition of the righteousness
of God which was something as follows: "The righteousness of God is that righteousness which the righteousness
of God requires him to require." Such is the person of
our blessed Lord.

Without this look at Christ on the cross, we can have
no eternal life, no eternal salvation, no forgiveness of sins.
But when we "look to the Lamb of God," we have, in

Him, all that we need for time and for eternity. "The wages of sin is death; but the gift of God is eternal life through Jesus Christ our Lord" (Rom. 6:23).

I wonder if things are as *personal* to us as they should be. Suppose you should come to me today and say, "I see by the papers that a man died today in Chicago." I probably would reply, "Yes, people are dying right along in every city all over the world." "But this man was a very wealthy man," you might say. "Yes," might be my rejoinder, "rich people die, just the same as poor people." "Oh, but this man left over a million dollars!" "Yes, if he left *anything,* I am sure he left it all," I would say, not exhibiting any great interest. "But, wait a minute," you might remark, "he left it all to *you.*" "Oh, well, that's different!" Now there is genuine interest, because it has become *personal.*

Christ died for *all,* but he died for *each.* God loves *all,* but He loves *each.* Salvation is offered to *all,* but it is offered to *each.* All who *will* may be saved; *you* may be saved. God's offer of grace is to *all;* it is personal to *you.*

Christ on the cross; "Christ, absolutely necessary." But, thank God, our blessed Lord did not remain on the cross, or in the tomb. The crucifix is not the true symbol of our faith.

And so the eye of faith, in the second place, looks at Christ, risen and *in the glory.* This view reveals *"Christ, instantly accessible."*

Having seen the Lord Jesus, dying *for* us and *as* us on the cross, bearing "our sins in his own body on the tree" (I Pet. 2:24), we need to see Him risen again out from among the dead, exalted to His present position at the right hand of the Father.

Paul, writing to his son in the faith, Timothy, (II Tim. 2:8) exhorts him to "remember that Jesus Christ was raised from the dead." He is alive; He is the man in the Glory; He is not some disembodied spirit; but He is the Glorified Man.

We must remember that no statement of "the gospel

of the grace of God" is complete without the declaration of the resurrection of our Lord.

A man stood in an art gallery, before a striking picture of Christ on the cross. As he gazes upon that solemn and significant scene, he was conscious of a little form standing at his side. He turned and saw a ragged urchin, whom he asked, "Do you know who that is?" "Sure," replied the boy, "don't *you* know?" "Who is it?" asked the man. "Why, that's Jesus." "What's He doing there?" "They killed Him, and He died for our sins." "Where did you learn that, sonny?" "At the Mission Sunday school." The man moved along the gallery arcade, but had not gone far before he heard the patter of little feet, and felt a tug at his coat. He turned and saw his little friend of a moment before. "Hey, Mister." "Yes?" "He came alive again." The little fellow remembered that which we so often forget, that the gospel is not complete without the resurrection.

Christ is at the right hand of the Father, our *High Priest,* to pray for us—One who can "be touched with the feeling of our infirmities" (Heb. 4:15). He is there, and "ever liveth to make intercession for them" (Heb. 7:25). He is there to be our *Advocate,* when we sin (I John 2:1, 2). He is there our *representative* with the Father. He is the "Firstfruits" of a multitude who shall one day be with Him and like Him in the Glory.

Because He lives, we may come boldly unto the throne of grace, into the very presence of the Father. to make our requests known. We are accepted in Christ. The Father hears us and receives us because now He sees us in His beloved Son.

We need no earthly, human priest, to intercede for us, for every true believer, however humble, has immediate, welcome access, through Christ, into the very presence of God.

'Tis not for *works* which I have wrought,
'Tis not for *gifts* which I have brought,
Nor yet for *blessings* which I sought,
  That I have been "accepted."

'Tis not for *tears* which I have shed,
'Tis not for prayers that I have said,
Nor yet for slavish fear or dread,
    That I have been "accepted."

'Tis not for *truth* which I believed,
'Tis not for *grace* which I received,
Nor yet for *thankful words* I breathed,
    That I have been "accepted."

'Tis not for *sorrows* which have grown
From *evils* which were all mine own,
Nor yet for *pleading* at the Throne,
    That I have been "accepted."

From these I turn my eyes to Him
Who bore my judgment due to sin,
And by His blood I enter in,
    And share in His acceptance.

Christ in the Glory; Christ, instantly accessible.

In the third place, the eye of faith looks at Christ *dwelling within the believer*. This view reveals Christ, exclusively sufficient.

The words of Galatians 2:20 come to mind, "I am crucified with Christ; nevertheless I live! yet not I, but *Christ liveth in me*: and the life which I now live in the flesh I live by the faith of the Son of God, who loved me, and gave himself for me."

The risen, glorified Christ, in the person of the Holy Spirit, has taken up His abode, His abiding place, in the body of every true child of God. He used seven wonderful words in John 14:20, "Ye in me, and I in you."

I Corinthians 6:19, "Know ye not that your body is the temple of the Holy Ghost which is in you, which ye have of God, and ye are not you own?"

As God the Father came to earth in the Person of the Son, so Christ the Son dwells within us in the Person of the Holy Spirit. Christ lives within us to strengthen, enable, and use us: *He does not ask us to imitate Him,* but to *yield* ourselves to Him, and our members as instruments of righteousness unto Him. He will use us. He does not ask us to use Him.

A Christian leader used to express it thus: "Supposing

— 67 —

I woke up in the morning and found the blessed Lord standing by my bedside, and He would say to me, 'My child, were you satisfied with your life yesterday?'"

"No, Lord, I was not."

"Rather bad, wasn't it?"

"Yes, very bad, Lord."

"What were you trying to do yesterday, my child?"

"Well, Lord, I was trying to imitate you."

"Well, now, suppose we try another way. I can enter into you; suppose you just yield your members now to Me as instruments of righteousness. That is all I ask of you—yield your thoughts, your whole nature to Me. Yield your passions to Me; yield to Me your entire being. I will enter in and take possession, and we'll try it that way for a day. Stop trying. Stop fighting. Let Me do the trying—everything."

Everyone of us would gladly welcome the Lord thus, wouldn't we? Ah, but He *is* within us. And when the eye of faith sees Him thus, it means victory in every department of our lives.

Christ indwelling the believer; Christ, exclusively sufficient.

Finally, the eye of faith looks at *Christ coming again*. This view reveals *Christ, perennially satisfying*. This view of Christ is called, in Scripture, "that blessed hope" (Titus 2:13).

The Lord Jesus Christ is coming again, personally, visibly, just as He came the first time, personally and visibly. He is coming *for* His own people first, and then *with* His own to rule and reign over the earth.

One of these days, we shall hear the "shout . . . the voice of the archangel, and . . . the trump of God: and the dead in Christ shall rise first: Then we which are alive and remain shall be caught up together with them in the clouds, to meet the Lord in the air: and so shall we ever be with the Lord" (I Thess. 4:16, 17).

The Psalmist said, "As for me, I will behold thy face

in righteousness: I shall be satisfied, when I awake, with thy likeness" (Psalm 17:15).

Christ coming again; Christ, perennially satisfying.
The things of earth do not satisfy. They are exceedingly uncertain these days. But the Christian has a glorious and satisfying prospect. His future is as glorious and as sure as is the future of Christ!

> Lord Jesus, I have found in Thee
> Abundant *life;*
> Life that as a river floweth,
> Life that deeper, fuller groweth
> 'Mid earth's strife.
>
> Lord Jesus, I have found in Thee
> Eternal *peace;*
> Peace which passeth understanding,
> Peace which day by day expanding,
> Shall not cease.
>
> Lord Jesus, I have found in Thee
> Exceeding *joy;*
> In Thy presence joy forever,
> Joy which even Satan never
> Can destroy.
>
> Lord Jesus, I have found in Thee
> The *love* of God;
> Perfect love that never faileth,
> Love which evermore availeth
> By Thy blood.

"YE MUST BE BORN AGAIN"

Message delivered by Dr. Archer Anderson,
Pastor, First Presbyterian Church, Duluth, Minn.,
Saturday, July 29, 1944

I would like to ask you some questions tonight and have you think about them. They are based on an experience recorded in the second and third chapters of the Gospel of John. Do you think it is possible for a young person actually to come to the place where he makes a profession of faith in Jesus Christ and still not be saved? I wonder whether it would be possible for someone to come into the presence of the Son of God, to hold His hand, to sit beside Him, to walk with Him, be in His school for three years and still not be saved? I wonder whether it would be possible for someone to preach in the name of Christ, yes, more than that, to be one of the group sent out to cast out demons—to have so much power that even the demons were subject to him in the name of Christ. Could a person be like that and still not be saved? My Bible tells me that he can! His name was Judas.

In the second chapter of John we read about a number of people who *said* that they were disciples of Jesus Christ. When our Lord was in Jerusalem at the Passover on the feast day, many believed in His name when they saw the miracles that Jesus did, but Jesus did not trust Himself to them. Why not? Didn't they *say* they believed in His name? Didn't they bear testimony to the fact that the miracles that Jesus was performing proved to them that He was the Messiah, the one that they looked for and expected and wanted to follow? Yes, just like a lot of folk today. You know, a lot of folk who talk about heaven aren't going there. But Jesus didn't trust these people. Why not? You read it yourself in the twenty-fourth and twenty-fifth verse: "But Jesus did not commit himself unto them, because he knew all men, And needed not that any should testify of man (here it is); for he knew what was in man." That's a tremendous statement.

In the early ministry of our Lord He turned the water into wine; He did other miracles and the great throngs rose up to follow Jesus, or so they said. Why? They wanted an easy life. They didn't want to be turned from sin but from work. This man could feed five thousand people—all they had to do was to sit down and eat the food as it was put before them. This man could heal anybody who was sick—they didn't have to worry about doctor's bills. This man could quiet the water—if there was a storm on the lake, they could go fishing and not be afraid. I would like to follow a man like that, wouldn't you? They didn't want salvation. They wanted a good time! They wanted a Saviour who could be cut down to their pattern. Just like an x-ray can see through your body, so the eyes of Jesus Christ can see through your heart as He saw through theirs. He didn't trust them—I wonder if He trusts you?

Is it possible to have your name on the rolls of the church and not be saved? Is it possible to be an officer in the church and not be saved? We had something that was like an earthquake in Duluth a couple of years ago in the Presbyterian Church. After a simple gospel message, I gave an invitation and to the utter consternation of all present, one of the elders came down the aisle to be saved.

Now that was not a modernistic church. It had its seventy-fifth birthday and never yet has it tolerated any man in the pulpit who doesn't preach the whole Word of God. I met with the elder in the inquiry room and said, "What are you doing here?"

I'll never forget his answer. He said, "Doc, you keep talking about being born again and I don't know what you're talking about."

He suddenly understood what had been the matter with him all the time, but it isn't the matter any more because he met Jesus Christ.

That brings us to this third chapter of John. I would like to have you get the picture because it is of tremendous importance. A lot of people saw His miracles and maybe some of them said, "Master, I'll follow you wherever you go . . . just so you'll feed me." That was in their hearts. But Jesus didn't trust them. He didn't reveal Himself to them because they weren't saved.

But there was one man, a man of the Pharisees, named Nicodemus. That man came to Jesus by night, just as you and I would do. He stepped over to where Christ was, greeted him with a very nice salutation, and paid Him high honors. I suppose he curtsied a wee bit and said, "Rabbi . . ." That was a tribute, for he was a graduate of many seminaries in Israel, and Jesus was just the adopted son of a carpenter. But this great religious leader said,

"Rabbi, we know that thou art a teacher come from God: for no man can do these miracles that thou doest, except God be with him."

The Lord Jesus turned and said, "Nicodemus, you just don't know me. You, Nicodemus, must be born again."

Let's jump across the centuries from Nicodemus. I wonder what would happen if you were to meet the Lord Jesus face to face as Nicodemus did? You would step up and say, "Good evening, Lord. I'm so happy I can meet you tonight. Lord, I have memorized 172 verses from the Bible, and I can say them all without any mistake. Yes, I can even give the references."

And Jesus would say, "You've got to be born again!"

Maybe you would meet Him and say, "Good evening, Lord. My dad is a deacon in the great Baptist Church." He would look at you and say, "Is that so? You've got to be born again."

That reminds me of a young lady at our church in Duluth. She and her boy friend were at a young people's conference, and as I was making the rounds I noticed that there was somebody in a car so I walked around carefully. I didn't want to surprise them too suddenly, and the car door pushed open and out came Bill. He said, "I knew this was one way to get to see you. Audrey wants to talk to you. Good night, Doc. I'm leaving." And away he went.

I stood by the door looking at Audrey and said, "What's the matter with you anyway?" I noticed that she didn't seem to be very happy, and she said, "Doc, you know I think I'm going to Hell and I can't believe it."

"What do you mean, you can't believe it?" I asked.

"Why," she said, "my father is an elder in the First Presbyterian Church."

"Yes," I said, "and his daughter, just like her daddy, is nothing but a sinner that needs to be saved. Girl, you need to be born again"—and she was!

You must be born again—that's what Christ would say to you tonight, everyone of you. He would cut right through all the superficial profession of faith that you and I have made. He wouldn't be satisfied with words from your lips. He would look right straight into your heart, and He would find one of two things. He would either find Himself, or He would find sin. He would say, "Young person, you need to be born again." Nicodemus did the natural thing. He was non-plussed; you would be too. He had an experience that took him down.

Some years ago I went as a missionary to Guatemala. I was full of life and anxious to go to work and said, "I wish I could speak Spanish." One of the co-workers said, "Thank God, you can't."

"What do you mean?"

"You'd be like a bull in a china shop if you could. You better get alone and study," he said.

What a rebuke that was. It would be like that if you met Jesus tonight. You would come up like Nicodemus and say, "We know you are a divine teacher. They taught me that you are the Son of God. Lord, they even taught me that you died on the cross and rose again. I can repeat the Apostle's creed in its entirety."

The Lord would say, "Stop, you have to be born again."

Nicodemus said, "HOW can I be born again? Can I become a babe again?" I'll tell you something. It wouldn't do me any good if I could. I would still be "just me," and "just me" is not good enough to go to Heaven, and neither is "just you," because "That which is born of the flesh is flesh; and that which is born of the Spirit is spirit." You must be born of God. But you say, "Didn't God make me?" Sure He did, but that doesn't mean you're His child.

Before going to Guatemala I happened to use a verse of scripture in a sermon taken from the Lord Jesus Christ when He said, "Ye are of your father the devil." After the service a couple of men came to me with doubled fists and were going to take me apart. I couldn't understand what it was all about. I said, "Why are you so angry?"

—73—

They said, "You told us that we are the children of the devil."

I said, "No, I didn't."

"You did so."

Again I said, "I did not.'

They said, "You said it and we heard you, and we are not the children of the devil."

"I didn't say that," I said. "That was Jesus Christ who said it. If you want to fight, fight with Him, don't fight with me."

I can still see that one fellow as he said, "So you think we are children of the devil. Let me ask you something. Who made us? Did the devil or God?"

I said, "You don't look much like it, but God made you." They didn't particularly like that, but I thought they had it coming.

He looked up and said, "That proves it. You yourself said God made us. Then we are the children of God."

I pointed to a bench and said, "Who made that?" They looked surprised and said, "We don't know." I said, "Sure you do." One said, "I suppose the carpenter did." I said, "That's right. That makes the bench the daughter of the carpenter, doesn't it?" They thought there was something wrong with me and they said so. I said, "No, I just followed your reasoning. Why isn't the bench the daughter of the carpenter?" The answer was, "Because the bench doesn't have the life of the carpenter in it." So I said, "You are the creation of God, but you are not the sons of God for exactly the same reason the bench is not the daughter of the carpenter—you do not have the life of God until you are born again." But how can you be born again? By simply accepting the gospel as given in that great text, John 3:16, that Christ was to become the sacrifice for us, that He would perform the greatest miracle of all history, that God could take your sins from you and nail them on His Son and let His Son on Calvary bear your sins and satisfy God's holiness and open the way for you to be born again—that's the greatest miracle of all time.

Have you ever had anybody offer to die for you? I did when I was in Guatemala. I sent a telegram one day to another member of the mission, and purposely made it ambiguous. One of the missionaries had done something she shouldn't have, and it looked like she might have to go home. However, I didn't know that there was a revolution to come off on the very day I specified in the telegram, in a place called Santa Anna. When I sent the telegram, the three key words of the revolution, unknown to me, were in the telegram. The telegram went not to the missionary, but to the president, and he sent out orders immediately to arrest Archer Anderson. They have a very convenient way of holding a trial there. They take the prisoner and shoot him first. Then, if they find that he wasn't guilty, they apologize to his family.

I didn't know anything about this until some time later when a man named Santiago was talking to me as we sat in my car. He said, "I'm sorry, but I have to ask you a personal question. What did you mean by your telegram?" I asked, "What do you know about it?"

Then he told me the story. He said, "Your telegram went to the president, and he sent it to the General. The General instead of arresting you, sent for me. He said, 'Look, there is a revolution in Santa Anna on Monday. This man sends a telegram mentioning Santa Anna and Monday. What is the meaning of all this?'"

Santiago said, "I took my hat off, stood up, and said, 'General, I'm his hostage.'"

He said, "Santiago, don't be a fool. Don't you know what will happen?"

"I certainly do, but I'm his hostage." He was standing instead of Anderson in the place of judgment.

The general said, "But Santiago, it might cost your life."

"That's all right, I'm willing."

"Why should you be willing?' the general asked.

"Because he led one of my children to Christ."

The general said, "If you are willing to trust him that

—75—

much, I'll trust him too. But you find out what that telegram was about."

He looked at me and said, "What are you crying about?"

I said, "That's the first time I had anybody offer to die for me." It got down under my skin because nobody ever did that for me before.

He said, "Shame on you, somebody certainly did."

I said, "Who do you mean?"

He looked at me and said, "I mean the Lord Jesus Christ. He didn't *offer* to die; He did it!"

Why was the Lord Jesus willing to die? Just because He loved me and because He loved you. Friends, I don't care how orthodox you may be in your theology. I don't care who your father or mother or grandmother or grandfather may be, nor who you are. The Word of God says, "You must be born again." How? Through the death of Jesus Christ, by a simple act of faith as you receive Him as your Lord and Saviour. I'll illustrate it to you:

Out in Colorado Springs a couple of years ago, there was a freckle-faced elevator boy. He was one swell kid, but he wasn't saved. There was another one who was, and one day he said to me, "I wish you would talk to. my friend. I've been trying to lead him to the Lord."

One day when I met him, I said, "Tell me something. Are you saved?"

He said, "I don't know."

I said, "You're not."

"What do you mean?"

I said, "If you were, you'd know. If somebody stepped up to me and asked me if I was an American and I said, 'I don't know,' they would take me to jail or to the cuckoo house. Fella, if you don't know whether or not you're saved, then you're not."

"You know," he said, "it has never quite clicked with me. I don't quite get it."

I said, "Do you believe that Jesus Christ died?"

"I've been taught that."

I asked, "Did you ever receive Christ?"

— 76 —

He answered, "That's just what I don't understand. How do you do that?"

I said, "Let me ask you something. Would you like to have a quarter?"

"Sure."

I said, "What do you have to do to get it?"

"I don't know."

"Well, if that's the case, I'll tell you," I said. "I'll give it to you as a gift. Now what?"

"I suppose I take it," he said.

He took the quarter, and I said, "Whose is it now?"

"It's mine unless you're a liar."

I said, "That's right. That's absolutely right. Now I want to show you something. I gave you a quarter and you took it and it's yours now. God gave you Jesus Christ, salvation, and everlasting life. To get the quarter you took it from my hand. To get Jesus Christ, you take it just like you did the quarter, but from the hand of God. Will you do it?"

And I could see his face light up as he looked at me and said, "Yes sir."

I said, "Tell me something, Bud. To whom does Jesus Christ belong?"

I can see him as he said, "He's mine."

Young folks, is He yours? Have you really been born again? Or are you hiding a heart full of sin behind the cloak of a lot of Scripture verses and other things? I wonder if God took you right now, if you are sure that you would go to Heaven? If you are not, make sure tonight.

THREE THINGS THAT NEED TO BE SETTLED

Message delivered by Rev. Robert Cook,
Associate Pastor, Midwest Bible Church, Chicago,
Saturday, August 5, 1944

I want you to think with me tonight about some verses from the twenty-first chapter of Luke. "Settle it therefore in your hearts, not to mediate before what ye shall answer: For I will give you a mouth and wisdom, which all your adversaries shall not be able to gainsay nor resist" (Luke 21:14, 15).

There are some decisions that may be put off—whether to go downtown today or tomorrow, whether to wear your red hat or your green one, and you, gentlemen, whether to wear your green tie or your yellow one with your brown suit. These are all unimportant decisions, but there are certain matters that can *never* be postponed. In fact, no life is effective until some decisions have been made. All of life is dependent upon certain things that need to be settled.

It is the admonition of our text that stirs my heart this evening: "Settle it therefore in your hearts." The authority of God's Word must be settled.

The reality of the message of the Cross must be settled. The Lordship and leadership of the Holy Ghost must be settled.

If I asked my audience how many really believe the Bible, I think almost all of you would say, "Yes, I believe the Bible from cover to cover. My parents had it in our home, and I was brought up to recognize the Bible as a holy and important book." You would probably say that your parents read to you from that Book, that you were trained to memorize certain Scripture passages, and that you have a very important place in your thinking for the Bible. I'm willing to admit that ninety-nine and forty-four one hundredths percent of our audience believes in the Bible. Still—I wonder whether you have ever settled in your heart the authority of the Word of God.

There are many people who believe in documents without believing in the authority of the document. For instance, here's a youngster who sees a cool, inviting pool of water. Before you can say, "Jack Robinson" this youngster is out of his clothes and into the water, enjoying a dip in the old swimming hole. In he goes, oblivious of the fact that there's a sign above him, a document that says, "No Swimming Allowed."

Now let us suppose that he sees a very imposing character coming over the brow of the hill, a man with shiny brass buttons on his coat, and all the marks of an officer of the law. My, isn't it wonderful what respect he has for *that* sign all of a sudden!

He believes in the authority of the sign—now! He believes that it means what it says. He puts his shirt over one arm and his stockings over the other, drapes his trousers over his shoulders and his shoes around his neck, hanging by their laces, and—all you can see is a cloud of dust. He got respect for the authority of that sign when he saw the person who could back it up.

I want to tell you that although you say, "I believe in the Bible and I'm trying to obey it," you really don't believe it or you would actually be obeying it.

A friend of mine some time ago said, "You say you believe God's Word," and then he asked me a very disturbing question. He said, "Just what part of the Bible did you believe today? You know, the Bible is full of promises. Just *what* did you believe today?"

I began to scratch my head and tried to think fast and my face got red. Here I was, a preacher—we are supposed to be super-holy!—and he was embarrassing me in front of people. I really hadn't believed any part of the Bible that day because I hadn't gotten down to business with God and decided what His Word had to say—to me! I had to make it part of my life, and then it carried some authority. My friends, until you settle the authority of God's Word, you will continue to flounder.

You say, "I'm interested in science." So am I, but did you ever check up on what the science books of a decade or so ago had to say? Back in nineteen hundred and . . . none of your business, I can remember some of the arguments I had with the science teacher. She did the best she could with what she had to work on, but I remember it was a rather feeble business. Whenever she said something I didn't quite agree with, I said, "The Word of God says so and so." She said, "Don't you realize that this is a scientific age and the Bible is antiquated and out-worn? You ought to believe science." We argued back and forth and finally compromised on a "C" average.

Today, if you go back and look at the science books we used back there, they just aren't up to date. As a matter of fact, some years ago I was going to sell some of my books. I took them to O'Leary's Book Store. (They take all the books that people want to sell when they are broke.) So I too them all down to O'Leary's and spread them out—a whole cardboard carton of them. Here was a literature book and a mathematics book. Here was the science book and a number of others.

The man said, "I'll take the mathematics book; that's still the same. You can take your literature book home, Sonny. It looks nice, and it has never been used. You can take your science book back, too."

I said, "Now listen, that was a good science book. I had to work hard to get a C average."

He said, "Yes, but you know, we don't believe the same things now." It wasn't many years ago *then,* and they don't believe the same things *now* that they believed *then* when they believed what they didn't believe when I went to school!

Can you beat it?

Yet they have the audacity to tell you that you're crazy and the Bible is old stuff because we have "science" today. But what can you do with science? Can science still the aching of your soul? Can you pillow your dying head upon the changing trends of science? Can you go to Heaven upon the wings of the Pythagorean Theorem? Can you do anything about your eternal destiny with a geometric proposition? No, you can't!

Tonight will you say, "O, God, I do believe Thy Word, and I'm going to take it seriously from now on—not simply carry it to a meeting and take someone else's word that it is the message of the Almighty without ever proving and living it. Right now, I'll settle the authority of the Word of God."

Another thing that needs to be settled is the reality of the message of the Cross. The same word translated "settle" in Luke 21:14 is translated in Luke 9:44 "sink down." "Let these sayings sink down." In other words, "Settle these sayings, for the Son of man shall be delivered into the hands of men." Jesus Christ was saying, "You better settle this matter about the crucifixion."

Let me ask you a question: What one factor contributed more to the confusion and disturbance of the disciples in the days immediately before and after the crucifixion than anything else? I think you will agree with me when I say that they *didn't really believe* He would be crucified and rise again. In other words, they had not settled the necessity for the message of the Cross in their hearts. What was it that the Lord said that day as He met those two disciples on the road to Emmaus? He said, "Why are you so sad?" They said, "Don't you know? Are you a stranger in town? They have crucified Jesus of Nazareth, and he was to redeem Israel." Then Jesus said to them, "O fools, and slow of heart to believe what the prophets have spoken: Ought not Christ to have suffered these things, and to enter into his glory?"

Much of the uncertainty that possesses people is traceable to the fact that they have never become absolutely sure that the message of the Cross is a necessity—for them! They know the story of the Cross—that Jesus died and was buried and rose again—but the reaction is very much like what I used to get some years ago when I would knock on the doors and tell the story of the Cross to folk on the West side of Chicago. I would begin to talk to them and tell them all about the Lord Jesus Christ. The response was almost always the same: "Ya, ya, ya"—BANG!—and the door was closed in my face. In other words, "Yes, I know all about it. Why are you bothering me with it? Get going!"

So many people are floundering because they have never come to the place of realizing that Jesus Christ had to die for *them*. If there had been no one else in all the universe

— 81 —

but you, He would have died for *you*, because it was in the eternal purpose of God, and His purposes are carried out.

When you really understand the importance of the message of the Cross, you will be saying as Paul, "Christ Jesus came into the world to save sinners: *of whom I am chief.*" When you have come far enough to do some real business with God, it will seem to you as though the whole universe had faded away and you stand in the presence of a Holy God as the greatest sinner of them all.

Do you remember the day you asked the Lord Jesus to come into your heart? You seemed to be the greatest sinner in all the world at that time. You need to settle tonight, my dear friends, the necessity of the message of a crucified Christ, not as a religious dogma, not as a doctrinal creed, not as a religious tenet to which you adhere, nor simply the basis of some religious relic you wear. You need to settle the fact that you *personally* needed to have a Saviour die for you, and that Jesus is that Saviour. I say frankly that a lot of people don't believe that. If you really believed it, you would already have received Jesus Christ as your Saviour. Have you settled that question?

The next thing you need to settle is the leadership and lordship of the Holy Spirit. The word translated "settle" in Luke 21, and "sink down" in Luke 9, is translated for us in Acts 19:21 as "purposed." "After these things were ended, Paul purposed in the spirit, when he had passed through Macedonia and Achaia, to go to Jerusalem, saying, After I have been there, I must also see Rome." He purposed where? In the Spirit. What Spirit? The Holy Spirit of God. Settle this thing in your heart, beloved! Not only the authority of the Word of God, and the necessity of salvation through faith in Jesus Christ, but now the leadership and lordship of the Holy Spirit of God.

You say, "Why bring that in here?" I'll tell you why: Because you must realize that only when the Holy Spirit is working in a life, does that life count for eternity. For instance, the beginning of salvation is brought about by the Holy Spirit. He does the convicting. "When he (the Spirit) is come, he will reprove the world of sin . . ." The very first pangs of suffering in your own conscience when you realized you were a sinner—who brought them there? Not the preaching, not the pleading, not the praying, but the working of the Holy Spirit of God. The work of regeneration when you are born again is the work of the Holy Spirit. Jesus said, "Except a man be born of water and of the Spirit, he cannot enter into the kingdom of God." The Holy Spirit actually brings you into the position of becoming a child of God, and after you are saved, the Holy Spirit tells you so. I never tell anyone that he is saved, because that is the work of the Holy Ghost (Rom. 8:16). If you are not sure you are saved, you ought to ask the Lord to make you sure. Then if you trust Him, the Holy Spirit will give you assurance because the Bible plainly says, "The Spirit itself beareth witness with our spirit, that we are the children of God."

The Holy Spirit helps you pray. Did you ever feel that you couldn't pray? Then perhaps you went to the Word (Rom. 8:26) and got a real background of Scripture and out from your heart came a real petition to God. The Spirit of God helped you pray.

The Holy Spirit leads people into service. "Ye shall receive power, after that the Holy Ghost is come upon you: and ye shall be witnesses unto me both in Jerusalem, and in all Judea, and in Samaria, and unto the uttermost part of the earth." The lordship and the leadership of the Holy Spirit—you need to settle that tonight.

A man whom I love in the things of the Lord told me that for years he was very active in Christian work. There was a period of several years during which he was preaching whenever he had opportunity. He gave out thousands of tracts and tried to do his best, but he told me rather ruefully that he could show very little evidence that anybody had ever been saved as a result of his hard work during that time.

Then one day he decided that there was something wrong with his approach. He got on his knees with his Bible and opened it to Romans 12:1 where it says, "I beseech you therefore, brethren, by the mercies of God, that ye present your bodies a living sacrifice, holy, acceptable unto God, which is your reasonable service." Somehow he saw the verse in a new light and said, "O, God, I've never done it before, but just now I do give my body and all that I am to Thee. Work through me, blessed Holy Spirit."

He went downstairs and said to his wife, "I've done something I never did before. I gave my body to the Holy Spirit, and I expect He's going to use me. I'm going to call you up as soon as I've won the first soul."

He went to work that morning with real victory: About ten o'clock the telephone rang. His wife answered and heard him say, "I just won two souls that the Lord sent in to me!" I wonder what happened? You know. He had settled the lordship and leadership of the Holy Spirit in his life.

Will you settle these things? First of all, whether you really believe the Bible is true: then settle whether or not you really believe you need Jesus, the crucified Christ; and, Christian friends, you settle the matter of whether or not the Holy Spirit has the use of your body—all of it.

Listen to our text again: "Settle it therefore in your hearts."

FIVE WORDS

Message delivered by Dr. Harry Rimmer,
Author and Lecturer, Los Angeles, Calif.,
September 2, 1944

The trouble with average Christian young people is that their mentality is like a disorderly house. They have no pegs whereupon to drape the garments of their thinking. They have no basic philosophy of Christianity. Tonight, in twenty minutes I have the impossible task of giving you that basic philosophy so that you will know *what* is a Christian, and *why* is a Christian, and *how* you can be saved. I'm going to give you an outline and let you build it up for yourselves. I'm going to drive five pegs into the wall of your mentality and let you hang your own thoughts upon those five pegs. The five pegs are five words, and in those five words are encompassed the whole horizon of God's dealings with man.

My first word, of course, if I'm going to be basically accurate, I take out of the first chapter of Genesis. Not only is that the foundation of belief, but it is also the most complete revelation of God we have anywhere in sacred literature. In the first chapter I find my first word, and that is *creation*. "And God said, Let us make man in our image, after our likeness: and let them have dominion over the fish of the sea, and over the fowl of the air, and over the cattle, and over all the earth, and over every creeping thing that creepeth upon the earth. So God created man in his own image, in the image of God created he him; male and female created he them."

If you are to have a basic philosophy of Christianity, you have to begin with the word *creation*. Without that you have no place to start. This word "creation" means to call into existence that which never had any form of existence before. Some people say that they believe in creation and evolution. That's just like trying to ride two horses that are going in different directions. The theory of evolution has man going one way and the theory of creation has him going the opposite way. When *man* tells the story of man, he starts it as low down as he can conceive, and then brags him as high as he can.

Do you know how the theory of evolution began? Let me boil it down and give it to you in a few words. In college the professor begins by saying, "Once upon a time a long time ago there was a little one-celled creature tossed upon the shore in some queer way. Instead of dying, this little creature lay right down and thought it over. Deciding that it was nicer to live on the ground rather than in the water, he began a process of development that is the most fabulous thing man has ever conceived. He decided that in order to get around he needed some legs, so he sprouted a pair. But he didn't get along on one pair of legs very well, so he got another pair. Then one day one of his enemies chased him up a tree."

"Where does the enemy come from?" I ask.

The professor yells, "Shut up!" and goes on.

"Then one day this little fellow made a startling discovery. He found that he had a tail that he could hang by. But one night a sudden wind blew up and before he realized what was happening, he landed on his ear. He stood up on his hind legs, and he's been that way ever since."

This is a brief condensation of the theory of evolution. I'm merely pointing out that they have man consistently going up. He starts in insignificance and he develops gradually until he is the creature that you see him now, and according to that, if man ever fell, he fell up. That's a good trick if you can do it.

The theory of creation says that God created man perfectly. God made man in the image and likeness of himself, but man stooped to sin until he was lower than the beasts of the field. I mean that literally. There is no animal that has to plead guilty to the awful indictment against the human race. And when man had fallen to be lower than animals, he never rose again until Christ came and lifted him out of his sin. When you start your basic philosophy of Christianity, my friend, you have to start somewhere, and since the theory of evolution has been utterly discredited and repudiated, and the theory of creation is the only thing left, you have to begin with the word *creation*.

Our second word is also from the book of Genesis, in the fifth chapter, the word *generation*. "And Adam lived an hundred and thirty years, and begat a son in his own likeness, after his image; and called his name Seth." It is not stated in the Scripture that any of us are born in the likeness of God. Adam was created in God's image, but we are born in the image and likeness of Adam. You say, "If Adam was created in God's image, what's the difference?" There is a vital difference. After Adam had sinned and fallen and had become the sin-ruined image and likeness of God, the generations that followed had a fallen nature. Those things that I determine to do, I catch myself never doing, and those things I swear I ought not to do, I do— I have a fallen nature. I have three strikes on me when I am born. I have no chance to succeed morally. I inherited from a long line of sinful ancestors a disposition to sin.

But if that is all I had to say, I never would have come. I have a third word from the eighth chapter of Romans. "For as many as are led by the Spirit of God, they are the sons of God . . . ye have received the Spirit of adoption, whereby we cry, Abba, Father." Here we have the word *adoption*. As many as are led, they are the sons of God. How about those that are not led? Obviously they are not the sons of God. All men are the children of Adam, but they have to be adopted into the family of God before they are his sons.

In my family we have three children, mine by right of birth. We always wanted four, and so we thought of adopting the fourth. There was a little fellow by the name of Thomas Kelly who spent a lot of time at our house. He didn't have a dad and so we thought very seriously of adopting him, and we would have were it not for a lot of legal impediments. If I had gone into court and adopted him according to the law, he would have come out with the name of Thomas Rimmer instead of Thomas Kelly. He would have come to my house and lived with me, and according to the laws of the state of California, he would be my son by adoption. When I died, if I left no will, the law would divide my estate equally among the four boys. He would have every right as a natural son. Therefore, when we are adopted by

God, we become heirs of God, and joint heirs with Jesus Christ. If I am adopted into the family of God, then, I have every right that Jesus has with the Father. That's a magnificent vista open to me, but I won't stop to enlarge on it.

There is one thing wrong with adoption. It doesn't change the nature of the individual. If I had adopted Thomas Kelly, his name would be changed to Rimmer, but as long as he lived there would be Kelly thoughts. He would have a Kelly heart and Kelly blood. He would have a Kelly nature until he died.

Here is God's difficulty. He is not willing to adopt the fallen children of Adam and leave them with an Adam nature. So we have to have a new word, and that word is *regeneration*. John 3:7 says, "Marvel not that I said unto thee, Ye must be born again." Jesus never said you ought to be born again. Jesus never said it's a grand experience you ought to have. He never said other people have enjoyed it, why don't you try it. If you will let me put that verse of the third chapter of John into the vernacular of the day, this is what He said: "Marvel not that I say unto you, you have got to be born again." When you are born again by the act of the Holy Ghost and the convicting power of the Word of God, there is formed in you a new nature, and the nature of Almighty God replaces the nature of Adam in you.

That brings me to my fifth word which comes from the verse which is my life motto: II Corinthians 5:17. "If any man be in Christ, he is a new creature: old things are passed away; behold, all things are become new." That's the verse that the preacher used on the night that I was saved. He wasn't much of a preacher, and it wasn't much of a meeting. I was walking up a street in San Francisco and a crowd of young people were holding a street meeting. The meeting was practically a failure; I was the only one saved. But as far as I was concerned, it was the greatest evangelistic campaign ever held at any time.

Now here's my word, and that word is *consummation*. "If any man be in Christ ... old things are passed away." Translated from the Greek it reads, "All things are in the process of becoming new." When you take Christ, never forget that there is a work continuing in you which never stops until you behold your Saviour.

I would like you to see that this new nature is not the old Adam nature fixed up so it will run a few years longer. God isn't in the junk business.

Years ago I formed the habit of stealing my two sons from their mother and taking them on a fishing trip. One day my wife said to me, "Did you ever stop to think about how selfish you are? You take the car and leave me to get around the best way I can."

I said, "That's right." The next morning I went to a used car dealer and bought a second hand Ford to go fishing with, and I paid forty-five dollars for it. When we bought that thing, it ran. All you had to do was to keep putting in gas and water. When we said we were going two hundred miles and back in the thing, my wife laughed and said, "I bet an apple pie against a box of candy it won't run a block."

We started out and it went two miles before anything happened. We got out and fixed it and went four miles more. We landed in San Francisco and found we had a broken landing gear. Finally that was fixed and we went merrily on our way.

It only broke four times on the way coming home. When we finally got that thing home on two cylinders and everybody pushing I said, "Phooey, I'll never try that again!" My wife played a mean trick on the colored boy. She sold it to him for fifteen dollars. That was the first time I ever bought a heap of junk, and that's the last time I ever will. I'm through trying to make a pile of junk run.

God feels that way about the Adam nature in you. When I came to Jesus Christ, Almighty God just put a new motor in me, and it's been running ever since, a streamlined job if you ever saw one!

This is what I'm trying to say. God wants to make out of you a complete new machine. I—that's the old Adam nature—am crucified with Christ. What is a Christian? Paul says, "It is 'Christ in you the hope of glory.' " What is a Christian? An ordinary human being like you and me into whom Jesus Christ has come to take up residence in the person of the Holy Spirit.

When you take Christ, He comes in and resides in you from that minute on. You remember what is written in the third chapter of the book of Ephesians. "That Christ may dwell in your hearts by faith; that ye, being rooted and grounded in love." Let me close with this one verse from Ephesians 2:10, "For we are his workmanship, created in Christ Jesus unto good works, which God hath before ordained that we should walk in them." Let me give you just one more passage—Colossians 3:9, 10: "Lie not one to another, seeing that ye have put off the old man with his deeds; and have put on the new man, which is renewed in knowledge after the image of him that created him."

We have completed the cycle. We began with creation. God created man in God's image and likeness. Man fell, but fallen man may be adopted into the family of God on condition that he will be born again and get a new nature which makes of him a child of God.

Are you a Christian? When we say, "Take Christ as your Saviour" do you know what we are trying to offer you? He'll blot out every sin against your record. You'll receive a new nature, and He'll give you victory day by day. There is no reason why you should be defeated. Take Christ as your Saviour and your present life is transformed.

That's the basic philosophy of Christianity. Do you know how to get this? He said, "Whosoever therefore shall confess me before men, him will I confess also before my Father which is in heaven." The Holy Spirit led Paul to write these words: "That if thou shalt confess with thy mouth the Lord Jesus, and shalt believe in thine heart that God hath raised him from the dead, thou shalt be saved."

If you want to be born again and become a child of God with present victory and future assurance, I'll tell you how. Just lift your heart right now and say, "I here and now take Christ as my Saviour. I surrender my life to him, and with the help of God, I'll live my life for Him from now on." That's all you need to do.

"THOU ART MY HIDING PLACE"

Message delivered by Dr. H. A. Ironside,
Pastor, Moody Memorial Church, Chicago,
Saturday, September 16, 1944

Psalm 32:7, "Thou art my hiding place; thou shalt preserve me from trouble; thou shalt compass me about with songs of deliverance."

In the early part of this Psalm we find a man hiding *from* God, and then when we get down to the seventh verse, we find him hiding *in* God. I wonder whether there are any here tonight who are trying to hide from God? I wonder whether there are any who have been pursued by God in His loving kindness and grace throughout the years, and yet you have been trying to get away from Him, where you wouldn't hear His voice . . . you're trying to silence the voice of your own conscience, and giving yourself to indulgence in things you know in your own heart are ruinous both to your soul and body—trying to find a hiding place from God.

That was David's condition. He had sinned—sinned terribly. Sinned so that to the present day, though three thousand years have rolled by, scoffers still smile as they talk of David, the man after God's own heart, and the awful sin into which he fell. If they only knew how broken hearted he was because of his sin! Think of him bowing before God and crying out, "Against thee, thee only, have I sinned, and done this evil." If they would follow him into the sanctuary of the Lord, where he prayed, "Thou desirest not sacrifice, else would I give it."

—91—

It was as if he said, "There is no sacrifice that man could offer that could ever atone for the sin that has marred my testimony and scarred my life." "Purge me... and I shall be clean; wash me, and I shall be whiter than snow."

Yes, David sinned, and he tried for a whole year to keep his sin to himself. He says in this Psalm, "When I kept silence, my bones waxed old through my roaring all the day long, For day and night thy hand was heavy upon me: my moisture is turned into the drought of summer."

There is nothing that will take away the joy of living like unconfessed sin. A person with a guilty conscience is the most miserable person. Of course, it is possible to fall so deeply into sin that the conscience at last will fail to register, and so we read in God's Word of some whose hearts are so hardened that they have no feeling and they no longer think anything of the depths of iniquity into which they have plunged.

Young man, young woman, be thankful if you still have a conscience that makes you unhappy when you sin against God. David's conscience was like that, and though he tried to keep from confessing it and didn't want to come face to face with God about his sin, yet he was miserable and wretched in hiding from God. Then, at last when he couldn't stand it any longer, he says, "I acknowledged my sin unto thee, and mine iniquity have I not hid. I said, I will confess my transgressions unto the Lord; and thou forgavest the iniquity of my sin." And so he could exclaim, "Blessed is he whose transgression is forgiven, whose sin is covered."

Now David lived a thousand years before the Lord Jesus Christ came into the world, and yet his sin was dealt with at the Cross of Calvary. It was because of what Christ was yet to do that God was able to send the message through Nathan, the prophet: "The Lord also hath put away thy sin."

Probably many of you have heard the story of the little Scotch lad. He was what the Scotch called "dull." This wee little laddie used to go to the kirk and listen to the great sermons. There were many that he couldn't understand very well. There were so many of the "Aurora Borealis" type of sermons that were away up in the air. The only thing he got of these great sermons was this, that away up somewhere beyond the stars, beyond the clouds, beyond the sun and moon, there was a terrible being that they called God. He had awful eyes that look right through the heavens. They could see in the dark, eyes that could look into the heart and could see every known thing that everyone ever did, and every thought that anyone ever thought, and someday this God was going to call everybody to account for all the wrong things done.

It used to stir the heart of little Jack, the Scotch laddie. He would walk up and down wringing his hands and saying, "I'm so afeared of God. Oh, I dinna want to meet Him. I wish I could run away from Him." People tried to explain to Jack that after all God might have mercy on a poor laddie. One day he went to the kirk and the great preacher was not there. Only a lay-man, a humble elder was there. He stood in front of the Lord's table and in a very simple way he spoke from the most wonderful of all texts, John 3:16, "For God so loved the world that he gave his only begotten Son, that whosoever believeth in him should not perish, but have everlasting life." He made it all so clear about why Jesus came and why He died on the cross. Why He shed His precious blood that we might be free, that guilty men and women and boys and girls might be forgiven and accepted of God. It all went straight to little Jack's heart, and he bowed his head and was thanking God for his wonderful Christ.

He didn't notice that all the people had left and he was there alone, save for the sexton. Finally the sexton said, "Come my little lad, it's time for you to be gang home noo."

He looked up and with a wonderful smile said, "Do ye ken, I'm no afeared of God, noo."

The sexton said, "You've been a bad laddie and you may well be afeared."

Little Jack replied, "Yes, I've sinned, but my sins have all been blotted out and I'm noo afeared of God noo, I'm gang to heaven."

The sexton said, "Explain yourself."

Jack scratched his poor addled pate and said, "Some day little John will see a great big white desk and on the desk He'll hae a great big Bible book with the names of everbody who ever lived and all the sins they have ever done. And when little John comes up before God, he'll turn to the big Bible book and find the page with John's name at the top and Jesus Christ will be there with his bleeding hand and put it down quick. God will say, 'I canna find a sin here. Let little John gang into heaven!'"

Little John's theology was pretty accurate. Come to God here and now for "He is faithful and just to forgive your sins," and "The blood of Jesus Christ cleanseth us from all sin."

So David, having put his trust in the promises of God and relying upon the pledge that God had given of the One coming, said with confidence, "Thou art my hiding place." Can you say that? He's not hiding from God any more—he's hiding in God.

My eldest son taught me a lesson when he was a wee lad. He was six years old before his brother came, and a lonely kind of a fellow for his father was away a great deal. When he would come home, he would have to try to be a big brother to his little son. He liked to play bear better than anything. Did you ever play bear? This is the way we played it. I was the bear and I would have to get down on all fours and my job was to growl.

The little fellow would come into the room as though he didn't know there was a bear there, and suddenly the bear would come rushing out of his den and the little fellow would run from room to room. The rule was that I had to keep down on all fours. That boy certainly could run and it was rather hard for a heavy old bear to catch a lively youngster.

We would go through one room after another, and finally he ran into the kitchen and found himself in a corner. It wouldn't open up to let him through, and there was that bear! The bear was actually upon him, and he was scared and alarmed. You know how real those things are to children. Suddenly just before the bear caught him, he wheeled around and caught his breath and said, "You're not a bear at all, you're just my own father!" and he jumped into my arms.

Then I thought that's just the way I was. I was running away from God. And one never-to-be-forgotten night in my soul's history, I ran right into a corner where, convicted of sin at last through the guidance of the Holy Spirit, I turned to the One who was pursuing me, and said as I turned, "Oh, God, you're not my enemy, but my loving, tender Father." Instead of running away from Him, I ran *to* Him and found a hiding place in Him.

> Rock of Ages, cleft for me,
> Let me hide myself in Thee;
> Let the water and the blood,
> From thy wounded side which flowed,
> Be of sin the double cure,
> Save from wrath and make me pure.

So tonight my soul can say, "Thou art my hiding place; thou shalt preserve me from trouble; thou shalt compass me about with songs of deliverance."

Do you know that Hiding Place from the storms of life and the covert from temptations that come your way? That hiding place is the Lord Jesus Christ. Will you come to Him tonight?

"CHICAGOLAND YOUTH FOR CHRIST"

Torrey M. Johnson, Director   Douglas Fisher, Managing Director

ADVISORY COUNCIL

Sten Benson
Walter Block
Freelin A. Carlton
Einar A. Comfield
Al J. Conn
Robert A. Cook

Howard Duntz
William Erny
Douglas Fisher
Floyd E. Gephart
Joseph Gunderson
Clifton B. Hedstrom

Torrey M. Johnson
Enoch J. Malmstrom
Henry Riemersma
Charles F. Stein
H. J. Taylor
Robert Van Kampen

THE BUSINESS WORLD

Ernest Alder
Roy E. Anderson
Roy Baumann
J. Paul Bennett, M.D.
Harold O. Benson
Stanley M. Berntson
Peter M. Black
Charles E. Bodeen
Kenneth J. Brouwer
Judith B. Carlson
LaVerne Carlson
Bruce E. Cederoth
Einar Christianssen
George Christophersen
Ardith M. Cornelius
Victor E. Cory
Stuart Crippen
Carl A. Dahlin
U. S. Deahl, Jr.
Clyde H. Dennis

Erling A. Dunhom
T. Wesley Eyres
Carl J. Frizen
William Garland
Audrey Gerken
William Gray
Carl A. Gundersen
Lacy Hall
Arthur Hansen
V. C. Hogren
Andrew H. Jessen
J. Martin Johnson
Mae Johnson
Ivan Lageschulte
Mel Larsen
Ferne Larson
Reamer G. Loomis
Mrs. Robert C. Loveless
Elmer Matthews
Mrs. George S. May
Blair Meeker

H. D. Mielke
Mabel Moore
Mrs. Donald M. Nelson
Chas. Palmquist, Sr.
E. Reeby
Theis Reynertson
Chester C. Scholl
R. Hugh Seffens
Beverly Shea
Mark C. Spencer, D.D.S.
Evelyn Stenbeck
A. J. Susans
Kenneth N. Taylor
Roy A. Thompson
Arnold Torsell
Cornelius J. Ulrich
Charles Warner
Helen Warner
Robert William Wyatt
Andrew Wyzenbeek

ORGANIZATIONAL LEADERS

Alvera Anderson, President, Chicago Christian Nurses' Fellowship
Amy Anderson, Chairman, Christian Business Girls' Association
Thelma Barnett, Secretary, Fox Valley Young People's Bible Fellowship
Sten W. Benson, Chairman, Northwest Gospel Fellowship
Nancy Carpenter, Chmn., Christian Business and Professional Women
Harry B. Cork, President, Chicago Camp, The Gideons
Peter Deyneka, Director, Russian Gospel Association
C. V. Egemeier, Executive Secretary, Greater Chicago Sunday School Association
Christian L. Eicher, Secretary, World Wide Prayer and Missionary Union
William Graham, Director, Suburban Men's Fellowship
Mrs. William Gray, President, Gideon Women's Auxiliary
Walter F. Hanselman, President, Christian Teachers' Fellowship
Kenneth Hansen, The Brigades
Olena Mae Hendrickson, Chicago Child Evangelism Fellowship

Maj. Dallas P. Leader, Terr. Y. P. Secretary, The Salvation Army
G. A. Lundmark, President, Pentecostal Young People's Fellowship
June Lundquist, Secretary, Miracle Book Club
Dorothy Marx, President, South District, Baptist Youth Fellowship
Eleanor Nerhus, Methodist Youth Fellowship
Edward Thoraldsen, Commander of Aaron Post No. 788, American Legion
Arnie Olsen, Luther League
Anna Penn, President, Chicago Christian Endeavor
Dora Reid, Executive Secretary, Christian Teachers' Fellowship
Elmer Sandberg, President, Free Church Youth Fellowship
Vaughn Shoemaker, Chairman, Gospel Fellowship Club
Lois Thiessen, President, Pioneer Girls
Dr. M. E. Wadsworth, Director, Great Commission Prayer League
Stacey Woods, Inter-Varsity Christian Fellowship

TWENTIETH CENTURY WONDER

Youth FOR Christ

By MEL LARSON

Introduction by
Percy Crawford

Zondervan Publishing House
GRAND RAPIDS, MICHIGAN

To
Vision-filled
Youth for Christ Leaders
Around the World

Introduction

Eternity alone will reveal the thousands of souls that have been sincerely won for Christ through the great modern Youth for Christ movement. It has truly been an influence for good and for God.

All of us rejoice in the wonderful way God moved on the hearts of men and women in this our day to bring forth in full blossom the moving of the Spirit of God upon the hearts of our youth.

I am sure as you read this volume your heart will be thrilled as you see God working and reaching the youth with the truth.

PERCY CRAWFORD, D.D.
Director, Young People's
Church of the Air

Philadelphia, Pa.

Foreword

Nothing in my short life has amazed and intrigued me more than the Youth for Christ movement. At times I could hardly believe that the organization was real. With lightning-like speed, Youth for Christ spread from its beginning in the United States, becoming world-wide almost overnight. Its speed rivaled the fastest and most modern inventions; its sparks touched all corners of the globe, startling Christian leaders around the world.

It has not been my privilege to do much research or study on revivals. As a young Christian, and as a young person, it has not been my privilege to witness any world-upheaving or nation-shaking movements of the Holy Spirit; consequently there can be no comparison of Youth for Christ with any similar outpouring of the past.

It would not be fair to begin this book without mentioning that the Youth for Christ movement has stirred my heart time and time again. The undeniable and clear-cut fact that souls bound for an eternity in hell have come to a saving knowledge of Jesus Christ, with assurance of eternity in heaven, has quickened and stimulated in a definite way. Luke 15:7 states, "I say unto you, that likewise joy shall be in heaven over one sinner that repenteth, more than over ninety and nine just persons, which need no repentance." Youth for Christ has brought some of that joy of heaven down to earth and has scattered it among the hearts of born-again believers the world around as thousands . . . yes, tens of thousands . . . of young people have been converted. Evangelical and nonevangelical, leaders alike have labeled Youth for Christ "The Twentieth Century Wonder of the Religious World."

FOREWORD

This book has been two and one-half years in the making. The main aim is to tell simply and completely the story of Youth for Christ. I have endeavored to be objective throughout. No attempt has been made to describe the movement elaborately; the facts tell the story.

Acknowledgment is due many individuals and organizations. The excellent co-operation received in this great interdenominational effort has warmed my heart. Every youth leader contacted has been exceedingly helpful and pleasant in supplying the needed information. Special acknowledgment must be made of the unusual assistance of the Youth for Christ International Office in Chicago, Illinois. Not only was the door thrown wide open to that busy beehive of activity for an unlimited and unhindered examination of everything in the office, but also a key for the office was given me; this enabled me to carry on research at any time convenient for me. Co-operation such as this assured me that the entire movement had nothing to hide or conceal. The office displayed its work readily and cheerfully.

I have received a great blessing from the study of the Youth for Christ movement. It is my hope that the readers of this book may receive in some small portion the blessing which has come my way as I have viewed and reviewed this great soul-saving movement.

MEL LARSON

Chicago, Illinois

CONTENTS

Chapter I

"...BUT NOW I SEE"

THE war was on.

It was September of 1942, and American soldiers by the thousands were streaming endlessly out of San Francisco's port of embarkation. Their destination . . . the wide, expansive South Pacific.

Many of those thousands walked down the gangplank in Australia, the first stop at the start of a long, long journey. Some stayed a short while; others remained for longer intervals.

It's a long way from Haddon Heights, New Jersey, to Australia, but through the free transportation of the United States Army a young fellow from that New Jersey town of five thousand found himself in Australia. He was normal, and along with many other American soldiers this young Yankee from New Jersey looked, and looked, and looked again at the Australian girls.

He looked until he found one he liked . . . and loved . . . and married. The war moved on. The American G.I. unwillingly but dutifully moved on. He continued to move until one day he found himself back in the United States, alive and unharmed, after many months and years of battle in the South Pacific. Several months later a young Australian war-bride arrived in the land of her husband and was met with open arms. There was joy in two hearts as husband and wife were together again.

All went well until he brought her home to his family in Haddon Heights. Frankly and bluntly, his parents refused to accept her as one of the family. She turned to the young fellow on whom she had been wanting to depend for so many long, dreary months. But he was not there. Seeing that his parents did not want her, this young husband decided that he, too, did not want her.

They were divorced. She found a job in Haddon Heights, hoping perhaps to earn money to go back to her native land. After a few months she lost her job. Lonesome, far from home and with an ache in her heart as big as the ocean over which she had traveled, she was far from the happiest person in this United States.

One Saturday night, not having anything to do, she was "just walking" along the street. She casually wandered into a Youth for Christ meeting in Haddon Heights. That same night God used the young speaker of the evening to convince her that she needed Jesus Christ as her personal Saviour.

The Holy Spirit convicted her of her sins . . . and she was saved!

*   *   *

Japan, powerful . . . but crushed. The war was over, and the bitter dregs of military defeat were being tasted by millions of Japanese.

Along the streets of Tokyo on a Sunday afternoon a

young girl of twelve walked aimlessly on. She had read in newspapers and heard from friends and neighbors of the many suicides of her countrymen. Suicide seemed attractive. Although only twelve years of age, she knew the difference between hope and despair, victory and defeat, joy and sadness. She walked blindly, but there was purpose in her heart. She, too, was on her way to take the "easiest way out"—to commit suicide.

As she made her way to the place where she planned to take her life, a friend stopped her on the street and said, "Won't you come to the Youth for Christ meeting with me today?" She started to refuse, but then just as quickly accepted the invitation. Her only thought was, "What have I to lose?"

An hour later, through the preaching of a young American sergeant as interpreted by a consecrated and soul-loving Japanese lady, a young twelve-year-old girl who might have been among the dead was a born-again Christian!

＊ ＊ ＊

The pastor of one of the leading churches in St. Louis, Missouri, finally agreed to attend a Youth for Christ meeting after his daughters had begged him to do so. At first the meeting annoyed him. It moved too fast. Gradually that irritation wore off. Analyzing the meeting, he realized that these young people were getting something real and genuine.

As he deliberated, he came to the conclusion that these young people had something which he, a minister of the Gospel, did not have. Upon returning home after the third visit to St. Louis Youth for Christ, he went to his study and prayed until he personally accepted Jesus Christ as his Saviour.

From that night on he was a different kind of preacher.

＊ ＊ ＊

Another unit of America's tank corps was going overseas. In those final hours on the California coast before the shipping orders came through, a young captain in that tank outfit sat down and wrote several letters. One went to the Middle West and was removed from a mailbox a few days later by a friend of the captain. The letter was brief, but pointed. It revealed a new aspect of the captain. He described his fear—fear of going to battle. In the eyes of his men he was dauntless; in his own heart and mind he was afraid—afraid to die—and he asked this friend to pray for him in the days immediately ahead.

That rugged tank unit of which he was the leader spearheaded the drive on Manila. In the fierce combat when life meant little, this captain proved his worth time and time again. His action was noteworthy, and soon after he found a Silver Star on his breast for gallantry.

Manila fell, and the captain was one of the many thousands of happy Americans who rode triumphantly into that city which the war had turned into a shambles. He took a few pictures to show the folks back home. He wrote to his friend in the Middle West, thanking him for his prayers. His unit had lost many men, but he had come through without a scratch.

During the days of battle he had thought much of God. He remembered his Sunday school days and the lessons and prayers taught him by his Christian parents. One day as he walked through the broken city of Mánila, someone handed him an invitation to a Youth for Christ meeting. The thought of a religious service on a Saturday night amused him. He had planned to spend this Saturday night just as he did any other—drinking with his friends. He had the distinction, if the term may be employed, of being one of the heaviest smokers and drinkers in his entire outfit.

But . . . for an unexplainable reason that Saturday night he went to a Youth for Christ meeting in Manila, held in a mortuary. A chaplain spoke, and spoke well.

An invitation was given to sinners to accept Christ as their Saviour. Without a moment's hesitation, a valiant, courageous captain walked forward and took Christ into his hitherto unsettled life and heart!

* * *

They had called it quits.

Married during the war, two young people, whom we'll call Jane and Dick, decided that their marriage had been a mistake. They separated. Jane stayed in Chicago, and Dick became a member of the United States Navy. Life for Jane went from bad to worse. It wasn't long before she was picking up servicemen on Chicago's Michigan Avenue. Without Dick, and deprived of his stabilizing influence, her life was barren and weak.

One night she was resting on a park bench directly across from Orchestra Hall. As she reflected, music—enthusiastic music—bounded across that busy thoroughfare. Three thousand young people were singing lustily. The music delighted her ears and touched her heart. She arose from the bench, slowly crossed Michigan Avenue, found her way into the balcony of Orchestra Hall and took the only vacant seat. She listened to every word and every song with an aching but eager heart; and God used every part of that service to impress her sin-sick heart with the need of a Saviour. When the invitation was given, she went forward with many others, knelt in one of the first two rows in Orchestra Hall and became a new creature in Christ Jesus!

In Los Angeles, on the very same night, Dick had gone to the Saturday Nite Jubilee at the Church of the Open Door. Going to church wasn't exactly routine for him, especially on Saturday night, but he was far from happy. He thought constantly of Jane and felt more and more that he was deeply in love with her. But there was something else that had to be straightened out first.

The meeting that Saturday night struck him. Young people here were actually enjoying a religious service. The young preacher spoke the language to which he was accustomed in the navy; his message was direct, with no mincing of words. The Holy Spirit worked in his heart and mind, convicting him of his sin. At the invitation, someone tapped him on the shoulder and asked him if he was interested in becoming a Christian. He walked down that aisle with a new friend who had the privilege of leading Dick to a personal knowledge of a "friend that sticketh closer than a brother."

On the very same night the Holy Spirit had worked in the hearts of two young people thousands of miles apart. Two young people sat down and wrote to each other, and there was amazement and joy when each received the other's letter. Needless to say, there was a happy reunion, a permanent reunion.

*   *   *

The quiet Chinese interpreter was realizing the truth of Romans 8:28, "And we know that all things work together for good to them that love God, to them who are the called according to his purpose." He had interrupted his studies at a college in the United States in order to enlist in the Marine Corps of the United States as an interpreter. The war at that time was far from over. In contemplating the big push into Japan by the way of China, the Marines had seen the need of interpreters in order to co-ordinate the work of China and the United States. This young Chinese student was not a "fighter," in the true sense of the word. He had been born in Hong Kong, and it was there that he accepted Christ as his personal Saviour. Through the influence of missionaries who had brought to his country the Gospel, the young fellow decided to study in America. Three years in a seminary had given him a definite and solid

Bible background. Then he went to college to prepare for preaching the Gospel to the people of his native land.

Now he was in the uniform of the Marines. During his indoctrination he was unable to find a single person who shared his beliefs; that was discouraging. But Romans 8:28 was still in his Bible.

Shipping orders finally came. He did not know where he was going, but he trusted the Lord, praying that he might be sent to his native China. When he finished his journey he was in Tientsin. Within a few days he had contacted Chinese Christian young people and pastors who were interested in the salvation of young people, and within three weeks Tientsin Youth for Christ was being held every Saturday night!

This young fellow acted as an interpreter for Uncle Sam during the day and for the Lord Jesus Christ at night. He was the key man in Tientsin Youth for Christ as it reached both the native Chinese and the American servicemen. While he was there, hundreds of young people were converted. And the meetings still go on!

*　*　*

In Oshkosh, Wisconsin, a young lad of eleven had such criminal tendencies that he was known as "Little Dillinger." One afternoon C. B. Cunningham, director of Winnebagoland Youth for Christ, was visiting the various schools in Oshkosh distributing invitations to the Youth for Christ meetings on Saturday nights. When he saw "Little Dillinger" he might easily have thought, "Why hand one to him? He'll never come."

However, Cunningham was working for the Lord, and into the hands of that little fellow went an attractive invitation.

Saturday night came, and "Little Dillinger" was in the audience. He felt uneasy at first, but the feeling gradually diminished. Once again the Holy Spirit worked through

His servants, and a little fellow whom everyone had tagged
as "an impossible case" came forward at the invitation
and accepted Christ.

That is not the end, glorious as it is. God touched that
little sinful heart in a wonderful way that night; the
young potential criminal is now preparing himself for the
ministry.

*   *   *

There are thousands of experiences of salvation as thrilling as those mentioned. The number of young people whom
God has saved through Youth for Christ is astounding.
God has blessed the movement in a remarkable and wonderful way. Every Youth for Christ group we have contacted—without exception—has had the wonderful privilege
of seeing souls converted. Each Youth for Christ group has
felt the power of the Holy Spirit, and that is the outstanding thing about Youth for Christ.

Without any central co-ordinating organization at the beginning, without any extensive organization plans, without
any lengthy conferences on procedure, Youth for Christ
sprouted simultaneously in cities, towns, villages and rural
areas all over the world. God provided youth leaders for
every place. Accepting the challenge, these active young
leaders put their abilities and resources whole-heartedly
into a great effort to reach the youth of the world for Christ.

To us it seems clear and definite that the movement is of
God. The presence of the Holy Spirit has been felt throughout. Even young servicemen felt the call to start Youth for
Christ meetings where they were stationed—Manila, Tokyo,
Paris. There were no definite rules to follow; each meeting
was a unit in itself, and each leader was free to carry on
the service in any way he desired.

This next fact is astonishing: although there had been
no organization meetings or consultations on methods, the
meetings of the groups were similar. As the movement

gained momentum, the leaders began to correspond with each other for ideas and suggestions. Various groups received national and international attention, and that recognition was a large factor in the spreading of the movement. The spread of the movement was so rapid—and the movement still is moving so fast—that we can be certain of supernatural power behind it. The thing moved so fast that even the progressive leaders could not keep abreast with it. There can be only one conclusion: God is in it.

As we will see in a later chapter, meetings similar to Youth for Christ were held as early as 1928 in New York, 1934 in Brantford, Ontario, Canada, in the 1930's in Washington, D.C., Detroit, Michigan, and Philadelphia, Pennsylvania. They did commendable work in their localities, but there was no nation-wide or world-wide spread. Percy Crawford and his great radio ministry, too, did much of the ground work.

Then came Jack Wyrtzen in 1940. With the advice and co-operation of Crawford, Wyrtzen went into the heart of New York on a Saturday night and held a youth meeting in connection with his radio program, The Word of Life Hour. Wyrtzen, converted dance-band leader and ex-insurance man, found that his methods and style of presentation clicked; the Saturday night meetings were crowded with young people from the New York area. During the war millions of servicemen from all parts of the United States were sent to New York, and they jammed his meetings. More important than the crowds was the fact that young people were accepting Christ as Saviour. During the week Jack and his Gospel teams traveled to nearby towns and cities and held evangelistic services.

The Word of Life Hour and similar programs in Detroit, Philadelphia and other places grew in size and effectiveness. Walter Smyth in his Philadelphia Youth Center and Oscar Gillian (and later Ed Darling) in Detroit were making definite and steady progress. In 1943 Wyrtzen, prompted somewhat by the casual remark of a policeman after a meeting, "Why don't you move from Carnegie Hall to Madison Square Garden? You turned hundreds away from here tonight," arranged for a meeting in Madison Square Garden.

The results were stupendous. No less than twenty thousand young people came to the Garden for the rally, and about ten thousand were turned away. News of the rally spread like wildfire, and vision-filled Wyrtzen found himself deluged with inquiries in regard to starting a rally similar to his. The Lord used this great rally to awaken youth leaders in all parts of the land to the possibility of establishing a powerful youth evangelism program. That youth leaders had been thinking about such a program seems evident from the way in which they reacted. No doubt they were encouraged by the success of Wyrtzen in New York; the impact of that first mammoth rally brought the idea into national focus.

Suddenly and quickly the idea took hold. Leaders making plans were encouraged by the results in Philadelphia, Detroit and New York. The groups started quickly and in many cities. With no central organization there was no way of keeping accurate records of the progress of the movement. Roger Malsbary, a young Christian and Missionary Alliance pastor in Indianapolis, Indiana, held his first meeting in May, 1943. Dick Harvey in St. Louis, Missouri, watched Malsbary's program grow, and Malsbary helped Harvey in the forming of an organization in St. Louis. Early in 1944 George Wilson in Minneapolis, Minnesota, was inspired, and the Minneapolis Youth for Christ Singspiration came into existence. In Chicago, Torrey M. Johnson, having contacted Wyrtzen, Harvey, Malsbary and others, brought Chicagoland Youth for Christ to Orchestra Hall in May, 1944.

They were popping up all over. Charles Templeton, a Toronto, Canada, preacher (former cartoonist), was supported by the Christian Business Men's Committee in bringing Youth for Christ into existence there. Servicemen in Honolulu started Youth for Christ meetings and the auditorium of the McKinley High School proved too small for the throng. Bermuda Youth for Christ opened up—the work of two sailors. All over the United States the units sprung up.

The pattern and formula of each group varied little. Good music, testimonies by young people who had been born again, and a God-centered message, constituted the main portion of the meetings. Servicemen were used whenever possible. An informal atmosphere was prevalent. Not a church service, each meeting was a youth rally. The message, with a definite appeal to young people, was short but pointed. Several groups even obtained radio time for their rallies.

As the sparks continued to ignite, the most successful groups were besieged with letters from interested individuals and organizations. Malsbary in Indianapolis, receiving many letters, began to compose plans for a national organization. In the summer of 1944 he was invited to speak at world-famous Winona Lake, Indiana, and later that summer he and Arthur W. McKee, executive director of the Winona Lake Conference Grounds, were hosts to several Youth for Christ leaders at an informal gathering. The group agreed to meet at Detroit in November, 1944, and at that meeting plans were made for a Youth for Christ Conference to be held at Winona Lake in 1945. Torrey Johnson was named temporary chairman of the conference. Since a national group was in the process of being formed, the inquiries were sent to the temporary chairman. The amount of correspondence received necessitated the establishment of an office in Chicago. From February 1, 1945, until the summer of 1945, the office in Chicago functioned as a service office for the hundreds of groups seeking information and help.

The amazing growth continued. Chicagoland Youth for

Christ sponsored a rally at the Chicago Stadium in the fall of 1944, which thirty thousand people attended; hundreds of them were saved. National magazines, both secular and religious, publicized the movement from time to time. From these magazine articles other leaders gained helpful information. The number of employees in the temporary office in Chicago necessarily was increased, but the office depended on God to supply the needed finances. Thorough and complete plans were made for the first convention to be held at Winona Lake in July. Leaders from all over the globe received invitations to that conference; over seven hundred letters were sent. But in all the planning there was full dependence on the Lord for His guidance at the conference and in the forming of a central organization.

Those at the conference decided unanimously that a central office should be established. Youth for Christ, they agreed, was here to stay for a while; therefore, an office was essential. Each leader had done outstanding work in his local area. Co-operatively, they united to form one central, national group which would be the spearhead of the campaign. Torrey M. Johnson of Chicago was elected president, the organization was given the name "Youth for Christ International" and a budget of $200,000 was adopted. The delegates returned to their homes with even greater zeal and vision for the glorious work of Youth for Christ.

At present there are over one thousand Youth for Christ organizations throughout the world. Youth for Christ has spread over the North American continent and stretched into at least forty-five foreign countries. One of the major reasons for its expansion is the consecrated work of American servicemen who proved to be true servants of God in all parts of the world. G.I.'s started at least three Youth for Christ meetings in Germany. They were instrumental in the organization of fifteen Youth for Christ rallies in China and sixteen in Japan. Manila, Guam, Okinawa, Frankfurt, and even ships returning to the United

States have been the scene of Youth for Christ Meetings. In a remarkable way young people have been won to Christ. Thousands of missionaries were forced home by the war, but soul-burdened G.I.'s took up the fight for Christ when they reached those areas. Not a few servicemen asked for their discharges overseas in order to continue the Youth for Christ work in those areas.

The call from Europe was strong and persistent. In the spring of 1946 four Youth for Christ leaders—Torrey M. Johnson, Billy Graham, Charles Templeton and Stratton Shufelt—flew to the continent for a period of six weeks to help in the organization of Youth for Christ. About six months later 22,000 people packed an auditorium at Oslo, Norway, to hear Hubert Mitchell, Asiatic representative of Youth for Christ, preach the Gospel. Youth for Christ was greedily accepted throughout the countries which were visited. Not only were souls converted but temporary organizations were formed, which in the course of time became permanent Youth for Christ groups.

The door to Holland opened after a baker on the south side of Chicago—Joe Biegel—proved the inspiration and the spark to send forth a Youth for Christ team to the Dutch. On the team were Rev. Spencer De Jong, a minister of the Reformed Church of America in Chicago, Don De Vos, assistant pastor of Calvary Undenominational Church, Grand Rapids, Michigan, and Douglas Fisher of Chicagoland Youth for Christ. Forty-two meetings were held on thirty-seven nights in twenty-four cities. Fifty-six thousand people attended, and so powerful was the working of the Holy Spirit that 3,500 responses were made to the invitations.

The call for more help in Great Britain was answered by Billy Graham and Cliff and Billie Barrows, Graham serving as speaker, Barrows as song leader, and Mrs. Barrows as pianist. For six months these consecrated young men couducted campaigns througout the British Isles, and thousands of young people accepted Christ. The culmination of their work came in Birmingham, England, on March 26-29, 1947, when 250 delegates from all over the Continent met and formed the British Youth for Christ.

South America, Mexico, China, Australia, Greece, Scandinavia—the calls for help kept coming in and, as we'll see later, much was done to meet those needs.

"It can't last," people said. But instead of dying out as had been predicted, Youth for Christ is still expanding and growing. This is true especially of the foreign countries and rural areas in North America.

Youth for Christ perhaps has caused more comment and criticism than any other Christian movement in decades. Being interdenominational in character, it has not been supported wholeheartedly by denominations which feel that they have adequate programs for their young people. One Christian periodical said of Youth for Christ, . . ."at least it is better than crime." In most cases it has received the unqualified disapproval of Christian liberals. The Communists in America have strongly opposed it, and are still opposing it; Communistic propaganda has extinguished at least two organizations. Pastors in many cities have raised the objection that the movement is not church-centered; other pastors, however, are using Youth for Christ to build up their churches. A Methodist pastor in Portland, Oregon, has twenty-eight young people active in his church as a result of the Youth for Christ movement in Portland. Opposition also has come from Christians who feel that the movement as a whole is too superficial for the attainment of permanent results. It also has been accused of being anti-Semitic and anti-Negro.

Youth for Christ, regardless of its temporary or permanent character, is recognized as one of the major religions phenomena of the twentieth century. In a day when juvenile delinquency presents a serious problem, Youth for Christ is pulling young people away from the paths of sin, and it is introducing them to the Saviour of the world, the stainless One. Were the movement to stop as suddenly as it started, Christians around the world could still testify for many years of the blessings the movement brought to them. It has revealed to thousands of young people the secret of happy living.

Apparently it is not yet going to die. It has lived through the embryonic and early stages of life and in the strength of the Lord is continuing to thrive. Youth for Christ is making an impression upon the lives of young people around the world. It has missionary vision, and it hopes to challenge the young people of this generation to bring the Gospel to the four corners of the earth.

Without a doubt Youth for Christ is winning young people for the Lord. It seems to be an agency of God outside the church through which He is reaching the unsaved.

As has been said many times, if Youth for Christ is of man it will come to nothing, but if it is of God there is no human limit to its effectiveness, and to oppose it would be futile. That the world needs a globe-rocking revival is evident.

Youth for Christ may bring it!

Chapter 2

WAS YOUTH FOR CHRIST NEEDED?

T HE minister of a church in London was concerned
about his young people. They seemed to be drifting
away from the church and from God. They had
grown up during the war, and they truly presented a problem to himself and to the community. One day he gathered
all of them into a room in the church and asked them a few
questions in order to know how best to proceed to win
them for the Lord.

His first question was, "What do you know about Good
Friday?"

Following are a few of the answers he received:

> Pancakes!
> A day when someone was supposed to look after the
> cakes and let them burn.
> One of Robinson Crusoe's gang.
> Theodore roasted an ox.
> The day when Jesus disappeared in a burning bush.
> The legendary figure said to be a friend of Robinson
> Crusoe.

The pastor was shocked and disturbed, although he knew that only one per cent of all of the young people in the entire British Isles went to church regularly. As the meeting continued the young people asked him several questions, "How can a dead man hanging on a piece of wood save me?" and "Did Jesus live before or after the stone age?"

The London *Daily Mail* published the Church of England's Commission on Youth report on November 10, 1945, and the report revealed an alarming situation. The young people of England were degenerating ethically and decaying spiritually.

* . * *

The United States was little different from England in the early 1940's. Early in 1946 newspaper readers all over the land read this headline:

TEEN-AGERS LEAD IN CRIME BOOST

The reporter's story stated:

"In a year in which the increase in crime was the greatest in fifteen years, seventeen-year-olds won the dubious distinction of leading the way in 1945.

"That is revealed today in the current issue of the Uniform Crime Report Bulletin. The F.B.I. has been analyzing crime trends and publishing the Bulletin since 1931.

"Of 543,852 persons arrested in the country, 21 per cent were under 21 years of age. Arrests of males increased 10.1 per cent, and although arrests of girls under 21 declined 10.6 per cent, the figure was still 109.3 per cent in excess of that for 1941.

"J. Edgar Hoover recently warned that an army of five million criminals was preparing an attack upon the nation.

"An estimated total of 1,565,541 major crimes were committed in 1945, or an increase of 171,886 over 1944."

Mr. Hoover, in the March, 1946, issue of *The American* magazine, said, ". . . in the United States today there is one criminal for every twenty-three inhabitants . . . It is an even larger army than that which did the actual fighting against the Germans and the Japanese." He then went on to warn the American people to "build up the dikes against the coming flood, for you will pay the price." He made it clear that failure to make contact with the citizen of tomorrow was also producing a field for future crime.

Thousands of articles and millions of words have been written on the juvenile delinquency problem which existed during and following the war. There will always be a youth problem, but the facts and the figures proved that there was something radically wrong with the youth of this period. Shocking titles appeared in magazines:

Challenge of Youth: Meet Delinquency and Unrest Through Recreational Centers, Progressive Teaching Method, and the Home
Teen Trouble. What Can Recreation Do About It?
What's the Use of Being Good?
Youth is More Sinned Against than the Sinner
New Lost Generation
Shall We Blame the Young?
Is Hitler Youth Incurable?
Sociological View of the Youth Problem

Divorce courts worked overtime to undo the ties which men and women had promised to keep "until death do us part." In Los Angeles County in California the divorce rate in 1945 reached a distressing ninety per cent! There were 37,090 marriage licenses issued in that year, and 33,267 filings for divorce, annulment or separate maintenance.

Across the country the children of broken homes crowded the reformatories and correctional institutions; soon the orphans thronged the jails and penal institutions. The undesirable conditions led a writer on a Chicago daily newspaper to begin one of her reports with, "The divorce court today—juvenile or boys' court tomorrow." Then she submitted statistics which showed that between seventy and eighty per cent of all juvenile delinquency could be traced to broken homes.

Above: One of the great Minneapolis Youth For Christ rallies.
Below: Platform scene from the huge Fair Grounds Rally held in Minneapolis. From left to right: Bob Pierce, Walter Smyth, Dr. Oswald J. Smith, Bob Cook, George Wilson, Spencer De Jong, Charles E. Fuller (at the microphone), Richard Harvey, Billy Graham, Charles Templeton T. W. Wilson and David Morken.

Top: Jack Wyrtzen   Center: Torrey Johnson
Below: Youth For Christ Cabinet. First row, left to right: Rex Lindquist, Cliff Barrows, T. W. Wilson, Ed Darling, Bob Murfin, Ken Anderson. Second row, left to right: John Huffman, Walter Block, Richard Harvey, Torrey Johnson, George Wilson, Charles Templeton, Charles White. Third row, left to right: Bob Evans, David Morken, Bob Cook, Bob Pierce, Billy Graham, Watson Argue, Walter Smyth and Emerson Pent.

The lack of religious knowledge among young people was deplorable. In a test given to 18,434 high school pupils in southern states, 16,000 of them could not name three major prophets; 12,000 could not name the four Gospels; 10,000 could not name three disciples of Jesus.

Sixty-six per cent, according to Dr. U. W. Leavell who conducted the survey, were not enrolled in Sunday school. The average Sunday school attendance in the area was fifty per cent of its enrollment. This meant that less than seventeen per cent of the population in that area was receiving any religious instruction at all.

Each month in the United States the boys and girls were reading 9,260,000 cheap adventure magazines, nearly 3,000,000 filthy sex stories, 3,250,000 detective stories revealing all the methods of committing crimes, and more than 10,500,000 movie magazines, noted for sex appeal pictures.

But facts are unnecessary to prove that the general moral life of the world in the 1940's was at a tremendously low ebb. Moral decadence was visible on every hand and even touched, to a small extent, the sturdy confines of rural life. Conditions in the armed forces did not tend to improve men morally. Liquor flowed freely on all fronts, home and abroad; and the degrading spirit, "We don't care about anything," seeped into the lives of many professing Christians. This hampered the effectiveness of the church.

These lamentable conditions were a matter of concern for leaders around the world. "Unless there is a moral regeneration throughout the whole world, there is no hope for mankind," said General Eisenhower.

Into such a situation . . . came Youth for Christ.

Chapter 3

JUST WHO DID START THIS THING?

O NE of the most interesting and amusing parts of the research on this book was the long, seemingly unending search to discover the originator of Youth for Christ. *Sunday* magazine, edited by Robert Walker and published in Chicago, printed in its "Reader, Write or Wrong" column a lengthy discussion on the matter, which discussion was carried on for several months. After reading the discussion and engaging in extensive research, one is inclined to agree with the lady in Greenwich, Connecticut, who wrote in *Sunday* of December, 1945: "The Lord is the one who originated the movement. He began it in behalf of young people (6 or 60) because He loves us with His whole heart. It's marvelous that such men as Jack Wyrtzen and all the others are willing to be 'promoters' for this department of the King's business. I'm sure it isn't the question with these men of 'who first,' but, rather, 'Who'll be next?' Where are those who should be promoting it in their own home town and aren't? Some twenty million young people need Him! What a challenge!"

It is evident that the movement is of such an extensive and inexplainable nature that no human being could be responsible for it. A. L. Dague of San Francisco, California, wrote in the *Sunday* panel discussion: "Just as Peter was not the founder of the Church and Martin Luther was not the author of the Reformation, so no mere man can be given credit for fathering Youth for Christ. Christ Himself, working through many widely separated locations, is calling out the youth in this great movement. God is not defeated by man's unfaithfulness. When one group, organization, or generation begins to hide the Gospel under a bushel, He raises up another and the torch is passed on to those who will hold it high. I'm sure the high honor of being chosen by Him for such an enterprise is all the credit that all these fine people would ask or want."

The youth leaders themselves take no credit for initiating the movement; they attribute Youth for Christ to God. Their spirit reflects their dependence upon the Lord. As mentioned previously, all the youth leaders contacted were unusually co-operative in supplying information for this book. This spirit of co-operation is one of the major reasons for the success of the movement. They have stated the unusual facts humbly, indicating a thankfulness in their own hearts for the privilege of being used by Him in the salvation of precious young souls.

Back in 1904 two young Irishmen, Frederick and Arthur Wood, heard and answered the call of God to step out in faith as evangelists. They were brothers, nineteen and twenty-one years old, respectively. For seven years God used them mightily in Great Britain in churches and campaigns. As they noticed that most of their converts were young people, they felt a growing burden for youth. They sensed that they should specialize in working with young life. The vision of a movement of Christian youth winning its own generation to Christ became clearer.

Traveling one day in a train one of them traced on the misty window the letters Y.L.C. as they discussed the possibility of a National Young Life Campaign. The train moved on, the letters on the window disappeared, but the idea remained. The advice of outstanding leaders of the day was sought. Dr. F. B. Meyer, winsome preacher loved by multitudes on both sides of the Atlantic, was particularly identified with the initiation of the movement. He and others called a conference of ministers and representatives of youth societies. As a result the Wood brothers were encouraged to form an advisory council and to launch a series of young life campaigns all over the country.

That occurred in 1911. Since then many developments took place. City after city was visited. Thousands of young men and women were reached and won for Christ. The largest halls were crowded. Even the Royal Albert Hall in London witnessed in 1920 an amazing gathering of youth.

Then came the problem of after-care or follow-up work. The converts united in order to strengthen the spirit of evangelism in the evangelical churches. The National Youth Life Campaign was organized, a board was formed, officers were appointed, branch offices were established, and a magazine was started.

Today the movement has twelve thousand members, all converted and all committed to lives of consecration and service. Its staff numbers twenty. It has 268 branches, twelve voluntary evangelists, and during the war it had fourteen youth centers for servicemen. In addition, it has sent more than three hundred workers into full-time service for the Lord on the mission fields and in the home churches.

Membership is arbitrary. The slogan of the movement is "Every Campaigner a Soul-Winner—Every Church an Evangelizing Center." The watchword is "The Utmost for the Highest." It is in no way a competitor of the church but is complementary to the church. Its aim is to help every department of the church by strengthening the individual Christian. Upon prayer, Bible study and soul-winning it places much emphasis.

Its national headquarters are in Memorial Hall, Farringdon Street, London, E. C. 4. The leaders are still very active in evangelistic work in England. Lt. Gen. Sir William S. Dobbie is one of the vice-presidents of the movement; the late Campbell Morgan was also a vice-president. D. Graham Scroggie is now president.

In 1937 Mr. and Mrs. Frederick Wood came to the United States and toured the country in a series of meetings sponsored by the Christian Youth Campaign of America, of which Rev. Lloyd Bryant is director. On their tour they met young, handsome, fiery Jim Rayburn in Dallas, Texas. Jim at that time was attending school in Dallas, and upon graduation he enthusiastically started the Young Life Campaign in the United States. It is now doing an excellent job of reaching the high school young people.

The British Young Life Campaign may be acknowledged as one of the forerunners of the Youth for Christ movement. As will be seen later, the seeds of the Young Life Campaign in England were sown in various places in the United States, and they brought forth fruit in this country in several different ways. The development in Britain has been solid and substantial, and the movement has contributed definitely to the growth in grace of many thousands of young people in the British Isles. It differs from Youth for Christ in a marked way, however, in that no Saturday-night meetings are planned or held, or at least a Saturday-night meeting does not constitute the main meeting of the group. But young people are being reached and won for Christ.

Now, back again to the North American continent.

First we stop to pay tribute to a young man who, although not termed a Youth for Christ leader in the real sense of the word, is one of the men who has been used of

God to reach the young people of America in a remarkable way. One writer described him as "the man who has in a great way been responsible for Youth for Christ in America."

His name is Percy Crawford and he directs the Young People's Church of the Air radio program, which program has been on the air since 1931. The program originates in Philadelphia, Pennsylvania, every Sunday afternoon, is heard over the Mutual Broadcasting System and is short-waved by ten stations throughout the world. In addition to the radio program, Crawford heads the Pinebrook Bible Camp, King's College and the Pinebrook Book Club, which club is the most popular and extensive of such organizations in the Christian literary field. In addition, he is known as one of the top youth speakers in the land. He was the main speaker for seventy thousand people at the Chicago-land Youth for Christ rally in 1945; he also gave the message at the Hollywood Bowl meeting in 1946 which twenty thousand people attended and which resulted in a truly remarkable outpouring of the Holy Spirit. His speaking schedule is heavy, and very often on Saturday night he can be found at a Youth for Christ meeting.

Percy Crawford was converted in 1923 at the Church of the Open Door in Los Angeles, California. After studying at the University of California at Los Angeles, Wheaton College and the Bible Institute of Los Angeles, he moved to Philadelphia and enrolled at Westminister Seminary. His first year was spent in preparation for the Lord's work. In his second year his vision of "reaching youth with the truth" flamed. He held rallies in the Barnes Memorial Presbyterian Church, and the program was broadcast over station WIT. As news of the meetings spread, people jammed into the church, and hundreds were turned away.

Not long after a young lady named Ruth Duvall became pianist for the meetings. Percy promptly fell in love with her, and they were married. She organized the first Young People's Church of the Air quartet, and she is responsible to a large extent for the excellent music on the program. The next forward step was taking on the powerful station WMCA in New York. The number of stations increased and the blessing of the Lord in the saving of souls was definitely felt. Two nation-wide tours were unusually successful. San Diego, California, was perhaps the high light of both trips—twelve hundred men at the San Diego Naval Base stepped forward as one man to accept Christ.

Unconsciously many Youth for Christ speakers have patterned their messages after Crawford's preaching. He speaks the language of youth in a frank, sincere and fearless way. He wavers not a whit from the old-fashioned Gospel. In a somewhat high-pitched voice, he speaks rapidly, and hammers his points home with plenty of Scripture. His influence on many present-day Youth for Christ leaders has been important, since his radio broadcast paved the way for the twentieth century youth movement. He brought his first message from a diving board in one of the toughest sections of Philadelphia, as a young, nervous would-be preacher. Today, after a Sunday broadcast, he may receive as many as three hundred letters telling of people who made decisions after hearing him over the air.

He showed it could be done . . . even by radio.

Before Crawford came on the scene, however, a national organization was in its embryonic stage in New York city. Boston-born Lloyd Bryant, reared in the Boston slums and the victim of a broken home, had a definite vision of reaching the 27,000,000 young people in America who had no religious connections. His heart was burdened with the drift away from the Sunday school. The thousands of unconverted young people in his own backyard were a challenge to "do something about it." The result was The Christian Youth Campaign of America.

Bryant conducted his first Christian youth broadcast in 1929, but there was no definite weekly program until 1932 when he went into Times Square, using the Christian Missionary Alliance Tabernacle at Forty-fourth Street and Eighth Avenue. From 1932 through 1939 he conducted approximately five hundred rallies, meeting not on Saturday but on Monday and Tuesday nights. Outstanding programs with recognized speakers were arranged. Such leaders as Erling C. Olsen, J. Wesley Ingles, Grace Livingston Hill and Rev. Wyeth Willard, spoke in 1934. The 1935 programs included Percy Crawford, Dr. Harry Rimmer, Harry S. Smith, Dr. Will Houghton; the Wheaton College Glee Club was featured on an evening. Walter MacDonald, Dr. Bob Jones, Sr., Dr. William B. Riley, Harry Vom Bruch, George Dewey Blomgren and others drew nearly thirty-five thousand young people during the 1936 meetings, with sixteen hundred as the largest crowd. A testimony to the entire area was given during Christian Mobilization Week from October 25 through November 1; this week of services in which as many as ten youth rallies were held simultaneously was concluded by a great mass meeting.

Bryant traveled extensively in furthering the movement. He toured America, riding about fourteen thousand miles, reaching 25,000 young people with the film, "Youth Marches On," and leaving in his trail a stirring challenge for personal soul-winning. Organization on a national scale came in 1935, with the name "The Association of Christian Youth in America" as the selected and official title. The association was patterned after the Young Life Campaign in Great Britain, and membership was also on an individual basis. Forty groups in about as many cities participated in this movement.

The movement was used to the saving of souls. There was evidence of a spiritual awakening in all places where it operated. In New York alone the organization had a mailing list of ten thousand, and from twelve to fifteen hundred attended the weekly rallies. Bryant proved that it could be done, even in New York City. Others saw his success and followed his example in their little corners.

The movement is still alive in some cities, and in New York it holds the New York Youth Forum at 340 West 55th Street each Monday night. A "School for Christian Leadership" was formed in 1945 as a part of the work. Dr. Will Houghton, president of the Moody Bible Institute, evaluated the work in these words, "Mr. Bryant has been wonderfully used of the Lord in organizing and developing youth activities. Always bearing in mind the right goals—evangelism and the building up of the faith—he has been successful in arousing and holding the interest of the young people." Evidence of this was the Christian Youth Center in New York City, which served as the meeting place for the rallies. He had much vision and in 1937 arranged the nation-wide tour of Mr. and Mrs. Frederick Wood of England, including a not-soon-forgotten Memorial Day parade in New York.

If anyone was working on the ground floor, even digging the basement in the building of a movement to reach American youth, it was Lloyd Bryant and his co-workers in the Association of Christian Youth in America. His work has been tested and proved. As a "national laboratory," it reports that "it works!" Twentieth-century methods to reach young people were used, and they proved workable. The seed was sown in a skillful and prayerful way. Lloyd Bryant has not seen his own organization used of God to the extent that Youth for Christ is being used of God today; but it can be said that the Youth for Christ movement had many of its roots in his plans. Jack Wyrtzen, aggressive Word of Life leader in New York, was once a member of one of Bryant's Gospel teams.

* * *

We move along to Washington, D.C.

In April, 1930, a group of young people felt a need for a deeper life in Christ and started to hold meetings in the vestry of the Metropolitan Memorial Church at 30 South Sixth Street. There were only eight or ten who met at first,

but the number grew rapidly. The meetings were held
on Tuesday nights and were similar to those of Youth for
Christ today. They lasted for an hour, and such men as
Jack Wyrtzen, Glenn Wagner, Clifford Lewis, James E.
Bennett and Phil Saint spoke for them. Young people
from all denominations began to come, and almost every
week there were decisions made for Christ. In the first six
months there were young people on hand from twenty-one
denominations and representing fifty-six churches.

The aim of the "Christian Youth Fellowship," as it was
called, was to lead unsaved young people to Christ and to
help those who were saved to lives of deeper devotion.
The C.Y.F. continued for twelve years, until 1942, under
the direction of Eugene A. Scheele, now general secretary
of the Tract Club of America. It published a monthly
paper, The Quest, which served as a rallying point for
through-the-week contact.

Still looking and moving around in the 1930's, we find a
group in the Evangelical Free Church in Brooklyn, New
York, holding Saturday-night meetings "for as long as I
[Jack Wyrtzen] can remember." We see the Plymouth
Brethren holding Saturday-night meetings to win the unsaved. We move up to Jamestown, New York, and observe
a group meeting in a home for Bible study and calling itself
"Youth for Christ." And Wyeth Willard, founder and director of the Good News and Good Cheer boys and girls
camp, printed and used millions of attractive stamps in
1936 with the banner "Youth for Christ" across the top.

We cross the Canadian border and reach Brantford, On-
tario. It is 1934, and we find a group of young people meet-
ing in a theater each Sunday night from eight forty-five
to ten o-clock. This group is named Brantford Youth for
Christ. How did it get started? A young Australian, Paul
Guiness, came to Canada with a burning desire to start a
Christian youth movement in the high schools and colleges.
After speaking in Brantford, his vision was imparted to the

hearts of Brantford young people. At first the meetings were held in the homes of the members, but they had to move from spot to spot to accommodate the crowds; finally the theater was rented. In the fall of 1934 the crowds reached five hundred several times. One of the speakers was a young fellow named Stacey Woods, now general secretary of the Inter-Varsity Christian Fellowship. They went on the radio for 207 consecutive broadcasts when a Christian lady in Brantford decided to help finance a radio program. Souls were converted regularly. In the spring of 1938 Dr. John Zoller and Douglas Hine of Detroit conducted a special campaign which brought forth a genuine spirit of revival. With the spirit of revival, the movement gained momentum, and a summer Bible conference was held. Attendance averaged between four and five hundred during the fall and winter months.

When the war came the group was forced to cancel its services, as the leaders and the majority of the young men went off to battle. Now that the fighting is over, it is again active and flourishing. With the aim of becoming dominion-wide the movement is spreading throughout Canada. Groups now exist in Niagara Falls, Hamilton, Brantford, Tilsonburg, London and Sarnia. Evon Hedley and John Stewart, now home from service, are energetically engaging in this work of reaching Canadian youth for Christ.

Thus we find Youth for Christ in Canada as early as 1934. As we look at the speaking roster of Brantford Youth for Christ, we find the name of Jack Wyrtzen. Another seed was being sown.

In 1934 a young fellow in southern California felt burdened for the young people of that great area. His name was Oscar Gillian, and his idea revolved around a group known as the Voice of Christian Youth. Radio broadcasts were the basis of the movement. Later Gospel teams were formed, which conducted meetings in various places. Once a month a great rally was held, and men such as Irwin

Moon, Charles E. Fuller and Clifford E. Lewis participated as speakers.

In 1937 Gillian crisscrossed Horace Greeley and headed east, not west. He went to Detroit and became the pastor of a Presbyterian church. A year later, after much prayer and persistent work, the Detroit Voice of Christian Youth came into being. Detroit was one of the first to use "Youth for Christ" in its program. A certificate used in its plans had these words, "Voice of Christian Youth—Our motto: Youth for Christ."

But just when it seemed as though the new group needed him the most, Gillian felt led to accept a pastorate call to Vancouver, British Columbia. Milton Strong took Gillian's place in the movement, and the Christian Business Men's Committee also decided to help. Initial meetings were held in the Missionary Tabernacle, which seats three hundred. In April of 1942 the services moved to the Wesley Methodist Church, seating one thousand. The next jump was to the Cass Technical High School, seating three thousand, where young people at night could learn of Christ and where they studied their school books during the day.

Growth called for another vital change in 1943, and it was decided to hold two meetings a month, one on the east side of town, one on the west. This arrangement worked effectively for a year, and then the two groups were united in one meeting on alternate weeks in the beautiful Art Institute Building. When hundreds continued to be turned away, another meeting place was necessary. Ed Darling, converted night club entertainer, and other Detroit leaders prayed . . . and the old Wilson Theater was remodeled into a cultural center to serve as the home of the Ford Sunday Evening Hour. It cost $50,000 to remodel the building and another $35,000 for the platform, "just so we could present Christ," Director Darling said.

Detroit now can humbly boast of being one of the oldest Youth for Christ groups in the world. It is well organized.

It supports five foreign missionaries. It carries on a varied and intensive ministry. On the Saturday nights on which rallies are not held the leaders can be found helping other Youth for Christ groups in the Great Lakes area. Decisions for salvation are followed up carefully, and many Detroit young people are on mission fields because of the challenge of V.C.Y.

And what of Gillian? As soon as he reached Vancouver he organized a Voice of Christian Youth. So successful was it in New Westminister and Vancouver that in October of 1944 he resigned his pastorate to go into the work full time. The groups there met on Monday and Tuesday nights since auditoriums are not available on Saturday nights. Here, too, we find a well-organized group doing a thorough and solid job.

Philadelphia—city of brotherly love—has a likeable young fellow by the name of Walter Smyth directing a youth center which is admirably reaching the city's youth for Christ. At the initial meeting in 1934 there were only fourteen. Now the number reaches one thousand. In addition to the work at the center, a regular meeting is held at which young people from all over the city gather for inspiration, singspiration and a message from a young people's speaker. This is another place where the youth movement was tested and proved itself worthy of the task to come.

Young men on fire for Christ . . . all over the North American continent. For years they have been proving that youth programs and youth meetings are not only possible but can do a mighty work for God. We have seen how God has blessed their individual ministries with souls and sent many young people forth into the whitened fields. As they have ventured out, others have watched them. Seed has been sown. As we look back in 1946, we see the many ways in which God has used various men and organizations. There likely are many which have not been covered in this brief survey, but we feel that the picture is synoptic.

We come to 1940. All the groups and men mentioned are doing their work for youth at this time, and God is blessing in a definite way. There seems to be but one thing necessary —someone to "start the fireworks." Once again, God has His man. For years He has been molding and shaping a young insurance salesman and ex-orchestra leader in New York. Now He pulls him forth, gives him the faith to start when he sees the "Go" sign, and we're on our way!

The name: Jack Wyrtzen.

The organization: Word of Life Hour.

The result: Youth for Christ in its present style and pattern.

Frank Mead, one of the able writers in *The Christian Herald*, said, "It was Wyrtzen who started the ball rolling," and added the following words:

"We've offered youth everything from the Golden Gate Bridge to a fifteen-cent box of candy at Christmas, thinking we could bribe them with that. And still they leave us! We're giving them milk bars, gymnasiums, summer camps, rumpus rooms, and picnics—and they want none of it and and none of us. We've made it ridiculously easy to join the church, we've watered down the requirements and apologized for the requirements we've kept; we've made a lot of our churches ninety per cent country club and ten per cent Gospel hall—and along comes Jack Wyrtzen and all the rest of the Youth for Christ leaders, offering nothing but the unvarnished Gospel we thought they didn't want, asking them only that they change their whole way of thinking and their whole way of living. And youth goes for it, not in dribbles, not by twos and threes, but by thousands! Something goes on here that cannot be laughed off. What all the denominations have not been able to do, with all their resources, organization and highly trained experts, these men have done outside the church. They have cut clean across denominational lines; they laugh at sectarianism; they even disregard the old division lines of the Gospel that has made them fishers of youth without equal in our times.

"Maybe they're wrong. Maybe Jack Wyrtzen is wrong; maybe what he is doing will not last. Only time and the Lord will tell us that, and Wyrtzen, for one, is willing to stand that test. But this much is as plain as the noses on our faces: This is a major religious phenomenon of our day, stirring youth as youth has not been stirred for a generation. It is a completely spontaneous spiritual eruption. Without the aid of any denominational or organized religious machinery whatsoever, without a single expert borrowed from any church board, these men are getting decisions for Christ that the church failed to get.

"Is it they who are wrong, or we? Can it be that we have the wrong technique with youth in our churches? And can it be that we have been offering them stones in the form of gyms and recreation rooms rather than bread in the form of the Gospel?"

Much has been written about Jack Wyrtzen and his co-workers on the Word of Life Hour for the simple reason that they have done much. Ever since the first Word of Life Hour radio program went on the air from a small station in Brooklyn, New York, Wyrtzen has been the center of a beehive of activity, and this activity has borne eternal fruit in amazing quantities.

He was born in Brooklyn, and his parents were Universalists. He was permitted to do as he pleased in matters of religion—and in other things, too. Before he was old enough to shave, he learned how to smoke, cuss and drink. He had a passion for two things—athletics and music. He could run the one-hundred-yard dash in ten seconds. He played the trombone in his school's orchestra; and he organized his own orchestra which played in the dimly lit dens of juvenile delinquency.

Jack's dad lost his job as a foreman in a glass factory during the depression in 1933, and that was the signal for

Jack to quit high school. In order to relieve the financial situation at home, he became an insurance salesman. The income which he received was supplemented by earnings from playing in a dance band which specialized in entertaining at sorority and fraternity parties. He joined the National Guard to play his trombone on horseback as a member of the cavalry band. There were plenty of cocktails, and there was plenty of sin in those days. Even in the matter of carousing he took second place to no one. He was young, good-looking, full of fun and intent on having a good time in the only way of which he knew.

Then "it" happened to his bosom friend, George Schilling. Schilling was converted in the Calvary Baptist Church in New York City. Schilling came back determined to win Jack and everyone else in the National Guard unit to Christ. Jack laughed at him even louder than did the others. Religion to him was for old ladies. Schilling gave Jack a Gospel of John, which he slipped into his pocket. One day, when looking for a match, Jack found it. He took it and tore out the pages one by one as he recited, "She loves me, she loves me not." He told Schilling about it, expecting him to be angry, but Schilling merely handed him another Gospel of John!

Jack was certain that Schilling would be "back with the boys" when they went to guard camp one summer at Pine Camp, New York, but he didn't slip once all summer. Jack began to wonder—perhaps Schilling had something. After they returned, George asked Jack one night to play his trombone at a Gospel meeting to be held in a YMCA building. Jack agreed; he was willing to play his trombone anywhere, even at a Gospel service. He played that night, but he also listened . . . to the testimonies, to the message, to the singing. When the meeting was over he went home and slipped up to his bedroom. After deliberating for a while, he quietly knelt by his bed, all alone, and accepted Christ as his Saviour; II Corinthians 5:17 be-

Top: Scene from Toronto Youth For Christ Rally.
Below: Youth for Christ float in Aquatennial parade, Minne-
       apolis.

Top: Publicity scene from Illinois Valley Youth For Christ, promoting their large Stadium Rally.

Below: Scene from outdoor rally in St. Petersburg, Florida.

came real to him, "Therefore if any man be in Christ, he is a new creature: old things are passed away; behold all things are become new."

From that night on Jack Wyrtzen was a new man. He had but one consuming passion in life—to know his Bible better so he could tell others of Christ. He didn't waste any time. With Schilling (now pastor of a Baptist church in Middlebury, Vermont,) and four other young fellows, Jack formed a Bible study class which met in his bedroom. As they studied they witnessed. He started to preach every noon to an assorted congregation in the City Hall Park, spending the better part of his lunch hour holding forth the Word of Life to an assembly of clerical workers, Bowery bums, Wall Street brokers and others. God honored his efforts, and souls were saved.

He was eager to do real work for the Lord. He met Percy Crawford, and Percy advised him to go into youth evangelism with the radio as his pulpit. Together with a few of his friends, he launched a Tuesday morning broadcast over WBBC in Brooklyn. It clicked. Soon he found that he didn't have enough time to work full time as an insurance man ("I was in the fire insurance business and Beverly Shea was in the life insurance business. Now we're working together in the eternal life insurance business") and do his religious work. The decision was hard to make, but he made it, and courageously set out. Before making the decision, he had sold insurance by day and spoken at night with Gospel teams and Pocket Testament League groups in all types of places—churches, jails, missions and C.C.C. camps.

His radio program was very successful; consequently, another big step was taken in October of 1941 when he brought his program to the powerful 50,000 watt WHN in New York. In his home town he had held his first youth rally in a local Lutheran church, and two hundred people had come. Within three months the average attendance was

635—as much as the auditorium could hold. The rallies had to be held in a larger auditorium. But where? Then it was that Jack took the matter to the Lord and received an answer which was of utmost importance. Even he himself was unprepared for the answer which came. The answer was, "Times Square."

Cautious friends advised against it, and perhaps justly so, as the downtown section of New York was known as an "evangelist's graveyard." When they heard that he was going to hold his meetings on Saturday nights, the disapproval became more pronounced.

But Wyrtzen waded in. He rented the Christian Missionary Alliance Tabernacle on Forty-fourth Street and Eighth Avenue and prepared to do business in the devil's backyard. The first night found only 250 people there, but soon after the Tabernacle was packed. The slim fingers of radio and WHN reached out and brought in the people until the crowds averaged one thousand a night.

Carnegie Hall was next, and it was at one of the meetings there that the policeman jokingly remarked, "You'll have to move into Madison Square Garden soon."

The seed was sown in Wyrtzen's mind. A few weeks later Jack mentioned that statement in a church in which he was speaking. A wealthy businessman was touched by God through that remark and dropped a check for one thousand dollars into the collection basket as a partial payment for a rally in Madison Square Garden. It took faith and courage to put on that first rally, but the Word of Life Hour workers had both. God honored the constant prayers offered in behalf of this project, and when the rally was held there were twenty thousand people on the inside and ten thousand turned away!

From that day on, April 1, 1944, in Wyrtzen's own words, "The movement seemed to spread like wildfire all around the country." His mail was filled with letters from interested youth leaders all over the land. He had been holding meetings in Times Square each Saturday night for two and one-half years, but not until the first giant rally did meetings start to pop out all over. Indianapolis had begun to hold rallies in 1943, and St. Louis, Minneapolis and Chicago were in the early stages of existence in the spring of 1944. Jack was more than willing to give to interested leaders all the help he could give, and his words of encouragement did much to get many rallies started. In the east he readily spoke at the initial meetings, and he also helped with organization plans.

The extent of Wyrtzen's Word of Life work is amazing. His radio program is heard from coast to coast and around the world by short-wave each Saturday night. The radio budget alone is $3,500 weekly. His Word of Life boat rides have attracted as many as 4,500 young people for a four-hour evangelistic cruise. A Word of Life men's banquet each winter draws as many as eight hundred men into such places as the Commodore and Astor hotels. Every Friday night he conducts a Word of Life Bible School in the National Bible Institute building at 340 West 55th Street. There is no charge, and over three hundred students were enrolled for the 1946 fall term. In addition, he offers free correspondence courses to radio listeners.

Three rallies in Madison Square Garden have drawn 67,000 people! At the first two rallies, fourteen hundred young people signed cards indicating a decision to accept Christ or to dedicate their lives to His service. At the third rally on September 29, 1945, the Holy Spirit moved in the great throng in a wonderful way and 2,400 decision cards were signed. Each convert receives a personal letter plus the book *The New Man* by Capt. Reginald Wallis. His other follow-up plan includes the use of the Navigator Bible Memory Plan and Bible Study. Eight stenographers are kept busy handling the mass of follow-up work necessary.

Months in advance plans for the Word of Life Hour

rallies are made. Prayer is the core of all the planning. Everything on the program is accurately timed, and the entire evening revolves around the thirty-minute broadcast. Forty-five-second testimonies speed out over the air to the radio audience. Wyrtzen usually brings the radio-message —"his feet braced behind the pulpit, his hands holding hard to the side and his words driving home the message with the speed and force of a machine gun." People don't go to sleep when he speaks. Following the radio program, the main speaker of the evening brings his message. Wyrtzen works hard to get the best in speakers—young men, especially, who know how to reach young people. Without exception, there have been souls saved at every rally. In one meeting there were 108 decisions; in another 204; in another 109. In the first three months of 1946 there were more decisions made than in any other previous three-month period.

Jack travels much. He spends only one night a week with his family. He tries to get back to New York for the Saturday-night broadcast, but if he cannot be in New York, he broadcasts from a large city along the way. In the early summer of 1946 the programs originated from Edinburgh, Scotland; London, England; Cardiff, Wales; and Belfast, Ireland, as he, Carleton Booth and Harry Bollbach spent thirty days in revival meetings throughout the British Isles.

Wyrtzen's youth fire kindled men all over the country. Washington, D.C. felt the glow in a new way as Glenn Wagner, former All-American Tackle at the University of Illinois, assumed the directorship of Washington Youth for Christ in addition to his duties as president of the Washington Bible College. Philadelphia's Youth Center increased in attendance and interest. Detroit's Voice of Christian Youth, as we have seen, started to feel its growing pains in a new way about this time. One spark jumped to the Middle West and lit the prepared heart of young Roger Malsbary in Indianapolis. Bucking the same kind of oppo-

sition which Wyrtzen had met and the taunts, "It'll never
work, it'll never work," Malsbary rented the English
Theater in the heart of Indianapolis and set up meetings.
One of his first speakers was a towheaded young preacher
from Chicago, Torrey M. Johnson, who later became the
first president of Youth for Christ International. Malsbary
held his first rally on May 27, 1943, and called it "Indianapolis Youth for Christ." As the Indianapolis unit grew and as
God blessed it with souls, leaders throughout the Middle
West queried him for information and help even as they had
questioned Wyrtzen. One day Malsbary, although sick,
went to St. Louis to meet with Dick Harvey and a group of
interested men there. The result, in February of 1944,
was St. Louis Youth for Christ.

Indianapolis stands high in the list of cities which first felt
the power of Youth for Christ. Youth for Christ there has
developed into one of the strongest units in the world.
There are Youth for Christ clubs in four of the city's high
schools. These clubs hold meetings once a week and prayer
meetings each morning at eight o'clock. A giant singspiration is held the first Sunday afternoon of each month.
Eighty young people are enrolled in a Bible training center
which meets evenings from Tuesday through Friday. This
training center also serves as an ideal arrangement for
effective follow-up work. High on the list of blessings which
have been showered on Indianapolis Youth for Christ are
the second anniversary rallies in 1945 which lasted for two
weeks; 209 professions of faith were made at that time.

By now the sparks are flying to all parts of the North
American continent so rapidly that it is difficult to keep
an accurate record. Here, there and everywhere youth
leaders who feel burdened for the young people of their
communities are led by God to step out in faith and start
rallies in their localities. Advice and help is passed around
freely; directors exchange experiences by mail and help
each other over the rough spots. Speakers say, "It's much

easier to preach in Youth for Christ meetings than any other place, as the power of the Holy Spirit is felt so much." Young people are saved by the tens, by the twenties, by the fifties and even by the hundreds! The growth of Youth for Christ startles and confounds even the most experienced of churchmen. Even the secular press notes that this is not "just another meeting."

How did it boom? What caused it to spread like wildfire? Someone had sown much seed in previous years. Others, perhaps, had watered it heavily with prayer. Now suddenly it is time for the harvest. Reapers who have been peculiarly prepared for this task are ready to go into the whitened fields. Even when millions of men were in the service there were still enough at home to begin the work. Servicemen did not shirk their duty either but established Youth for Christ in London, Paris, Manila, Tokyo, Frankfurt.

Big trees from little acorns grow. Some trees grow too fast; that has been one criticism of Youth for Christ. Critics feel that because it grew so fast it will wilt very soon. Whether Youth for Christ will endure remains to be seen. One thing is certain—it is here.

Now let's watch the bonfire blaze!

Chapter 4

"HERE WE GO!"

YOUTH for Christ's spontaneous beginning and rapid growth are amazing. Due to its sudden outburst, it was somewhat difficult to check the facts on the manner and circumstances in which Youth for Christ started. It was also difficult to keep pace with its phenomenal growth.

Being not too concerned about exact chronology, we go first to St. Louis, Missouri, where we meet a young Christian and Missionary Alliance pastor named Richard Harvey. The results which Percy Crawford had been experiencing convinced Harvey that a youth rally could also be successful in St. Louis. He knew of Wyrtzen and Malsbary, and he contacted both of them. Harvey spoke at one of the early meetings of Indianapolis Youth for Christ and kept his eyes open during the meeting to see how Malsbary was working. Harvey started to plan for a Youth for Christ

51

organization in St. Louis in the fall of 1943, and Malsbary came from Indianapolis to speak to the committee of leaders which Harvey had selected. The "kickoff" took place the first Saturday night in February, 1944, after months of praying and planning. Dr. Robert G. Lee of Memphis, Tennessee, was the first speaker. Naturally, Harvey and his committee wondered what kind of response they would have that night. They did not have long to wait. The Municipal Auditorium was packed with one thousand young people, and several hundred were turned away. Souls were won to Christ at that very first meeting and in every meeting following. Not only have young people found Christ, but the mayor of St. Louis told Harvey one day that Youth for Christ had done a great deal to reduce delinquency in St. Louis.

St. Louis was one of the first, if not the first, to use the Bible Quiz which has proved to be so popular. It provided excellent contact with the churches and allowed for church recognition. Servicemen were used as ushers during the war. Each Saturday night servicemen were given the opportunity to call home from the platform of the auditorium. Along with the regular Saturday-night program, the leaders sponsored three successful Master Rallies, patterned after Jack Wyrtzen's Madison Square Garden meetings. From the very beginning St. Louis Youth for Christ proved to be a spiritual success. People heard about the meetings, and Harvey received about one hundred requests for information and advice. He was able to help these interested leaders because of the careful way in which he had planned the entire organization. A man of vision and faith, Harvey was willing to risk his salary and modest home in St. Louis in order to launch Youth for Christ.

From St. Louis we move to Minneapolis, Minnesota. In August, 1937, George Wilson, a young Baptist layman, had gone to Atlanta, Georgia, for a long, long look at the Baptist World Alliance Conference held there. A crowd of 100,000 had gathered for an entire week, and George Wilson received a vision at that time of reaching young people. A graduate of the Northwestern Bible School in 1936, and having spent two years in the Northwestern Theological Seminary's religious education course, Wilson went into the publishing business instead of the ministry. He took specialized training in journalism at the North Dakota State University and at the University of Minnesota. After completing his course, he established the Northwestern Bible and Book House in Minneapolis, which has since been expanded to include Wilson Press and other affiliate organizations.

It was April, 1944—the last Saturday. For several months Wilson, Mervin Rosell and other youth leaders in Minneapolis had been planning a great Saturday-night musicale and singspiration as the feature of the annual Homecoming Week at Northwestern Bible School. They spent more money for advertising the Saturday-night meeting than for the advertising of the entire conference. They opened the doors that Saturday night . . . and three thousand young people jammed the auditorium of the First Baptist Church!

George asked them if they would like to come back two weeks later for more singing, and they shouted, as if in one voice, "Yes!" So it was that on April 27, 1944, the first real City-wide Minneapolis Youth for Christ Singspiration was held. Again the church was packed, so much so that a young pastor from Chicago by the name of Torrey M. Johnson (he was holding meetings at the Central Free Church in Minneapolis), who came after eight o'clock, had to stand for the entire service!

During the summer a temporary committee was formed and a meeting was announced for the Municipal Auditorium on October 21, 1944, with R. G. LeTourneau as the main speaker. A week before the rally *Life* magazine carried its lengthy article on Mr. LeTourneau and this recognition helped to bring 7,500 people to the service.

There had been much prayer in behalf of that meeting, and God honored it in a wonderful after-meeting at which sixty-five young people accepted Christ as Saviour.

Working hand in hand with a pastor's committee, Wilson holds meetings every-other Saturday night in the Municipal Auditorium, which seats ten thousand people. The Minneapolis group has become known as the largest Youth for Christ group in the world. On several occasions the auditorium has been filled to capacity. At the beginning the program was broadcast over WLOL and WDGY. The talent which has been made available to Minneapolis young people is the best in the world. Wilson is chock-full of ideas, one resulted in an outstanding New Year's Day "Swedish Smorgasbord," a fellowship supper which started at five-thirty on the first day of the New Year, and which was followed by an evangelistic service in the auditorium upstairs. Dr. Wilbur Smith of the Moody Bible Institute spoke in 1945 and Dr. Charles E. Fuller in 1946. Easter sunrise services are sponsored each year. When Gil Dodds, holder of the world's indoor mile record, spoke in Minneapolis, an indoor track was prepared and Dodds ran an exhibition race against two leading high-school runners from the Minneapolis area. The crowd was thrilled to see Dodds run, but it was given an even greater thrill when both of the fellows accepted Christ as Saviour following the race. Minneapolis Youth for Christ has proved to be a "big brother" to innumerable Youth for Christ groups throughout the Northwest and served as host of the Second Annual Youth for Christ Convention in July, 1946, at nearby Mission Farms on Medicine Lake.

God has blessed the Minneapolis organization with much talent. Gerhard Lee directs the Minneapolis Youth for Christ Band. George Edstrom, an outstanding soloist, is in charge of music, and Adora Norlander, with her beautiful soprano voice, sings at most meetings. The follow-up of converts is thorough and sincere. Each Monday morning Wilson sits down and writes a personal letter to every person who accepted Christ on the previous Saturday night. Various young people telephone the converts, inviting them to the church of their choice or to some fundamental, Bible-believing church if no choice has been made. Twenty-five billboards around the town carry the message of Youth for Christ and an invitation to the rally. From ten to twenty-five souls find the Lord at each meeting, on an average.

Each Saturday night as Wilson leaves his home his three-year-old daughter says to him, "Daddy, I'll pray for you at the rally."

With those words ringing in his ears Wilson is on his way to lead the largest Youth for Christ meeting in the world, a unit which drew thirty thousand people to the Minneapolis State Fair Grounds in the summer of 1946 to hear Dr. Charles E. Fuller at the mammoth rally held in conjunction with the Second Annual Youth for Christ Convention.

As we leave Minneapolis and move to Chicago we pick up an issue of *Colliers*, dated May 26, 1945, and read these words from the pen of William A. McDermott, one of the outstanding free lance writers of our day and a born-again Christian: "It's a spontaneous sort of thing which mushroomed in a dozen different places at once and has spread like a prairie fire!"

Now as we watch the bonfire grow we see that some of the highest flames come from sin-sick, sin-weary and sin-burdened Chicago. It took God a long time to convince a young man, Torrey Johnson, that he was the man for the job in Chicago. As pastor of the successful Midwest Bible Church in Chicago, Torrey had done outstanding work with young people. During the winter months of 1944 the Holy Spirit was talking to Torrey about starting Youth for Christ in Chicago. Torrey saw Youth for Christ operating in St. Louis, Indianapolis and Minneapolis, but he felt that he was not the person to begin meetings in Chicago.

But a midnight prayer meeting at the conference of the National Association of Evangelicals in Columbus, Ohio, in April, 1944, was the deciding point. He grabbed a telephone and called Douglas Fisher in Chicago. Fisher stumbled out of bed to hear what Torrey had on his mind. The idea clicked with Fisher and the next morning he went to Radio Station WMBI in Chicago and tendered his resignation in order to become managing director of Chicagoland Youth for Christ.

Chicago's inspiration had come from many sources. Beverly Shea, one of the outstanding male soloists in Christian circles, had worked for many years with Jack Wyrtzen in New York, both in selling insurance and in selling the Gospel. He was willing to lend his talent and advice. From Washington, D. C., came Lacy Hall, a student at the Moody Bible Institute, who had worked with Glenn Wagner in Washington Youth for Christ. A month previous the Midwest Bible Church had called a young Baptist preacher from LaSalle, Illinois, to become Torrey's associate at the church. His name was Bob Cook, and not only could he play a trombone, lead the singing, and preach, but he also knew how to handle publicity. All these talents merged under the leadership of Torrey, and after several city-wide meetings of youth leaders and businessmen, Chicagoland Youth for Christ came into existence. From the very beginning the planning was on a "miracle basis." Four weeks before the first service the group had no meeting place. Suddenly the acoustically perfect Orchestra Hall in downtown Chicago became available. Almost as miraculously, a half-hour spot on 'Radio Station WCFL was obtained. The speaker at the first meeting on May 26, 1944, was a young Southern pastor named Billy Graham. Orchestra Hall was nearly filled; but best of all, following the service the front rows were filled with young people seeking Christ.

The complete story of Chicagoland Youth for Christ cannot be covered in this book. The first three chapters of

Reaching Youth for Christ, written by Torrey and Bob, tell the heart-warming and encouraging story in a unique way. It may be correct to say that Chicagoland Youth for Christ, because of its faith, sensational growth, success, and the recognition it received, has done more to spread Youth for Christ than any other single movement. In the fall of 1944 a rally at the Chicago Stadium drew thirty thousand people, and there were hundreds of decisions for Christ. Upon its heels came a flood of requests for help and advice in organizing other groups. Each letter was answered and help given. On May 30, 1945, the first anniversary was marked with an outdoor rally in Soldier Field which drew seventy thousand people to hear a Spirit-guided program and a message by Percy Crawford. During the winter months the meetings are held in the Moody Memorial Church as the downtown auditoriums are not available.

As in St. Louis when Dick Harvey advanced his own money to get Youth for Christ started, so in Chicago Torrey Johnson made a personal financial effort to establish Youth for Christ. When the holding of a Stadium rally was considered, Torrey was faced with "doubters" even as Wyrtzen had encountered "doubters" in New York when he launched out. The officials at the Stadium thought Torrey "a bit crazy" for wanting every available seat put into the Stadium for the rally. They told him that twelve thousand to fifteen thousand people was his limit. Even the officials of the city streetcar and bus systems believed "Torrey and tribe were talking too big" when they asked for the transit officials to plan for thirty thousand people.

Twenty minutes before the program started the Stadium was filled. Between five and ten thousand people were turned away. God used the program and speaker, Merv Rossell, to the salvation of hundreds of people. The meeting drew the attention of people the world around; it brought a definite challenge to "go thou and do likewise" to many who attended. The deluge of mail received was too much for the local unit to handle; and, as we will see later, Youth for Christ International came into being at about this time to help handle the correspondence. Prior to the organization of the International office, however, Chicagoland was the hub of a great deal of expansion work, and Torrey Johnson was the spark plug of the Chicagoland leaders. Together with his co-laborers, he wasn't afraid to do what others thought impossible. The result: The city of Chicago, the entire Middle West, the North American continent and the world came to know of a spiritual movement among young people that was truly phenomenal.

The next step, following a banquet which drew fifteen hundred young people to the Stevens Hotel, was the first Memorial Day Rally in Soldier Field. Here again some of the "wiser" heads thought Torrey was tearing off too big a piece to chew. But they prayed and planned, prayed and planned. An all-day prayer meeting was held, with much interceding for favorable weather. It rained the night before the rally, but Memorial day was perfect and seventy thousand turned out for a great religious and patriotic service. Percy Crawford spoke at the conclusion, hundreds of hands were raised for salvation and cards indicating decisions were signed by the converts. Once more the event drew national and international attention both in the secular and religious press.

In the fall of 1945, instead of holding a rally in the Stadium, the group held evangelistic meetings seven consecutive nights in Moody Memorial Church. Seven thousand young people were reached during the week and over three hundred decisions were made.

The best in consecrated singing and speaking talent has been sought at all times. Prayer keeps the many activities going. That this was not a one-man affair was evident when Torrey stepped down and Bob Cook assumed the duties of director. The organization is working on the same high spiritual plane.

But by now our bonfire is completely out of human control. Groups are starting Youth for Christ all over. When we examine the ways and means that are used, we are struck by the similarity between them all. God seems to be challenging and speaking to leaders in the same way and at the same time, giving them the same pattern to follow.

We now stop at Winnipeg, Canada. In the fall of 1944 Youth for Christ started under the direction of Watson Argue. It was backed by thirty churches and the Christian Business Men's Committee. On June 9, 1945, sixty-five hundred young people filled the Amphitheater Rink to celebrate the first anniversary of the initial plans. Torrey Johnson spoke, the Holy Spirit worked in that big throng, and many young people came to Christ.

We move on to Los Angeles, California, and find Hubert Mitchell, a young missionary returned from Sumatra, in charge of a "Saturday Nite Jubilee." The Lord brought Rudy Atwood of the Old Fashioned Revival Hour to the Jubilee as pianist. He laid it on the heart of Johnny Shearer to lead the singing. The burning zeal for the lost souls of men which sent Hubert Mitchell to Sumatra was being used to win the sin-sick young people of Los Angeles to Christ. Hollywood Bowl was obtained, and eighteen thousand were on hand. Mitchell left for the mission field again. Another great rally was scheduled, this time under the leadership of David Morken. Twenty thousand gathered to hear Percy Crawford. Thousands—yes, thousands—found Christ at those two meetings!

Flying cross-country to Boston, Massachusetts, we find a young preacher by the name of John Huffman getting up enough courage to hold his first meeting in the Hatch Memorial Shell in Boston. God honored that courage and five thousand young people filled that great shell to launch New England Youth for Christ. A month or two later

Huffman went to Havana, Cuba, to help American service-men with Havana Youth for Christ.

Honolulu Youth for Christ meets in the McKinley High School Gymnasium and draws crowds of 2,200. Here again servicemen provided the spark which set the movement working. Ten churches co-operated in the meetings. Cornelius Keur, a chaplain's assistant who had worked for WMBI in Chicago, was the director. The group held meetings for some time but disbanded for military reasons. Now four of the men who were active there are going back to Honolulu to start a Christian broadcasting station and promote Youth for Christ once again.

The city of Paris, France, found itself being visited more and more after its liberation by American G.I.'s. Not all of them came to spend their time and money on "wine, women and song"; some came with a burden to reach unsaved men and women for Jesus Christ. A Fisherman's Club was organized, and Al Sedgwick became the leader. Then the Youth for Christ idea sprouted, developed and burst into full bloom.

There were thirty-five at the first meeting. As prayer and work persisted, the crowds grew. Although not more than 125 attended, the meetings were used of God to win men for Christ. The meeting place: the parish room of the American Cathedral in Paris. The meetings lasted for two hours. About fifteen per cent of the crowd was French civilians. The plucky group planned a large rally in the American Methodist Church on September 22, 1945, and the church was packed. The message was first given in English and then in French. Souls were saved. There, in the sinful city of Paris, American "missionaries in uni-form" preached the Gospel on "the devil's night," and God gave them a harvest. Over there, even as over here, the most important meeting of the Youth for Christ schedule was the midweek prayer service; there were usually between sixty and eighty G.I.'s on their knees in behalf of the rally.

Where would you expect a crowd to go—to Youth for Christ or to a dance?

Youth leaders in Wetaskiwin, Alberta, Canada, started their Youth for Christ meeting on the same night that a town organization sponsored a dance. God honored their faith and the dance operators closed their doors when only three or four couples came. The rest of the young people were at Youth for Christ!

It is Friday, October 5, 1945. In Montreal, Canada, a young Frenchman by the name of LaGemere is realizing one of his dreams. *La Jeunesse Pour Christ* a chapter of Youth for Christ for those who could understand French, started that night. The burden for the lost condition of French-speaking Canadians had led him to begin the rally. So well had he done his planning that at the first meeting he was able to announce the speakers for the next eight meetings.

Manila—a book in itself!

If ever a city felt the effect of modern war, Manila did. But it wasn't long after the American troops reached Manila that a great sign, "Manila Youth for Christ," was stretched across the main street.

Cpl. William Deese and Sgt. George Overlander were perhaps the first two men to have the idea of starting Youth for Christ in Manila. The manner in which that idea grew and developed is one of the remarkable religious stories of the entire war. In reality, there were two meetings each week. The first, held on Saturday night, was known as the G.I. Gospel Hour and was a Youth for Christ meeting dressed up in military garb in order to attract servicemen. It was held in a funeral parlor on Rizal Avenue, Manila's great "White Way." The funeral parlor was owned by a Catholic, but G.I.'s were permitted to use it free of charge for their services. An army generator provided the means of light for the meeting. Seats were at a premium, and not a few G.I.'s found themselves seated on empty coffins . . . and some which were not empty! Army trucks brought the G.I.'s from all parts of the Islands. The generator made a great deal of noise, but no one noticed that very much. Chaplains were the main speakers, and the meetings were patterned after those in the United States—special numbers, quartets, choruses, announcements of the growth of Youth for Christ back in the States, testimonies of those converted at the rallies, a WAC trio, and so forth. This proved to be a wonderful place to meet friends, but most of all it proved to be a wonderful place to meet the Lord Jesus Christ as Saviour. As one chaplain said, "It was like receiving a shot of plasma in my arm."

On Sunday night the regular Youth for Christ service was held at the Elinwood Malate Church (Presbyterian)`, on the south side of Manila. Deese and Overlander had started this service, and when they left for duty in various parts of the globe other G.I.'s assumed responsibility for the service. The offerings taken were put into a fund to assist in the rebuilding of damaged churches in Manila. The gifts averaged $150 a week, and by November 1, 1945, $3,000 had been received for the nine months previous.

Manila Youth for Christ owes no little debt to the Reverend and Mrs. Edwin C. Bomm and their family. This missionary couple of the Association of Baptists for World Evangelism had been interned at Santo Tomas. After being released from the Japanese, they obtained a place to live in Manila and promptly opened it to all G.I.'s as "home away from home." But the Bomms were scheduled to leave for home to recuperate, and this presented a new problem. God again worked wonderfully, however. A lot was obtained, and a concrete floor was laid. Two fabricated buildings were erected by voluntary help. Some of the most important work was done at night when the guards watched the building. The result—a Christian service center!

Youth for Christ in Manila was but one of the several efforts put forth by the G.I.'s. A radio program was conducted every Sunday afternoon over the Office of War Information Station KZFM, starting at one-thirty. The program was heard all through the Islands and reached even China and Japan on the five-thousand-watt station. The servicemen were the main speakers on the radio program, but chaplains spoke every third Sunday.

Prayer was the hub of the wheel of activity, and the Wednesday-evening prayer meetings were thrilling, as answers to prayer were told each week. Unsaved buddies prayed for on Wednesday night were often converted at Youth for Christ the following Sunday and gave their testimonies in the prayer meeting the next Wednesday. Manila Youth for Christ had a definite part in the Far Eastern Bible Institute and Seminary (FEBIAS), an interdenominational Bible School in Manila which was started by G.I.'s and which was scheduled to open in the fall of 1946.

Not only in Manila did Youth for Christ take hold in the Philippines. In at least eight other places in the Islands Youth for Christ organizations operated efficiently and effectively.

Tsingtao, China, Youth for Christ is next. The first meeting was held on January 1, 1946, in the Christ (Lutheran) Church. American Marines were partly in charge, with Dr. Frank Connelly, an American missionary, as the speaker. Testimony time was taken care of by a nurse, a Chinese layman and two G.I.'s who told what Christ had done for them.

Peiping, China, Youth for Christ is about to start. Shanghai Youth for Christ is ready for its first meeting. Before we leave China we hear that at least sixteen cities and towns hold Youth for Christ meetings!

Back in the United States we find ourselves at Olympia,

Washington, the capital of that great state. The President
of the United States, the Honorable Harry S. Truman,
was vacationing for a few days with Governor Monn
Walgren before going to the San Francisco Peace Conference. Youth for Christ leaders in the Olympia area received permission from the Governor and the President to
hold a youth rally singspiration in the Capital Building
from nine-fifteen to ten-fifteen one evening. There were
choruses, there were hymns, there were testimonies—and to
these the President listened attentively and with interest.
When he was asked to say a few words he said, "I have
been in this kind of a service for fifty-five years now, and
this is the best one I've ever attended. This has been
a fitting climax to my visit to the state of Washington,
and it would have been well worth the trip all the way
from Washington, D.C., just for this service tonight. That
which we have been considering tonight is what our boys
out there are fighting for."

Glasgow, Scotland, is next. Aberdeen University in that
Scottish city was playing host to not a few American
divinity students under the "exchange system." Ten of
these students were sufficiently interested in the spiritual
welfare of the youth of Scotland to start Aberdeen Youth
for Christ. One of them, Cpl. Maurice Schultz, had become
burdened enough to write to the United States to get the
necessary information on organization. Prayer meetings
followed, and on October 24, 1945, Aberdeen Youth for
Christ was on its way.

It is not far from Glasgow to London, where we next
find ourselves. In 1943 six American G.I.'s definitely felt
the need of a Bible study meeting. They formed the "G.I.
Victory Bible Class." The infant class grew in size and
fervor as servicemen from all over the world joined in
servicemen Bible study. The attendance soon reached 225.
Each Wednesday night an informal discussion of one chapter of the Bible was held. Out of the group came a

smaller unit called the "United Nations Gospel Team"; this group of earnest soul-winners spoke and sang for churches all through England, and almost every time they conducted a service the house was packed.

Letters started to come from the United States telling of the remarkable progress of Youth for Christ. The idea took root in the hearts and minds of these young servicemen. On August 18, 1945, the Westminister Chapel, just around the corner from Buckingham Palace, was the scene of the first London Youth for Christ rally.

The crowd? No less than two thousand! Several of them found Christ as Saviour. A September meeting was announced that night when Tom Rees, a young British evangelist holding tent meetings during the month of September, asked the group to take over the entire service at one of his meetings. Youth for Christ asked for Thursday night, September 13, and the meeting was scheduled for Central Hall, Westminister. Again the auditorium was packed and hundreds were turned away. The rally was addressed for a few moments by Lady Montgomery, mother of the famous English general, and Robert Nelson, vice-president of the LeTourneau Company, also gave a testimony. Servicemen from Great Britain, Canada and Australia gave their testimonies, and the great throng included men in uniform from Holland, New Zealand and Tasmania, as well as Great Britain and the United States. At the invitation, one hundred young people came forward for salvation, and fifty of them signed cards indicating an acceptance of Christ as Saviour.

God continued to bless. The next rally drew ten thousand people to London's largest meeting place, Royal Albert Hall, and Gypsy Smith was on hand to bring a greeting and short message. On October 6 the regular Youth for Christ meetings started in Farringdon Hall, and five hundred people attended. The next Saturday Youth for Christ was held at Westminister Chapel and 2,800 came out to hear

Harry Young, member of the United Nations Gospel Team, who had been a school teacher. Scores of young people stayed after the service to pray. Two thousand hymn books had been donated by the Morning Cheer Center of Philadelphia, Pennsylvania. Part of the spark for the London Youth for Christ group came from Don Chittick, a young fellow who worked in the Good News Fellowship youth meetings in Philadelphia before going into the service.

Incidentally, the work is being carried on even though the servicemen are now back in their longed-for homes. Mr. Rees is London director, and Roy Cattell is aiding him. As a part of their program, these leaders are using Hildenborough Hall as a weekly conference center for youth leaders; and they are holding rallies on Saturday in the Royal Albert Hall. September of 1946 marked the beginning of twenty-six consecutive Saturday-night rallies, and campaigns were also planned for Liverpool and Glasgow by this energetic group.

This next scene could have occurred anywhere, and it perhaps did occur wherever American servicemen were found. The meeting wasn't called "Youth for Christ," but it showed the desire and hunger which existed in the hearts of young people the world around. The story was told by Lt. Roland Meiners of Barrington, Illinois, a twenty-two-year-old Army Air Corps man who was interned in four different German prison camps. He told of the reading of the Bible by the men in those camps, but he also told of the miniature Youth for Christ meetings which were held in the largest foxhole available. These servicemen congregated regularly to sing, pray and testify of the Lord Jesus Christ and what He was doing for them daily. The inspiration for those gatherings came from the folks at home, as they had written of the spread of Youth for Christ all over the North American continent.

Our next stop is Mentone, Indiana, a town of 731 people.

E. C. Ralston, director of Youth for Christ there, one night took a poll of the young people at the rally. He found fifty-eight towns, four countries and numerous counties represented. There were twenty-three ministers present, six servicemen, one servicewoman and hundreds of young people interested in the Lord Jesus Christ. A little town had caught the fervor and spirit of Youth for Christ. God had moved into the rural areas, also, to reach the millions of young people so situated.

Alaska—most of us think of it as being purchased from Russia or as a place where it's cold all the time. But there are people there, and they need Jesus Christ. Peter Deyneka, fiery and beloved leader of the Russian Gospel Association, one night sent a telegram to the International headquarters in Chicago with this message, "We had our first Youth for Christ meeting in Anchorage tonight. Two Russian women and one Eskimo accepted the Lord."

You may wonder how Youth for Christ reached Alaska. Many Christian workers had been thinking of Alaska for some time. Doris Franz, one of the missionaries supported by the Voice of Christian Youth in Detroit, was working in Alaska, and she told a few of the Christians there of what God had done for the young people in Detroit. They prayed much and long, and Anchorage Youth for Christ was the result. One young person accepted Christ a little later; consequently, there were four conversions the first night!

A flare in Neosho, Missouri, directs us on a June night in 1945 to the opening meeting of Neosho Youth for Christ. The man in charge is Cpl. Charles Gilles, a young fellow who promised God on the battlefields of Europe that if and when he returned to the States he would do something to help win young people to Jesus Christ. Youth for Christ proved to be his means of service. He wanted to launch his meeting in an outstanding way and he trusted God for courage to step out. God answered his faith and his prayer. On the platform that night as guest of honor sat . . . General Mark Clark!

Canada calls once more, and we find ourselves in Toronto. We run into an amazing story and an amazing man . . . with amazing results. Charles Templeton is the man, and the story begins with him as a sports cartoonist on the Toronto *Daily Globe*. His life's ambition was to become an internationally known cartoonist or athlete. He tripled the amount of his salary on the Toronto paper by syndicating his cartoons to twenty-three newspapers in Canada. One night after an evangelistic service he went home, knelt by his bed and took Christ as Saviour.

In 1941 he saw a "For Rent" sign on a Toronto church and rented it for $100 a month. Today that church Avenue Road of the Nazarene, is filled Sunday after Sunday, and souls continually are won to the Lord. When Youth for Christ hit Toronto, Templeton seemed the logical man to handle it. The Christian Business Men's Committee became the sponsoring group, with Templeton as director. Even when he is not present the rallies continue with the same large crowds, the same fine spirit and, thanks to God, the same results. The crowd averages three thousand per week, and this fact puts Toronto on top of the record as the largest *weekly* Saturday-night youth rally in the world. Success breeds success, and Toronto has been able to help smaller cities and towns in Canada to get their movements started. The crowds are big, yes, but the main thing as in all Youth for Christ meetings, is that young people are being born again.

South America. What a missionary challenge! And what a difficult time the Protestant missionaries were having in that priest-dominated continent.

Young Bob Savage and his co-workers at HCJB, the Voice of the Andes, were burdened about the young people of Ecuador. Try as they would, they could not draw a crowd for a Gospel meeting. Fearful of retribution, the people would not attend the services. The thought of a week end of Youth for Christ meetings gripped their hearts, and after much prayer they decided to launch out. The dates set were November 16, 17 and 18, 1945, and the meeting place selected was the seaport town of Guayaquil. From the beginning the rallies were saturated with prayer. The final rally was held on Sunday night after the church services were over. The result: 850 people, an unheard of number to attend a Gospel meeting in South America, were on hand! Twenty-seven found Christ as Saviour and twenty others dedicated their lives to His Service. Once again the unusual power of the Holy Spirit in Youth for Christ had done it.

One day Youth for Christ International received a letter from a man in Massachusetts asking for information to start Youth for Christ meetings in Greece! The office was eager to give advice and information. A few months later a letter came from another man in Massachusetts, written upon his return from a missionary trip to Greece and its nearby lands. The letter stated that four hundred young people, challenged through Youth for Christ in Katerini, Macedonia, already had evangelized eight nearby villages; that a Youth for Christ group had been formed in Canea, on the island of Crete; and that informal groups were meeting in Thessalonica, Alexandroupolis and Athens!

"You'll never get into Germany with the Gospel!"

That statement had been hurled at more than one evangelical Christian who longed to reach into the festered spot of World War II and scour it with the cleansing blood of the Lord Jesus Christ. But Youth for Christ got into Germany through the consecrated lives of the American G.I.'s. Not only did it influence the lives of the Yanks, but it also touched the lives of the German people.

The rallies at Frankfurt, Germany, were held in the "Roundup Chapel," and G.I.'s composed the major part of the audience. Even though many of the troops were deployed from time to time, the meetings grew in attendance. Streaming across the main street in Frankfurt was a large banner "Youth for Christ on Saturday night." Many G.I.'s passing through gave testimony at the rallies that the sign had irresistible drawing power. Chaplains proved to be the best source of speaking talent, although occasionally a G.I. was the main speaker. A male quartet was recruited from the 508th Infantry Parachute unit; and, believe it or not, a Girls' Trio sang at the meetings. Of the great number of governmental employees in Frankfurt there were three girls who knew Christ as Saviour and who were more than willing to sing praises unto Him each Saturday night. A medico named Bert Russell was the original soloist; and, in the words of the *Frankfurt Youth for Christ Magazine,* "A violinist who could give Fritz Kreisler competition—at least we think so," completed the program.

As in most places, the "power meeting" was the Wednesday-night prayer service. The nature of the prayer meeting seemed to determine the nature of the rally on Saturday night. In addition to the monthly mimeographed paper which it published, the enthusiastic Frankfurt group was hoping to go on the Armed Forces Network in Europe with the Gospel story.

Other spots in Germany also had Youth for Christ meetings. Way up in the mountains in Austria a young lad wrote for song books, hoping in the near future to get a group of fellows together for a singspiration and rally. Even though most of the German people did not attend the rallies, the G.I.'s witnessed to them by distributing German tracts. Each Sunday afternoon the servicemen went various areas and gave out the Gospel. Pfc. Fred Rodman, a young fellow who served as chairman of the Frankfurt Youth for Christ for a while, wrote home that one Sunday afternoon the group handed out five thousand

tracts! "And," he added, "the children and the grownups
run for them!"

Were there results? Another letter read, "Just last
night three men accepted Christ and two others returned
to living for Him. One little German girl—she's just seven
years old—accepted Christ at a rally. That's the purpose
of Frankfurt Youth for Christ."

We could go on . . . and on . . . and on. Okinawa . . .
Guam . . . Korea . . . the Philippines . . . Peru . . . Lisbon,
Portugal . . . Stockholm, Sweden . . . Belfast, Ireland . . .
Edinburgh, Scotland . . . Oslo, Norway . . . (where 22,000
young people gathered for a Youth for Christ rally in the
fall of 1946) . . . Le Havre, France . . . Johannesburg,
Africa . . . and we touch only the fringe of what Youth
for Christ has done and where it has gone. The hotbed of
it all is in the United States. The great mammoth rallies
in Madison Square Garden, Chicago Stadium, Soldier Field,
Hollywood Bowl, Minnesota State Fair Grounds and other
places did more than bring the unsaved to Christ—they
stirred an entire nation as secular and religious periodicals
imparted the thrill of those mass Christian testimonies
to their readers.

To report on all the Youth for Christ groups in the
United States would be an unending task. Even to make
a report on the unusual experiences of Youth for Christ
would require a great deal of time. However, we have
jotted down little items from "here, there and everywhere"
which may prove interesting. So come along.

We stop at *San Francisco, California,* Youth for Christ and
the active group there publishing a monthly paper, *Victory
News,* and holding forth for thirty minutes each Sunday
afternoon on Radio Station KSFO . . . In Saskatchewan,
Canada, we pick up Clare Richardson. He has been waiting
for John Brown, head of the schools which bear his name,
to conduct a series of meetings. Brown, flying his own
plane, couldn't go all the way by air, but he arrived

nevertheless. Fourteen meetings had been scheduled for eight days, and every meeting was held, despite a temperature of twenty-four degrees below zero and heavy snows! The people laughed at Brown when he mentioned the "blizzard." "No blizzard," they said, "until it's forty below and the snow is five feet deep!" In eight days, more than nine hundred people responded to the invitations, and John Brown came back all warmed up!

The twenty-two Hearst newspapers have given Youth for Christ much favorable publicity. This publicity undoubtedly has done much to put the movement before the secular world. On July 1, 1945, for example, every Hearst paper in the country carried full-page story and pictures on the movement. This effort alone reached ten million readers. Nation-wide coverage followed the first anniversary Chicagoland Youth for Christ rally on May 30, 1945. *Newsweek* said of the good weather, "It was a gift of God Almighty." the San Francisco *Examiner* supplied the uniforms for the San Fransico Youth for Christ band, and the Chicago *Herald American* did the same for the Chicagoland band . . . Negro Youth for Christ meetings were started by Negro leaders in Chicago. The leaders received help from, and worked in conjunction with, Chicagoland Youth for Christ . . . *Baltimore, Maryland* Youth for Christ crowded 3,200 people into the Lyric Theater on November 24, 1945, to listen to Torrey Johnson; 150 of them made decisions that night.

Youth for Christ has sought to co-operate with the churches in all ways. The Los Angeles Saturday Nite Jubilee slogan is, "Gang, this is yours. How about turning in early on Saturday night and rolling out early on Sunday morning? We'll be seeing you." Eighteen thousand people crowded into the Hollywood Bowl on October 6, 1945, to hear Jack Shuler preach. The Los Angeles *Examiner*, in describing the rally, wrote, "Nearly one thousand came to the stage and made a decision for Christ and confessed

Him as Saviour." . . . Young people around *LaSalle, Illinois,* came to the opening meeting in a hayrack . . . Mississippi Valley Youth for Christ at *Moline, Illinois,* meets in the Scottish Rite Temple. It conducted two eight-day evangelistic campaigns in its first year and a half of existence; it has a regular broadcast over WHBF.

The official Youth for Christ song book was compiled by Douglas Fisher of Chicago, Gordon Johnson of Indianapolis and Dick Harvey of St. Louis. It moved into its third edition in a hurry . . . A few years ago a young fellow named Carroll Blakeslee played the violin in the Rochester, New York, symphony orchestra. Today he is head of *Orlando, Florida,* Youth for Christ, which meets regularly in the San Juan Hotel . . . Unusual features keep young people coming to the meetings. *Birmingham, Alabama,* Youth for Christ had three hundred young people marching in a parade before one big rally, carrying the Christian and American flags and singing patriotic songs and hymns . . . At *Winston-Salem, North Carolina,* the mayor of the city was on hand for the first rally . . . *Denver, Colorado,* tried something new in the way of a week end conference for its young people, and the conference was wonderfully successful . . . Publicity attention-getters flow freely from young people's heads. The four I's of Publicity, as outlined by one director, included "International, Interdenominational, Inspirational and Interest-filled." . . . Celebrities have been on hand for many meetings. Governor Earle Warren of California attended the *Santa Monica* rally and encouraged the young people with a word of greeting . . . *Cleveland, Ohio,* Youth for Christ sponsored a banquet and invited only those under thirty years of age. And they packed the place!

When Lady Montgomery spoke at London Youth for Christ she used as her topic "The Importance of Keeping a Daily Tryst with God". . . Several rallies are held in

Philadelphia each Saturday night and on Friday night there is a roundup rally, with Walter Smyth as director.

Humor flows like a steady stream through the meetings, but it is not excessive . . . At *New Britain, Connecticut,* the lights went out one night just as the rally started. Leader Everett S. Graffam used a flashlight to see his notes for the first twenty minutes, and everything went according to schedule . . . At *Toronto, Canada,* Youth for Christ a man actually tried to force his way into the meeting by using a crowbar. The rally was so packed that 150 young people stood outside on the fire escape to listen to the program . . . At a rally in *Charleston, West Virginia,* the speaker spoke on "The Parable of the Hen and Chickens." As he went along he gave various chicken calls to illustrate certain points. As he imitated the call in one place he asked, "Now what does this one mean?" A little boy spoke up quickly, "She's choked!" . . . At *Fort Wayne, Indiana,* a photographer took about twenty pictures of Billy Graham; finally Graham said, "If you get a good one be sure to send it to my wife because that's all she sees of me," . . . At *LaSalle, Illinois,* a speaker referred to slightly bald Cedric Sears, the leader, as "no longer having waves but just being a beachhead." In the general laughter that followed Sears almost fell off of the platform into the orchestra pit below!

There have been many problems and many conflicts. The city council at *Riverside, California,* for example, was called upon to decide whether the city auditorium should be used for a dance on Saturday night or for Youth for Christ . . . *Santa Rosa, California,* Youth for Christ found itself barred from use of the high school on the grounds that it was sectarian and denominational. The school board had approved the request, but the attorney general's opinion was sought and he said "No."

At one of the Chicagoland Youth for Christ rallies a group of deaf and dumb young people was able to listen to the entire program through an "interpreter." . . . In looking over the field, we find thirty Christian Business Men's Committees sponsoring or co-sponsoring Youth for Christ rallies . . . The manner in which Youth for Christ has spread has been remarkable and unusual; this is illustrated by the experience of a group of Swedish Baptist churches in Minneapolis and St. Paul. These churches had operated a Christian Cheer Service Center in St. Paul for the men at nearby Fort Snelling. In August of 1945 five of the young men who had found Christ as Saviour at the center went off to ports unknown. They landed in Tokyo. One of them wrote back, "This afternoon I attended two Youth for Christ meetings. At the first, the Spirit of God certainly broke over the meeting. Six precious souls came at the invitation . . . At the second service, four souls were led to Christ. One of them, a girl, told me that she saw the love of Christ in our soldiers, in their kindness to her as one of the defeated nation. Some of our Christian G.I.'s, though they cannot speak a word of Japanese, are preaching a fine sermon with their lives. I have true victory now and may come back here someday as a missionary."

Cleveland Youth for Christ was alert when it entered a beautiful float in the city's V-J Day parade. One hundred fifty young people walked behind it carrying Christian flags and singing the great hymns of the faith . . . *Elgin, Illinois,* originated the "Top o' the Town" as a recreational center for use during the week to conserve the results of the Saturday-night meetings . . . *Memphis, Tennessee,* also used this means of making available a meeting place during the week when it opened a Youth for Christ Lounge right across from the city auditorium . . . *Lincoln, Nebraska* Youth for Christ sponsored a city wide campaign of tent meetings. The attendance each night averaged 1,100, and there were 220 converts. One pastor said after the meetings were over, "We're now having morning prayer meetings which I hope will continue until Jesus comes!" . . . There was much support from businessmen as the movement continued to grow and expand. One business leader wrote, "The most practical investment today is in young people and in Youth for Christ." . . . Following the great rally in Chicago Stadium on October 14, 1944, head-usher Andy Frain said, "I was really astonished at seeing the huge crowd that night. In my seventeen years of handling crowds I have yet to find a more orderly and courteous crowd than attended this affair. Because of these courtesies a job which ordinarily would have been a headache developed into a most pleasant experience. This gathering constituted the largest attendance the Stadium has ever had—approximately thirty-thousand people. It would please me greatly if all public gatherings were as easy to handle as this one and the people attending such affairs were of the same caliber." The only people who didn't enjoy that rally were the bartenders in the basement of the Stadium and across the street. They didn't sell a drop all night to that crowd!

Youth for Christ came with such a suddenness and proved to be such a tremendous success that church leaders around the world examined it to see if it had something which they might be able to use. One of the first things they discovered was that Youth for Christ was making use of a night hitherto regarded as utterly hopeless for religious gatherings. As they studied the movement, they took from it ideas which they thought would work in their own groups.

So it was that the Baptist youth movement labeled "Adventurers for Christ" came into being. It aimed at the participation of young people from thirteen to twenty-five. The technique used followed closely the Youth for Christ pattern—music, prayer, Scriptural quotations, testimonies, brief addresses and general congregational singing. The executive board of the Baptist Training Union of Texas planned for 3,250 such meetings in the Baptist churches in Texas.

Top   Choir in Honolulu, Hawaii, Youth for Christ Victory Rally.
Below: Scene from Bible Study hour in connection with G.I. Gospel Hour (Youth for Christ) in Tokyo.

Top: Bob Finley with young people responding to Gospel invitation at Youth For Christ rally.

Below: Gil Dodds with high school athletes in attendance at a Youth For Christ rally.

Because of the feeling that Youth for Christ was not sufficiently church-centered, the Christian Endeavor started on November 11, 1945, in Detroit, Michigan, a campaign which it called "Youth Marches for Christ and the Church." These campaigns were to be held in twenty of the largest cities in America; they were prepared at the annual meeting of the Board of Trustees of the Christian Endeavor in Niagara Falls, New York, November 5, 1945. In the words of that meeting's report, ". . . Christian agencies and churches will be united to marshal Protestant young people under the banner of their faith for the highest goals of citizenship, community service and brotherhood . . . The entire program will be youth led and will have its own answer for intolerance, indifference and everything else that is un-American. While it will be first of all evangelistic among Christian youth, it will also be a call to that unity which, without uniformity, makes us 'Americans all.' "

As we have said, the secular press took notice of Youth for Christ in a way not seen since Billy Sunday's time. One of the hundreds of articles on the movement and its growth was written by Charles Neville for the Saturday *Home Magazine* of August 18, 1945. We feel that it is worthy of being quoted in part:

"A million and more teen-age girls and boys have decided that boogie-woogie is old stuff and definitely on the way out. They don't sing the blues anymore. They sing of joy and hope in a world they intend to change for the better. Why is this? Because there is a new Saturday-night swing to salvation that is sweeping the country, and youth is in command. In five hundred towns and villages the Youth for Christ movement is drawing the bobby-soxers and their boy friends away from the juke boxes and dark-boothed hideaways to a streamlined revival of that indestructible thing—the human soul.

"Youth for Christ has chosen to combat evil at its most potent hour, Saturday night, and therefore is doing more to discourage juvenile delinquency than all the curfews, threats and even punishments could accomplish.

"There are no mournful Christians at the Saturday-night rallies. I've seen no frenzied shouting about hell and damnation, none of the hysterical tricks that have done so much to keep many would-be church-goers out of the church instead of in them. Youth for Christ talks turkey to its young audiences, and they love it! Jack Wyrtzen's message is short and pithy and delivered in a homely, midwestern voice unspoiled by elocutionary mannerisms. This is particularly effective when later in the meetings he calls for converts. Youth is there to advise youth. Youth for Christ realizes that healthy young people are mass-minded.

"There were not, and I searched every tier, any of the bilious, moody, introspective types that unbelievers regard with mistrust because they seem to carry their religion as though it were a calamity. The ones I saw were first-rate ads for sound bodies and consciences. When they sang in a great shower of melody I thought of the old response, 'And our mouths shall show forth Thy praise.'

"Youth for Christ has a job on its hands, but those hands are mighty capable hands. The aftermath of war has been hard on the young. Moral bars are down, homes are broken up, the crime reports swell to record proportions. As the Apostle John said, 'The truth shall make you free.' It will take the youth to keep us that way!"

As we have seen, the movement sprouted in so many places that the requests for help streamed steadily into the office of Youth for Christ International. For the most part these letters had to be answered by mail, although, as the work grew more and more, field men were added to the staff. As the movement became established in North America, Youth for Christ International leaders could turn their attention to the calls from foreign lands. Many lands were calling and after much prayer and deliberation the decision was made to go first to Europe.

On March 18, 1946, four leaders—Torrey M. Johnson, Billy Graham, Charles Templeton and Stratton Shufelt—boarded a plane of the American Airlines in Chicago to take them direct to London. They spent six weeks in Europe, visited ten European capitals and a host of other cities. God granted them journeying-mercies all along the way, and they made many valuable contacts. The purpose of their trip was twofold—to win European youth to Christ and to encourage youth leaders on the continent to set up Youth for Christ organizations of their own to carry on the work.

We pause briefly at a few places along the way.

Manchester, England—two thousand on hand forty minutes before the meeting started; hundreds turned away. Twenty took Christ as Saviour. A strong invitation to come back for meetings in the fall of 1946. Entertained by 150 pastors and laymen.

Stockholm, Sweden—More than five thousand heard Torrey in Filadelfia-kyrken, Europe's largest church, with two thousand turned away. A temporary committee set up.

Aberdeen, Scotland—fourteen hundred packed historic Gilcomston South Church . . . thirty-five teen-agers converted at one meeting. American servicemen had prepared the ground well.

So it was all over. Graham remarked on returning that never had he felt it so "easy to preach." This, of course, can be attributed to the fact that thousands of young people on the North American continent daily prayed for the group. Some thirty cities were reached, and in each of them a tentative organization was set up or preliminary arrangements were made to set up one. When the leaders returned in the early part of May to make their report to the executive council at its quarterly meeting in Boston, Massachusetts, they came with a thrilling story of what God had done and a challenge of what God could do in war-weary and war-devastated Europe. They came back with hundreds of invitations to return for longer periods of time.

As we have seen, the Dutch team of De Jong, De Vos and Fisher flew into Holland and "the dykes of blessing opened up" in their brief but well-planned campaign. There was opposition before they arrived and even after they came, but the power of the Holy Spirit overruled in a wonderful way and the results outwardly and inwardly were amazing. One veteran Dutch Reformed pastor was led to say, "This is the greatest thing that has happened in Holland in this generation!"

When the team came home, a national Holland Youth for Christ group had been established and by May, 1947, when the team was scheduled to return, there were no less than fifty Youth for Christ rallies throughout the land.

The "British Team" of Graham, Cliff and Billie Barrows began its work in England in November of 1946. Notwithstanding one of the hardest winters England has experienced in recent years, with crippling strikes and lack of coal and food on every hand, the week and two-week campaigns proved to be unusually successful in every instance. As mentioned previously, the first British Youth for Christ conference was held in Birmingham during the last few days of March, 1947, and when it was over, a national organization was formed to help the 200 rallies in their work.

From that Birmingham conference the representatives from the United States went into various lands. Torrey M. Johnson and William Bond journeyed to Holland first, where they were received by Queen Wilhelmina and continued the work of encouraging the Dutch rallies. Then Torrey moved into Germany alone to prepare the way for the coming of the Dutch-German team of DeJong, Fisher, Stratton Shufelt and Gene Jordon, marimbist of Chicago.

David Morken of Los Angeles, California, and Bond flew together to the Orient to visit the rallies there. Dr. V. R.

Edman of Wheaton College, Wheaton, Illinois, and Dr. Joseph Evans of Boston, Massachusetts, continued from Birmingham to Greece for work there with the Greece Gospel Association. Before coming home, Harold Stockburger of the Moody Bible Institute went to Holland to help with the work there.

South America was not forgotten. Immediately after the quarterly Youth for Christ council meeting in Tampa, Florida, in January, 1947, the Rev. Watson Argue of Winnipeg, Canada, flew to the West Indies and through South America in answer to many invitations from those areas. Dr. Frank Phillips of Portland, Oregon, moved into Cuba and Mexico to help the leaders in those areas and had the privilege of discussing the matter of Mexico Youth for Christ with President Miguel Aleman.

Even as God supplied the personel of the teams He supplied the necessary finances. Even as the calls from foreign lands answered the work at home under field representatives T. W. Wilson and Bob Pierce went on at full steam. The only real problem was one of trying to keep up with the pace at which the program was moving. From July 1, 1946, to January 1, 1947, rallies across the North American continent increased 25 per cent as region after region felt the need for engaging full-time men to meet the increasing needs.

We have had a world's-eye view of Youth for Christ. Even since the start of this book there has been a tremendous advance in the movement, and the closing of this chapter on growth and progress will have to wait—perhaps years. Youth for Christ is still moving, and the people who predicted an early death for it seem to be in error. The leaders themselves take a very practical, down-to-earth view of the entire thing. They feel that, although it may not last forever, it has a definite ministry to perform before it leaves the scene. At this writing it is definitely on the upswing, both in the United States and in foreign lands.

Chapter 5

THE FIRE SPREADS

IT had to come." That is one competent observation of the origination of Youth for Christ International. It was only logical that young men with identical convictions and similar plans for youth rallies should unite in an attempt to win youth for Christ.

The idea of an international group suggested itself to Roger Malsbary when he̅ had a pastorate in Danville, Indiana. Malsbary was one of the speakers at the Winona Lake Bible Conference at Winona Lake, Indiana, in 1944. In the early summer of 1944, when conversing with Arthur W. McKee, executive director at Winona Lake, Malsbary broached the topic of a Youth for Christ conference. McKee was interested and consented to help in any way he could. At the invitation of Malsbary and McKee, Youth for Christ leaders from various sections of the country met at Winona Lake in August to consider a summer conference for 1945.

It clicked! Everyone present was enthusiastic about it. On hand for the meeting, among others, were Ed Darling of Detroit, Dick Harvey of St. Louis, Torrey Johnson and Bob Cook of Chicago, Ray Schulenburg of Moline, Malsbary,

McKee, and Dr. Palmer Muntz, program director of the Winona Lake Conference. They met for two days and agreed to meet again at Detroit in November to lay plans for the coming summer conference. Before they left they had a lengthy prayer meeting, and every day from then until November each individual prayed about the prospective conference plans.

At the Detroit meeting a temporary committee was named to plan for the conference to be held at Winona Lake from July 22 through July 29, 1945. The committee consisted of Dr. V. R. Edman of Wheaton college, Harvey, Malsbary, Schulenburg and Johnson; Johnson was made temporary chairman. Thirty-five leaders from eight states and twenty-one cities were present, and the vote to hold the conference was unanimous. A constitutional committee composed of George Wilson of Minneapolis, William Erny of Chicago and C. B. Cunningham of Oshkosh, Wisconsin, was appointed to prepare a constitution for presentation at the conference.

Those at the Detroit meeting returned to their various cities with quickened steps and new vision. They had heard afresh of what God was doing in other cities, and the possibilities of a great offensive through united action thrilled them. They looked forward to the summer of 1945 with eager and prayer-filled minds and hearts. The conference plans which they helped to formulate, looked very, very promising.

But things moved faster than they had planned . . . or hoped.

Inquiries and requests for help continued to come to the various leaders. The leaders forwarded this correspondence to Torrey Johnson as head of the temporary committee. Torrey's Chicagoland group was proving to be a great center of growth and inspiration, and it had also been doing an excellent job of replying to the many queries which came its way. The book, *Reaching Youth for Christ*, by Torrey Johnson and Bob Cook helped many leaders in getting started. Torrey could not answer the many calls asking him to speak at various rallies. In the late months of 1944 he felt led of God to ask Billy Graham, young and dynamic pastor of the Village Church of Western Springs, Illinois, and director of the radio program, Songs in the Night, to work full time in behalf of Youth for Christ. Billy accepted the call and went to work to meet as many of the hundreds of demands coming in as he possibly could.

A meeting of the temporary committee named at Detroit was called on January 8, 1945, in order to do something about the showers of requests being received and to start planning for the summer conference. It was decided to set up a temporary Youth for Christ International office to handle the flood of inquiries. The meeting also authorized *Youth for Christ Magazine,* and named Clyde Dennis of Chicago as editor. Indianapolis Youth for Christ relinquished the title of the magazine and turned over its entire subscription list of eight hundred to the national group. The first issue came out in March of 1945.

The sentiment at the January meeting was that the international organization should consist of leaders and groups who were holding Youth for Christ meetings in various localities. The feeling expressed was, "If God wants this job done, by His grace we'll do our best to do it right." They took with them into the International organization the enthusiasm and vigor which characterized their Youth for Christ activity.

It is good to examine even at this early date the plans and aims of the international group. The ideas and resolutions adopted in those preliminary meetings proved to be the guiding principles for the further work of the international group. The three words which best explain Youth for Christ International are "Channel for Service." It was to be a melting-pot of ideas. It was to help the groups already established and to promote the starting of rallies in other places. A member of that early committee stated one of the basic policies: "It was strictly understood then, even as it is now, that Youth for Christ International shall not in any way dictate the policies of any local center but shall be for the purpose of providing service, suggestions and help in doing a better job."

As Youth for Christ International developed, it helped the local groups in many ways. It gave encouragement and it disseminated information through the magazine. A *Leads for Leaders* bulletin was sent each month to the rally directors listed in the International office. Aids for advertising and other publicity were given as suggestions. When interested leaders wrote or visited the office, they were fortified by literature and other helps. A "Speaker List" was issued; the Number One Problem of any rally, to obtain a speaker who would preach Christ in a way to reach his young audience, was partially solved as the list circulated. Advice was given to remedy organizational difficulties. Suggestions for follow-up work were sent out frequently.

Things were moving at a tremendous pace. By May of 1945 two additional field men had been added to the staff. They were Emerson Pent of Kansas City, Missouri, and Bob Finley of the University of Virginia where he distinguished himself as Student Council President and intercollegiate boxing champion. Torrey Johnson was sharing his time with the Chicagoland rally, the International office and the planning for the constitutional convention. An office was rented at 130 North Wells Street in downtown Chicago. Expansion of this office has been necessary on three occasions.

There was a great spirit of enthusiasm when the first conference from July 22 through 29 was held. The first Chicagoland Soldier Field rally had drawn seventy thousand people just six weeks previous. Other meetings had not only proved to be outstanding testimonies to the secular world but had resulted in the salvation of thousands of precious souls. Seven hundred invitations were sent out for the conference, and groups all over the North American continent made the conference a matter of special prayer for months previous.

We look at the conference through the eyes of Wesley Hartzell, reporter of the Chicago *Herald American* and himself a born-again Christian:

"Not a longing eye was cast at the inviting beaches of cool Winona Lake as the Youth for Christ International meetings opened here today. They were here for business. Much the same atmosphere of enthusiasm and energy must have characterized the early church fathers who streamed in from every section of the then-known world to attend the annual Nicea.

"But these young men are not gathered to outline a new creed or religion. They have met here to bring new methods into the Christian faith, to draw young people back to the church and found their every deed upon the Bible."

There were forty-two delegates representing forty-two different Youth for Christ rallies at the first business meeting on the morning of July 23 at 10 o'clock. (Delegates were limited to fifty by wartime restrictions.) Mitchell Seidler of Danville, Illinois, led in prayer, a deep, moving prayer, and the formation of Youth for Christ International was on its way.

Perhaps it should be mentioned here that Jack Wyrtzen was not active in the formation of the International organization nor is his Word of Life Hour affiliated with it today. He explained it this way: "We have no direct tie-up with Youth for Christ International except through the blood of Jesus Christ. We believe in fellowship with all believers." Because of his Brethren background, Wyrtzen believes in keeping organization at a bare minimum, although his own Word of Life program is well planned and well organized. He feels that a movement should be spread through the

Holy Spirit, unhampered by any organizational methods. There has been, however, a good spirit of fellowship between Youth for Christ International and Wyrtzen. Many of the International men have spoken on the Word of Life Hour, and Wyrtzen in turn has spoken at many Youth for Christ rallies. Wyrtzen had been invited to the initial meeting in 1944 at Winona Lake, the meeting in Detroit and the constitutional convention.

One of the key problems of the convention was the selection of a president. There were many possible candidates—Malsbary, Harvey, Darling, Johnson, Mitchell and others. As chairman of the temporary committee for the conference, much of the publicity had been handled by Torrey Johnson, and a large number of the delegates thought that he would be the logical choice for president. Before the convention, however, even his closest friends were certain that he would not accept the leadership. He had mentioned on an occasion that he felt that he was in the spot where God wanted him to be—pastor of his Midwest Bible Church and head of Chicagoland Youth for Christ. He did see, of course, the need for a leader and prayed with the others that a director would be forthcoming from this convention.

The nominating committee named Harvey and Johnson. Harvey stood up and withdrew his name. After a lengthy discussion a white ballot was cast for Johnson. He refused to accept, but he was prevailed upon to pray about it and to give his decision later in the conference.

During the night of Wednesday, July 25, God met Torrey Johnson on the shores of Winona Lake. There were few people awake at that hour. Until midnight many of the delegates had tried to convince Torrey that he should accept. In his own mind he could not see that he should. But that night, not far from dawn, a young, husky Norwegian got up from his knees, wiped his eyes and in his heart said, "I'll do it, Lord, if you'll give me the strength."

His acceptance the next morning at the business meeting

thrilled the group, and a lengthy prayer meeting was held in his behalf. The atmosphere of the entire conference changed that moment—the ship had received a captain!

Other decisions in this history-making conference were soon made. Harvey was elected vice-president, George Wilson of Minneapolis, secretary, and Walter Block of Kenosha, Wisconsin, treasure. The following regional vice-presidents were elected:

Pacific Northwest—Bob Pierce, Seattle, Washington

Southern California—Hubert Mitchell, Los Angeles, California

Rocky Mountain—Rex Lindquist, Denver, Colorado

North Central—George Wilson, Minneapolis, Minnesota

Central—Dick Harvey, St. Louis, Missouri

Great Lakes—Ed. Darling, Detroit, Michigan

New England—John Huffman, Boston, Massachusetts

Eastern—Walter Smyth, Philadelphia, Pennsylvania

Southern—Daniel Iverson, Miami, Florida

Western Canada—Watson Argue, Winnipeg, Manitoba

Eastern Canada—Charles Templeton, Toronto, Ontario

Dr. Edman of Wheaton college handled the elections in a masterful way. The brief but completely satisfactory constitution was accepted at one of the night sessions. Article One set forth the four-fold aim of Youth for Christ International: (1) To promote and help win youth for Christ everywhere, (2) to encourage evangelism everywhere, (3) to emphasize radiant, victorious Christian living and (4) to foster international service of youth through existing agencies.

The seven-point doctrinal platform, which was unanimously adopted, is as follows:

1. We believe the Bible to be the inspired, the infallible, authoritative Word of God.

2. We believe that there is one God, eternally existent in three persons: Father, Son and Holy Spirit.

3. We believe in the deity of our Lord Jesus Christ, in

His virgin birth, in His sinless life, in His miracles, in His vicarious and atoning death through His shed blood, in His bodily resurrection, in His ascension to the right hand of the Father, and in His personal return and glory.

4. We believe that for the salvation of lost and sinful men, regeneration by the Holy Spirit is absolutely essential.

5. We believe in the present ministry of the Holy Spirit by whose indwelling the Christian is able to live a godly life.

6. We believe in the resurrection of both the saved and the lost; they that are saved unto the resurrection of life, and they that are lost unto the resurrection of damnation.

7. We believe in the spiritual unity of believers in Christ.

The over-all policy adopted did not infringe upon established evangelistic organizations. It aimed to supplement the activity of all Bible-believing agencies and institutions in harmony with the stated doctrinal position. Torrey said, "If anyone else can do the job, we stand ready to help him do it." To carry out the extensive program a budget of $200,000 was adopted.

But all was not business in the seven-day convention. The evening meetings proved to be soul-winning rallies in every sense of the word. God used Billy Graham, Jack Shuler, James Bennett, Torrey and others to challenge and change many a life. The radio was used to good advantage —three meetings a day were broadcast over radio station WMBI. Bud Tichy of Chicagoland was voted the most friendly boy and Helen Meloff of Indianapolis the most friendly girl. Greetings were sent to President Truman, to Prime Minister MacKenzie King of Canada and to Secretary of State Byrnes. Dr. John Brown flew to the conference in his own plane and was so thrilled by it all that he announced that he was ready to give the next five years of his life to the promotion of Youth for Christ!

The conference proved to be a real melting-pot. Hearts were melted together and denominational lines were completely forgotten as the great task of reaching youth presented itself. Not only did the leaders go home having established an international organization, but they went home inspired by the fellowship which had been theirs. Torrey stated during the week, "The various individual rallies knew nothing of the other rallies. Now the Spirit of God has moved upon the hearts and minds of men and revealed to them the need of reaching youth for Christ, and all of them are going about in just about the same way."

It has been said that Youth for Christ moved along miraculously. This convention proved that statement again. The origin of Youth for Christ was astonshing; its development to all parts of the globe was unusual; and the formation of an efficient International organization in one short week was marvelous.

The conference ended, and leaders from all parts of North America hastened home to disclose what had occurred, to work harder in their localities and to support the International set-up which God has brought into being. International, faced with the tremendous task of co-ordinating all the movements in all parts of the globe, took off its coat, rolled up its sleeves and went to work.

Additional help was needed immediately. Gil Dodds, well-known runner who holds the world's record of 4:06.4 minutes for the indoor mile, joined the International staff in August of 1945. Charles White, a young fellow who spent four years with the Army Air Corps, came home to Chicago to take up the position of business manager. At a meeting of the Executive Council in Chicago on September 5 and 6, 1945, Billy Graham was appointed field representative, Charles Templeton promotional director, Dick Harvey executive secretary, and Dr. Lee Roberson of Chattanooga, Tennessee, vice-president of the southern region. A training school and the organizational meeting of the north central region was held in Minneapolis late in the summer, and directors from four states were on hand. Another training school was held from December 2 through 5,

1945, in Detroit, which fifty leaders attended. These two schools proved to be so successful that twenty others were tentatively scheduled.

After repeated calls from Europe plans were made to send a group of leaders there as early as November of 1945. God supplied different plans, however, and the trip was postponed until March of 1946 in order to allow the young International organization to gain strength. When the Executive Council met in Los Angeles from January 2 through 4, 1946, all the leaders were present. This council meeting proved to be outstanding in many ways. So rapid had been the growth of International that four full-time employees were hired to care for the replies for assistance. Ex-Navy Chaplain Robert Evans came in as executive secretary, T. W. Wilson of Ashburne, Georgia, as field representative, Cliff Barrows of Ceres, California, as a field man, and Bob Murfin, Navy hero from the south Pacific, as co-ordinator of itineraries. It was at this session that Hubert Mitchell gave Youth for Christ International a stirring world vision as he spoke on sending sparks—not missionaries—to all parts of the world to inspire the Christians in those lands with Youth for Christ fervor and to encourage them to start rallies in their own areas.

Criticism had been flowing in freely, and, in order to clarify the stand of Youth for Christ on various matters, the following important resolutions were passed:

1. Youth for Christ is a positive movement, seeking to create unity and good will through the spirit and message of Christ. It is definitely not anti-Semitic or anti-racial but is sympathetic to all oppressed peoples and desires to show forth the love of Christ to all mankind.

2. Youth for Christ is a positive spiritual movement, free from all fanaticism on the one hand and formalism on the other, free from all fighting, and free from all sectarianism, but extending a definite challenge to youth to give their hearts to Christ and their lives to the Saviour.

3. Youth for Christ is an international organization and evangelistic movement with a co-operative spirit, seeking to win the lost, co-operate with all established churches and help them with their God-given message to evangelize the world.

4. Youth for Christ International has no alliances or commitments to any political, religious or secular organization or individuals. It is out to do a positive job for Christ and His church among the youth of our generation.

Also receiving much attention at the Los Angeles meeting was the important problem of follow-up work for converts.

We step along briskly as we see Youth for Christ International maturing. On March 18, 1946, four young fellows boarded a giant airliner in Chicago and flew to London for six weeks of meetings on the Continent. As we have seen, they went, came back, and were abundantly blessed by God. Even in the farewell services before they left souls were saved. A farewell service in Charlotte, North Carolina, for Graham brought out a capacity crowd and resulted in the salvation of souls. The same thing happened in a three-day farewell for Templeton at Toronto. Two days before the departure, eighteen thousand people filled the Olympia Stadium in Detroit, and five thousand were turned away. Best of all, one thousand young people (by actual count) came forward to make a decision for Christ, following the message of the evening. On Sunday night, March 17, Moody Memorial Church in Chicago was packed with five thousand people as the final farewell service was held. Telegrams from forty-nine groups in twenty-one states and six provinces were read and acknowledged. The wires brought pledges totaling $3,700, and Ed Darling of Detroit submitted a check for $4,000 as Detroit's part in financing the trip.

The next morning about one thousand people came to the Chicago Municipal Airport to say "good-bye" to the

Top: British team leaves Chicago airport for first trip to Great Britain.

Center: President Torrey Johnson with his efficient secretary, Miss Amy Anderson.

Below: British team with Gavin Hamilton and Lord Mayor of Belfast, Ireland.

Top: Chuck Templeton interviews young quiz contestants
           in Toronto rally.
Right: Mayor William F. Devin of Seattle.
Lower left: Bob Finley and Gil Dodds.
Lower right: Bob Cook and Dr. Percy Crawford at Chicagoland
           rally.

four messengers. After a short, prayer-filled program, the group knelt by the plane for a moment of prayer. Then in they went, and a few moments later the plane tilted its nose into the air, London-bound.

This was the kind of trip for which Youth for Christ International had been organized. By pooling the strength of all of the groups, the various rallies in North America could send four first-rate young men to tell what God had done through Youth for Christ in America. Alone they could not have done so.

The movement took on global proportions faster than any Christian work in many years. When the executive council met in Boston in early May, 1946, Hubert Mitchell was named the Asiatic Youth for Christ representative. Gavin Hamilton previously had been named the Great Britain representative, and he did much in the arrangement of the meetings for the first team.

The delegates, richer for their experiences, leaders, and various interested Christian workers gathered at lovely Mission Farms on Medicine Lake, eight miles northwest of Minneapolis, Minnesota, on July 22 through 28, 1946, for their second annual convention. The egg that had been hatched just a year previous had developed strength, courage and wisdom. In some regions the number of rallies had increased ten times in just one year. The European trip had shown what could be done overseas. The second annual convention took hold of the hand of God once more and made the following decisions:

1. To send five Youth for Christ Gospel teams to foreign lands—Great Britain, Scandinavia, Holland, South America, Australia, Japan, and so forth. (So quickly did God answer the prayers of that conference that two months later the first team of three men was in Holland. Three months later the second team was in England!)

2. To adopt a world-wide evangelization policy to be

financed by the tithing of offerings received at the local rallies.

In addition, they re-elected Torrey M. Johnson and the other officers for another year, elected regional vice-presidents, chose Winona Lake as the site of the third convention in 1947, adopted the constitutional by-laws, and went through a maze of other business.

The seven hundred delegates, directors and visitors came from thirty-two states, six provinces of Canada, the Philippines, England and Africa. They heard such outstanding men as Dr. Charles E. Fuller, Dr. Oswald Smith, Torrey, Dave Morken, Templeton, Graham and Dawson Trotman. Highlight of the week was a mammoth outdoor rally in the Minnesota State Fair Grounds which drew thirty thousand people, despite the prevalence of infantile paralysis in Minnesota in the summer of 1946. They heard reports of growth such as these: Pacific Northwest, eight rallies a year ago, sixty-five now; Eastern Canada, one rally in 1945, twenty-four now; Central, eight rallies in 1945, thirty-nine now, and "more rallies starting in the last three months than in the entire nine before put together"; Eastern, from twenty-five to sixty-eight in one year.

If the young people and youth leaders were inspired after the 1945 conference at Winona Lake, they must have walked home on air after the 1946 sessions. There was a challenge in even the dullest business meetings, and very few of the meetings were dull. Once again the prime motive of Youth for Christ was apparent: About four hundred young people made decisions to accept Christ during the week. (This figure includes the 115 who accepted Christ when Dr. Fuller spoke at the great outdoor rally.)

As we look at Youth for Christ International, we find ourselves at 130 North Wells Street in Chicago. This office is a beehive of activity at all times of the day and often during the night. The swirl of detail work which so often hits the valiant group of office workers more than once came close to engulfing them. They were able to keep their heads above water, however, and now have things well under control for any and all emergencies.

The office has consecrated typists, secretaries, stenographers and bookkeepers who feel without a bit of doubt that they are working in one of the greatest movements of our day. They enjoy their work, and plenty of banter flows back and forth; but underneath is the soberness and seriousness that is prevalent in all offices where the work of Christ is done. At present Youth for Christ International employs eighteen men and women and the average salary is $2,500. This includes all the leaders. The girls in the office come from six different denominations and fuse their talents into an effective and efficient job under Business Manager Charles White.

The International office is no exception to the rule that all Youth for Christ work is based on prayer. Prayer meetings can be and are held at all times of the day in the various smaller offices, but each morning the entire group gathers for a fifteen-minute devotional period. A prayer list is kept in the office, and these specific requests are remembered from day to day.

Youth Publications is one of the busiest spots in the organization. It handles all literature published by the organization and supervises the *Youth for Christ Magazine*. The magazine took over the mailing list and work of *Youthcast*, a Philadelphia publication, in the winter of 1946. *Youth for Christ Magazine* has grown into a healthy and well-edited publication. Ken Anderson, one of the top Christion fiction writers in the United States, is the editor. Subscriptions came in on an average of ten a day throughout the first year.

In connection with fulfilling requests for speakers and musical talents, International has jurisdiction over only the men and women on its payroll. The "Approved Speakers List" includes hundreds of names, but only a small percentage of that group can be supplied by International. Arrangements in other cases are handled by the individuals themselves, and the International office co-operates in as many ways as possible.

As we have looked at Youth for Christ International, we have seen the definite contribution which it has made to the effective carrying on of the work. It seems to have justified its existence at every turn. Often, when it becomes necessary for a movement to be organized, the very step of organization saps the strength instead of increasing it. Not so with Youth for Christ International. Because the organization impetus came from the individual leaders themselves and not from one or two leaders anxious to establish the formal organization perhaps to further their own cause, it has been blessed of God in a real way. One thing is certain. If a young fellow wants to start a Youth for Christ rally, he can receive advice from an organization which specializes in helping to establish new rallies. It came through prayer; it moves along on wings of prayer; and therefore it is not surprising that it leads the way in answering prayer and in serving as the channel through which blessings flow to and from the local Youth for Christ rallies.

We have looked at the flames and the center of the fire. Someone has to feed the fire; in our case the Holy Spirit is the main "feeder" of the Youth for Christ blaze. God uses Spirit-filled men to win souls to Him. A fire needs men at various times to add fuel, to stir things up, to remove burned-out embers or to give new life to a flickering ember. The individual rallies form the logs in the fire and Youth for Christ International serves as the fireplace.

Chapter 6

WHOM GOD HATH TOUCHED

... And there went with him a band of men, whose hearts God had touched (I Sam. 10:26).

WHEN on Sunday, March 17, 1946, at crowded Moody Memorial Church of Chicago, Torrey Johnson said good-bye with four fellows leaving for Europe the following morning, these words from First Samuel were the keynote of his message. He spoke correctly when he referred to his co-workers in Youth for Christ as "men whose hearts God had touched." And because God did touch them, He now is touching the sinful lives of young people in all parts of the globe with the Gospel of the Lord Jesus Christ.

A lady once wrote to the Youth for Christ International office and said, "I think it's so wonderful that the Lord saw fit to use Torrey M. Johnson despite the fact that he is such an ignorant man."

A writer in the Chicago *Daily News* picked that up and went on to say, "If Torrey Johnson is ignorant, so is Einstein . . . Young people of today want to hear the language of youth, down to earth and straightforward. Torrey Johnson has a philosophy of making it easy for people to come to church, and they're coming."

It has been extremely interesting to read the life stories of some of the hundreds of Youth for Christ leaders. There is something vitally different about each and every one of them. The entire movement is unusual, and they also are unusual. On the other hand, they rightfully could be classed as "just a bunch of guys named Joe" through whom God is working in a marvelous way to win thousands of young people to Christ. They have ability; and God is using it. But that ability is not the main reason for their being leaders of the movement. They are young men of vision, young men of prayer, young men of uncompromising Christian character. Above all, they depend on the Lord for any results which may come from their efforts. As Gil Dodds once said about his running, "I run as though everything depends on me and pray as though everything depends on God." The same shoe fits our many leaders.

You may be interested in knowing their average age. In the 152 questionaires which were returned, we found the following information:

Average age of directors—33.37 years

Average age when directors were converted—15.6 years

Denominations represented among directors—20

Denominations with most directors—Baptist (64)

The age runs from a fifteen-year-old junior in high school who acts as co-chairman of a rally, to a spry old man of fifty-four whose heart is some thirty years younger. The greatest age group is between twenty-five and thirty with thirty to thirty-five as second and twenty to twenty-five as third. Several elderly leaders raise the average to thirty-three.

Regarding the vocations of the leaders, youthful pastors rank first and laymen second. A few of the leaders are in schools of learning. It is interesting to note that the average age at which the leaders were converted was 15.6 years, and this perhaps explains to a large degree the burden for the lost souls of teen-agers felt so keenly by the leaders. They undoubtedly know the struggles of the teen-agers as others do not, and they want to help as many young people as possible find the key to the problems of teen age. The vast majority were converted when young, some as young as seven years of age. But there are exceptions: One leader was converted at thirty-seven; at forty he is leading a successful Youth for Christ meeting.

One critic disliked the lack of training of the leaders. The question of training appeared in the questionaire. We found that fifty-six of the leaders had college and seminary training. Thirty-six had high school plus either seminary or Bible institute. Twenty-two had high school and college work. Seventeen had high school only. A few had only eighth-grade educations and for significant reasons could go no further.

Several comprehensive things characterize almost every Youth for Christ director. He usually has a pleasing personality. He is happy about his Christian experience and life. He makes no "bones" about his one chief aim in life—winning people to the Lord Jesus Christ. He has had training and experience which help to qualify him for work with young people. The young people like him, which is one reason why they come back. He has a sense of humor and is not afraid to try the unique. He has vision and the faith to do what that vision tells him to do. He is a good organizer, unfettered by denominational ties or insignificant differences between believers. He is a man of prayer, realizing the utter dependence on God for any and all spiritual blessing which He may shower on his group. He knows his Bible and what it teaches, especially if week after week he finds himself asking the questions in the Bible quizzes. He may play an instrument, or sing, or do something else in addition to his position as leader and organizer. He has a keen interest in sports and may even have been an athlete when he was in school.

It has truthfully been said time and time again that a Youth for Christ group will succeed or fail even as the leader succeeds or fails. This has proved true. An outstanding thing is that so very few of the movements have failed, and even those that fell by the wayside may have done so through no fault of the leader but because of the opposition in the locality. Local rallies may have failed somewhat in their task of winning *as many* young people to Christ as might have been possible, but in only a few instances have we come across the skeletons of organization which once were. This seems to say even more loudly that God is in the movement from beginning to end.

Torrey Johnson could fit well into the above description, except for the playing or singing ability. If they had swimming pools in Youth for Christ auditoriums, however, Torrey could hold his own with the best of them. He was a "crack" swimmer in high school and won the breast stroke meet in a national tournament soon after graduation from high school. When he was at Wheaton college he played tackle and end on the varsity football team. He has carried that enthusiasm right into his religious work and found that it is contagious and invigorating. And God has honored it.

As head of Youth for Christ International and founder of the Chicagoland group which has been so widely publicized, Torrey perhaps has received more individual publicity than anyone else in the world-wide movement. It has not changed him a bit. He is still the same sincere, frank, clean-cut, above-board young fellow he always has been. He is a true leader. If you could swing yourself into the chair in which I sat interviewing him, you would be impressed by his sincerity and his spirituality. He likes to have a good time, but at the same time he is a serious young man, burning himself out to preach the Gospel. He is a good listener; he will let you tell him everything on your heart before he will offer any advice or help.

Perhaps the best way to describe him is to label him as an "All-American boy" who grew up to be an "All-American young man." Torrey is thirty-seven at this writing, but he feels and acts about ten years younger. He was ready to commit suicide only a few months after he was converted because of an inner conflict which gave him only agony of mind and soul. He was resisting a call to go to Africa as a missionary. When he yielded, however, and said, "Yes, I'll go to Africa, Lord," that burden rolled away! Instead, he found himself with a deep, burning, seemingly unquenchable desire to win people to Jesus Christ. First, last and always he is a soul-winner—no matter where he may be. Two examples: While flying to Tulsa, Oklahoma, one night, he felt led to talk to the stewardess about her soul. When they landed, she took Christ as Saviour. In England he invited three waitresses to one of the rallies there. They came, and one was converted.

Torrey is "Chicago" from beginning to end. Born of Norwegian parents on March 15, 1909, he proved to be the cause of his parents having to move because "the family was now too large." (Torrey was the third child.) Someone has said that Torrey has been moving ever since. He sat through many evangelistic meetings at the Salem Norwegian Free Church in Chicago but didn't accept Christ. He was definitely "a problem child" but had good company in that two of his cronies were the sons of the preacher.

His dad sent him to nearby Wheaton college to see if that institution might not be used to bring salvation to a lad who thought not too much about the religion of his mother and father. Torrey went willingly—he was set to tear the place apart. He did just that for a while, but one

Sunday night in the college chapel he went forward at the personal invitation of his football team-mate and captain, Evan Welsh, and accepted Christ. Only one person was saved that night, but how God was to use him.

He studied dentistry for a period at Northwestern University; but, after the inward battle of consecration was over, he returned to Wheaton and graduated in 1930. After that he was with a Baptist church in Chicago for a year and on the road in evangelistic work for two years with Rev. Ray Schulenburg of Moline, Illinois. Then he went to Northern Baptist Seminary in Chicago for more study. In his senior year he started to teach Greek and history at the seminary, and after graduation he continued his work at Northern Baptist, working for his doctor's degree while he was pastor of the Midwest Bible Church in Chicago. In 1940 it was decision-time again—a teacher or preacher. God gave him the answer—a preacher.

All during these years he was making the Midwest Bible Church one of the outstanding evangelical churches in the city. Souls were saved continually. The church was and is a real lighthouse. When the challenge of Youth for Christ came, Torrey was given a free hand by the church. He was given a year's leave of absence by the church when he became head of the International group.

Torrey whips out a big hand at a challenge and says, "Let's go!" Very seldom does he overstep himself. Two things keep him from cracking physically under his terrific schedule. One is a definite conviction in his own heart that he is "doing the work of two men." A younger brother, Arling, died in 1933 at the age of twenty-one. He was going to be *the* preacher in the family and had yielded his life to the Lord for His service. According to everyone in the family, Arling had the personality, the voice and the speaking ability for the ministry. But after being stricken with a disease while on a tour of Europe, he came home to die. As Torrey stood by his coffin he vowed to God, "Lord, if

you give me strength I'll do his work and mine, too."
Torrey was sincere in that vow, and he is certain that God
is giving him strength over and above his own. He gets
things done in quantities which seem almost impossible.

The other thing revolves around two bits of philosophy:
"Never do anything yourself which you can get someone else
to do for you," and "Everyone can do something, and it's my
job to find out what it is and to get him to do it."

Although Torrey was not the one who had the original
idea of an International organization, it can be said that
he, perhaps more than anyone else, was responsible for
its coming into existence. He was the key man, but he was
not the only man. Once the world vision reached him,
however, he was not able to let it go without doing his
best to carry it through.

Torrey is a good organizer, uses his head, knows his
advertising, knows how to handle people, but above all
he knows Christ in an intimate, refreshing way. He prays
about everything. One day he leaned against a tree on an
empty lot and said, "God, if you want us to have this lot
for our church, let us have it." At that time it was in a
seemingly endless tangle of litigation, but God unraveled
it. The Midwest Bible Church now stands there.

A sense of humor is his, also. He likes to have a good time
himself, and he doesn't mind if others do, too. One night
in the middle of his message a little girl in the front row
stood up, slowly put on her hat, coat and overshoes. Torrey
asked her, "Where are you going?"

She replied in one word, said so all could hear her,
"Home."

Everyone laughed. As the little girl left, Torrey said,
"Good-bye," and then added that there were probably plenty
of others in the church who felt the same way but who
didn't have the nerve to follow it through.

Until the time that he became active head of Youth for
Christ International, he received not a penny for his services.

Every time the appreciative group gave him a gift, he
slipped it back into some worthy project. So it was that
on the night of the farewell rally in the Moody Memorial
Church the office group presented him with a cash gift. He
promptly placed it in a fund for Jewish evangelism. The
work among the Jews is near and dear to him, and he
served as chairman of the Chicago Hebrew Mission for
a number of years.

One writer said of Torrey, "His courage for Christ is rich
and deep, and his vision is boundless." He symbolizes the
entire movement as he flies to all parts of the world to
spark this great twentieth century revival. He is home so
seldom that his lovely wife and three children rightfully
could question his using of 3717 West Wrightwood in Chicago as his residence. But when he is gone, four hearts are
in prayer in behalf of "Daddy"; the front-room davenport
gets a rest from serving as a diving board; the rug relaxes
from its task of serving as a swimming pool for Torrey
and the three children.

We move along to *Billy Graham*. Billy is from Charlotte,
North Carolina, or nearby Montreat. So great an impact
did he leave on one of his grade-school teachers in Charlotte
that when the first troupe went to Europe she took an
offering from the children in her class to help defray
his expenses! Eight dollars came in.

Billy is executive vice-president of Youth for Christ International and was its first full time employee, starting
in the fall of 1944. Six feet three, wavy-haired, jovial,
likeable, he is said to typify American youth at its best.
He was converted at seventeen and started to preach
shortly thereafter. He attended the Florida Bible Institute
and served as associate pastor in the Gospel Tabernacle
at Tampa, Florida, for four years. In 1941 he moved to
Wheaton Illinois, to succeed Dr. V. R. Edman as pastor of
the Wheaton Gospel Tabernacle. While there he also
finished his schooling. In college he was outstanding. He

served as president of the student council and participated
in many school activities. Later he moved to Western
Springs, Illinois, becoming pastor of the Village Church and
director of the radio program, "Songs in the Night." When
Chicagoland Youth for Christ began, Billy was the first
speaker, and he's been heart and soul in the movement
ever since.

Three words best describe him, "He can preach."

God has given him unusual speaking ability, and this,
together with a heart which has been touched by the Holy
Spirit, has made a man who has been wonderfully used by
God to the salvation of many thousands of souls. His energy
and strength is seemingly boundless. During the winter
of 1945-1946 he visited Youth for Christ groups in forty-
seven of our forty-eight states, and then flew to Europe
with the other three leaders! His messages are straight,
simple, Biblical and powerful. As many as 270 young people
have made decisions following one of his messages. When
he was in England he spoke in an Episcopal church. Not
being familiar with the order of worship, he did not know
how to conclude the meeting, so he did not give the usual
invitation. After he sat down, the pastor of the church
came to him and said, "Why don't you give an invitation?"
Billy did; and eighty-two people, including four deacons,
came forward for prayer!

Billy has served as No. 1 "trouble shooter" for the International. He also has worked hard in helping new groups
get started. Many Youth for Christ rallies throughout
the North American continent and Europe received a real
"lift" after a visit from Billy. At twenty-eight he has had
eleven years of preaching experience. Should the Lord
tarry, he seems likely to become one of the great evangelists in America and in the world.

As the "travelingest" man in International (he is in
England for the second time as this is being written), he
has had an opportunity to see the actual scope of Youth

for Christ. After a few moments of conversation with him, one can easily see that Youth for Christ has thrilled his own soul to its depths. He has the ability to impart information in a challenging and thrilling way, and his enthusiasm is contagious. His manner of speaking is similar to that of the other leaders—straightforward, right from the shoulder, definite and clean-cut. He is married and has one child. He saw his little baby girl only four days in the first six months of her life. As he said, "Everytime I get home she wonders who the stranger is coming in the door."

We move across the Canadian border for another brief look at Charles Templeton and Toronto Youth for Christ. His work in Toronto has been so noteworthy that the Canadian edition of *Liberty* magazine carried a full length article on him and his work as pastor of the Avenue Road Church of the Nazarene. Until 1937 he never went to church; now he seldom goes anywhere else. At the time of his conversion he was sports cartoonist for the Toronto *Daily Globe*, and his cartoons were syndicated to twenty-three papers in the dominion. He made eighteen dollars a week on the *Globe* and about sixty dollars a week through the syndicate. He was completely sports-minded, and had no thought for religion. Then his mother was converted; and his two brothers and three sisters, were also saved. The transformation in them intrigued him; so one night he went to church to hear the Cleveland Colored Quintet. The Holy Spirit worked in his heart. Following the service he went home, knelt by his bed and accepted Christ.

Not long after he went on a tour with his pastor, making drawings and giving his testimony. When he reached the United States border he had only forty cents in his pocket, but the officials permitted him to cross after hearing his case. One of the men said, "Go on across; you'll get along all right."

A few months later he was in Grand Rapids, Michigan,

attending a conference. He heard Constance Orosco, a converted opera star, singing. Cupid's arrow pierced him, twelve days later he proposed and two months later they were married.

When Templeton left the sports field, he took a good deal of "ribbing" from his co-workers, but he had all the answers. After leaving the paper, he was thrilled when able to lead one of those fellow employees, a man sixty years of age, to Christ.

The Christian Business Men's Committee of Toronto decided to sponsor a Youth for Christ rally, and there was just one man whom they felt would qualify as director. Templeton was that man. He had many ideas. He put his energy into the organization, and God blessed Toronto Youth for Christ in a remarkable way. As stated previously, Toronto Youth for Christ has the distinction of being the largest *weekly* rally in the world, with an average crowd of over three thousand throughout the year. Templeton works hard and long. His previous schedule has been increased. He is the typical Youth for Christ leader in that he has a pleasing personality and a straightforwardness in preaching and giving of the invitation which reaches young people and convinces them of his sincerity. The article in *Liberty* stated, "He preaches a positive religion and believes that no one can be truly happy unless happy internally." One of his basic ideas is that you can't reach people who don't come to hear you; so he does everything he can to get them to come to his meetings. He enjoys Christianity immensely, and his laugh rivals Wyrtzen's. Because of his outstanding abilities, he soon moved into a prominent position in the International office. He serves as promotional director and Eastern Canada representative. As an artist he has been able to help greatly in the promotional literature.

When Graham moved into the position of executive vice-president, in walked T. W. *Wilson* of Ashburne, Georgia, as the new field representative. "T.W." is from the same town as Graham, and they were pals as youngsters. They were born two months apart and were born again two months apart. Wilson is the only man in Youth for Christ International who uses initials instead of his first name, and gets away with it. (His first name is Thomas, the second unobtainable.) A rich and smooth southern accent and a jovial and happy face characterize "T.W." the best liked young man in Youth for Christ work. He simply radiates the warm spiritual glow which is his. A graduate of Bob Jones College, he left his pastorate work at Ashburne, Georgia, to enter Youth for Christ work at a cut in salary. In his own words, he "wouldn't be any other place right now." An excellent contact man, Wilson is even better as a preacher. He is on the lookout for souls everywhere he goes. One time in a restaurant in Chicago he bowed his head to thank the Lord for the food. The waitress came running up and said, "What's wrong with the food that you have to look at it that way?" Wilson told her, in a way in which only he can, that he was thanking the Lord for his food, and then left her with a personal testimony of what Christ meant to him.

One time he was on a plane in the South and was taken off because there were too many passengers on board. He could not understand it at all, especially since he would miss his next engagement. He jumped on a bus as soon as he could, and as he rode along he thought of the miserable situation in which he was—having to miss one of his engagements. But God had His hand in the matter. When Wilson arrived at his destination, he picked up a paper and read that the plane had crashed only a short time after he had gotten off. Once more he thanked God for His goodness.

Youth for Christ has used the sports appeal a great deal in its work. Two of the young men who have been used are *Gil Dodds* and *Bob Finley*. Dodds, the son of a preacher, was known throughout the world because of his feats on the track. He holds the world indoor mile record. His testimony has brought many to the Lord. Dodds took his college work at Ashland college, Ashland, Ohio. From there he went to Boston, Massachusetts, and enrolled in Gordon School of Theology and Missions. There he was under the track tutelage of Jack Ryder, "maker of champions." A friendship with Wyrtzen put Gil into a close relationship with his Bible, and his testimony has been even stronger since that time. Gil often gets to a town early in the afternoon in time to have a workout with the local high school trackmen. While there he invites the fellows to the evening service, and they usually come in droves. He did just that at Rockford, Illinois, and when the invitation was given following the service a whole row of trackmen stepped out to take Christ as Saviour! Thousands of people the world around were moved when he told a crowd of thirteen thousand in the Chicago Stadium and the nationwide listening audience, "Running is only a hobby with me. My real job is serving the Lord Jesus Christ."

Bob Finley used to throw punches while a student at the University of Virginia. He handled himself well enough to be the recognized 155-pound intercollegiate champion of the United States. The national meet was not held the year he was at his peak, but he defeated everyone. Finley also knows how to win souls to Jesus Christ, and he realized that there were greater laurels than having the right hand raised after a few rounds of glove-throwing. Both Dodds and Finley started to work full time for Youth for Christ in 1945, and they spanned the country telling sportsminded young people of the greatest thrill that ever had come their way—acceptance of Jesus Christ as personal Saviour.

Cliff Barrows, fresh from graduation at Bob Jones College and with a liking for sports and flying, developed into one of the top song leaders in the land as he traveled extensively with Jack Shuler and then later by himself. In high school and college he was an outstanding tennis player. He is a pilot and has dreams of having his own plane, someday. He joined the Youth for Christ International staff early in 1946, and went with Graham to England on the second trip to that needy land.

Bob Evans came home from the war with a Purple Heart on his chest and a keen desire in his heart to reach the youth of America. He had seen what it meant to be without Christ in the service—seen it in hundreds of men as he worked as a Navy Chaplain. Evans was one of the few Navy chaplains to ride the deadly PT boats in the initial assault on Normandy. In that tremendous clash he visited the forty ships for which he was responsible by plane, jeep, motorcycle and small boats. One time while riding along on a motorcycle in Normandy, he struck a land mine and was severely injured. When the fighting was over, he was led of God to accept the position of executive secretary of Youth for Christ International, and he also became one of the regular speakers.

Another "Bob,"—*Bob Murfin*—heard a doctor say that he never would walk again on one of his legs after an experience in the South Pacific. But Murfin prayed, and God answered. Today he is not only walking on it but standing before Youth for Christ rallies across the land telling them what Christ did for him and what He can do for them.

Co-ordinating the activities of these many men through the International office was *Charles White,* who came after four years of work with the Army Air Forces in Orlando, Florida, to serve as business manager of the office. Previous work on railroads plus the experience gained in the air force work served as perfect training for his Youth for Christ job, and into the work he went.

There are hundreds of others who could be mentioned if space would permit. Walter Block, head of the Quaker

Stretcher Company in Kenosha, Wisconsin, has served as the treasurer of the International group. Bob Cook, co-author of *Reaching Youth for Christ* and successor to Torrey as head of Chicagoland Youth for Christ and the Upper Central region, has been a pillar in the movement's growth. Bob was converted at the age of five. He attended the Moody Bible Institute, Wheaton College and Eastern Baptist Seminary and served churches in Glen Ellyn, Illinois, LaSalle, Illinois, Philadelphia, Pennsylvania. Then he went to the Midwest Bible Church in Chicago where he served as associate pastor until Torrey left. Alert, full of ideas and the ability to put them into action, Cook also has become known for his spiritual insight. It was Cook who directed the great Soldier Field Rally in 1946, at which seven hundred people came to the cross in the middle of the field to accept Christ following the message by Dr. Charles E. Fuller. He stepped into big shoes when he succeeded Torrey Johnson, but through God he has been able to fill them effectively. The marvelous work in Chicago goes on.

Walter Anderson, leader of Charlotte, North Carolina, Youth for Christ, was the Chief of Police of that city until he was promoted to head of the Federal Bureau of Investigation in the state of North Carolina. Anderson spent a period of time in evangelistic singing but went back into police work when God assured him that He wanted him there. He has sought the positive approach to crime— preventing it before it happens—and feels that it is cheaper to save a youth when young than to handle him as a criminal. His statement about Youth for Christ bears weight. He said recently, "Youth for Christ is doing more than anything else I know to stop juvenile delinquency."

It would be impossible to list the outstanding musicians and soloists used in Youth for Christ rallies around the world. The importance of music in the success of Youth for Christ rallies cannot be estimated. Such men as Carleton Booth in New York, Rudy Atwood in Los Angeles, Beverly

Shea and Doug Fisher in Chicago, to name *only a few,*
have been mightily used of God through their consecrated
talents. Atwood's piano playing is known internationally
through the Old Fashioned Revival Hour and also through
Youth for Christ rallies. Booth and Norman Clayton work
with Wyrtzen in New York. Beverly Shea is used in rallies
all over the land and now is heard on a nation-wide
broadcast originating in Chicago. Fisher compiled the Youth
for Christ song book and has planned music for many of the
largest rallies in the country.

Maurice Carlson of Muskegon, Michigan, led a dance
band and worked on a newspaper for four years before he
was converted. Then Youth for Christ came along, and he
is now leading it . . . .C. E. Hershey of Marion, Ohio, was
another dance band leader who accepted Christ and
turned into a soul winner. He was the radio accordionist
over stations KDKA and WFBG in Marion before he was
converted. God used him to start Youth for Christ in
Juneau, Alaska.

William Ross Pusaure of Honesdale, Pennsylvania, Youth
for Christ was a professional fighter before going into the
ministry and, later, into the Youth for Christ . . . Dr.
Frank Phillips, a veterinarian, found Youth for Christ
in Portland, Oregon, taking so much of his time that he
had to give up his practice and go into Youth for Christ
full time. Phillips had an unusual background. A graduate
of the University of Toronto, he spent two years in China
as a veterinarian with the China Inland Mission. He came
home in 1937 because of war and went to Portland to study
at the Western Baptist Seminary, from which he obtained
in 1944 his B.D. degree. For a while he took care of his
pets in the morning and did Youth for Christ work in the
afternoon. When God continued to pour out His blessing
on the work, Phillips left his work with the animals and
went out seeking young people for Christ.

The leaders have come from all walks of life and from

many denominations. Many of them are preachers, but not all. George Wilson in Minneapolis is a publisher. Gene Lind of Springfield, Illinois, is a school teacher. Charles Anderson of Kenosha-Racine, Wisconsin, Youth for Christ is a personnel manager. Ted Engstrom of Grand Rapids, Michigan, is an editor. And on and on.

Templeton is a Nazarene. Dr. Paul S. James, the early leader in Atlanta, Georgia, is a Baptist. Dr. Daniel Iverson of Miami, Florida, is a Presbyterian. Myron S. Boyd, one of the early leaders in Seattle, Washington, is a Free Methodist. T. C. McCulley of Milwaukee, Wisconsin, is a Brethren. Watson Argue of Winnipeg, Canada is from the Assembly of God. Ray Schulenburg of Moline, Illinois, is from the Evangelical Free Church. Allen Blegen of Elgin, Illinois, is Lutheran. Richard Harvey of St. Louis is from the Christian and Missionary Alliance. Dr. Russell Purdy of Hammond, Indiana is a Baptist. Ted Engstrom of Grand Rapids, Michigan is from the Mission Covenant group.

In addition to these leaders there are men who, in a way, have been leaders of Youth for Christ. They include Percy Crawford of Philadelphia, Mervin Rosell of Rochester, Minnesota, Jack Shuler of California (a son of "Fighting Bob" Shuler), Dr. Bob Jones, Jr., and many others. In the main they have been used as speakers and evangelists. Being young themselves, they have a tremendous appeal to youth. Youth for Christ is a new outlet for their abilities and talents, and they have been able to reach many more young people because of Youth for Christ units in a city or area.

As we have studied the men and the situations, we have felt more and more that the leaders have been appointed by God—and by no one else. We have noticed that God selected busy young men. Whatever their vocation or calling, they have been God's men. Some had to leave not long after the rallies were started, but in most cases the rallies continued, as God raised up other men to fill the vacancies.

One of the criticisms of Youth for Christ has been that it "plays up the man too much and does not glorify Christ enough." This criticism undoubtedly has come because of the methods of advertising. Phil Kerr answered this in writing in *Sunday*:

"The answer is partly in understanding that *there is a great difference between 'sheep feeding' and 'fish catching'* . . . It's not necessary to use fishing bait to attract sheep to the feeding trough. Natural hunger is sufficient . . . *But the sinner is not hungry!*" He then goes on to say that the "bait" used is often in the form of outstanding athletes, businessmen, war heroes, musicians, singers. Then he said: "Care must be taken that the 'bait,' having served its purpose, should be faded into the background and the sinner's final attention be focused on Christ alone."

Young people tend to be hero worshipers. Because of that natural human trait Youth for Christ leaders have sought to reach them through outstanding men and women in various fields. The crux of the matter lies in switching their attention from the individual to Christ; and this has been done in the vast majority of cases. Personal contact with many of these leaders and outstanding Christians has led us to believe that they are truly consecrated servants of Jesus Christ, desiring only that young people come to know Christ through their testimonies or messages. It is not for us to judge. God knows the hearts of all His children and the reasons for their service.

In Youth for Christ God is using young men with outstanding personalities, abilities, love for Christ, to win other young people to Christ. In the next chapter we shall share with you some of the jewels which have been won through Youth for Christ. The fire is blazing high.

Chapter 7

THE THRILL OF
YOUTH FOR CHRIST

THE sailor lad was far, far from home. He was in Norfolk, Virginia, but his home was in China. He did not mind too much being far from home, but he did often get a longing for home.

It was Saturday night. He walked the streets of Norfolk aimlessly. He looked across the street and saw a great many "men in blue" going into a building, and he decided to go in, also. A few minutes later he found himself sitting in Norfolk Youth for Christ.

When the invitation for salvation was given, he went forward. A personal worker spoke to him at length, and the young sailor seemed to drink in every word, although he did not say very much. Finally he turned to the worker and said, "I trust the Lord."

That was all he said—just that simple, straightforward sentence. A few Saturday nights later he was back. The same personal worker, eager to learn how he was getting along, said to him, "Jimmie, there's one thing I didn't tell you the other night. That's this—you've got to pray. You've got to pray to grow in grace."

Jimmie smiled and replied, "Oh yes, I've been praying."

"And what have you been praying for?" the personal worker asked.

The answer silenced the personal worker, and sent him away with a lump in his throat, "I pray for myself and that the Lord will bless my testimony aboard my ship. Then I pray for the people in China who still worship their ancestors. Then, Eddie, I pray for you, that the Lord will help you to speak to many more fellows about their souls, as you did to me. You know, you're the first person who ever talked to me about being saved!"

* * *

This happened in Chicago. A sixteen-year-old girl sat in her first Youth for Christ meeting. She enjoyed it from the beginning and was soon singing and rejoicing in the service. Enjoyment turned into conviction. When the invitation was given, she was one of twenty-two young people who responded.

Where had she come from? What did she do?

Bob Cook, Chicagoland director, discovered after hearing her testimony that she was a Chinese-American teenager who had known *only Buddhist ceremonies*. But she found the living God that night!

* * *

The thrill of Youth for Christ lies in the results. Young people, and older ones too, are finding Christ as Saviour. Its main purpose is to lead souls to Christ, and God is showering His blessing upon the work.

In the aforementioned questionaire appeared the following item: "Greatest number of souls saved in one night—"

There were 125 replies to that question. When the sums reported were totaled, this was discovered: 5,144 *people were converted on only one night in one-fourth of the rallies going at that time!* In one night 5,144 people came to Christ for salvation.

Dr. Herbert Lockyer said, "God save us from numbers," and Youth for Christ shares that feeling. The figure is quoted merely to show the amazing extent to which Youth for Christ is being used.

The "main fruit" of the rallies—the salvation of souls— will be considered first. Later the effect that Youth for Christ has had and is having on young Christians and on young people's work and churches will be mentioned.

A young lad, hardened by the most cruel warfare, had this story to tell to Bernice Scheu at Detroit's Voice of Christian Youth: "I came near to accepting Christ when flying a plane over Anzio, but . . . I didn't do it. Thank God, I made that decision tonight at the Voice of Christian Youth!" Miss Scheu learned later that this young technical sergeant had stopped to visit friends in Detroit before going to Ohio to receive his discharge. His heart was touched at a meeting, but he did nothing about it. The Holy Spirit continued to speak to him, and a few weeks later he had an excuse to go to Detroit again and attend the Voice of Christian Youth. That night he gave his heart to Christ. Today he is attending Ohio State University.

Toronto Youth for Christ invited the girls from the Toronto Girls' Reformatory to a Youth for Christ meeting. The girls were asked to vote on the invitation, and they decided to attend in a group. When the call to accept Christ was given, a number of them responded.

In Oakland, California, a Jewish sailor one Saturday afternoon sat on a park bench reading. He was reading a Bible. Someone had given him one, and he had become interested enough to read it. He came to Isaiah 53 and read verse six: "All we like sheep have gone astray; we have turned every one to his own way; and the Lord hath laid on him the iniquity of us all." The light came, and he saw Jesus as the Messiah. That night he found his way to East Bay Youth for Christ at Oakland where he publicly accepted Christ as his Saviour.

In Hartford, Connecticut, an unsaved sailor offered a Christian girl an engagement ring. She refused it, saying "No, not until you know Jesus." The sailor's leave allowed him to attend a great victory rally of Hartford Youth for Christ. Later the girl was all smiles. She had a ring on her finger, and her sailor fiancé was on his way to a navy base having settled two very important problems. He was one of 209—yes, 209—who had accepted Christ at the great rally when Jack Wyrtzen gave the invitation; also, he had the promise of a sweet, consecrated Christian girl to be his future wife.

Holland, Michigan, is known for more than its tulips. Holland has a good Youth for Christ rally. One night a young lad prevailed upon his brother who was home on leave to go to the rally with him. The younger brother was saved and had been praying often that his brother might accept Christ before going back into the thick of the battle. On that last Saturday night of his leave, it happened! God answered those prayers, and a born-again sailor went back to his ship with a new "Captain." Also in Holland a young girl was saved at a rally. So burdened was she for three of her girl friends that she successfully coaxed them to attend the next rally with her. You know the result—all three came to know the Lord at that rally.

Boston, like most other large American cities, has its share of soap-box orators. One of the men was an avowed atheist and freely advocated atheism from his soap box. But one night he went to a Youth for Christ meeting and before finishing his "investigation" of it, he allowed Jesus

Christ to come into his heart and life. From that day on he *truly* had something about which to talk.

The cab should have been there long ago, but it didn't come . . . didn't come. Finally the girl went back upstairs, thoroughly disgusted, and took off her formal gown. There was no ball for her that night at the sorority to which she had been pledged a few weeks previous. The phone rang and a girl friend asked if she cared to go to a Youth for Christ rally. "Anything," she thought, "to get away from my disappointment in not going to the dance." A few hours later at Minneapolis Youth for Christ, held in the Municipal Auditorium not far from the University of Minnesota which she was attending, she was converted. Four weeks later she stood on the platform and gave a thrilling testimony of what Christ had done for her just a month previous. Now she is continuing in her studies for foreign diplomatic service: she has the conviction that the Lord will use this training for missionary work.

Three pastors in Grand Rapids, Michigan, were in their studies one Monday reflecting on the work of the previous day and thinking about the future week. As if by arrangement, three young fellows walked into those pastor's studies. Each had the same thing to tell his pastor, "I was converted at Youth for Christ last Saturday night, and I want you to pray for me."

Merchant after merchant in Washington, Pennsylvania, was visited one morning by the same lad. At each store he had the same story, but he told it with his chin up: "I was at the Youth for Christ meeting on Saturday night and took my stand for Christ. I have been stealing from you for several months, and now I want to pay you back for all I've taken . . ." It was a long, long walk through town that morning, but the lad had courage and spirit. He had learned the truth of II Corinthians 5:17, "Therefore if any man be in Christ, he is a new creature:

old things are passed away; behold, all things are become new."

Gil Dodds was scheduled to speak in the evening, but he arrived at Rockford, Illinois, early in the afternoon. He immediately went to the high-school track and had an enjoyable afternoon "working out" with the prep trackmen. When he had a chance to talk with them for a few minutes, he gave them pointers on track and then invited them to the rally in the evening. They came, and they heard him tell in a sincere and straightforward way what Christ had done for him. He gave the simple invitation to accept Christ. Almost a whole row of fellows, and many of them on the track team he had talked to that afternoon, came forward for prayer and confession of Christ.

Two young lads from Plattesville, Wisconsin, had been arrested for theft and placed on parole. A few weeks later a Youth for Christ rally was held in their town, and they responded to the invitation at the end of the service. They had attended church and Sunday school when younger but had drifted away. They went back to church with a new fire in their hearts.

All young criminals and potential criminals who attend Youth for Christ rallies do not accept Christ. Chicagoland Youth for Christ discovered that one night. A sixteen-year-old boy attended Chicagoland Youth for Christ one Monday night in order to hear Gil Dodds. After the meeting he said to the chum who had brought him, "I don't get it. These kids, are they serious? Do they mean they accept Christ?" His Christian friend told him that it was one of the most serious steps they would take in their entire lives. The young fellow, urged by his saved friend, promised to come back in five days . . . maybe . . . Five days later he called and said that he had a "big deal on" and couldn't make it. The "big deal" was the theft of a car and the kidnaping of a filling-station attendant. The police came on the scene, and the sixteen-year-old lad was killed when the get-away car crashed into a pole during the wild chase. It was too late for him.

Staff Sergeant Jacob DeShazer was one of the famed Doolittle fliers. After their courageous flight to Tokyo he was shot down and sent to a Japanese prison camp. No words can describe conditions in that camp. He lived in constant fear of being executed. Three of his buddies were put to death, and one starved to death. Then it was that DeShazer accepted Christ as his Saviour. "I had a long time to think," he said, "and that's where the Holy Spirit started talking to me. Now . . . I'm going back as a missionary because I feel that it must not happen again to any man."

DeShazer spent forty-one months in Japanese camps. All along the way he felt that Jesus would "carry him through." Now his thoughts are expressed in the following verse, "Love your enemies, bless them that curse you, do good to them that hate you, and pray for them that despitefully use you, and persecute you (Matthew 5:44).

Lowell Thomas, well-known radio commentator, told the thrilling story of Jacob DeShazer over the air one night. Thomas received a letter from a war-material manufacturer in Massachusetts, John W. Young, who wanted to use some of the profits from his fuse-making business to finance the education of Jacob DeShazer so that DeShazer could return to Japan with the Gospel of Jesus Christ. "I believe," Young wrote, "that unless we have a revival of Christianity throughout the world, to give this generation a spiritual and moral foundation that will make it possible for them to know how to use our scientific achievements, we will find that the next generation will be destroying itself completely . . . I want to increase my expenditures for the preaching of the Gospel of Jesus Christ in a way that will make our country great."

Indianapolis Youth for Christ has had many wonderful conversions. Sixteen Catholics were converted during the

"City-wide Awakening Rallies" in 1945. A professional gambler and a Hindu young lady were converted. A man chained by the liquor habit was referred to Malsbary at the Youth for Christ office. The man accepted Christ in Malsbary's office and called the personnel manager at his place of employment to tell him of the decision. Malsbary also talked to the manager. The man later told Malsbary that the owner of a bootleg joint had stopped him and shoved a bottle of whiskey under his nose. He took a sip ... then just as suddenly stopped himself, handed the bottle back, and said, "No thanks. I took Jesus Christ as my Saviour this afternoon in the Youth for Christ office, and I'm through with liquor." The bootlegger laughed, but the man left him. He now spends his nights taking a Bible course which Malsbary teaches.

A missionary who had served in China and South America was home on furlough. His wife was the daughter of a missionary; he was the son of a missionary. But they had worked on two different fields *without knowing the Lord Jesus Christ personally!* Louis Talbot, head of the Bible Institute of Los Angeles, came to St. Louis, Missouri, Youth for Christ to speak, and that night the wife accepted Christ. The husband made a decision later. He is now filling a pulpit in his own denomination. He had never before experienced the joy of winning a soul to Christ.

Many people have tried to analyze Youth for Christ. One night following a Chicagoland rally two students from the University of Chicago walked up to director Bob Cook and asked, "What makes this thing work?"

At that moment a counselor came to Cook with two attractive girls of eighteen who had just been converted. Cook introduced the three young people to the university students, had a few words of conversation with the girls, and heard the testimonies as to what Christ had done for them. As the two girls walked away, Cook said to the students "There, fellows, is your answer. As long as young people are being saved, Youth for Christ will keep on growing."

Two girls from Chicago had run away from home and reached St. Louis. It was the Saturday night to which they had looked forward with the wildest dreams. Away from home . . . free . . . no need to go home early. But the situation lacked joy. They were troubled, so they turned for advice and help to Youth for Christ. They asked Director Dick Harvey, "Do you think our folks would want us back?" An hour later, after a long-distance call to Chicago, they were on their way home.

Min-Cheng Liu was one of nine hundred Chinese college graduates sent to the United States by the Chinese government to receive industrial training. One night at Milwaukee Youth for Christ Min-Cheng Liu did what so many other young people around the world have done in recent years—accepted Christ. He testified of his acceptance in these words: "I have opened my heart widely without any reservation to accept Jesus Christ as my personal Saviour. It is really a wonderful thing to be a Christian. I regret that I didn't get a chance before now to come in contact with Christians. However, God is so kind to me as to show me the way of salvation very soon after my arrival in this country through Milwaukee Youth for Christ . . . In the Lord Jesus Christ my every desire was fulfilled and He gave me salvation. I am grateful to God for such a wonderful gift. I was born again into God's family. God loves me, and I deeply appreciate my new life . . . I know that I am saved and that I have eternal life. Our Lord Jesus Christ gives me perfect satisfaction such as I never had before. He becomes more and more precious in my life."

The newspaper in a little town in Alaska assigned a lady photographer to cover the monthly Youth for Christ rally. In addition to taking the pictures, she had the job of interviewing the speaker of the evening. During the interview he asked her a few questions about her personal relationship to Jesus Christ. The Holy Spirit used that two-way interview, and a young newspaper photographer that night accepted Christ as her personal Saviour.

The way in which God has used the Word of Life Hour in New York has been amazing. A chaplain once told Jack Wyrtzen, "The last time I heard the Word of Life Hour I was flying a B-29 from the Philippines to Tokyo." A missionary standing nearby said, "That's interesting. Just before I left Alaska I was walking down the streets of Anchorage. As I passed a saloon I heard the Word of Life Hour going full blast on the gin-mill radio."

Youth for Christ in Frankfurt, Germany, was mainly for G.I.'s because of the language problem. But not too infrequently a few Germans would attend. One of the regular visitors was a young German girl of fourteen. She understood a little English, and the G.I.'s helped her by translating much of the service for her. When the invitation was given one Saturday night, six soldiers went forward to accept Christ. And following in their footsteps was a German girl of fourteen!

We could go on . . . and on . . . and on.

We could tell you in detail about the young lad who called a Youth for Christ director and said, "I got saved tonight, but I didn't sign a card. Is it all right?"; or about the little son of a preacher who broke the silence in his daddy's car as they drove home from the first rally in Soldier Field by saying, "Daddy, I saw Gil Dodds run tonight . . . and I accepted Jesus as my Saviour." There have been thousands of incidents as interesting as those which have been cited. Many people have found Christ as Saviour through Youth for Christ. The Holy Spirit's power has been felt in rallies all over the world. A pastor told us, "I preached just about the same sermon in my own church as I did at a Youth for Christ rally hundreds of miles away. Nothing happened in my own church, so far as visible results were concerned. But in the Youth for Christ rally there was tremendous power of the Holy Spirit, and many young people came to Christ. It seems as though you can almost feel the power of the Holy Spirit each time you walk into a Youth for Christ meeting place."

Were we to stop at the soul-saving aspect of Youth for Christ, we would be more than justified. Thousands of young people have come to know Christ as Saviour, a great host of Christians have been strengthened in their spiritual lives, and many have dedicated their lives for full-time service for the Lord. What a thrill it was to stand in Soldier Field in Chicago on Thursday, May 30, 1946, and see 685 people kneel at the cross in the center of the field and accept Christ as Saviour; and what a heart-warming thrill it was to see 2,500 young people file out of that great outdoor arena and stand in front of the platform to indicate their decision to go anywhere in the world should Christ ask them to do so. One young fellow said, " 'Fraid I'll have to be a missionary now . . . thank God!"

There have been thousands of such dedications for life service. Frank Ford Jelsma, whom you may have heard a few years ago playing solo parts in a band directed by Sammy Kaye, was converted at a meeting held by Percy Crawford and dedicated his life for missionary service in South America at a Denver Youth for Christ rally. In Cleveland, Ohio, a young son of a minister was a faithful and active worker at Youth for Christ. One night the Lord spoke to him in a new way, and today he is studying to enter the ministry.

The proof of the depth and the extent of such decisions can be seen in the large enrollment at Christian colleges and Bible schools. To be sure, the G.I.'s are home and are getting back to school as fast as they can. But many other young people are asking admission to Bible schools and colleges. Young people, touched at Youth for Christ rallies, are preparing themselves for service around the globe.

The movement has made soul-winners of many young

people. At the Soldier Field rally in 1946 a teen-age girl fairly bubbled over with joy as she told Bob Cook. "I led my first soul to Christ tonight!"

Another young girl attended Youth for Christ regularly. Her pastor took advantage of her interest, along with that of other young people in the church, and started a series of messages on "Soul-winning." One Sunday night he asked this question. "How many of you will say, 'I'll do my best, God willing, to talk to someone this week about salvation?' "

She raised her hand. From Monday through Thursday she wondered to whom she would speak. She lived a consistent and sweet Christian life at school, and her friends knew by her life that she was a Christian. On Thursday night the phone rang. She answered it. On the other end of the line was a girl friend who wanted her to come over that very night and show her how to be saved!

Young people have learned to pray. Youth for Christ is based on prayer. One night seventeen young people gathered for two hours during the regular Youth for Christ rally. They asked God to save at least one person for each one in that prayer room. God answered that prayer, and seventeen people found their way to the prayer room that night!

Entire churches and youth groups have felt the impact of the movement. One pastor told us that his young people's work had been transformed by Youth for Christ. Another said that his youth work had been completely revitalized. Another stated that his young people were using Youth for Christ as a means of winning their friends who would go to a civic auditorium but who would not enter a church. They would hold a prayer meeting first and then invite their friends to Youth for Christ. God honored their plans, and several of their friends accepted Christ at the rallies. The young people immediately took the new converts into the society and put them to work. Another pastor told

McDermott for his article in *Collier's*, "I've got a new church since my young people caught the thrill of this new youth crusade."

Many churches have been affected. Youth for Christ has transmitted its emphasis on soul-winning, service and missionary effort to churches in all parts of the world.

The influence on the general public might be called a fourth result of Youth for Christ. Not since the days of Billy Sunday have evangelism and the church received such widespread notice in the press. Youth for Christ has been getting the crowds, and crowds draw stories. Some people have decried the crowds. But if an editor knows that five thousand people in his city will be at a certain building on a certain night, he likely will have a reporter there. If crowds appear time and time again, he will assign a man to the rally. The valuable space given to Youth for Christ has been a welcome respite from the tawdriness and undesired muck of the juvenile delinquency upswing. As the story spreads and as the movement increases, more and more people tend to look on Youth for Christ as the possible solution to the greed and materialism of the day.

Unsaved people are impressed. Make no mistake about that. A policeman told a reporter, "If anyone would have told me that so many kids would go for religion on a Saturday night, I'd have said he was nuts."

And an amazed usher at the Chicago Stadium rally in 1944 said as he looked at the thirty thousand people packed into that great indoor arena, "What do you know! More people got religion than belong to the Republican Party. Anyway, it looks like there are more here tonight than came to the G.O.P. convention a few months ago."

This has been—"The Thrill of Youth for Christ." This chapter on "fruit" is necessarily incomplete. Only the fringe has been touched. Just a few examples of the manner in which Youth for Christ has influenced both unsaved young people and young Christians have been presented. Youth for Christ could stop today, but the praises to God for what it has done will keep rolling on through eternity.

But . . . it does not look as though it is stopping, or that it is even beginning to stop. As this chapter is being finished, an amazing new story has been written in Holland by a team composed of Spencer De Jong, Don DeVos and Doug Fisher. One report—954 souls saved in a single rally!

How long will the fire keep burning?

Chapter 8

WHITHER . . . YOUTH FOR CHRIST?

How long will Youth for Christ last?

There is one definite answer—as long as God wants it to last.

One thing is certain—its effects are eternal. In that way of thinking, it will never stop. But in the human way of appraising movements and men and women, we like to look at the future and speculate in regard to the duration of Youth for Christ.

It will never stop for lack of a goal: It has as its incentive the salvation of souls. As it serves as a stimulant for world-wide missionary work, its scope will expand each time a new door opens.

Torrey Johnson said in the early days of Youth for Christ that its goal was to reach a million people every Saturday night. Later, in a message in Orchestra Hall on June 16, 1945, he stated the four-fold plan of Youth for Christ: (1) to

reach every city, town, village and rural community in
North America with the good news that Jesus saves,
(2) to promote and encourage great city-wide revival
meetings, (3) to lift up our eyes and see the world that
needs the Gospel and (4) to "Go ye into all the world" in
this generation!

If Youth for Christ is to achieve those goals, it will be
with us for a long, long time. In God's plan, it may be the
channel through which He will pour out His blessing in
a new way over all the world.

At another time, when Torrey was asked to explain the
purpose of Youth for Christ, he said:

> Youth for Christ must be of God. It has come in the most
> unusual way and is moving in the most unpredictable fashion.
> All we know is that God is in it and is blessing it to the
> salvation of many souls. We believe that it is God's answer
> to the sin and unbelief of the present hour.
>
> For two thousand years it has been found that those who
> sought to do the will of God were progressive in their
> methods. The Wesley brothers preached in church yards,
> standing on tombstones, on street corners, in houses, halls, and
> other places. D. L. Moody was very unorthodox; he rented
> circus tents and introduced the evangelistic song leader
> into church programs. He was accused of violating good
> taste when he used Sankey, Bliss and others. In line with
> that, and in looking at the use made by the Apostle Paul
> of all the means available in his day, Youth for Christ leaders
> seek the courage to enable them to blaze the trail and meet
> the need of reaching the crowd of our day.

Without a doubt, much of the future success of Youth for
Christ will depend on the extent to which it receives
the co-operation of the churches. One of the most severe
criticisms of the movement is that it is not church-centered.
But it can truthfully be said that Youth for Christ seeks
in a definite, well-planned way to relate its program to
the local church in every way it possibly can.

In the follow-up work of converts, Youth for Christ
clearly shows that it is not a competitor of the church.
There are several methods of follow-up of converts, and
each method seeks to bring the new-born creature into

the church—the church of his choice. One system used is the "chaperone" or "counselor" plan. Each new convert is assigned a "chaperone" of the same age and sex, and it is the duty of that chaperone to call on the new convert the following Sunday morning and go to the church of his choice with him. He also will do everything he can in those first critical weeks of new life to help the convert as he makes known his stand for Christ. He goes with the new convert to visit his pastor and helps him tell the pastor just what happened. He arranges to have other friends contact the convert and seeks to find Christian young people in the church to take an interest in him. If he is in high school, the chaperone will try to place him in contact with the Bible club in his school. Many groups use this system: Indianapolis, St. Louis and Los Angeles have used it very effectively.

Another method used in follow-up work is the "letter system." Three letters are mailed on the Monday morning following the rally. One is sent to the convert, another to the church he has indicated as his choice, and third to an interested and co-operating group, such as the high school Bible club, inter-varsity, or a like organization. The group contacts the convert and invites him to their meetings and fellowship.

The matter of follow-up of converts is an important one, and the second annual convention of Youth for Christ International studied it thoroughly. There is one danger which must be avoided. If the follow-up is too thorough, the convert may be become Youth for Christ minded and not church-minded. The majority of the Youth for Christ groups co-operate with the churches (they refer the converts to the churches of their own choice) and then depend upon the churches to take care of the converts. That is the church's work; but in many instances the church does not do the job. This it true especially if the convert is a member of a modernistic church. When he tells a modernistic pastor of his conversion, the pastor often tries to explain it away and undermine its importance.

Jack Wyrtzen encountered the typical example of indifference on the part of pastors. At one of Wyrtzen's meetings in the South five young men came forward and accepted Christ. Wyrtzen had to leave the next morning, but he asked them where they went to church or where they would like to go. They told him, and that night he called the pastor and gave him all the information, including their names and addresses. Several months later he was back in that city and contacted the pastor to see how they were getting along. The pastor's reply was, "Oh, those fellows. I guess they weren't much interested. I sent each of them a postal card inviting them to our services, and they never showed up." That was the extent of the follow-up!

However, there are also many, many pastors who do the follow-up work thoroughly. As a result, they have active, progressive young members in their churches.

Another criticism of Youth for Christ, which has been declared to be one of the reasons why it will not last, is that it is superficial. The danger of its being superficial and shallow is one of the things about which Youth for Christ leaders constantly pray. The seeming levity of the average Youth for Christ meeting frequently offends Christians. Young people do have a good time at the rallies—there is no denying that. That is one reason why they continue to come back. When older people, or even younger Christians, visit the rallies, they sometimes feel that the meetings are not serious enough. Bob Cook of Chicagoland Youth for Christ said this in connection with the problem:

> We feel much the same way that you do about it; but the fact is that we aren't trying to reach people such as yourself. We're trying to reach unsaved young people, young people who have been used to good entertainment in their worldly pursuits, who have been accustomed to having a good time

on Saturday night. So we plan our programs that way, but with a toning down and a sobering down in the last forty-five minutes or hour, and especially at the end when the invitation is given. And . . . God is honoring that plan, as we pray to Him for guidance in our planning of each program.

Torrey Johnson, in a statement to a reporter, said:

We don't look like a church, we don't sound like a church, we don't sing like a church, and we don't act or dress like we're in a church. The reason is simple—we're not a church. Youth for Christ . . . is a religious movement to get young people to return to God and to the reading of God's Word. We are anxious to get them to go to church—their own church of whatever denomination or wherever its location . . .

. . . Back of it all, young people have found that God is no faraway, gloomy being who lives solely in edifices of stone, brick, or concrete, and who habitually casts a look of disapproval on a good time . . . They've found that He's young in spirit, vigorous, full of joys and blessings, and, best of all, that He's someone with whom they can have daily fellowship and who can help them meet the tremendous problems they meet today.

. . . Might God give us the sense not to use too much showmanship . . . and the courage to use enough!

Charles Templeton of Toronto, speaking to a regional Youth for Christ meeting in Detroit, gave an adequate solution when he said, "Youth for Christ cannot be a Sunday-night service, nor can it be pure entertainment. It should be sparkling and entertaining, *and yet spiritual*."

Whether these methods will last for any length of time depends, of course, upon the way in which God blesses them. At the present moment, they are being used in an almost miraculous way. Frank Mead wrote in *The Christian Herald*, "You don't laugh off success." Denominational groups and churches, as a rule, are not at present doing the job of winning souls in great numbers. Youth for Christ is.

One of the most successful Youth for Christ directors analyzed the movement of the day. "My wholehearted interest lies with this movement because *God is in it*. He is using it today to the salvation of many precious souls and to the edification of Christians. My primary interest is in the souls of men. Since Youth for Christ is a movement winning souls to our blessed Lord, I must lend my support."

Will the converts become church members? Will they give their support to the onward progress of the Gospel? Dr. Frank C. Phillips of Portland, Oregon, Youth for Christ wanted to know the same thing. In the seventeen-month period which he checked, Phillips found that 1,056 people in Portland Youth for Christ had signed cards and been dealt with personally. He found that 32 young people were attending Bible colleges because of Youth for Christ. He made a thorough check with 45 pastors of 116 conversions which had occurred more than a year previous and received these figures: 66 still active; 16 in need of further religious instructions; 10 not contacted; 12 not attending church; six moved away; and six were prior conversions.

Where to next?

Torrey Johnson says:

> We expect to let God open the doors for us as we move ahead. We will serve only as sparks as we move from country to country, igniting the young people in the various lands and inspiring them to do the job in their localities . . . German youth, Swedish youth, Japanese youth . . . can be re-born the same way that New York or Podunk youth have been re-born.. As our youth goes, so go our countries. If Communism, materialism or wide indifference capture our youth, we shall go down the road to Fascism. Youth for Christ is determined that young people in the United States—and over all the world—shall get a chance to know about the Lord Jesus Christ and what He can do to transform a life.

* * *

The day is over . . . The day—the book—is over, but the fire burns on. It moves on into the night—into a Saturday night which once was thought to be the sole property of the devil. Young people on one side of the world are going to bed; but as they retire, other young people are attending Youth for Christ rallies. On and on they go, rally after rally. The languages vary but the message is the same, and the young people are the same.

The fire glows and grows. The fire cannot go out, for the Fireman is God. Human hands cannot quench it, nor human weaknesses dim its glow.

Burn on, Youth for Christ, burn on! May millions of embers from your blaze shine through eternity. And, oh, may your flames spread rapidly . . . and burst into a world-sweeping revival!

TITLES IN THIS SERIES

The Evangelical Matrix
1875-1900

■ 10. Arthur T. Pierson, ed.
The Inspired Word: A Series of Papers and
Addresses Delivered at the Bible Inspiration Conference,
Philadelphia, 1887
London, 1888

■ 11. Moody Bible Institute Correspondence
Dept. *First Course — Bible Doctrines, Instructor—*
R. A. Torrey; Eight Sections with Questions,
Chicago, 1901

The Formation of
A Fundamentalist Agenda
1900-1920

■ 12. Amzi C. Dixon,
Evangelism Old and New,
New York, 1905

■ 13. William Bell Riley
The Finality of the Higher Criticism;
or, The Theory of Evolution and False Theology
Minneapolis, 1909

■ 14.-17 George M. Marsden, ed.
The Fundamentals: A Testimony to the Truth
New York, 1988

Fundamentalism Versus Modernism
1920-1935

■ 24. Joel A. Carpentar, ed.
Modernism and Foreign Missions:
Two Fundamentalist Protests
New York, 1988

■ 25. John Horsch
Modern Religious Liberalism: The Destructiveness
and Irrationality of Modernist Theology
Scottsdale, Pa., 1921

■ 26. Joel A. Carpenter,ed.
Fundamentalist vesus Modernist
The Debates Between
John Roach Stratton and Charles Francis Potter
New York, 1988

■ 27. Joel A. Carpenter, ed.
William Jennings Bryan on
Orthodoxy, Modernism, and Evolution
New York, 1988

■ 28. Edwin H. Rian
The Presbyterian Conflict
Grand Rapids, 1940

Sectarian Fundamentalism
1930-1950

■ 29. Arno C. Gaebelein
Half a Century: The Autobiography of a Servant
New York, 1930

■ 30. Charles G. Trumball
Prophecy's Light on Today
New York, 1937

■ 31. Joel A. Carpenter, ed.
Biblical Prophecy in an Apocalyptic Age:
Selected Writings of Louis S. Bauman
New York, 1988

■ 32. Joel A. Carpenter, ed.
Fighting Fundamentalism:
Polemical Thrusts of the 1930s and 1940s
New York, 1988

■ 33. *Inside History of First Baptist Church, Fort*
Worth, and Temple Baptist Church, Detroit:
Life Story of Dr. J. Frank Norris
Fort Worth, 1938

■ 34. John R. Rice
The Home — Courtship, Marriage, and Children: A
Biblical Manual of Twenty-Two Chapters
on the Christian Home.
Wheaton, 1945

■ 35. Joel A. Carpenter, ed.
Good Books and the Good Book: Reading Lists by
Wilbur M. Smith, Fundamentalist Bibliophile
New York, 1988

■ 36. H. A. Ironside
Random Reminiscences from Fifty Years of Ministry
New York, 1939

■ 37 Joel A. Carpenter,ed.
*Sacrificial Lives: Young Martyrs
and Fundamentalist Idealism*
New York, 1988.

Rebuilding, Regrouping, & Revival
1930-1950

■ 38. J. Elwin Wright
*The Old Fashioned Revival Hour
and the Broadcasters*
Boston, 1940

■ 39. Joel A. Carpenter, ed.
*Enterprising Fundamentalism:
Two Second-Generation Leaders*
New York, 1988

■ 40. Joel A. Carpenter, ed.
Missionary Innovation and Expansion
New York, 1988

■ 41. Joel A. Carpenter, ed.
*A New Evangelical Coalition: Early Documents
of the National Association of Evangelicals*
New York, 1988

■ 42. Carl McIntire
Twentieth Century Reformation
Collingswood, N. J., 1944

■ 43. Joel A. Carpenter, ed.
The Youth for Christ Movement and Its Pioneers
New York, 1988

■ 44. Joel A. Carpenter, ed.
The Early Billy Graham:
Sermons and Revival Accounts
New York, 1988

■ 45. Joel A. Carpenter, ed.
Two Reformers of Fundamentalism:
Harold John Ockenga and Carl F. H. Henry
New York, 1988